Minimalism Beyond the Nurnberg Funnel

Minimalism Beyond the Nurnberg Funnel

edited by John M. Carroll

 society for technical communication

The MIT Press
Cambridge, Massachusetts
London, England

© 1998 Massachusetts Institute of Technology

This book was set in Sabon on the Monotype "Prism Plus" PostScript Imagesetter by Asco Trade Typesetting Ltd., Hong Kong and was printed and bound in the United States of America.

Library of Congress Cataloging-in-Publication Data

Minimalism beyond the Nurnberg funnel / edited by John M. Carroll.
   p.   cm.
 Includes bibliographical references and index.
 ISBN 0-262-03249-X (alk. paper)
 1. Communication of technical information. I. Carroll, John M.
(John Millar), 1950–
T10.5.M56   1998
004′.071—dc21   97-36124
                                         CIP

Contents

Preface

Early in my technical career, I was fortunate to become involved in a project investigating how people learn to use what would now be regarded as routine computer applications, like word processors. I had excellent colleagues (Clayton Lewis, Robert Mack, and later Mary Beth Rosson) and rich opportunities to learn about the use of technology. We quickly tumbled to a simple and obvious realization: people experience difficulties in these situations *because* of their strategies and plans, deductions and inferences, prior knowledge and expertise. This elementary glimpse into the nature of practical learning sparked many empirical studies and design projects, and engaged us with a large network of colleagues. Through the 1980s, the work of this community helped to change instruction and documentation design practices.

In 1994, I was honored by the Association for Computing Machinery's Special Interest Group on Documentation (ACM SIGDOC) with its Rigo Award, given for contributions over a number of years to the fields of documentation. In my case, the award was for *The Nurnberg Funnel* (MIT Press, 1990) and the minimalist approach to instruction and documentation described in that book. I went to Banff in October to receive the award and to present a lecture at the SIGDOC meetings. I drove back to the airport in Calgary with a group from the conference that included Stephanie Rosenbaum. Stephanie suggested that I organize a workshop on new directions and developments in minimalism. This book is the result of that workshop.

This is the moment to take stock of minimalism. The early work from the 1980s has had its impact. But the progress, or perhaps I should say the changes, of the 1980s—in both instruction and documentation, and in computer systems and applications—have helped to pose new questions and to recast old ones. There is now both the need and the opportunity to push minimalism ahead with respect to its foundation in cognition, education, and design and with respect to its application in a broader range of tasks and technology contexts.

Stephanie's suggestion came at a good time for me. I had spent the summer of 1993 visiting Twente University in the Netherlands and had established a collaboration with Hans van der Meij. Our two papers clarifying the minimalist approach are reprinted here. Both push beyond *The Nurnberg Funnel* in providing more specific guidance to practitioners who wish to use minimalism and specific clarifications to practitioners and researchers who encounter conflicting descriptions and interpretations.

The timing was also opportune in that by 1994 I had (finally) met most of the people who had played central roles in developing and disseminating the minimalist approach. I knew who to invite! I asked the Society for Technical Communication to support a workshop to bring together a group of these researchers and practitioners to exchange perspectives and experiences with minimalism beyond *The Nurnberg Funnel*. We met over a weekend in mid-November 1995 in Blacksburg, Virginia, on the campus of Virginia Tech.

I felt fortunate all over again: excellent colleagues, rich opportunities. Minimalism is still developing; it is already beyond *The Nurnberg Funnel*. This book is a good summary of where minimalism is today, of the challenges and activity that now define it. But this book is also filled with new challenges and possibilities for what minimalism can be tomorrow. I hope and expect that the book will guide and excite the broader community of researchers and practitioners working with minimalism.

I am grateful to the Society for Technical Communication for sponsoring the workshop. I thank the authors for sustaining the workshop goals and spirit during the year following the workshop, as we wrote and rewrote chapters. I particularly acknowledge Ginny Redish and Hans van der Meij, who kept me on track with timely, practical, and wise advice at critical moments.

1

Reconstructing Minimalism

John M. Carroll

Seventeen years ago, I was working in a research group of young cognitive psychologists. We were young enough to be astonished by the profound difficulties people routinely experienced in using what appeared to be carefully designed documentation and self-instruction material. These initial observations propelled us down a path of investigation and analysis that we are still pursuing.

In this introduction, I will survey the emergence of minimalism as an approach to technical communication—from my personal perspective. Although I coined the term as it is now applied in technical communication and played a role in launching and developing the minimalist approach to technical communication, I regard the minimalist movement as more a matter of zeitgeist and refinement than of radical innovation. The scientific and philosophical foundation for minimalism was well established before 1980; indeed, it was writ large by giants like John Dewey, Jean Piaget, and Jerome Bruner. Many other investigators, including some of the chapter authors of this book, were developing what now might be called minimalist approaches at the same time I was getting started.

In this reconstruction, I will distinguish four phases in the emergence of minimalism: the very start of our project in late 1980; the early to mid-1980s when we developed the experiments, case studies, and interpretations that comprise *The Nurnberg Funnel*; the late 1980s, when we began to extend minimalism to supporting object-oriented programming and design; and the present, in which the themes of the past continue to develop and to be reconstructed further in a variety of networked information and education projects.

1.1   Less Is More

As the 1980s began, many people were discovering ease of use and ease of learning, most of them in fairly unpleasant ways. In the midst of a revolution in technology to support human activity, people were being terrorized by word processors. The user population for computers was increasing and diversifying rapidly; programmers and engineers were being replaced by secretaries and professionals as the typical users. But companies did not understand the needs of these new users, and they were not prepared technically to support them. The IBM Corporation, where I worked as a research scientist, was enjoying enormous expansion in office products. It was about to transform the industry with its PC. But market success was taken for granted in IBM at that time; what was more salient to technical leaders in the company were the open problems.

In IBM, one approaches uncertainties by commissioning task forces. I served on a task forced created by the Research Division in late 1979. Our job was to survey the leading research and development groups in the world and to propose a plan for IBM to achieve technical leadership in usability. One of the first projects established within the division under this mandate was directed at characterizing the problems of new users in a way that could provide design direction for user interfaces, training, and documentation. Clayton Lewis, Robert Mack, and I undertook this project. Our empirical approach was protocol analysis; we watched learners closely for hours upon hours, periodically asking them what they were thinking, what the things they noticed meant to them, and what they wanted to do.

What we found in these protocols—in the thoughts and actions of our test subjects—was not dearth of understanding and failure to notice and interpret; rather we observed incredibly complex attributions, elaborately reasoned abductive inferences, and carefully performed, ritual behaviors. People were not so much being merely stumped by this learning task as being drawn into a nightmare in which things frequently made a little bit of sense but generally ended in disaster. This was unpleasant to watch and intriguing to ponder. But what could we do about it?

Our interpretation of our subjects' struggles was that they were actually making rather systematic attempts to think and reason, to engage their prior knowledge and skill, to get something meaningful accomplished. They did not seem to be getting appropriate guidance and feedback from the systems and documentation they were using, even though they were being presented with a huge amount of information through these channels. For example, although they often tried to attempt real tasks, their training materials did not support this. Although they made a great variety and number of errors, their materials did not support error recognition, diagnosis, or recovery, and the systems did not provide general undo functions (Mack, Lewis, and Carroll 1983).

The minimalist design approach we pursued emphasized encouraging and supporting work on realistic tasks from the start and throughout training: learning by doing rather than learning by reading. We wanted to engage the learner and evoke positive motivation toward meaningful activities. If we could do this, we felt confident it would more than make up for perhaps presenting a smaller volume of information; people able to get started effectively could learn on their own as necessary. We stressed coordinating documentation with system information and supporting error handling in both the system and documentation. We insisted, for example, that if people tended to jumble the instructions they read and executed, then instructions should be absolutely modular; they should make sense in any order.

This contrasted with the then-pervasive systems approach (Gagne and Briggs 1979), which emphasized carefully sequenced, thorough practice on individual steps to support learning and further practice on methods, but ignored learner motivation to undertake realistic tasks rapidly. The systems approach emphasized structural decomposition and completeness of information but ignored the context of use (e.g., coordination of the system and documentation) and support for error.

1.2   Iterative Design

In our earliest work on minimalism, we wanted strong and simple principles to drive an initial "ruthless" design analysis and first-pass design, with subsequent iterative evaluation of both formative and summative sorts. Indeed, I think my understanding and practice of minimalism over the years has been linked strongly to my more general views on design.

When I joined IBM's research division in the late 1970s, John Thomas, Ashok Malhotra, and I formed a project to study the software design process. The context for the project was a then-current schism in the basic understanding of design activity. On the one side were a set of naive and prescriptive views of design, originating in the psychology of problem solving and in the "waterfall" methodologies of software engineering. These views held that design problems could be systematically decomposed into sets of routine puzzles. On the other side were the somewhat fuzzy and often disturbingly naturalistic views of theorists like Horst Rittel and Fred Brooks—people who had actually seen real design projects.

I think we were fortunate to be working in an industrial laboratory; our colleagues were real software designers. I was still close enough to graduate school to try persistently to see software design as hierarchically organized, simple information processes. But it was not working. Our studies showed, for example, that software designers do not work from hierarchical decompositions; rather, they interleave top-down and bottom-up development. We found that the design process involves the development of partial and interim solutions that play no concrete role in the ultimate solution. Indeed, we found that the goals of a design project routinely change through the course of the process (Carroll, Thomas, and Malhotra 1979).

The design practice we observed in the late 1970s was more complex than contemplated by psychology and software engineering, but it was still woefully oversimplified. User testing was generally seen as a validation process tacked onto the very end of system development. In those days, the objective of user testing was to identify glitches that could be papered over before the system was delivered. Indeed, users played almost no role at all in system design. The requirements gathered early in the system development process, and used to develop the initial goals for a project, came from managers, often with no involvement of the workers who would ultimately be the users of the system.

Our work found a place within the broad shift in thinking about the role of prototyping, usability testing, and user models in the system development process. We ended up helping to articulate a prescriptive design methodology that is now widely taken for granted: iterative development. Today one just assumes that usable and useful systems cannot be specified first-time final, that the real needs and practices of users must be understood as design requirements, and that the extent to which the designed system meets these needs must be directly and continuously evaluated throughout the development process via mock-ups and prototypes.

What is the connection to minimalism? Someone who imagines that design is a process of systematic decomposition, specification, and implementation will seek hierarchically detailed models and structured methods. And this is precisely the process assumed in the systems approach (Gagne and Briggs 1979). However, someone who understands design as a process of iterative development and goal discovery will seek a strong and concrete starting point, a coherent design vision that may (perhaps must) entrain design dilemmas and trade-offs. That is the way to get the most out of a process of iterative redesign.

1.3   The Human Need for Sense Making

The ideas that guide us in technical communication are necessarily bound to the technology contexts within which they develop. The systems and documentation materials that served people so poorly in our early studies belong to a bygone era. Indeed, in 1980, better models for information design were already in hand; they were merely waiting to be applied, and innovations in systems and user interface software were already implemented in commercial products. Maybe the time for minimalist information slashers was to pass as quickly as it came.

In 1983, Sandra Mazur-Rimetz and I made a detailed study of professionals as they learned to use the Apple Lisa. The Lisa incorporated many of the user interface ideas pioneered in the Xerox Star system, and it was the direct precursor of the Apple Macintosh. Our study was circulated internally in IBM for three years before being cleared for outside publication, so we had plenty of time to ponder our results. For me, the most important outcome was a strong encouragement to generalize the descriptions and interpretations we had been making of the problems and experiences of secretaries learning to use IBM systems like Displaywriter. Although the Lisa incorporated genuine advances in user interface presentation and although our professional users were far more knowledgeable about computers than were the secretaries we had studied earlier, the basic problematic patterns of user and learner interactions remained. This point is most directly argued in chapter 3 of *The Nurnberg Funnel*.

In 1985, Mary Beth Rosson and I wrote a paper, "Paradox of the Active User." We argued that although people need to learn in order to engage effectively in activities, their compelling orientation to meaningful activity continually undermines the motivation to spend time and effort "just" learning. We showed that this mechanism could explain a variety of the new user problems that had originally innervated our minimalist design work, but that it also explained phenomena associated with more experienced users, for example, the tendency for skill to asymptote at relative mediocrity (Carroll and Rosson 1987).

These two projects transformed the minimalist enterprise for me. They led me to see our inventory of learner problems not as reflecting merely a set of design blunders (which, of course, they do) but also as exemplifying types of problems that are necessarily entrained when knowledgeable people try to acquire new cognitive skills through self-instruction. People want to learn by doing, but this inclines them to jump around opportunistically in learning sequences. They want to reason things out and construct their own understandings, but they are not always planful, and they often draw incorrect inferences. They try to engage and extend their prior knowledge and skill, but this can lead to interference or overgeneralization. They try to learn through error diagnosis and recovery, but errors can be subtle, can tangle, and can become intractable obstacles to comprehension and motivation.

I came to understand that the very dispositions that make people good sense makers are also causes for characteristic learner problems. I came to see our project more as managing design dilemmas that can never merely be solved rather than as correcting design blunders tout court. In rereading my own expressions of minimalism, I do not now find as sharp a shift as I then felt in my own thinking about what we were trying to create. Prior to 1984, I was truly captured by the aesthetic of presenting less information, of responding to learner problems by cutting rather than adding. After 1984, I was more centrally concerned with better-supporting self-initiated sense making. Both aspects were always there.

1.4   Managing Design

As my understanding of educational philosophy and technology grew, and as minimalism took on for me a more extensive, more articulate, and more general meaning, I was becoming increasingly dissatisfied with merely iterative development as an attitude toward understanding and managing design. I still regarded the insights of Rittel and Brooks (and by this time, like everyone else, I was also reading Donald Schön) as empirical bedrock. However, I began to recognize that a strong starting point and a continuing responsiveness to evaluation was not enough. What was the guarantee that iterative design would not merely produce local optimizations and thrashing. What was the guarantee of global convergence or coherence in the final design result? Replacing the un-realizable ideal of systematic decomposition with a chaos of local pertur-bations, unguided by any overall design concept or integration, seemed to me to be an advance from the frying pan to the fire.

I became interested in techniques for managing the process of iterative development. Our first notion was that a set of written usability specifi-cations could be created early in the system development process and then be carried along through the process as a living goal statement (Carroll and Rosson 1985). Usability specifications were to be measur-able claims about the use of the system being developed. They could be updated if and when necessary, but they would be maintained as a precise description of the usability commitments and performance of the system—analogous to functional specifications. This approach is fundamentally different from merely emphasizing testing and design refinement.

Our initial conception of usability specifications strongly emphasized user performance (e.g., "secretaries will be able to type, edit, format, and print a one-page memo after two hours of instruction"). Over the next several years, we continued to develop concrete approaches for man-aging iterative design. These evolved in the direction of becoming more qualitative; for example, in *The Nurnberg Funnel*, the design analysis of training-wheels interfaces—interfaces that block the consequences of typical and/or serious user errors—(pp. 188–200) is filled with hypotheses about the inferences users might make when they encounter a blocked function and a message such as, "The Request key is not available on the Training Displaywriter."

This approach was more explicitly developed in papers written with Robert Campbell, Wendy Kellogg, and Mary Beth Rosson on what we eventually called "psychological design rationale." We suggested that the usability trade-offs implicit in a design should be made explicit and managed as part of the system documentation. For example, we described the scenario in which a person learns to type and print using training wheels as incorporating the following trade-off: "Immediate feedback on blocked device state instigates evaluation while relevant intentions, plans, and actions are still active in memory, but could also encourage nonplanful action" (Carroll, Kellogg, and Rosson 1991, 94). A thorough set of such trade-offs provides guidance in planning and evaluating iterative design refinements.

1.5 Scaling Up: The "Simple Domain" Challenge

By the time I wrote *The Nurnberg Funnel* (1990), and certainly by the time the book appeared in print, minimalism was fairly well known. I read more than two dozen reviews and review articles of *The Nurnberg Funnel*. Naturally, most of these suggested directions in which the work could be developed further. I also wished to move on from this work.

I was attracted to three possible continuations of the project. The first of these was longer-term outcomes. We had demonstrated transfer effects of initial training with minimalist manuals and interfaces (Carroll et al. 1987–1988; Catrambone and Carroll 1987), but these were very limited investigations, and we had not considered how to design minimalist reference materials. The second area I was attracted to was better specifying the underlying psychological dynamics of using minimalist materials. Our analysis had followed the social cognitivism of Dewey, Piaget, and Bruner; we had eschewed information-processing models (basically because they tend to specify behavior and experience at uselessly fine grains of detail from the standpoint of practical design). Much remained to be done in better specifying particular elements of minimalist designs: inference, examples, error recovery activity.

The third area that especially interested me was the question of whether minimalism would scale up to complex domains, that is, whether minimalist materials and techniques could support learning highly technical concepts and skills. There is a fundamental difficulty with the very statement of this challenge: that the complexity scale alluded to in fact does not exist. Word processing is less complex than rocket science but more complex than tic-tac-toe. Is it a simple or a complex domain? These examples suggest a few guides: complex tasks may have many subtasks or options, many steps per subtask, and many conditions or dependencies on subtasks and options. In my work environment at IBM, the general issue was finessed: there was a broad, tacit understanding there that routine office tasks are simple and that programming and software design tasks are complex.

In the spring of 1988, there was a groundswell of interest in the programming language Smalltalk and object-oriented software design in my research area. We had been using and exploring Smalltalk for several years already, but at that time it seemed to click more widely in the work of a number of my colleagues. This presented an opportunity to me. I was finishing the first draft of *The Nurnberg Funnel*; the rest of what I still had to do would be edits and refinement. The most obvious way that I could contribute to the groundswell, and allow it to carry me along as well, was to tackle the problem of helping experienced procedural programmers—something IBM had lots of—attain a practical understanding of Smalltalk and object-oriented design. In the next six years, we created and studied a variety of programming environments to support learning and programming. We found that although the main thrusts of minimalism still provided useful guidance, the specifics did require some reworking.

A key principle of minimalism is that people need to engage in real tasks. However, the real tasks of complex domains can be overwhelming for learners and unmanageable for instructional designers. In our work on Smalltalk, we developed a set of realistic projects, analysis, enhancement, and debugging activities directed at intrinsically interesting software systems (many of them interactive games). For example, we gave learners a blackjack game and suggested they try to make a specific enhancement to the user interface; we created a gomuko game that occasionally stole moves and invited learners to discover how it cheated and to correct it. These are not the real tasks of professional programmers, but they include the elements of real tasks.

Minimalism assumes that people engaged by a task will creatively reason and improvise, that they will make sense. Complex domains often encompass immense content, myriad entities, relationships, and rules. For example, Smalltalk includes thousands of software building blocks in its classes and methods. Of course, it is possible (necessary, really) to practice Smalltalk programming without knowing or using all of these. The point is that there is an order of magnitude more to learn about Smalltalk than there is about even the most function-laden word processor. We decided not to try to provide instruction for a general core of domain content. Instead, we tried to convey and support meta-skills of the domain that could help learners make sense on their own. For example, we tried to convey the utility of causal analysis of code and to encourage reflection and self-critique in programmers (Alpert, Singley, and Carroll 1995; Carroll et al. 1990).

Minimalism emphasizes getting learners started quickly. Because the tasks of complex domains tend to incorporate many subtasks, and many steps per subtask, "getting started fast" becomes more a matter of sustaining interest and activity than of quickly dispatching a task. We had to give up our early commitment to absolute modularity—for example, of the sort embodied in our "guided exploration" cards, self-contained support for individual tasks (Carroll et al. 1985). We adapted Bruner's concept of scaffolding and tried to design chunks of intrinsically motivating, task-oriented activity that were as self-contained as possible but that cumulated within a discovery-based curriculum (Rosson, Carroll, and Bellamy 1990; Rosson and Carroll 1996). Structuring and managing the presentation of such dynamic projects is difficult using only paper materials; we found tool-supported exploration particularly critical.

Minimalism supports error handling: recognition, diagnosis, and recovery. However, it becomes intractable to enumerate all possible errors and their interactions in a complex space. We found it more useful to provide a higher level of support, for example, critiquing strategies instead of individual actions (Alpert et al. 1995). When we could not be certain about the exact nature of an error, we made suggestions, explicitly warning the learner that the advice was our best guess but that it could be wrong (Singley, Carroll, and Alpert 1993).

1.6 Design Rationale

Design iteration was always the process touchstone for minimalism. We encouraged risk taking in design analysis and initial design, assuming that the best guidance ultimately would emerge from observing real people trying to learn and use prototypes. Complex domains challenge this orientation. When too many dimensions are involved and too many aspects of a design situation can change, attributions in formative evaluation become indeterminate. The shift in our technical work toward the more complex domain of programming and software design had more strongly encouraged our interests in psychological design rationale. Building explicit theories about how designs are expected to affect situations of use, as illustrated earlier for training-wheels interfaces, constrains and focuses the interpretation of formative evaluation data. This is the same hypothetico-deductive logic as in the scientific method.

In the early 1990s, we developed a framework in which the design rationale for particular artifacts could be abstracted to design archetypes or models. For example, we developed a minimalist tutorial and tool ensemble for Smalltalk (Minimalist Tutorial and Tools for Smalltalk, MiTTS) and showed how its psychological design rationale could be seen as a specialization of the rationale for the minimalist model. Five trade-offs summarize a psychological design rationale "view" of minimalism (Carroll, Singley, and Rosson 1992, 254–255):

1. Working on a realistic task provides the learner with an appropriate framework for integrating and applying learning experiences, but realistic tasks may be too difficult, and there may be too many kinds of task settings to support.

2. Working on a familiar task orients and motivates learners by engaging prior knowledge, but it may encourage task-specific learning and engage inappropriate prior knowledge.

3. Incorporating planning and acting throughout the learning experience helps orient the learner to applying knowledge and supports skill transfer, but it increases task complexity.

4. Retrieval, elaboration, and inference making engage and sustain learner attention and make skills more robust and accessible, but learners might not have access to enough information to reason successfully and may be anxious about bearing such responsibilities.

5. Diagnosing and recovering from errors focuses and motivates learners and helps sharpen a concept of correct performance, but errors can be frustrating and disrupt task goals.

One trade-off in the MiTTS design was a specialization of the second proposition: exploring the execution stack in the Smalltalk environment orients and motivates learners by engaging their prior knowledge of call stacks, but inappropriate procedural programming knowledge may also be engaged. Another MiTTS trade-off specialized the fourth proposition: specifying the function name but not the message name in instructional projects forces learners to infer or retrieve the connections between goals and methods, but they might not have access to enough information to reason successfully and may become anxious about bearing such responsibilities. We argued that building design rationales for models or archetypes could make design work scientifically cumulative by allowing formative evaluation results to be adduced not merely to the particular artifact being evaluated, but to the model (or models) instantiated by that artifact.

1.7   Reflections on the Future

Much of the future is the continuation of themes from the past. I am pleased that the minimalist results and design interpretations of the mid-1980s have proved sound and replicable. A growing number of colleagues around the world have been able to apply, refine, and extend both the practice of minimalism and our understanding of why and how it works. Many questions remain open; many challenges remain ahead. I believe that there cannot be an ending to the project of reconstructing minimalism, because I believe there cannot be an ending to the project of learning how to design information. We do better, but we can do better still.

My own research interests have focused largely on learning in the context of networked community information systems. As in the object-oriented programming work, this has been a minimalist revelation to me. The vision of an information highway affording universal access to vast libraries of digital information is bold and exciting, but it is incomplete. People want to share, discuss, and create information, not just retrieve it (Carroll and Rosson 1996). For example, our ongoing work augments the community information available through the Blacksburg Electronic Village network with a community "historybase" to which residents can contribute their own stories, reflections, and perspectives, as well as their comments on the contributions of their neighbors (Carroll et al. 1995). Our most ambitious current project is directed at a collaborative environment for middle and high school science students to work together on simulated experiments (Chin, Rosson, and Carroll 1997).

The balance of this book presents a sample of the most important current developments of minimalism. The next two chapters, written in collaboration with Hans van der Meij, summarize and update the statement of what minimalism is. Chapter 2 presents a set of principles and heuristics intended to facilitate the understanding and application of minimalism; chapter 3 discusses a set of typical misconceptions about minimalism, to clarify what was originally intended and to focus analysis and investigation of open questions.

The next twelve chapters present a variety of original developments and analyses by some of the people who have contributed the most toward pushing minimalism beyond *The Nurnberg Funnel*. Tricia Anson gives a practitioner perspective on minimalist design, emphasizing the need to incorporate minimalist principles throughout the system development life cycle, and not just to the production of documentation. She argues that the complexity of contemporary systems and documentation provides new, powerful, and multifaceted incentives to adopt a minimalist approach. Stephanie Rosenbaum discusses her experiences teaching minimalist design to experienced technical writers; she analyzes their problems in identifying appropriate instructional tasks and managing inference in these tasks. In a follow-up study of how her students used minimalism, she found relatively conservative practices and applications, and indications of intra-organizational contention regarding more aggressive minimalism (for example, between information development and marketing groups).

JoAnn Hackos describes experiences with a development project in which a minimalist approach was employed for a system whose users were both highly experienced with computers generally, and experts in various areas of science and engineering, such as medical imaging, seismology, and cryogenics. She discusses why the approach was selected and how it was implemented for this increasingly prominent type of user and usage context. Barbara Mirel also examines the challenge of designing information for experienced users and complex task domains, arguing that these circumstances require a task perspective that incorporates social, cultural, organizational, and technological dimensions of the user's work. She argues that minimalist information should incorporate this larger context in supporting realistic learning.

Janice Redish argues that minimalism must take into account several ways that users and situations of use can differ: cognitive mode (learning to do versus doing), learning style, and type of system. Differences among users is an important issue, often difficult to address in design, but a major direction of enhancement for minimalism. Like Anson, Rosenbaum, Hackos, and Mirel, Redish emphasizes the importance and also the difficulty for technical communicators of always describing the task in *users'* terms.

David Farkas discusses the general strategy of layering user support as a fail-safe for minimalist documentation. Drawing on examples from a variety of online technologies, he shows how minimalist procedures, tutorials, and helps can be supplemented by more comprehensive sources of information that are encountered only if the primary material fails. Hans van der Meij develops the important point that most of what we know about minimalism has come from studies contrasting the minimalist and systems approaches. He suggests that we are ready to move on to more focused studies of particular minimalist techniques. He analyzes the role and design of visual coordinative information in minimal manuals and reports on an experimental study of the efficacy of visual presentations.

Karl Smart focuses on organizational obstacles to adopting a minimalist approach; he examines minimalism as a component of strategic managerial decision making based on principles of quality management. Most discussion of minimalism has addressed the worlds of designers and users, but in some sense the final decisions depend on managerial acceptance, which seeks grounding in relatively aggregated views of product differentiation, cost effectiveness, and customer satisfaction.

Robert Johnson analyzes minimalism as a rhetorical "art," emphasizing the process of creating particular experiences and effects for the user. He argues that a theoretical rationale based in rhetoric enhances the relevance of minimalism for technical communicators. Steve Draper provides a similar interpretation of minimalism, emphasizing the principle of being user centered and the objective of providing support for user tasks as the root content from which the minimalist approach can be derived.

John Brockmann reviews the emergence of minimalism as a case study of technology transfer. He discusses readiness of the profession to change, the context and foundation of task orientation, the early advocates and slogans, the research program, and the radical edge of minimalism as causal factors in the process of its adoption. And he poses the challenge of how and whether this process can continue to develop. Greg Kearsley outlines a broad agenda for further research and practice of minimalism, focusing on both its theoretical foundation and practical issues of technology adoption, applicability, and impact. He has constructed an ambitious work plan for minimalism, as well as suggesting some new areas to look for and to create impact. There is a lot to do to achieve more with less.

My view of minimalist design continues to evolve, driven as always by the particular domains and materials with which I am working, and in the case of this project, by the insights and activities of an excellent group of colleagues. Our current projects are all vehicles for pursuing a Deweyan vision of design as participatory inquiry and of inquiry as necessarily involving design. No doubt these most recent directions will both develop and, in their turn, be reconstructed. At times, these latest endeavors feel a long way off from making tiny manuals; at times, they seem like the inevitable consequence.

References

Alpert, S. R., Singley, M. K., and Carroll, J. M. 1995. Multiple mutimodal mentors: Delivering computer-based instruction via specialized anthropomorphic advisors. *Behaviour and Information Technology 14*, 69–79.

Carroll, J. M. 1990. *The Nurnberg funnel: Designing minimalist instruction for practical computer skill.* Cambridge, MA: MIT Press.

Carroll, J. M., Kellogg, W. A., and Rosson, M. B. 1991. The task-artifact cycle. In J. M. Carroll (Ed.), *Designing interaction: Psychology at the human-computer interface*, pp. 74–102. New York: Cambridge University Press.

Carroll, J. M., Mack, R. L., Lewis, C. H., Grischkowsky, N. L., and Robertson, S. R. 1985. Exploring exploring a word processor. *Human-Computer Interaction, 1*, 283–307.

Carroll, J. M., and Rosson, M. B. 1985. Usability specifications as a tool in iterative development. In H. R. Hartson (Ed.), *Advances in human-computer interaction*. Norwood, NJ: Ablex.

Carroll, J. M., and Rosson, M. B. 1987. The paradox of the active user. In J. M. Carroll (Ed.), *Interfacing thought: Cognitive aspects of human-computer interaction*, pp. 80–111. Cambridge: MIT Press/Bradford Books.

Carroll, J. M., and Rosson, M. B. 1996. Developing the Blacksburg Electronic Village. *Communications of the ACM*, 39(12), 69–74.

Carroll, J. M., Rosson, M. B., Cohill, A. M., and Schorger, J. 1995. Building a history of the Blacksburg Electronic Village. *Proceedings of the ACM Symposium on Designing Interactive Systems* (August 23–25, Ann Arbor, Michigan), pp. 1–26. New York: ACM Press.

Carroll, J. M., Singer, J. A., Bellamy, R. K. E., and Alpert, S. R. 1990. A view matcher for learning Smalltalk. In J. C. Chew and J. Whiteside (Eds.), *Proceedings of CHI90: Human Factors in Computing Systems*, pp. 431–437. (Seattle, April 1–5). New York: ACM.

Carroll, J. M., Singley, M. K., and Rosson, M. B. 1992. Integrating theory development with design evaluation. *Behaviour and Information Technology, 11*, 247–255.

Carroll, J. M., Smith-Kerker, P. S., Ford, J. R., and Mazur-Rimetz, S. A. 1987/1988. The minimal manual. *Human-Computer Interaction, 3*, 123–153.

Carroll, J. M., Thomas, J. C., and Malhotra. A. 1979. A clinical-experimental analysis of design problem solving. *Design Studies, 1*, 84–92.

Catrambone, R., and Carroll, J. M. 1987. Learning a word processing system with guided exploration and training wheels. In J. M. Carroll and P. P. Tanner (Eds.), *Proceedings of CHI+GI87 Human Factors in Computing Systems and Graphics Interface*, pp. 169–174. (Toronto, April 5–9). New York: ACM.

Chin, G., Rosson, M. B., and Carroll, J. M. 1997. Participatory analysis: Scenario-based requirements development. In *Proceedings of CHI'97 Human*

Factors in Computing Systems (Atlanta, March 25–27), pp. 162–169. New York: ACM.

Gagne, R. M., and Briggs, L. J. 1979. *Principles of instructional design*. New York: Holt, Rinehart and Winston.

Mack, R. L., Lewis, C. H., and Carroll, J. M. 1983. Learning to use office systems: Problems and prospects. *ACM Transactions on Office Information Systems, 1*, 254–271.

Rosson, M. B., and Carroll, J. M. 1996. Scaffolded examples. *Communications of the ACM, 39*(4), 46–47.

Rosson, M. B., Carroll, J. M., and Bellamy, R. K. E. 1990. Smalltalk scaffolding: A minimalist curriculum. In J. C. Chew & J. Whiteside (Eds.), *Proceedings of CHI90: Human Factors in Computing Systems* (Seattle, WA, April 1–5), pp. 423–429. New York: ACM.

Singley, M. K., Carroll, J. M., and Alpert, S. R. 1993. Incidental reification of goals in an intelligent tutor for Smalltalk. In B. duBoulay and E. Lemut (Eds.), *Cognitive models and intelligent environments for learning* programming. Proceedings of the NATO Advanced Research Workshop (Genova, Italy, March 17–21, 1992). New York: Springer Verlag.

2

Principles and Heuristics for Designing Minimalist Instruction

Hans van der Meij and John M. Carroll

Minimalist instruction is heavily learner oriented. It takes the need that learners have for meaningful activity and sense making as the primary requirement and resource for designing effective training and information. Of course, no serious approach to the design of instruction would set out to ignore or thwart these needs. But for many approaches, objectives of logical decomposition and structuring ultimately subordinate learners' preferences and propensities.

Research has repeatedly proved the effectiveness of minimalist instructions (Black, Carroll, and McGuigan 1987; Carroll et al. 1987; Carroll 1990b; Frese et al. 1988; Gong and Elkerton 1990; Lazonder and Van der Meij 1993; Oatley, Meldrum, and Draper 1991; Ramsay and Oatley 1992; VanderLinden, Cocklin, and McKita 1988; Van der Meij 1992; Wendel and Frese 1987). However, since the conception of minimalist instruction in the early 1980s, only a limited number of its ideas have found their way into more conventional approaches to instruction. One of the obstacles to a wider application is that its design principles sometimes lack the detailed specification that practitioners expect (Hallgren 1992; Horn 1992; Nickerson 1991; Tripp 1990). In this chapter, we present a comprehensive overview of four major principles of minimalist instruction and their corresponding heuristics.

The minimalist ideas presented here are intended primarily for the instruction of novice learners or users who are becoming acquainted with a new application or tool (e.g., word processor, object-oriented programming language). But their usefulness is not restricted to this audience, nor are they useful only for writing tutorials (whether on paper or online). Instead, we believe they are suited for optimizing instruction in general, and illustrations are offered to support this stance.

These minimalist principles and heuristics are guides and grist for thinking about instruction rather than prescriptions to be followed strictly. The heuristics are our solutions to design problems. As such, they should be concrete enough for readers to follow in developing their own minimalist instruction. At the same time, they do not fully detail everything there is to know, nor do they guarantee success in all situations. Some problem solving will always be needed. As environments, programs, audiences, and purposes of instruction vary, there will always be a need to adapt the design to particular situations, to incorporate other, new ideas, and to *not* follow some of the suggestions. Indeed, for this very reason we speak of principles and heuristics rather than of norms, standards, guidelines, criteria, rules, or prescriptions. Some of the descriptions already suggest a varied usage as we show that certain heuristics are better suited to the design of manuals, whereas others have more to offer for (re)designing the programmatic support to users.

We introduce these ideas with a mixture of theoretical and empirical background information. Throughout, we show that the heuristics have a strong bond with theoretical models, that they hinge on observations of users, or that they have proved their usefulness in comparative experiments. In addition, numerous examples are given to detail how particular heuristics can be used. The majority of these examples are drawn from the main fields of study in which we are working—that is, the design of manuals for word processors (i.e., WordPerfect 5.1) and the design of an instructive environment (paper and online) for an object-oriented programming language (Smalltalk). Together, they illustrate the wide range of situations in which the design principles and heuristics of minimalism can be applied.

An overview of the four major principles and their corresponding heuristics is presented in figure 2.1. We have tried to describe each section as an independent unit as much as possible to allow readers to browse, skip, scan, read, and study this chapter in the way that best addresses their personal agenda.

Principle 1: Choose an action-oriented approach
Heuristic 1.1: Provide an immediate opportunity to act.
Heuristic 1.2: Encourage and support exploration and innovation.
Heuristic 1.3: Respect the integrity of the user's activity.

Principle 2: Anchor the tool in the task domain
Heuristic 2.1: Select or design instructional activities that are real tasks.
Heuristic 2.2: The components of the instruction should reflect the task structure.

Principle 3: Support Error Recognition and Recovery
Heuristic 3.1: Prevent mistakes whenever possible.
Heuristic 3.2: Provide error information when actions are error prone or when correction is difficult.
Heuristic 3.3: Provide error information that supports detection, diagnosis, and recovery.
Heuristic 3.4: Provide on-the-spot error information.

Principle 4: Support reading to do, study and locate
Heuristic 4.1: Be brief; don't spell out everything.
Heuristic 4.2: Provide closure for chapters.

Figure 2.1
Four major design principles and their heuristics for designing minimalist instruction

2.1   Principle 1: Choose an Action-Oriented Approach

People trying to learn a skill are eager to act, to do something meaningful. This eagerness is at the heart of their motivation to learn the skill, but it also is the source of a fundamental production paradox (Carroll 1990a, 1993). To learn to do, it may be psychologically necessary to act. At the same time, we can clearly see from their misconceptions and errors that users need to learn in order to act (Carroll and Rosson 1987). Designing usable materials will therefore require a constant balancing of the learner's need to act with the learner's need for knowledge with which to plan and evaluate action. To manage the production paradox, we must always make genuine activity available to the learner and to scaffold, stage, and structure this activity to ensure that it is tractable and understandable.

Minimalist instruction is always action oriented. It is a priority in designing such materials to provide users with an immediate opportunity to act meaningfully (Carroll 1984, 1990b; Carroll et al. 1987). Minimalist instruction should also encourage and support exploration and innovation (Van der Meij 1993) and respect the integrity of the user's activity. We consider these points in turn.

Heuristic 1.1: Provide an Immediate Opportunity to Act

A priority in designing minimalist instruction is to invite users to act and to support their action. Of course, instruction for skill domains always seeks to support user activity, but often it does not make immediate activity a high enough priority. For example, tutorials often begin with an explanation of how the application and instruction work or an orientation to the semantics of the domain. Such explanations are valuable to the learner, of course, but, positioned at the very entrance to the manual, they constitute a distraction. The learner is confronted with prerequisites to action instead of the opportunity to act.

An alternative approach is to begin by giving the user less to read but more to do. The manual may, for example, first present a simple but realistic activity that conveys some of the explanatory content and then follow this with the balance of the explanation. In this approach, the learner still gets the explanation, but after having been given a chance to experience an activity.

Providing immediate opportunities for action is so central to minimalism that any example of minimalist instruction would illustrate it. An example is the Minimalist Tutorial and Tools for Smalltalk (MiTTS) (Rosson, Carroll, and Bellamy 1990; Rosson, et al. 1993). MiTTS consists of a brief tutorial to be used in concert with a set of programming tools and instrumented programming projects; it is directed at giving programmers experienced with traditional procedural languages (like Pascal and C) a rapid introduction to the object- oriented language Smalltalk. The manual is thirty-five pages long and is used in conjunction with an instructional environment that opens itself with a graphical animation of a blackjack card game. The intention is that both the slender manual and the graphical demonstration will impress the user as invitations to act.

In MiTTS, the programmer is exercising real code in the blackjack application within fifteen minutes of starting, and in two hours, the programmer is making changes to its design and implementation. After four to six hours, the programmer is working on open-ended projects enhancing other applications and their graphical user interfaces in novel ways. In many comparable tutorials for programming languages, students must endure a descriptive overview and rationale for the language they are learning and the instruction they are using before they get to do anything. For example, the instructional manual that accompanies the Smalltalk software (Digitalk 1989), a highly refined commercial manual that we take as representative of the state of the art, begins with a substantial sales pitch for object-oriented programming and a detailed argument that Smalltalk is more efficient to write than is Pascal.

In our minimal manual for WordPerfect (Lazonder and Van der Meij 1993; Van der Meij 1992, 1993; Van der Meij and Lazonder 1992) users receive their first instructions to act on page 2. Again, the contrast with other manuals is striking. A brief inventory of ten commercially available tutorials for WordPerfect reveals that, on average, they give the first instruction on page 15 (not counting the title page or the table of contents). Even if we exclude one extremely long-winded tutorial in which users started doing something on page 56, the other manuals still required users to read seven pages more than our minimal manual.

In general, we feel that it is important to take serious the idea that users are never convinced by talk alone. Documentation should become more compatible with guided tours and graphical user interfaces that provide users with a direct access to "things." Users who bother to pick up the manual at all are probably more than ready to be convinced by example activity.

Heuristic 1.2: Encourage and Support Exploration and Innovation
Users should always feel in control of their own activities. People are more engaged by self-directed activity; they prefer it and learn more from it (Carroll 1990b; Kluwe, Misiak, and Haider 1990; Mack , Lewis, and Carroll 1990; Rettig 1991; Van der Meij and Van Stapele 1993; Wendel and Frese 1987). Minimalist instruction provides users with opportunities to act that are, to the greatest extent possible, under the user's control (Carroll et al. 1987; Van der Meij 1992).

These are not unguided explorations, however, because such activities can be very ineffective and frustrating (Carroll 1993; Charney and Reder 1986; Charney, Reder and Kusbit 1990; Williams and Farkas 1992). Nor are they instructions that ask users to carry out exercise steps couched at a very low level, because such activities are perceived as trivial and unengaging. In minimalist instruction we try to strike a balance between activities that are sufficiently open-ended for users to understand and undertake as meaningful projects and yet are defined clearly enough that they can orient to specific goals and perhaps specific methods in pursuing activities. We will illustrate three points in this respect: use a language that invites users to explore, consider carefully when users should be offered suggestions for other strategies, and focus more on student evaluation and less on expert evaluation.

In various places in our WordPerfect manuals, users are encouraged to try things out for themselves (Lazonder and Van der Meij 1993; Van der Meij 1992, 1993; Van der Meij and Lazonder 1993). A critical aspect of these action prompts is the specific way in which they are formulated. Users are clearly given the message that exploration is welcome because most action prompts are accompanied by expressions such as, "Please try it," "Try and see for yourself," and "See what happens" that invite users to act. In contrast, when conventional manuals describe alternative options, they tend to use relatively neutral statements. They describe rather than invite (e.g., "You can also ..." and "Another possibility is ..."). This difference in style makes the minimalist action prompts more seductive. Our research indicates that these prompts in our minimal manual lead to 33% more explorations than do the descriptive prompts in our control (conventional) manual (Van der Meij 1994; Van der Meij and Lazonder 1992).

One of the situations in which users are especially receptive to suggestions about other strategies or possibilities is immediately after completing a project. For this reason, we decided to create a "Guru" (an expert programmer) that users could call up at the end of a tutorial project in Smalltalk programming. This Guru (Alpert, Singley, and Carroll, 1995) was designed to help novices exploit more fully the capacity of existing (sub)programs (classes and methods in Smalltalk). For example, many novices would fail to use the existing program for "Arrays" class to create an arrangement of integers by changing just one line of code. Instead, they would create a completely new program. The Guru was intended to suggest to users the more efficient use of the inheritance mechanism in Smalltalk and to convey the insight that the expert strategy is easier to maintain. We believed that users would be in the best position to appreciate these insights after having practiced creating their own code.

For any nontrivial programming problem, there are infinite solutions. Indeed, students are often highly engaged by the task of fooling instructional systems that purport to be able to evaluate programming solutions. One solution to this problem is to focus less on evaluation of student efforts. Particularly for new users, it may be more important to obtain an interpretable result than an exactly correct one. Thus, instead of checking the student's program line by line, the instruction could indicate some tests and criteria or provide an instructor's solution and allow the student to do the evaluation. If the student is satisfied or the program produces the right results at the level of the tests and criteria, we can consider it a correct result. It probably is close enough.

We are taking an approach like this in designing a tutorial system for the skill of object-oriented software design. This design skill is so complex that managing and evaluating student efforts closely would force us to trivialize the projects. Instead, we decided to instruct at a very conceptual level and to provide checkpoints at which the students can measure a design against a teacher's solution annotated with its design rationale (Robertson et al. 1993). We encourage comparisons but candidly note that many correct solution are possible. We offer one solution only to help the students reflect on their own work. In this approach, we have thus off-loaded the management and evaluation task to the student, thereby turning it into a further learning activity.

The optimal balance point between instructing and supporting exploration and innovation may vary considerably from project to project. An important factor to consider is the guarantee of safe progress. It is stimulating to veer off the prescribed path only if users have some confidence that the prescribed path is still there and can be rejoined. In providing immediate opportunities for action, it will often be useful to scale down the initial problem space in which users will be acting (Carroll and Carrithers 1984). Under these circumstances, explorations support active elaborations that can be very effective in promoting comprehension and memory.

Heuristic 1.3: Respect the Integrity of the User's Activity

To the designer, the learner's activity can often seem ancillary: the designer's goal is to impart information and help the user develop skill and understanding. It is critically important for designers to keep in mind that the moment-to-moment goal of the user may be much less sophisticated and much shorter term (Carroll 1990a, 1990b; Hill 1989; Landauer 1988; Mack, Lewis, and Carroll 1990). Instruction and documentation must respect the integrity of the user's activity. In some cases, this will mean subordinating the presentation of information or explicit instruction to the continuity of the user's project-oriented activity. A variety of passive help techniques that support this heuristic have been developed.

For example, with the release of the new operating system for the Apple Macintosh (System 7), balloon help was introduced. This help appears only on request; users must select the Show Balloons command from the Help menu. When they do, objects are documented as the cursor sweeps over displayed objects. Thus, balloon help mimics the main purpose of a glossary, providing users with the meaning of an object at any time (Brockmann 1990; Farkas 1993).

We too have experimented with passive help tools in some of our recent systems. Our work on the MoleHill intelligent tutoring system for Smalltalk illustrates two ways to offer help without imposing on the user (Singley, Carroll, and Alpert 1991, 1993). MoleHill's GoalPoster (see figure 2.2) displays a best-guess analysis of the user's programming plan. This goal analysis can be used, for example, as an aid for reflection and as an index into help facilities (Singley, Carroll, and Alpert 1993). We leave it to the user to decide whether to use or ignore the goal analysis; we cannot be certain it is the correct analysis unless we ask the user and because we can never be certain when the time is right to interrupt the programming project to initiate a dialogue about programming plans.

MoleHill's Commentator takes a similar approach in documenting the code for particular classes and methods (figure 2.2). The Commentator inhabits a small pane in the MoleHill window and passively displays stored documentation for the currently selected chunk of code. It makes a best guess as to which coherent code structure the user meant to select (indicated to the user by a lined box, drawn around that code constituent). The corresponding documentation is displayed in the Commentator pane. It can be ignored, but it can also be annotated; it is user

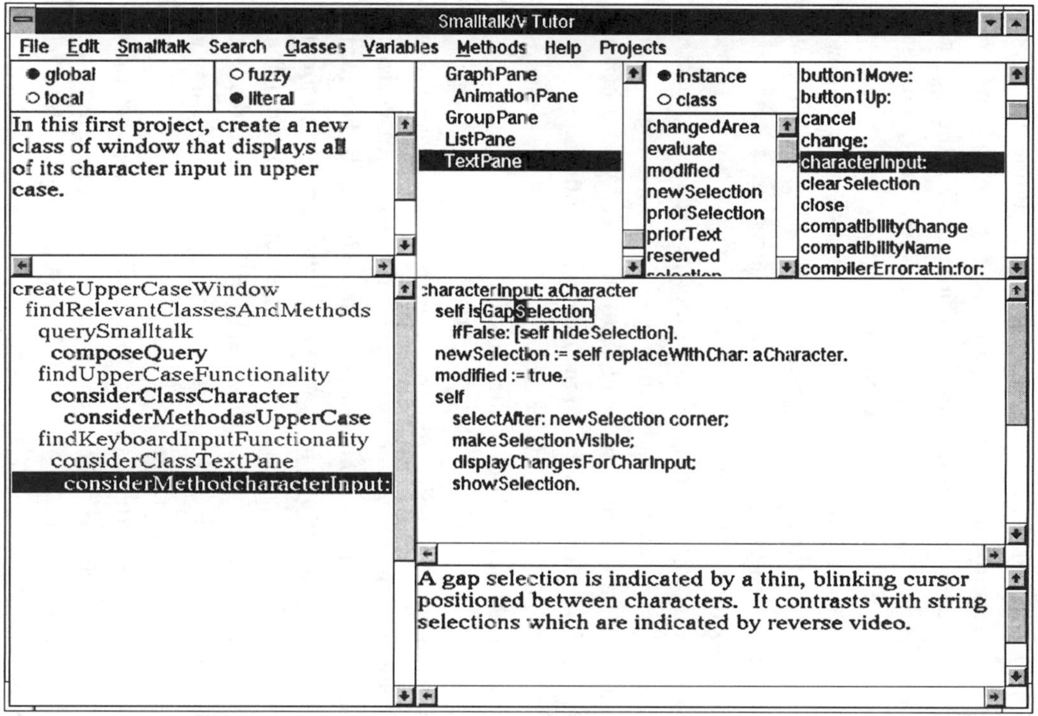

Smalltalk/V Tutor

File   Edit   Smalltalk   Search   Classes   Variables   Methods   Help   Projects

● global   ○ fuzzy
○ local   ● literal

In this first project, create a new class of window that displays all of its character input in upper case.

createUpperCaseWindow
findRelevantClassesAndMethods
  querySmalltalk
    composeQuery
  findUpperCaseFunctionality
    considerClassCharacter
    considerMethodasUpperCase
  findKeyboardInputFunctionality
    considerClassTextPane
    considerMethodcharacterInput:

GraphPane
AnimationPane
GroupPane
ListPane
TextPane

● Instance
○ class

changedArea
evaluate
modified
newSelection
priorSelection
reserved

button1Move:
button1Up:
cancel
change:
characterInput:
clearSelection
close
compatibilityChange
compatibilityName
compilerErroratin:for:

```
characterInput: aCharacter
    self isGapSelection
        ifFalse: [self hideSelection].
    newSelection := self replaceWithChar: aCharacter.
    modified := true.
    self
        selectAfter: newSelection corner;
        makeSelectionVisible;
        displayChangesForCharInput;
        showSelection.
```

A gap selection is indicated by a thin, blinking cursor positioned between characters. It contrasts with string selections which are indicated by reverse video.

Figure 2.2
MoleHill, the Smalltalk tutor, presents passive help to users in different ways. In the lower left is the Goal Poster, which offers a best guess of a programmer's plans. The lower right view is the Commentator tool, which explains the currently selected code.

editable (Singley et al. 1991). Thus, far from interrupting the user's activity, the Commentator offers itself as a resource to be employed for the user's purposes and interests. For example, in figure 2.2 the user has selected the *s* in the Smalltalk message *is Gap Selection*. The Commentator parses the line of code and determines that *Gap Selection* is the smallest meaningful code constituent. Therefore, it displays a comment for that constituent (see the pane at the bottom of the MoleHill window).

To respect the integrity of users' activities, designers must often step aside a bit. They can create help but should not impose this on users. However, this does not mean that users cannot be seduced into other actions. If the designer succeeds in creating effectively meaningful activities for the user, these will become genuine to the user. At any instant, they will become the activities to which the user is committed.

2.2   Principle 2: Anchor the Tool in the Task Domain

For most users, an application is a tool they want to use to achieve objectives in the task domain for which that application has been designed. The tool is merely a means; it is almost never an end in itself. For example, the user of a hypertext application may be interested in gathering and organizing notes for a report. But such a person is not fundamentally trying to build a card stack or a relational database; these are merely vehicles for the person's real concern. This observation is implicit and obvious to the user, but it can easily escape the writer.

Instructions are often written as if the tool itself were the user's principal objective. For example, one HyperCard manual presents, on its second page, an argument that card stacks are more flexible than relational databases—and this before the reader has ever been allowed any experience with a card stack! This, of course, is much like the introductory statements of tutorials for word processors that promise novice readers that macros have wonderful possibilities. Such an approach can be distracting, even confusing, for users; and perhaps worse, it may increase anxiety (e.g., "This is too difficult for me") and waste the opportunity to leverage the user's intrinsic interest in and knowledge about the task domain in instructing on the use of the application.

Minimalist instruction is always anchored in the task domain. To the greatest extent possible, tasks are selected from the core tasks of the application domain (Carroll 1990b; Van der Meij 1992). The users' interest in and understanding of these tasks is what motivated their original interest in the application. Building the instruction from within such tasks capitalizes on this original motivation and helps to satisfy it. The basic tasks of a domain provide a structural template for learning activities; they are a rubric and a meaningful context for the presentation of information. In addition, they provide concepts and terms with which to present and explain an application. Two enabling heuristics are enumerated below.

Heuristic 2.1: Select or Design Instructional Activities That Are Real Tasks

We recommend presenting the user with instruction activities that can instantly be recognized as genuine (Carroll 1984, 1990b, 1993; Van der Meij 1992). These tasks can be quite modest. For example, early on in the documentation for Northern Telecom's Norstar system, the task of customizing the ring on one's own telephone is suggested (figure 2.3), a very elegant idea. Office workers may be unsure of the scope and potential utility of a telephony system like Norstar, but they will immediately understand the task of changing the ring signal on their own phone. In addition, the procedure required to accomplish the task is quite simple, and the result is concrete and personal. Thus, the task is a meaningful achievement in itself. It suggests a general action schema for further interactions with the system, and, perhaps most important, it may help orient and interest the user in identifying and attempting other tasks.

The programming domain is of special interest with respect to providing real tasks because it is so general. It is not obvious what the core tasks of programming are, in the sense that it is obvious that the core tasks of word processing are creating, revising, and printing documents. One approach we took to remedy this was to guide students to create small applications or to provide them with applications and suggest that they extend or debug these. We have created a set of small games for this purpose (tic-tac-toe, gomoku, blackjack). For example, we presented a graphical gomoku game with a special stealMove method that permitted

Introduction	Your Norstar M7310 Phone offers the simplicity of a standard telephone plus the versatility of many special features. This card will help you to use your new Norstar phone and to customize some of its features. When using your phone refer to the detachable Feature List and the Receiver Card under the receiver for quick reference.

Telephone Buttons	⬛ Rls	To release a call or a feature press this button.
	⬛ Hold	To put a call on hold press this button.
	⬛ Feature	To use a feature press this button and then enter a feature code.
	[dialpad]	Press the dialpad to make a call or to enter feature codes.
	◀》 ◀》	When using the receiver, handsfree speaker or headset, press this button to adjust the volume.

Adjusting Ring Volume	Try using some of these buttons now to set the volume of your phone's ring.
	1 To make your phone ring press ⬛Feature ⬛* ⬛8 ⬛0 .
	2 To reach desired volume press ◀》 ◀》 repeatedly.

Display and Display buttons	**Display** The top line shows you the time and date, and call information. The display helps you use Norstar features. Follow the instructions. **Display buttons** Function-names for the three display buttons appear on the second line of the display.

Selecting Ring Type	Now select a distinctive ring to help you distinguish between your phone and others nearby.
	1 Press ⬛Feature ⬛* ⬛6 .
	2 Press the ⬛Next display button until you hear the ring type you want.
	3 Press ⬛OK display button to finish.

Figure 2.3

An illustrative page from the Norstar system. Brief explanations next to the headings make the goals accessible and understandable. Note the early positioning of customizing the ring signal.

the game to take two moves at once occasionally. The bug was fairly obvious and easy to correct, but repairing it is a representative programming task, and the results of making the correction are immediate and tangible.

In word processing, sample files can be used to get users to work on real tasks without burdening them with too many additional activities. For example, users may be offered templates that help create a fully formatted text but do not hinge on having to specify all the codes for headings, fonts, or margins. Users can also be stimulated to change some formatting codes to accommodate their own particular situation. Similarly, tutorial programs may present users with a paper manual that asks them to activate and make changes in training diskettes with sample files.

Users will be able to recognize an activity as genuine only to the extent that they have had adequate prior experience in the task domain to underwrite such a judgment. Therefore, to capitalize most effectively on the users' interests in and knowledge about the task domain, instructions must build on their prior skills, knowledge, and experience by directly recruiting the scenarios and procedures of the task domain that are familiar to the users (Carroll 1990a, 1993; Davis Baker 1988; Kay and Black 1990; Mack et al. 1990; Ramey 1988).

Heuristic 2.2: Create Components of Instruction That Reflect the Task Structure

The structural organization of a manual, often codified in its section headings, is salient to the user and can be a powerful resource to the instructional designer (Byrnes and Guthrie 1992; Hager 1992; Hartley 1985, 1990; Matchett and Ray 1989; Spyridakis and Wenger 1992; Wright 1987). The headings should therefore be crafted to convey the major procedural elements in the instructional tasks. Such headings help the user keep in view the big picture of the skill being learned. For example, presenting the basic create-and-print word processing scenario through a series of subsections entitled "Starting a new memo," "Working in the typing area," and "Requesting a print" suggests the major structural components for the create-and-print scenario.

Examples of ineffective headings are "You can typeset your own letters," "Switching to and from the DOS command line," and "Tips

Topic 1: Exploring the blackjack game	**Topic 1: Exploring an application**
Starting up the Bittitalk browser	Starting up the class browser
The blackjack game	Finding the application game
Creating an instance of blackjack	Creating an application instance
Sending messages to the blackjack instance	Sending messages to the application instance
Exploring other objects and message used in blackjack	Exploring other objects and message used by the application class

Figure 2.4
Headings should give an overview of the main tasks in a domain. Generic headings (right column) may be more useful than specific headings (left column) to support the development of a general schema and subsequent reference use.

for users of WordPerfect." Although it is easy to imagine important content under these headings, they do not suggest anything at all about the organization of the basic domain tasks. They do not give the big picture and instead draw users into the lowest level of the procedure, the individual steps.

In the MiTTS manual, the headings convey an overview of the main tasks in the domain (Rosson et al. 1993). The major subheads for chapter 1 are shown in the left column of figure 2.4. This sequence of phrases is a fair summary of what the user does in this chapter: open a browsing tool, use the tool to survey the code for a blackjack game application, use the code to create an instance of the blackjack class, further explore the code by sending some simple messages to the blackjack instance, and then continue to explore some other objects used by blackjack and some further message-sending relations. Indeed, this is also the basic structure of the prototypical scenario for code exploration in Smalltalk programming.

These headings focus the learner's attention on working on the blackjack project but leave it to the learner to generate the analysis of that specific project. To extract the general schema of Smalltalk programming activities, general headings can be more effective. For example, in our work on the Reuse View Matcher, a documentation tool, we found that even when people consider very concrete examples useful, they sometimes are hampered by example-specific headings in the presentation of the examples (Rosson and Carroll 1994). In addition, general headings allowed us to couch some explanation at the most general level. Since users typically try to make subsequent use of instructional material as reference material, more general headings, such as those shown in the right column of figure 2.4, may subsequently serve as better search keys.

A similar heuristic can be applied in designing online instructional tools. In our View Matcher tool, several views of a running Smalltalk application are displayed simultaneously. These different views comprise a structural analysis of concerns users can pursue: a graphical presentation of the application (e.g., the blackjack game) displays a particular task state, a method execution stack details the computations that correspond to that application state, a commentary pane links the two by providing a description of the currently selected computation (message send) in the application semantics, and a Bittitalk browser displays the code that underlies the currently selected computation in the method execution stack (figure 2.2 presents another example of multiple views from the MolcHill tutoring system).

In short, headings that reflect the task structure may support users in different ways: they can offer scenarios that users otherwise (must) create themselves, support the different points of view users (should) take in task execution, and help users locate information easily when the manual is consulted for reference.

2.3   Principle 3: Support Error Recognition and Recovery

Software users make many mistakes, and correcting these mistakes may be very time consuming. Research shows that learners spend between 25 and 50 percent of their time correcting errors (Arnold and Roe 1987; Bailey 1983; Card, Moran, and Newell 1983, 1990; Carroll et al. 1987; Graesser and Murray 1990; Lazonder and Van der Meij 1994a; Van der Meij 1993). Reducing mistakes and streamlining detection, diagnosis, and recovery may substantially reduce the frustration and anxiety of learning about and using computers. In addition, it may make such learning and use more productive (Wendel and Frese 1987).

In our research, we distinguish the following categories of mistakes: semantic, syntactic, and slip (Allwood and Eliasson 1987; Lazonder 1993, 1994a, 1994b; Lazonder and Van der Meij 1992, 1994a; Lewis and Norman 1986). A semantic error occurs when a method that cannot possibly achieve a given goal is chosen. For example, users make a semantic error when they try to save a file by clicking one of the buttons controlling the presentation of files (e.g., the maximize or minimize button on the title bar). When a correct method is followed but its execution is performed improperly, a syntactic error occurs. A typical example is that of a user who selects a bold font and then selects a text target (instead of performing the two actions in the reverse order). Slips are small mistakes that occur at the keystroke level (e.g., mistyping the name of a file when conducting a search for it).

In general, we have found it easier to support the detection, diagnosis, and correction of syntactic errors than of semantic errors or slips (Lazonder and Van der Meij 1994b, 1995). Of all error types, syntactic mistakes are the most foreseeable. They can be predicted with reasonable accuracy, and therefore precise and well-placed error information can be given for these errors. Semantic errors and slips are more difficult to predict. Consequently it is harder to provide error information at the right place and with the right (i.e., specific) content. The described correction method is often a general method that works for different kinds of mistakes and in many different situations (e.g., choose Undo or press the Escape key; Van der Meij 1992).

For detecting errors that are difficult to predict, usability testing is indispensable. So although our experience concurs with Schriver's (1992) observation that writers with extensive usability testing experience develop a third eye for the problematic places in a manual, iterative testing remains necessary. It is absolutely essential to test the manual with a sample of subjects from the intended audience (Carroll 1984; Karat 1990; Mack, Lewis, and Carroll 1990; Schriver 1989, 1992, 1993; Thimbleby 1991). In general, we have found that six to eight subjects suffices for locating most of the "hot spots," or areas where most users are likely to make mistakes, in a manual.

With regard to the minimalist philosophy of presenting less information to users, the provision of error information takes a special position in that it is often desirable to present more than the bare minimum. Our research suggests there should be ample error information in the manual (Carroll 1984, 1990a; Lazonder and Van der Meij 1994a, 1994b;

Thimbleby 1991). In general, we have found it desirable to include error information at a rate of about once for every three actions. The frequent inclusion of this information provides a safety net, supports more flexible and ambitious action-oriented learning, and helps deepen the users' understanding of how the program works. Without the error information, action-oriented instructions can be forced to a low-level focus on training mere playing-back scripts (Charney, Reder, and Kusbit 1990; Way 1991).

Another argument for the frequent inclusion of error information in the manual is that programs often do not have adequate help systems for novices. For example, in our research with word processors (for MS DOS), we registered only about ten successful instances of such consults. Given a sample of over 350 users working about fifteen hundred hours with this word processor, this does not speak favorably of its support. Other research reports the same miserable state of affairs. Allwood and Kalén (1993), for example, mention that on 93 percent of the occasions when help was needed in a patient registration system, it was not even available.

If the manual supports error detection, diagnosis, and correction according to the heuristics that follow, user mistakes may help rather than hinder. They can substantially contribute to the users' confidence and skills in using a program (Carroll et al. 1987; Lazonder 1994; Lazonder and Van der Meij 1993; Seifert and Hutchins 1992; Van der Meij 1993). For example, in a recent study, we compared subjects who used a manual with error information designed according to our minimalist heuristics with subjects who used the same manual but with most of the error information excluded. Significant effects were found on many aspects of error detection, diagnosis, and correction. For example, the presence of error information helped subjects detect errors 33 percent faster during training and led to 28 percent better diagnosis and 73 percent more successful correction after training (Lazonder and Van der Meij, 1995).

Heuristic 3.1: Prevent Mistakes Whenever Possible

The best way to remedy some mistakes is to help users avoid making them in the first place. Prevention can be found in different guises, for example, by following well-known guidelines such as providing a safe trajectory of activities, using short and simple sentences, signaling action information clearly, and minimizing jargon.

Mistakes can sometimes be prevented by including hints in the manual. For example, in our MiTTS tutorial, we have used hints such as, "Upper and lower case matter in Smalltalk. Type the expression exactly as it appears in the instruction" (Rosson et al. 1993). Because of their distinct signaling and the high interest value of hints in general and because the pages are not crowded with hints, we feel that there is a fair chance that users will actually follow the advice.

Some errors can be prevented by using the results from user tests to rewrite certain sections (Gould and Lewis 1985; Karat 1990). Tests may indicate that users often make mistakes in executing a particular task, signaling that a further decomposition of the task (e.g., making subgoals and choosing smaller chunks of action steps) may be helpful. For example, stimulated by the demands for creating a user guide for the athletes and officials using the 1984 Olympic Message System, Gould and his coworkers tested 200 pilot versions before reaching a final product (Gould et al. 1987). In general, recordings and analyses of user errors can prompt a redesign of the manual or of the program (Gould et al. 1987; Mantei and Teorey 1988).

Errors can also be blocked. Certain options can be made unavailable to the user, or users may not be given a chance to explore certain options. An important rationale behind such a training-wheels technology is that users can get themselves in serious trouble when exploring (Carroll and Carrithers 1984). For example, one system we studied had an extremely inflexible response to the misspecification of a disk name: it froze in the state prompting for that disk. Most users responded to this error by turning the system off and restarting it, which took several minutes (and caused a disk recovery error as a side effect). When we designed our training-wheels error-blocking software, we made sure to include this error among those blocked.

The best place to prevent errors is probably in the program itself. For both writers and programmers, defensive programming should be the ultimate goal. For example, many programs currently warn users who wish to close a file without saving the changes that were made by asking, "Would you like to save your changes?" In MS DOS, giving the command Delete *.* can have such catastrophic consequences that users are always asked to verify that action first: "All your files will be deleted! Are you sure? (Y/N)." Because of the high risk, even the default is special. Normally a default value is automatically indicated; here it is not. Users must type the response; an inadvertent Enter merely repeats the question. Clearly such error prevention can never be as timely or as effective in a paper manual.

Heuristic 3.2: Provide Error Information When Actions Are Error Prone or Correction Is Difficult

Error information is often needed when actions are error prone. Typically these situations arise because of a mismatch with the users' knowledge or because the required actions deviate from a standard routine. For example, in WordPerfect 5.1, users often got stuck when they wanted to exit the Print Preview mode. Activating the menu—the standard routine—failed because the program did not accommodate it. In addition, there was no information on the screen suggesting how to exit. As a result, many users were lost, and many mistakes were made.

Failures also often occur when the users' real-world experience conflicts with the way in which the program should be operated or when prior knowledge is insufficient (Carroll, Mack, and Kellogg 1988; Douglas and Moran 1984; Payne 1991). Typically this is the case when users forget to create a text block before underlining existing text. Users overlook the marking of a block of text because they do not have to perform these actions in a noncomputer environment. They are simply not part of the way in which they normally deal with issues of text presentation.

The presence of error information may also be called for when correction is difficult. Often, but not always, this is the case when the consequences of some actions are hard to understand or when error recovery truly depends on correcting the mistake.

Recuperating from mistakes is possible in two ways: by following a (re)constructive approach or a corrective approach (Lazonder 1994a, 1994b; Lazonder and Van der Meij 1995). In a (re)constructive approach, users merely reposition themselves, which suffices for task continuity. In a corrective approach, the user must really correct (remove) the mistake. Especially in the latter situation, the manual should provide error information. For example, when users give a wrong file name after activating the File Retrieve option in WordPerfect, they are trapped on the status bar until they correct their mistake. The manual should inform users how to make this correction.

In designing MiTTS, we identified several seemingly trivial syntax errors that produced outcomes uninterpretable to new Smalltalk programmers. For example, omitting the return symbol ($\wedge$) produces a method that returns nothing—an outcome for which it is difficult to find specific causes. We paid careful attention to the way this detail was introduced in the manual to avoid the occurrence of the error and to support its recognition and correction.

Error information is nearly always called for when two or more of the above factors appear simultaneously, that is, when standard routines fail and there is no other information to guide the user. Users also need help with mistakes when there is a mismatch with prior knowledge, the cause or consequence of an incorrect action is difficult to understand, or error recovery depends on a true correction of the mistake.

Heuristic 3.3: Provide Error Information That Supports Detection, Diagnosis, and Correction

After committing a mistake, users need to recognize and locate their error, understand and analyze it to an appropriate extent, and then take some corrective or evasive action (Allwood 1984; Lazonder 1993, 1994a, 1994b; Lazonder and Van der Meij 1994a; Van der Meij 1993). For error recovery, detection and correction are requisite; diagnosis is optional. These processes are detailed below along with illustrations of how they can affect the type of error information given in the manual.

Detection of a mistake can be triggered internally or externally (Allwood 1984; Lazonder 1993). Internal triggering takes place when users feel they have done something wrong but lack a visible cue to support this. Typically this kind of triggering is set off by questions like, "Did I do this right?" and "Is this wrong?" External triggering takes place when some information on the screen sets off these questions. For example, a program message may warn the user that a file is about to be removed without saving the changes. Questions can also arise when users are confronted with some unexpected and unintended outcome. For example, when users forget to mark a piece of text as a block and then try to set it into italics, nothing visibly happens. This, in turn, will set them wondering.

In diagnosis, the nature of the error is established; users try to find out what kind of error they have made (Lazonder and Van der Meij 1994a, 1994b). When triggering is stimulated externally, detection and diagnosis often are one process. The presence and the nature of a mistake are then cued simultaneously. Typical examples are on-screen messages such as "syntax error" and "ERROR—File CHATPER1.DOC not found" or warnings such as "All files will be deleted." Diagnosing after internal triggering is much more difficult because users have no visible cue suggesting what mistake(s) may have been made.

In diagnosis, yet another process may take place: an analysis of the cause of the error (Lazonder and Van der Meij 1992). For some program messages, this cause can be located easily. A message like "ERROR—File CHATPER1.DOC not found" speaks for itself. In many cases, however, these messages do not reveal the cause (e.g., "Cannot change ... setting"), and this step in diagnosis must be made by the user. Think-aloud protocols of users then typically reveal some inferential reasoning such as, "Ah, of course, I pressed F1 instead of Shift plus F1" and "Oh, I forgot to type the dot" or "I don't want to do that."

In correction, users set themselves a new goal (Allwood 1984; Arnold and Roe 1987; Lazonder and Van der Meij 1994a, 1994b). This goal may be to recoup: to correct the mistake and get on with the work. It may also be that users try to get back to where they were right before the mistake, merely putting themselves into a position to start afresh (Lazonder and Van der Meij 1995).

The error information in our manuals is designed so that it supports all these processes when necessary. That is, users may be given information to detect, diagnose, and recover from a mistake (Lazonder 1994a, 1994b; Lazonder and Van der Meij 1994a, 1994b; Van der Meij 1992, 1993). The examples shown in figure 2.5 illustrate that these processes are not always treated in the same detail. Among others, variations depend on whether the mistake must be corrected or whether only a repositioning is needed. Some variations also stem from a fine-tuning of

1. "If the statement **A:\coins.wp** does not appear on the status-bar, you have forgotten to clear the screen first. Press the F7 key and type a **N** twice to clear the screen."

Error type: semantic
Problem: detection and correction
Solution: specific detection information correction information

2. "If the statement **Document to be retrieved:** does not appear on the screen, you have chosen a wrong command. Press the F1 key to undo your choice."

Error type: semantic
Problem: detection and correction, diagnosis may be impossible
Solution: specific detection information, general correction information

3. "If the text has been inserted at the wrong place, you have positioned the cursor wrongly after pressing the ENTER key. Remove the text again."

Error type: syntactic
Problem: diagnosis
Solution: specific detection and diagnostic information, prompts for correction

4. "If the statement **Drive not ready reading drive A.** appears, you have not inserted the diskette deep enough into the drive. Insert it so that the button pops up. Then type a **1**"

Error type: syntactic
Problem: detection, diagnosis, and correction
Solution: specific information for detection, diagnosis, and correction (note that no full stop is given after the last sentence to prevent an accidental typing error)

5. "Typing mistakes can be corrected by pressing the BACKSPACE key. Thereafter type the correct text."

Error type: slip
Problem: none
Solution: general correction information

6. "If your screen remains empty, you may have made a typing error. Again type the name of the file and press the ENTER key."

Error type: slip
Problem: diagnosis and correction
Solution: specific correction information

7. "If the statement **Document to be saved: A:\letter1.wp** does not appear on the screen, you have made a typing error. Press the ENTER key once and then answer the question the program asks you."

Error type: syntactic or slip
Problem: detection
Solution: specific detection information, prompt to interact with program for correction

Figure 2.5
Error information given in the WordPerfect Minimal Manual. The left column presents seven examples of error information. The right column characterizes each example by type of mistake, user's main problem, and the corresponding rationale for the content of the error information.

program and manual and from the suitability of specific or general correction methods. In addition, when a program provides prompts for recovery, it can be desirable to give incomplete correction information in the manual, suggesting that, from a certain point onward, users should follow these prompts (example 7 in figure 2.5).

Heuristic 3.4: Provide On-the-Spot Error Information

Manuals often fail to support the users' error recognition and correction at the right spot (Van der Meij, 1995, 1996a). We believe that error information should be placed where users need it most: as near as possible to the wrongly executed actions or methods (Carroll 1984, 1990a; Carroll et al. 1987; Van der Meij 1993, 1995, 1996a).

Proximal positioning of the error information is crucial for a number of reasons. First, it can help users catch mistakes early, before they lead to possibly even greater mistakes that can be nightmares to restore. Second, when only one or two actions have been executed before the user notices the mistake, there is a fair chance the user can easily diagnose what went wrong. Diagnosing is much more difficult, or downright impossible, when a multitude of key presses lie between the mistake and the moment of detection. Third, proximal positioning helps overcome the problem of giving the right contextual information and of being specific enough. When all error information is placed in a separate section, it can be extremely difficult to describe the problem state so that the information is both easily accessible and readily understood by the reader (Hunt and Vassiliadis 1988).

In our research, we discovered yet another reason that proximal positioning of error information is desirable. We found that users exploit the error information to explore error correction out of curiosity, even when they can execute the particular task faultlessly (Van der Meij 1992, 1994). Such exploratory usage of error information is neither incidental nor unusual. Around 15 percent of all error information in our minimal manuals is used to practice making a mistake and recovering from it. For one manual this meant an average of seven such error simulations during a practice period of around four hours (Van der Meij 1994). When the error information is placed in a separate section in the manual, this type of usage is probably zero.

2.4   Principle 4: Support Reading to Do, Study, and Locate

The various ways in which people process a manual have been qualified under such colorful names as the penguin syndrome, the nose-in-the-book phenomenon, and the kick-and-rush strategy (Bethke et al. 1991; Carroll 1984; Rettig 1991). All of these names signal that users do not systematically process their manual from beginning to end. Instead, their behavior is more flexible. Sometimes they read to study, and sometimes they read to locate some information. Most of the time, however, they read to do; that is, their reading is task and action oriented (Bethke et al. 1991; Carroll 1984; Debs 1988; Redish 1988; Sticht 1985). Observations from users suggest they can be classified roughly into three main groups.

A small group of users is likely to read a conventional manual cover to cover. Penrose and Seiford (1988) suggest this may constitute less than 15 percent of all readers. In contrast, for our minimal manuals we have found figures of 90 percent and higher. These users follow the sequencing of the chapters and process the whole manual, but they do not process the manual in a completely linear fashion. Instead, their behavior is recursive; they reread chapters and frequently look back to earlier sections. By presenting only the necessary preliminaries and little text overall, writers can increase the chances that a large group of users will process the manual in this fashion.

A second group of users typically begins at the beginning but abandons the manual after a while, and then processes it in a more random fashion, using a lot of browsing. When certain tasks in the manual are attempted, these users must go back and forth in the manual to find out how prerequisite actions can be performed. To support such explorations, browsing, and look-backs, the manual should be designed in a modular fashion, making sections like chapters and paragraphs as independent of previous sections as possible. In addition, prerequisite actions must clearly be indicated, and headings and signaling techniques must support reading to locate (Dreher 1993; Dreher and Guthrie 1993).

A third group of users uses the manual as a last resort. Usually they turn to the manual only when they are stuck, browsing the body text to find the right information. They may also use the front- or backmatter of the manual in order to conduct a more directed search. These users profit from the same design techniques as those in the second group. In addition, special attention is needed for the front- and backmatter. For instance, the careful construction of a proper table of contents, including a judicious wording of headings, is called for.

The manual should somehow support all of these users and all their reading strategies, and to achieve this, the manual must make a favorable first impression. It is vitally important to avoid giving the manual a massive appearance (Brockmann 1990; Thing 1984). Just by looking at its size, users should get the idea that working through the manual will not take them long and that learning to use the application will not be too difficult. Minimization of content is therefore necessary; the manual must cut down considerably on substance. Combined with adequate presentation techniques, the old Bauhaus notion of doing more with less can come true. The heuristics presented below detail how to achieve this.

Heuristic 4.1: Be Brief; Don't Spell Out Everything

Remember that users are generally not seeking explanations for their own sake (Carroll 1990b; Wright 1989). Manuals traditionally present explanatory material as a prerequisite to procedural material. For instance, how information is stored magnetically on disks is discussed before the user is introduced to procedures for creating and manipulating such information. If explanations are needed, they should be short to give users the impression of being easy to work through (Markel, Vaccaro, and Hewett 1992; Meyer 1986), and we suggest they may often be more effective when given after, rather than before, task completion.

Another way to be brief is to create chapters of two to four pages (Arnold 1988; Weiss 1991), to give users the impression that working them through does not require an inordinate amount of time or the endurance of a long-distance runner. The manual must live up to these expectations; chapters should not only look short, they also should take a short time to work through. We have found that designing for a mean time of around twenty minutes per chapter works well. This generally enables 95 percent of all users to complete a chapter within thirty minutes, which seems about the right time for them to concentrate on the task and stay motivated.

Rather than explaining or showing it all to users, writers can use pointers and prompts to have users infer certain facts or procedures. A key principle for not spelling out everything is to omit information that can be inferred easily (Carroll 1990b; Carroll et al. 1987; Lazonder and Van der Meij 1993; Van der Meij 1992). For example, manuals often discuss how certain keys work. One manual for a word processor even introduces the metaphor of the Pied Piper of Hamelin to explain how pressing the Backspace key makes all signs preceding the cursor disappear. The Delete key is linked to black holes. In a minimalist approach, no such explanations are given; users merely exercise the use of the Backspace and Delete keys. These actions are supposed to speak for themselves; users should be able to see how these keys work and infer how they differ.

For tutorials, it is often desirable not to give full screen information (Carroll 1984, 1990b; Horton 1993; Nowaczyk and James 1993; Van der Meij 1993, 1994, 1996b). Full screen information typically consists of two types of information presented in context: a particular content, (e.g., icon, warning, question, or menu option) and some locative information (e.g., top, bottom, right, left). Incomplete screen information can be created by leaving out one of the two and by making the information less explicit. For example, stimulating users to attend to a message of the program can be achieved by a statement such as, "A warning appears at the bottom of the screen." Users can be prompted to locate information with a statement like, "Check if the following sentence appears on the screen: Name Document: .... " Another solution is to show only the important area. Some prompts may even be vague on content and location to make users depend less on the manual for support: "Look at the screen to see what further actions you should perform."

In general, reducing the text of a manual is a matter of exploiting actions and the context in which they appear. By being brief, the manual communicates to users that their task does not require a formidable effort. By not explaining everything, the manual stimulates users to activate relevant prior knowledge and depend more on their own thinking.

Heuristic 4.2: Provide Closure for Chapters
For random-access readers, it would be ideal if chapters could be worked through in random order. When chapters are made completely indepen-

dent of one another, users can jump around in any direction. Unfortunately, total independence is impossible to realize; some dependency will always be the case. What writers can do, however, is to make chapters as independent as possible by providing closure (Arnold 1988; Van der Meij 1992; Weiss 1991). In other words, each chapter depends on as little outside information as possible. Users should need to consult other chapters (and books) only by exception. It also means that tasks are rounded off in each chapter. One might say that closure means starting and ending with a clean desk. To achieve closure, writers should attend to deciding on a home base, avoiding dependency of products, and avoiding dependency of process skills across chapters as much as possible.

The writer must choose a home base from which to start and end each chapter. This home base can be the computer turned off, but most often it is the start screen, or window, that users see after opening an application. The main menu bar is visible, and perhaps some of the working area is displayed. The start screen is a good home base because it is an easy point from which to exit or enter an application further. In addition, it is the screen most users should become intimately familiar with. When all chapters in a manual start from home base, there is a common entry point for all users: those who come from the previous chapter and those who just step in.

Closure also depends on avoiding dependency of products across chapters. Manuals sometimes are designed around a single case, or file, the contents of which become more and more complex as users work through the chapters. Because all sorts of things can go wrong and because users may not want to start at the beginning, such dependencies should be avoided. It is desirable to have users create independent products in each chapter. There are at least two ways to achieve this: by offering different sample files prepared specifically for the task(s) at hand in each chapter for users to practice on, or by providing backup files that users can activate when starting a new chapter, which maintains the buildup of a case, or file, without the dependency.

How one handles prior knowledge and skills must also be considered. What users learn in one chapter may be needed in another. In our first design of a minimal manual, we intended to be as minimal as possible, asking users merely to achieve a certain goal if the procedure for reaching that goal had been presented earlier in the manual. For example, in chapter 3, the action information would merely say, "Open file *x*." Users were expected to know by then how to do this or to look back to the precise steps described in the previous chapter. Tests revealed that this led to too many mistakes and lookingbacks; therefore, we decided to fade out the action information more gradually. We built in more reminders and made each reminder less complete. For example, we would say what users had to do, not how to do so: "Open file *x* by selecting the File Retrieve option." These later manuals were more successful in reducing the number of mistakes and lookingbacks.

When users start and end at home base in each chapter, some tasks are repeated frequently in the manual. When a start screen is the home base, these repetitions concern fundamental managerial tasks such as opening, saving, and closing files. We have found that these repetitions make users fast at and very comfortable with file management (Lazonder and Van der Meij 1993; Van der Meij 1992). These repetitions are beneficial rather than obstructive because these management skills are probably among the most important ones novices should acquire.

2.5   Conclusion

We have outlined the theoretical and empirical rationales for four minimalist design principles and their corresponding heuristics. The chapter expresses our understanding of the foundation, application, and development path for a minimalist approach to instruction. It should make possible a further development of this knowledge and of the ways in which it can be applied.

We have emphasized here the codification of the minimalist approach as a set of practical techniques and specific heuristics for designing action. Our objective is to provide a view of minimalism that complements other published material and integrates the many narrower research studies, while decomposing the minimalist approach into action-oriented heuristics. Thus, this chapter is a summary of what we now know about minimalist design of instruction and how to use what we know.

We hope that this chapter can help to initiate a broad-based discussion, development, and codification for minimalist designs. Much has been accomplished in the past decade, but, as always, much more remains to be done.

Acknowledgments

We thank Ard Lazonder for comments on the first draft. We also acknowledge the incisive review of Karen Ann Schriver and Deborah Andrews for help with editing.

References

Allwood, C. M. 1984. "Error detection processes in statistical problem solving." *Cognitive Science* 8:413–437.

Allwood, C. M., and M. Eliasson. 1987. "Analogy and other sources of difficulty in novices' very first text-editing." *International Journal of Man-Machine Studies* 27:1–22.

Allwood, C. M., and T. Kalén. 1993. "User-competence and other usability aspects when introducing a patient administrative system: A case study." *Interacting with Computers* 5:167–191.

Alpert, S. R., M. K. Singley, and J. M. Carroll. 1995. "Multiple multimodal mentors: Delivering computer-based instruction via specialized anthropomorphic advisors." *Behaviour and Information Technology* 14:69–79.

Arnold, W. A. 1988. "Learning modules in minimalist documents." In *Proceedings of the 35th International Technical Communication Conference (ITCC)*, pp. WE16–19. Washington, DC: Society for Technical Communication.

Arnold, B., and R. Roe. 1987. "User errors in human-computer interaction." In Psychological issues of human computer interaction in the work place, ed. M. Frese, E. Ulich, and W Dzida, pp. 203–222. Amsterdam: Elsevier.

Bailey, R. W. 1983. *Human error in computer systems*. Englewood Cliffs, NJ: Prentice Hall.

Bethke, F. J., W. M. Dean, P. H. Kaiser, E. Ort, and F. H. Pessin. 1991. "Improving the usability of programming publications." *Journal of Computer Documentation* 15, no. 2:3–22.

Black, J. B., J. M. Carroll, and S. M. McGuigan. 1987. "What kind of minimal instruction manual is the most effective?" In *Proceedings of the Second IFIP Conference on Human-Computer Interaction*, ed. H. J. Bullinger, B. Shackel, and K. Kornwachs, pp. 159–162. Amsterdam: Elsevier.

Brockmann, R. J. 1990. *Writing better user documentation: From paper to hypertext*. Version 2.0. New York: Wiley.

Byrnes, J. P., and J. T. Guthrie. 1992. "Prior conceptual knowledge and textbook search." *Contemporary Educational Psychology* 17: 8–29.

Card, S. K., Th. P. Moran, and A. Newell. 1983. *The psychology of human-computer interaction*. Hillsdale, NJ: Erlbaum.

Card, S. K., Th. P. Moran, and A. Newell. 1990. "The keystroke-level model for user performance time with interactive systems." In *Human-computer interaction: Selected readings*, ed. J. Preece, and L. Keller, pp. 327–356. Hemel Hempstead: Prentice Hall.

Carroll, J. M. 1984. "Minimalist training." *Datamation* 30:125–136.

Carroll, J. M. 1990a. *The Nurnberg funnel: Designing minimalist instruction for practical computer skill*. Cambridge, MA: MIT Press.

Carroll, J. M. 1990b. "An overview of minimalist instruction." In *Proceedings of the Twenty-Third Annual Hawaii International Conference on Systems Sciences (IEEE'90)*. Washington, DC: Institute of Electrical and Electronic Engineers Computer Society Press Reprint.

Carroll, J. M. 1993. "Techniques for minimalist documentation and user interface design." Paper presented at the Conference Quality of Technical Documentation, May 6–7, Enschede, Netherlands.

Carroll, J. M., and C. Carrithers. 1984. "Training wheels in a user interface." *Communications of the ACM* 27:800–806.

Carroll, J. M., R. L. Mack, and W. A. Kellog. 1988. "Interface metaphors and user interface design." In *Handbook of Human-Computer Interaction*, ed. M. Helander, pp. 67–85. Amsterdam: Elsevier.

Carroll, J. M., and M. B. Rosson. 1987. "The paradox of the active user." In *Interfacing thought: Cognitive aspects of human-computer interaction*, ed. J. M. Carroll, pp. 80–111. Cambridge, MA: MIT Press.

Carroll, J. M., P. L. Smith-Kerker, J. R. Ford, and S. A. Mazur-Rimetz. 1987. "The minimal manual." *Human-Computer Interaction* 3:123–153.

Charney, D. H., and L. M. Reder. 1986. "Designing interactive tutorials for computer users." *Human-Computer Interaction* 2:297–317.

Charney, D. H., L. M. Reder, and G. W. Kusbit. 1990. "Goal setting and procedure selection in acquiring computer skills: A comparison of tutorials, problem solving and learner exploration." *Cognition and Instruction* 7:323–342.

Davis Baker, L. 1988. "The relationship of product design to document design." In *Effective documentation: What we have learned from research*, ed. S. Doheny-Farina, pp. 317–327. Cambridge, MA: MIT Press.

Debs, M. B. 1988. "A history of advice: What experts have to tell us." In *Effective documentation: What we have learned from research*, ed. S. Doheny-Farina, pp. 11–24. Cambridge, MA: MIT Press.

Digitalk. 1989. *Smalltalk/V 286: Object-oriented programming system*.

Douglas, S. A., and Th. P. Moran. 1984. "Learning text editor semantics by analogy." In *Proceedings of the Computer and Human Interaction 1983 Conference on Human Factors in Computer Systems*, pp. 207–211. New York: Association for Computing Machinery.

Dreher, M. J. 1993. "Reading to locate information: Societal and educational perspectives." *Contemporary Educational Psychology* 18:129–138.

Dreher, M. J., and J. T. Guthrie. 1993. "Cognitive processes in textbook chapter search tasks." *Reading Research Quarterly* 25:323–339.

Farkas, D. K. 1993. "The role of balloon help." *Journal of Computer Documentation* 17, no. 2:3–19.

Frese, M., K. Albrecht, A. Altmann, J. Lang, P. von Papstein, R. Peyerl, J. Prümper, H. Schulte-Göcking, I. Wankmüller, and R. Wendel. 1988. "The effect of an active development of the mental model in the training process: Experimental results in a word processing system." *Behavior and Information Technology* 7:295–304.

Gong, R., and J. Elkerton. 1990. "Designing minimal documentation using a GOMS model: A usability evaluation of an engineering approach." In *Proceedings of the CHI'90 Conference*, ed. J. Carrasco Chew and J. Whiteside, pp. 99–106. New York: Association for Computing Machinery.

Gould, J. D., S. J. Boies, S. Levy, J. T. Richards, and J. Schoonard. 1987. "The 1984 Olympic Message System: A test of behavioral principles of system design." *Communications of the ACM* 30:758–769.

Gould, J. D., and C. Lewis. 1985. "Designing for usability: Key principles and what designers think." *Communications of the ACM* 28:300–311.

Graesser, A. C., and K. Murray. 1990. "A question-answering methodology for exploring a user's acquisition and knowledge of a computer environment." In *Cognition, computing and cooperation*, ed. S. P. Robertson, W. Zachary, and J. B. Black, pp. 237–267. Norwood, NJ: Ablex.

Hager, P. J. 1992. "Teaching students the verticality of technical documentation." *Technical Communication* 39:182–188.

Hallgren, C. 1992. "The Nurnberg Funnel: A minimal collection." *Journal of Computer Documentation* 16, no. 1:11–17.

Hartley, J. 1985. *Designing instructional text*. London: Kogan Page.

Hartley, J. 1990. "Textbook design: Current status and future directions." *International Journal of Educational Research* 14:533–541.

Hill, W. C. 1989. "How some advice fails." *Proceedings of the Computer and Human Interaction (CHI) 1989 Conference on Human Factors in Computer Systems*, pp. 85–90. New York: Association for Computing Machinery.

Horn, R. E. 1992. "Commentary on the Nurnberg Funnel." *Journal of Computer Documentation* 16, no. 1:3–11.

Horton, W. 1993. "Dump the dumb screen dumps." *Technical Communication* 40, no. 1:146–148.

Hunt, P., and K. Vassiliadis. 1988. "No easy answers: Investigating computer error messages." In *Effective documentation: What we have learned from research*, ed. S. Doheny-Farina, pp. 127–142. Cambridge, MA: MIT Press.

Karat, C. M. 1990. "Cost-benefit analysis of iterative usability testing." In *Human Computer Interaction—Interact '90*, ed. D. Diaper et al., pp. 351–356. Amsterdam: Elsevier.

Kay, D. S., and J. B. Black. 1990. "Knowledge transformations during the acquisition of computer expertise." In *Cognition, computing and cooperation*, ed. S. P. Robertson, W. Zachary, and J. B. Black, pp. 268–303. Norwood, NJ: Ablex.

Kluwe, R. H., C. Misiak, and H. Haider. 1990. "Learning by doing in the control of a complex system." In *Learning and Instruction*, vol. 2.1, ed. H. Mandl, E. de Corte, N. Bennett, and H. F. Friedrich, pp. 197–218. New York: Pergamon Press.

Landauer, T. K. 1988. "Research methods in human-computer interaction." In *Handbook of human-computer interaction*, ed. M. Helander, pp. 905–928. Amsterdam: Elsevier.

Lazonder, A. W. 1993. "Tutorial documentation and the effective control of errors." Paper presented at the Conference Quality of Technical Documentation, May 6–7, Enschede, Netherlands.

Lazonder, A. W. 1994a. "Minimalist documentation and the effective control of errors." In *Quality of technical documentation*, ed. M. Steehouder, C. Jansen, P. van der Poort, and R. Verheijen, pp. 85–98. Amsterdam: Rodopi.

Lazonder, A. W. 1994b. "Minimalist computer documentation: A study on constructive and corrective skills development." Ph.D. dissertation, Twente University.

Lazonder, A. W., and H. van der Meij. 1992. "The effective error control in computer documentation." Paper presented at the Second EARLI-SIG Work Conference on Comprehension of Verbal and Pictorial Information, Nijmegen, Netherlands.

Lazonder, A. W., and H. van der Meij. 1993. "The minimal manual: Is less really more?" *International Journal of Man-Machine Studies* 39:729–752.

Lazonder, A. W., and H. van der Meij. 1994a. "The effect of error information in tutorial documentation." *Interacting with Computers* 6, no. 1:23–40.

Lazonder, A. W., and H. van der Meij. 1994b. "Towards a theory of effective error control in computer documentation." In *Process-oriented instruction, verbal and pictorial aids and comprehension strategies*, ed. F. P. C. M. de Jong and B. H. A. M. Van Hout-Wolters, pp. 165–174. Amsterdam: VU University Press.

Lazonder, A. W., and H. van der Meij. 1995. "Error information in tutorial documentation: Supporting users' errors to facilitate initial skills learning." *International Journal of Man-Machine Studies* 42:185–206.

Lewis, C., and D. A. Norman. 1986. "Designing for error." In *User centered system design: New perspectives on human-computer interaction*, ed. D. A. Norman and S. W. Draper, pp. 411–432. Hillsdale, NJ: Erlbaum.

Mack, R. L., C. H. Lewis, and J. M. Carroll. 1990. "Learning to use word processors: Problems and prospects." In *Human-computer interaction: Selected readings*, ed. J. Preece and L. Keller, pp. 185–204. Hemel Hempstead: Prentice Hall.

Mantei, M. M., and T. J. Teorey. 1988. "Cost-benefit analysis for incorporating human factors in the software lifecycle." *Communications of the ACM* 31:428–439.

Markel, M., M. Vaccaro, and T. Hewett. 1992. "Effects of paragraph length on attitudes toward technical writing." *Technical Communication* 39, no. 3:454–456.

Matchett, M., and M. L. Ray. 1989. "Revising IRS publications: A case study." *Technical Communication* 36, no. 4:332–340.

Nickerson, R. S. 1991. "A minimalist approach to the 'paradox of sense making,' " *Educational Researcher* 20, no. 9:24–26.

Nowaczyk, R. H., and E. C. James. 1993. "Applying minimal manual principles for documentation of graphical user interfaces." *Journal of Technical Writing and Communication* 23, no. 4:379–388.

Oatley, K., M. C. Meldrum, and S. W. Draper. 1991. "Evaluating self-instruction by minimal manual and by video for a feature of a word-processing system." Unpublished manuscript, University of Glasgow.

Payne, S. J. 1991. "A descriptive study of mental models." *Behaviour and Information Technology* 10, no. 1:3–21.

Penrose, J. M., and L. M. Seiford. 1988. "Microcomputer users preferences for software documentation: An analysis." *Journal of Technical Writing and Communication* 18, no. 4:355–366.

Ramey, J. 1988. "How people use computer documentation: Implications for book design." In *Effective documentation: What we have learned from research*, ed. S. Doheny-Farina, pp. 143–158. Cambridge, MA: MIT Press.

Ramsay, J. E., and K. Oatley. 1992. "Designing minimal computer manuals from scratch." *Instructional Science* 21:85–98.

Redish, J. C. 1988. "Reading to learn to do." *Technical Writing Teacher* 15:223–233.

Rettig, M. 1991. "Nobody reads documentation." *Communications of the ACM* 34, no. 7:19–24.

Robertson, S. P., Carroll, J. M., Mack, R., Rosson, M. B., Alpert, S. R., and J. Koenemann-Belliveau. 1993. "ODE: The object design exploratorium." IBM Research Report, J. T. Watson Research Center. Yorktown Heights, NY.

Rosson, M. B., and Carroll, J. M. 1994. "The role of examples in Smalltalk reuse." IBM Research Report, J. T. Watson Research Center, Yorktown Heights, NY.

Rosson, M. B., J. M. Carroll, and R. K. E. Bellamy. 1990. "Smalltalk scaffolding: A case study of minimalist instruction." In *Proceedings of the Computer and*

Human Interaction 1990 Conference on Human Factors in Computer Systems, pp. 423–429. New York: Association for Computing Machinery.

Rosson, M. B., J. M. Carroll, R. K. E. Bellamy, S. R. Alpert, and J. A. Singer. 1993. "MiTTS: Minimalist tutorial and tools for Smalltalk/V." Computer Science Department, IBM J. T. Watson Research Center, Yorktown Heights, NY.

Schriver, K. A. 1989. "Evaluating text quality: The continuum from text-focused to reader-focused methods." *IEEE Transactions on Professional Communication* 32, no. 4:238–255.

Schriver, K. A. 1992. "Teaching writers to anticipate readers' needs: What can document designers learn from usability testing?" In *Studies of functional text quality*, ed. H. Pander Maat and M. Steehouder, pp. 141–157. Amsterdam: Rodopi.

Schriver, K. A. 1993. "Quality in document design: Issues and controversies." *Technical Communication* 40. no. 2:239–257.

Seifert, C. M., and E. L. Hutchins. 1992. "Errors as opportunity: Learning in a cooperative task." *Human Computer Interaction* 7:409–435.

Singley, M. K., J. M. Carroll, and S. R. Alpert. 1991. "Psychological design rationale for an intelligent tutoring system for Smalltalk." In *Empirical studies of programmers IV*, ed. J Koenemann-Belliveau, T. Moher, and S. P. Robertson, pp. 196–209. Norwood, NJ: Ablex.

Singley, M. K., J. M. Carroll, and S. R. Alpert. 1993. "Incidental reification of goals in an intelligent tutor for Smalltalk." In *Cognitive models and intelligent environments for learning programming*, ed. B. duBoulay and E. Lemut. New York: Springer Verlag.

Spyridakis, J. H., and M. J. Wenger. 1992. "Writing for human performance: Relating reading research to document design." *Technical Communication* 39:202–215.

Sticht, T. 1985. "Understanding readers and their uses of texts." In *Designing usable texts*, ed. T. M. Duffy and R. H. Waller, pp. 315–340. Orlando, FL: Academic Press.

Thimbleby, H. 1991. "Can humans think? The Ergonomics Society lecture 1991." *Ergonomics* 34:1269–1287.

Thing, L. 1984. "What the well-dressed manual is wearing today." *Technical Communication* 31, no. 4:8–12.

Tripp, S. D. 1990. Book review of *The Nurnberg Funnel*. *Educational Technology Research and Development* 38, no. 3:87–90.

VanderLinden, G., T. G. Cocklin, and M. McKita. 1988. "Testing and developing minimalist tutorials: A case history." In *Proceedings of the 35th International Technical Communications Conference (I* (pp. RET 196–199). Washington, DC: Society for Technical Communication.

Van der Meij, H. 1992. "A critical assessment of the minimalist approach to documentation." In *Conference proceedings of the 10th Annual International*

Conference on Systems Documentation (SIGDOC92), October, Ottawa, pp. 7–17. New York: Association for Computing Machinery.

Van der Meij, H. 1993. "Learning by doing it on your own." *Performance and Instruction* 32, no. 10:18–22.

Van der Meij, H. 1994. "Catching the user in the act." In *Quality of technical documentation*, ed. M. Steehouder, C. Jansen, P. van der Poort, and R. Verheijen, pp. 201–210. Amsterdam: Rodopi.

Van der Meij, H. 1995. *Does the manual help? An examination of problem solving behavior and the support manuals offer*. Research report 12-7-1995. Twente University, Faculty of Educational Science and Technology, Enschede, Netherlands.

Van der Meji, H. 1996a. "Does the manual help? An examination of the problem solving support offered by manuals." *IEEE Transactions on Professional Communication* 39, no. 3:146–156.

Van der Meij, H. 1996b. "Examining the role of screen captures in manuals." *InterCom* 43, no. 4:35–38.

Van der Meij, H., and A. W. Lazonder. 1992. "A constructivistic approach to computer documentation." Paper presented at the Second EARLI-SIG Work Conference on Comprehension of Verbal and Pictorial Information, November, Nijmegen, Netherlands.

Van der Meij, H., and A. W. Lazonder. 1993. "Assessment of the minimalist approach to computer user documentation." *Interacting with Computers* 5, no. 4:355–370.

Van der Meij, H., and P. Van Stapele. 1993. "Self-managed media education." *New Era in Education* 74, no. 1:26–36.

Way, E. C. 1991. *Knowledge representation and metaphor*. Dordrecht: Kluwer.

Weis, E. H. 1991. *How to write usable user documentation*. 2d ed. Phoenix, AZ: Oryx Press.

Wendel, R., and Frese, M. 1987. "Developing exploratory strategies in training: The general approach and a specific example for manual use." In *Proceedings of the Second IFIP Conference on Human-Computer Interaction*, ed. H. J. Bullinger, B. Shackeland, and K. Kornwachs, pp. 943–948. Amsterdam, NH: Elsevier.

Williams, T. R., and D. K. Farkas. 1992. "Minimalism reconsidered: Should we design documentation for exploratory learning?" *SIGCHI Bulletin* 24, no. 2:41–50.

Wright, P. 1987. "Writing technical information." In *Review of research in education*, ed. E. Z. Rothkopf, pp. 327–385. Washington, DC: American Educational Research Association.

Wright, P. 1989. "The need for theories of not reading: Some psychological aspects of the human-computer interface." In *Working models of human perception*, ed. B. A. G. Elsendoorn and H. Bouma, pp. 319–320. London: Academic Press.

3

Ten Misconceptions about Minimalism

John M. Carroll and Hans van der Meij

The minimalist approach to designing instruction and documentation leverages task orientation to produce more effective learning and performance outcomes more rapidly. It emerged through the course of the past decade as a broad attempt to bring theory, empirical research, and practical design experience to bear on design practice. Accordingly, it is at once a body of psychological theory, a body of empirical research, and a body of design practice and discourse. The approach has attracted attention from a diverse group of researchers and practitioners with a variety of interests and disciplinary backgrounds. Not surprisingly, this interest has created an expansive and sometimes confusing literature pertaining to minimalism.

In this chapter, we provide focus for the continuing discussion on minimalism by critiquing aspects of the literature. To begin, we acknowledge that what we will call misconceptions are in every case understandable as legitimate interpretations of minimalism. Frequently they are simplifications of what we intend by minimalism, useful in particular cases. We applaud the self-initiative and creativity of our colleagues in helping to explore and develop the concept of minimalism. Nevertheless, it is important occasionally to rein in the concept, question the simplifications, and call attention to inconsistencies and contradictions. Our hope is that this effort will cause more, not less, debate, research, and practical development of minimalism.

The central principle in minimalism is task orientation. But many other principles play a role in this design approach, either because they support task orientation or because they follow from it (Carroll 1990). One could hardly expect otherwise of a broad design philosophy. However, this architecture can be problematic. There is a temptation to see minimalism as constituted entirely of one or another of its constituent principles.

For example, it is not uncommon to see minimalism glossed as "cut text." Brevity is a key element of minimalism, but only because it can facilitate task-oriented activity and learner-initiated reasoning, not as a self-sufficient end in itself. Wantonly slashing text and leaving other design characteristics unchanged will not lead to a minimalist design. It is easy to see the attractions of this misconception. Random slashing is an inexpensive design transformation; if it really did produce better instruction and documentation, it would comprise the mother of all panaceas.

The first group of misconceptions we will discuss has this character: minimalism means the designer does not have to produce a complete design; minimalism means that all learning is learning by trial and error; minimalism means preventing learners from making errors; minimalism means that job aids can be employed as instructional manuals (see figure 3.1). Each exaggerates a single aspect of minimalism, often taking it more simply and more extremely than we intended. Unfortunately, these misconceptions are subsequently sometimes attributed to minimalism *tout court* (that is, instead of to a simplified and exaggerated caricature of minimalism). In essence, we argue that a general view of minimalism cannot be reduced to any of these simplifications; the effectiveness of the minimalist approach hinges on taking a more comprehensive, articulated, and artful approach to the design of information.

A second group of misconceptions devolves from the first group. These pertain more to the meta-strategy of minimalism than to its technical

1. Minimalism means brevity.
2. Minimalism means incomplete instructional analyses.
3. Minimalism means trial-and-error learning.
4. Minimalism does not support people who learn by reading.
5. Minimalism over-emphasizes errors.
6. Minimalism is just another word for job aids.
7. Minimalism works only for simple domains.
8. Minimalism merely reflects the preconceptions of users.
9. Minimalism offers a complete documentation solution.
10. Minimalism has no theoretical foundation.

Figure 3.1
Ten misconceptions about minimalism

content. For example, because the original examples of minimalist documentation were developed in relatively simple application domains, it is sometimes concluded that the approach is suitable only for such simple domains. Another example is that because the leading idea of minimalism is to leverage the learner's task-oriented motivation and reasoning, it is sometimes concluded that a critical requirement of minimalism is to fit the pretheoretical expectations of users. Because minimalism describes an expansive program for the design of documentation and training, it is sometimes concluded that the intent of minimalism is to offer a comprehensive design model for all documentation. Because minimalism is a design philosophy, often conveyed or illustrated by sets of design heuristics (Van der Meij and Carroll 1995), it is sometimes concluded that minimalism comprises only heuristics, without a systematic foundation in science.

The most serious consequence of these assorted misconceptions is that they may confuse or deter prospective researchers and practitioners. Therefore it is important to consider how the misconceptions arise and to try to clarify them with sounder conceptions, thereby improving the relevance and substantiveness of subsequent discussions. In the balance of this chapter, we consider the ten misconceptions enumerated in figure 3.1.

3.1   Minimalism Means Brevity

Brevity is clearly implied by the term *minimalism*, and brevity certainly has always been a part of the minimalist approach to instruction and documentation. However, it has never been the totality of the approach. In some presentations, it is explicitly enumerated as one of several principles that work together to produce minimalist designs (Van der Meij and Carroll 1995; Carroll 1984). In some presentations, it is identified as a derivative property of minimalist designs, caused by more central principles (Carroll 1990).

Nevertheless, it is typical to see mere brevity taken as the central thrust of minimalism, for several apparent reasons. First, simplifying in this way makes minimalism easier for commentators to explain and discuss. Nevertheless, it also yields a view of minimalism that is a caricature. For example, Hallgren (1992) complains that Carroll, in his book *The Nurnberg Funnel*, "feels the need to make lengthy explanations to fellow practitioners on reducing their writing to the essentials" (p. 16). The irony in this appraisal seems witty, but in fact *The Nurnberg Funnel* is one presentation of minimalism that explicitly treats brevity as a derived property. The "lengthy explanations" Hallgren apparently did not view as worthy of analysis are in fact the principles of minimalism from which brevity derives.

A second possible reason for this misconception originates in the politics of the development process. There is still a substantial tendency for development managers to see instruction and documentation as a kind of tax on their budgets. Many of these managers may not care a whit about producing more effective training and documents; they just want to think less about supporting users and spend less of their resources on it. They may wish to believe that designing and publishing fewer pages and panels will cost less. But this reasoning rests on serious fallacy. Minimalist design in documentation, as in architecture or music, requires identifying the core structures and content. It hinges on being able to make good decisions on what to do, say, or show and on what not to include. This typically requires more skilled (expensive) developers and greater development effort.

The standard, systematic approach of responding to new design requirements with functions, new conditions, and new pages or panels of documentation will not lead to minimalist results, but neither will the approach of slashing or simplifying. Developers must create genuine and intellectually engaging instructional opportunities for users. They must include just the right amount of information, not too much or too little. This goal typically involves more development effort, particularly when it is first adopted by a given designer or by an organization. It typically costs more, not less, as writers and developers need to reconsider some of most basic strategies and assumptions that guide their work (Carroll 1990; Brockmann 1990; Vanderlinden, Cocklin, and McKita 1988).

Minimalism can be cost-effective for managers, but not because it makes documentation insignificant or inexpensive. Its focus on responding creatively to actual users and actual tasks entrains a development process in which prototype documents are continually redesigned and tested. Feedback from users and their work contexts pervades the process. A current-best prototype is always available to give managers a concrete status summary, enabling more fruitful discussions. The key savings in effort are to the user, not to the developer. Minimalism significantly reduces training time while supporting better user performance. Experiments have shown reductions of between 25 and 40 percent training time (Carroll et al. 1987–1988; Gong and Elkerton 1990; Lazonder and Van der Meij 1993).

3.2 Minimalism Means Incomplete Instructional Analyses

A key technique in minimalist documents is the use of incomplete descriptions and instructions. As in the case of brevity, this technique has always been presented as part of a more comprehensive set of techniques, not as a one-line design philosophy unto itself. And, also as in the case of brevity, this technique should be seen as the consequence of deeper principles. Incomplete descriptions and instructions can pose problems to the learner, suggest goals and activities, and guide self-initiated investigation and discovery.

Incompleteness has sometimes been misconceived by commentators and managers. The general misconception is that incomplete documentation is obtained through incomplete analyses. Of course, completeness is always a matter of degree; no document can be a complete description of a product or procedure. Writers and information developers always must find a balance in the detail they present. Creating effective but deliberately incomplete documentation requires some sort of theory of user inference—not a simple matter (Mirel, Feinberg, an Allmendinger 1991). It hinges on making just the right assumption about the prior knowledge and skills of the intended audience.

Figure 3.2 presents an example of an instructional procedure for starting up a program (Glasbeek 1992, 1994). The procedure that users must follow involves changing the current directory, selecting a program, and completing a log-in/password dialogue. Three steps are presented at a fairly high level of precision with respect to the task element of changing

Chapter 1: How to start the program

You can start the program as follows:
1. After the 'C:\' type: cd\hours
2. Press: Enter
3. Choose: 'sawmenu'
The main menu now appears on the screen.

Figure 3.2
An example of incomplete instructions from a manual developed by Glasbeek (1992)

the current directory, but absolutely no guidance or even information is provided with respect to the log-in/password dialogue or menu navigation actions that are also required in the situation.

This approach would be appropriate for users who were quite familiar with the log-in/password dialogue and menu navigation elements but who did not know how to change the current directory. It is possible that people like this could exist, but unlikely: all three of these elements are basic skills. In fact, it turned out that two of five subjects tested in this study experienced considerable difficulties with the omitted topic of menu navigation. This kind of incompleteness is not guided by any theory or analysis of what the user knows or can infer. At best, it can convey an impression of sloppiness; at worst, it can leave users bewildered.

The attractiveness of this simplification of minimalism is analogous to the case of brevity. If documents could be made more incomplete by random omission of steps and conditions, and indeed thereby become more effective to users, it would be possible to realize huge savings in development and production costs. However, as the example in figure 3.2 shows, incomplete analyses of user knowledge, skills, and needs lead to poor documents, whether they are more or less complete.

As in the case of brevity, designing effective instruction and documentation that is incomplete requires more, not less, analysis. Determining what can be left out of a document involves analysis of users' prior knowledge and skills, task and needs analysis, and an empirical identification of likely hot spots. Draper and Oatley (1990) draw the critical distinction: "An instruction to 'open the header and add a phrase' need not be expanded into 'go to the Format menu, execute the Open Header command, click in the new window and type a phrase, close the window' if users can be relied on to search the menus for commands they do not know.... Such instructions are not designed by thoughtless omission however. If users do not already know about opening headers, it is important that the phrase used ('open the header') be a close match to the command name they must search the menus for, or the search will be poorly constrained" (p. 228).

To implement the minimalist approach reliably, it is necessary to assess user knowledge and skill against the tasks that users will be carrying out. A good approach is scenario analysis: creating and walking through scenarios of use, often in collaboration with real users (Carroll 1995). In some cases, it may be useful to carry out structured task analyses or information-processing analyses (e.g., Gong and Elkerton 1990; Jonassen, Hannum, and Tessmer 1989; Merrill 1987).

A particular focus of such scenario analyses must be potential sites of user error. Research consistently indicates that error-free performances of users are the exception rather than the rule (Carroll et al. 1987/1988; Arnold and Roe 1987; Bailey 1983; Card, Moran, and Newell 1983, 1990; Graesser and Murray 1990; Lazonder and Van der Meij 1994, 1995). No matter how hard writers try, users are prone to make errors. Locating the hot spots in the program and manual is therefore a crucial part in the prewriting analyses in a minimalist approach. We believe as well that writers should, in this stage, examine the best ways for dealing with the problems of users (Carroll 1990; Van der Meij and Carroll 1995; Lazonder and Van der Meij 1995).

The problems users may have with the program and the manual are often found by logical analyses as well as by testing with the intended audience. After finding a problem, the writer must decide whether it should lead to changes in the program, changes in the manual, or the provision of error information (Lazonder and Van der Meij 1995). Unfortunately, most task-analytic procedures ignore breakdowns or mistakes; what-if scenarios are hardly ever analyzed, yet they are an essential part of an instructional analysis in a minimalist approach.

People do not learn everything in one pass. Just as it can be wise to employ progressive disclosure in the number of menu options presented on-screen to novice users, so it can be wise to use fading as a way of gradually decreasing the support for users. For example, when designing for an audience of adults with no computer knowledge, even simple tasks such as choosing from a menu may best be taught by gradually decreasing the support users are given. This is not inconsistent with an approach in which every chapter can be worked through independently from other chapters, but it surely is much more difficult to take this notion into account in designing a modular approach that works well for the user.

In an early version of our minimal manual for WordPerfect, we asked users merely to achieve a given goal if the procedure for that goal had been presented earlier. Testing revealed that we assumed too much learning, leading to mistakes and look-backs on the part of some of the users. We therefore decided to fade the information more gradually, adding reminders but making successive reminders less complete (figure 3.3). These later manuals were more successful in terms of reducing the number of mistakes and look-backs.

Testing keeps one in touch with reality. As people become more and more experienced computer users, they can forget the difficulties they had as a novice. For example, Hayes (reported in Wright 1988) showed that the more knowledge of a topic writers have, the poorer their predictions of difficulties for users.

Open a File (first presentation)
1. Press the Alt key
2. Press the ⇩ key
3. Press the Enter key

Open a File (second presentation)
1. Go to the menu bar
2. Press the ⇩ key
3. Press the Enter key

Open a File (third presentation)
1. Go to the menu bar and choose File
2. Press the Enter key

Open a File (fourth presentation)
1. Open file x by activating the menu and selecting Retrieve

Open a File (fifth presentation)
1. Open file x

Figure 3.3
The use of a fading technique can reduce the number of mistakes and look-backs.

3.3   Minimalism Means Trial-and-Error Learning

Discovery learning is clearly a key element in the theoretical foundation of the minimalist design philosophy. Minimalism assumes that learners should be active, working on real or realistic tasks as they learn. Part of the reason is that real and realistic tasks are highly motivating (Keller 1987). Engaging in genuine activities during learning also better supports transfer to real situations by bringing the learning situations and transfer situations into closer correspondence (Duffy and Jonassen 1992). In addition, solving real problems helps students become independent learners (Bruner 1966, 1973).

It is easy to confuse discovery learning with learning by trial and error (DeWeaver and Bauman 1992; Farkas and Williams 1990; Kamouri, Kamouri, and Smith 1986). As Williams and Farkas (1992) put it, "We believe that the stated minimalist goal of enabling the learner to accomplish real work while learning a program is often thwarted by the act of compelling that learner to induce, *through trial and error*, the correct procedures needed to accomplish that work" (p. 41, emphasis added).

The confusion hinges on taking systematic (i.e., rote) curricula and trial and error as exhaustive possibilities, which they are not. Discovery learning is not equivalent to the absence of all curriculum and support; rather it entails fundamentally different kinds of curriculum and support from passive and rote-structure approaches. This distinction has always been drawn in minimalism (see Carroll 1990, 104–110, describing research from 1981 contrasting guided exploration with learning by unguided immersion in a problem situation), but perhaps not clearly enough.

Effective discovery learning must be carefully supported. Learners must have enough knowledge to form appropriate goals, pursue relevant activities, and draw correct conclusions. Implementing this support requires knowledge analysis of what learners can be expected to do at various points throughout a discovery learning curriculum. Learners must be enabled to learn from mistakes and simultaneously be protected from distracting errors and confusions. Opportunities to discover must retain the motivating aspects of real tasks but also be tractable for learners.

Searching a Text

You can position the cursor quickly to a word or part of a sentence by searching for this text.

1. Position the cursor at the beginning of the file
2. Go to the menubar and press twice on the → key
3. Choose the command FORWARD and press the ENTER key

WordPerfect asks what you want to search for. Check to see if the prompt -> **Search:** is on your screen.

4. Type any word(s) from the text
5. Press the F2 key

*If the code **[Hrt]** appears after the word, you have pressed the ENTER key instead of the F2 key. Remove the code by pressing the BACKSPACE key. Then press F2 for searching the word(s).*

WordPerfect automatically positions the cursor at the first occurence of the word(s) in the text.

*If your hear a bleep and the text ***Not found**** appears, you may have made a typing mistake. Try again.*

On your own: Searching text

The commands NEXT and PREVIOUS enable you to find out if the word you have been searching can also be found elsewhere in the text. You can find these commands under the SEARCH option. Try them and see.

Figure 3.4
An example of the "On Your Own" section in a minimal manual developed by Van der Meij and Lazonder (1993)

A technique for ensuring that learners have the prerequisite knowledge to benefit from exploration, will want to explore, and will have a fair chance of success is to place invitations for exploration immediately after practice on a related task (figure 3.4).

The "On Your Own" section in figure 3.4 does not merely ask students to explore. It cues them to consider what other goals they might want to pursue in relation to searching a text. The suggested goals for exploration are related conceptually and procedurally to the operations practiced in that context. This proximity helps to create what Bruner (1973) called the "well-prepared mind"; the student has just been thinking about forward search and thus is prepared to discover backward search. And the exploration is quite tractable. In this case, searching backward requires only two slightly different actions (position the cursor at another place, and select another option from the Search menu).

Our research indicates that preparing and cueing exploration strongly encourages learners to explore. For example, in one study, we found that such cues induced 81 percent more exploratory episodes than occurred with a control manual (Carroll et al. 1985). In another study, we found that 74 percent of all invitations to explore in a minimal manual for WordPerfect led to explorations by the users. In contrast, the invitations to explore in a control manual were significantly less tempting. Only 41 percent of all invitations were followed by explorations (Van der Meij 1994).

How much cueing is appropriate for effective exploration depends on the knowledge and skill of the learners. For some audiences, fewer cues may suffice, and more extensive examinations into the menu options (e.g., "search and replace") may be possible and challenging. The manual presented in figure 3.4 was intended for an adult vocational audience with no prior computer experience. Therefore, it has a fair degree of cueing in the "On Your Own" section.

The role of errors in learning is not ignored in conventional instructions and documentation, but it is given too low a priority (Van der Meij 1995). Errors play a distinctive and central role in approaches that incorporate discovery learning. Discovery learning tends to view error as a natural event in inquiry, a kind of event that should be put to use. Accordingly, a substantial amount of attention is directed at supporting the recognition and diagnosis of errors. At the same time, instructional environments must protect learners from making choices or performing actions that can severely disrupt task flow. One of the ways to create a fairly safe environment for exploration is to use a training-wheels technology in which errors are identified to the user but their consequences are blocked (Carroll and Carrithers 1984). This preserves the original system state and makes it easy for the learner to continue.

Among the various ways in which it is possible to retain the motivating aspects of real tasks while reducing the complexity of reality is the use of sample files that enable users to create or revise a complete product without burdening them with all of the tasks that usually need to be performed for such a product. For example, users may be offered templates that help create a fully formatted text but do not hinge on having to specify all the codes for headings, letter types, margins, and so on.

Another way of helping users cope with a complex and real task is to offer information sources in the environment. For example, to assist Smalltalk programmers with a debugging task, we have combined passive help with a Commentator explaining the specific expressions used by the programmer, a Goal Poster offering a best-guess analysis of the programmer's ongoing activity, and a Guru providing strategic critique of the programmer's solution.

3.4 Minimalism Does Not Support People Who Learn by Reading

Minimalism finds it important to value and support the reading strategies that people spontaneously apply. At the same time we also believe in Wright's (1994) adage that "quality writing provokes quality reading." In other words, we try to find the right balance between accommodating to the users' reading strategies and using principles and techniques of good instructional design to evoke action-oriented reading.

The pervasive emphasis on learner activity in minimalism has led some to question whether minimalism is intended to serve learners who wish to read or whether it can serve them. This is a more complex issue than it first appears; it involves several misconceptions about learners, minimalism, and alternatives to minimalism.

First, it is by no means clear that there are people who can learn skills merely by reading about them, without any active practice or performance of those skills or their components. Those who criticize minimalism for emphasizing learning activity, and thereby failing to support those who learn by reading, have not always been clear about what they take "learning by reading" to mean (Glasbeek 1994; Horn 1992). They have not produced any compelling reasons or evidence to believe that skills can be learned by reading alone. They imply that minimalism emphasizes learning activity too much, but they have not been specific as to how much is enough.

Many reader-oriented alternatives to minimalism incorporate strong assumptions about reading. One of the assumptions is that users do as requested by the experimenter. Another is that users read everything before doing anything. These assumptions lead to certain design principles that writers should be very cautious in following when designing a manual whose usage is not artificially constrained. In our experience, even learners who declare that they typically read everything before trying to do anything quickly and spontaneously begin interacting with the system as they read (Carroll and Mazur 1986). By way of illustration we discuss the important studies of Charney, Reder, and Kusbit (1990) and of Sweller and Chandler (1994).

Sweller and Chandler (1994) argue that some programs are hard to learn because they require the user to integrate information from different sources (e.g., manual, keyboard, and screen). The training materials they designed to support such integration were found to be superior to the ones that did not support these. We agree with the need to support integrative (in our term, coordinative) activities (Carroll 1984). However, Sweller and Chandler were interested in learning by reading, and so the subjects were required to study the entire manual before they were permitted to practice with the system. We view this assumption about reading as a severe and quite unnatural constraint, and is reflected in the manual Sweller and Chandler designed and studied.

Figure 3.5 displays a page from the Sweller and Chandler manual presenting linkages among cursor location information in the drawing area, the status area, and the keyboard of a computer-assisted design/computer-assisted manufacturing (CAD/CAM) system. This information is presented in a strictly descriptive style without reference to user tasks or activities. As a result, it does not capture and support the dynamic relations that constitute coordinative information.

Charney et al. (1990) suggest that it can be advantageous for people to engage in problem solving (rather than merely executing prescribed instructions) when learning about a new program, and their research supported that notion. We agree with the need to have users engage in problem-solving activities such as inferencing and with the emphasis on devising one's own plan for achieving a task (Carroll 1990). However, Charney, Rodes, and Kusbit (1990) studied strictly sequential reading; they did not allow users to look backward or forward in the manual. Indeed, each piece of information appeared on its own separate page (figure 3.6). This approach affords well-controlled laboratory experiments. However, its implications are unclear for circumstances in which manuals are designed, and not merely controlled, and for situations in

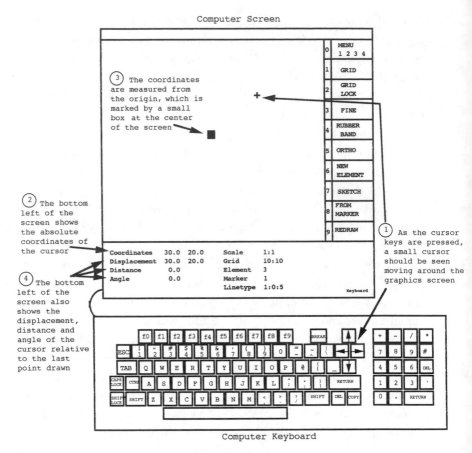

Figure 3.5
A page from a CAD/CAM manual developed by Sweller and Chandler (1994)

which people are free to use materials as they wish (see Mirel, Feinberg, and Allmendinger 1991, 81).

A main idea in the design of our manuals has been the attempt to encourage sequential processing and to support a random-access approach as well. One of the ways to realize this is by carefully structuring the manual around user scenarios. The user scenarios for structuring the content of our manuals typically lead first to the presentation of a few key tasks that are expanded later. For example, in our text processing manuals, the core is formed by a create-save-print scenario. After having acquired these basic skills, users are presented a number of chapters that

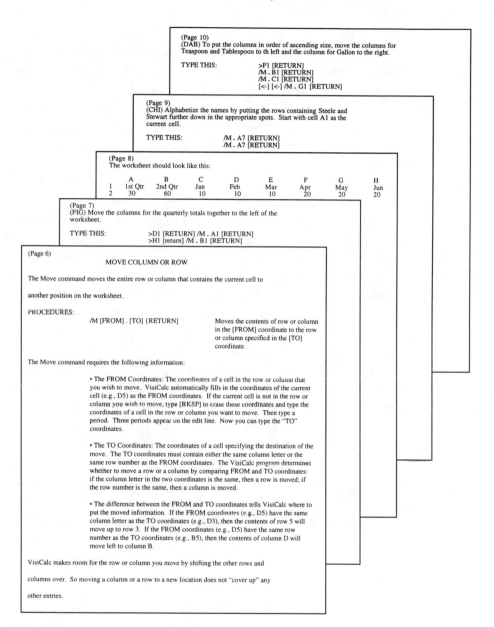

(Page 10)
(DAB) To put the columns in order of ascending size, move the columns for
Teaspoon and Tablespoon to th left and the column for Gallon to the right.

TYPE THIS: >F1 [RETURN]
                    /M . B1 [RETURN]
                    /M . C1 [RETURN]
                    [<-] [<-] /M . G1 [RETURN]

(Page 9)
(CHI) Alphabetize the names by putting the rows containing Steele and
Stewart further down in the appropriate spots. Start with cell A1 as the
current cell.

TYPE THIS: /M . A7 [RETURN]
                    /M . A7 [RETURN]

(Page 8)
The worksheet should look like this:

	A	B	C	D	E	F	G	H
1	1st Qtr	2nd Qtr	Jan	Feb	Mar	Apr	May	Jun
2	30	60	10	10	10	20	20	20

(Page 7)
(FIG) Move the columns for the quarterly totals together to the left of the
worksheet.

TYPE THIS: >D1 [RETURN] /M . A1 [RETURN]
                    >H1 [return] /M . B1 [RETURN]

(Page 6)
                    MOVE COLUMN OR ROW

The Move command moves the entire row or column that contains the current cell to

another position on the worksheet.

PROCEDURES:
        /M [FROM] . [TO] {RETURN}   Moves the contents of row or column
                                           in the [FROM] coordinate to the row
                                           or column specified in the [TO]
                                           coordinate.

The Move command requires the following information:

        • The FROM Coordinates: The coordinates of a cell in the row or column that
        you wish to move. VisiCalc automatically fills in the coordinates of the current
        cell (e.g., D5) as the FROM coordinates. If the current cell is not in the row or
        column you wish to move, type [BKSP] to erase these coordinates and type the
        coordinates of a cell in the row or column you want to move. Then type a
        period. Three periods appear on the edit line. Now you can type the "TO"
        coordinates.

        • The TO Coordinates: The coordinates of a cell specifying the destination of the
        move. The TO coordinates must contain either the same column letter or the
        same row number as the FROM coordinates. The VisiCalc program determines
        whether to move a row or a column by comparing FROM and TO coordinates:
        if the column letter in the two coordinates is the same, then a row is moved; if
        the row number is the same, then a column is moved.

        • The difference between the FROM and TO coordinates tells VisiCalc where to
        put the moved information. If the FROM coordinates (e.g., D5) have the same
        column letter as the TO coordinates (e.g., D3), then the contents of row 5 will
        move up to row 3. If the FROM coordinates (e.g., D5) have the same row
        number as the TO coordinates (e.g., B5), then the contents of column D will
        move left to column B.

VisiCalc makes room for the row or column you move by shifting the other rows and

columns over. So moving a column or a row to a new location does not "cover up" any

other entries.

Figure 3.6
The full text from five consecutive pages of the problem-solving manual developed
by Charney et al. (1990)

belong to a revise scenario (e.g., chapters on locating text in a document, moving text within a document, and changing the presentation of words and a document as a whole). But we do not expect users to process the manual in a linear fashion. Indeed, such reading is quite uncommon; in our studies about one of every twenty subjects read everything in this order, by and large. As a rule, users frequently look back to earlier sections and chapters, peek at chapters and sections ahead, and redo chapters or tasks.

Our observations also reveal they attend to most of the information presented in the minimal manual and process that information as intended. For example, 94 percent of all action steps were executed rather than read or skipped; 78 percent of learners checked the screen when prompted by coordinative information; 60 percent of learners who made an error used the error information in the manual to correct it.

When people are free to direct their own learning, motivation becomes a central issue. The first thing to do is to make a favorable initial impression. It is vitally important to avoid giving the manual a massive appearance (Brockmann 1990; Thing 1984). The manual text must make the same impression. This can be done by creating short chapters that take around thirty minutes each to work through. Nothing motivates more than success (after effort). For this reason, we propose to use real or realistic tasks as soon as possible, provide a safety net where needed, and vary direct instructions with built-in problem-solving activities that offer a conquerable challenge. Interestingly, a fair number of these minimalist principles and heuristics are also mentioned as design suggestions that positively affect motivational aspects such as attention, relevance, confidence and satisfaction. For example, Keller (1983, 1987) argues that real or realistic tasks are important for relevance and satisfaction and that a safe trajectory of activities and challenging but conquerable tasks or problems is important for building confidence.

3.5   Minimalism Overemphasizes Errors

User errors are a major focus of minimalism. Most important, the mere fact that errors occur is acknowledged in minimalism. It is still quite typical for approaches to the design of instruction and documentation to ignore errors as a central phenomenon of using information, to assume implicitly that errors do not occur (Charney, Reder, and Kusbit 1990, 324) The facts go another way: error detection, diagnosis, and recovery consume somewhere between a quarter and half of the user's time (Card, Moran, and Newell 1983; Lazonder and Van der Meij 1994, 1995; Carroll and Carrithers 1984; Prümper et al. 1992, and studies of Davis and Magers mentioned in Arnold and Roe 1987). Any realistic approach to instruction and documentation must focus substantial attention on errors. There are many trade-offs and complexities; substantial design effort is always required. Recognizing and recovering from some particular error might be a good pedagogical opportunity for the user. Another error might be a snakepit of side effects. Yet another might be pedagogically unproductive but difficult to block in the software, it might best be handled by a warning.

Some commentators have suggested that minimalism overemphasizes error and error support, making a fuss about something that "most of us would endorse as good, old-fashioned, common sense" (Williams and Farkas 1992, 41) and that "it is fairly common for manuals to anticipate users' errors and to provide correctives for errors" (Farkas and Williams 1990, 186). These assertions are wishful thinking. A recent survey on the presence and design of problem-solving information (i.e., error information) in conventional manuals revealed that six of the eight manuals for a word processor failed to help users deal with a set of specific problems. In addition, an analysis of sixty conventional manuals in that same survey revealed that when there was problem-solving information, it was hard to find. For example, 33 percent of the tables of contents and indexes in the manuals gave no references to problem-solving information, and 86 percent of the problem-solving information on the page was not marked in any way, (Van der Meij 1995).

Other commentators have taken a single technique investigated in one or another minimalist project as a general approach to all error. For example, the training-wheels technique of blocking error consequences (Carroll and Carrithers 1984) has been critiqued in this way (Frese and Altmann 1989; Frese et al. 1991). Errors are not homogeneous. Some errors immediately intrigue learners; they wonder what caused the error, and they want to replicate it, analyze it, and try variations. These are good candidates for which to encourage error diagnosis and recovery. Other errors annoy users from the first keystroke to the final recovery.

When the frustration a learner experiences obstructs the possible insights, the error recovery can no longer be seen as productive.

On the one hand, minimalism seeks to capitalize on error. Errors raise questions to users and prepare the mind to draw new insights. For example, our MoleHill tutor for Smalltalk incorporated a tool we called the Guru, which provided a critique of the student's strategy, delivered immediately after the completion of a project (Alpert, Singley, and Carroll 1995). The critique focused on errors of programming and design style. For more serious errors, we have employed more directive interventions: warnings, checkpointing, and explicit error recovery suggestions. We do not advocate structured practice with error handling to address potential negative effects of error (e.g., demotivation, anxiety, stress, and points of no return; see Frese and Altmann 1989; Frese et al. 1991). Our view is that such training compromises too much the goal of being task oriented. Moreover, the error information in a minimal manual sufficiently deals with the negative effects of error.

On the other hand, minimalism seeks to provide a safety net for errors that are difficult, distracting, or unilluminating to recover from. For example, the training-wheels interface intercepted and blocked user actions that would have led to serious error consequences. Instead of allowing the error to occur, the system displayed a message saying that the selected function was not available in the training-level system. Such a message conveys a lot: it confirms for the user that the selected command was indeed selected, while making it clear that the command was not executed by the system. By saying that the command is not available in the training-level system, it suggests that the command will be available in some other level of the system. Thus, the user is encouraged to remember that function and try it again later, yet is spared the effort and potential complications of trying to recover from the error consequences that would have ensured if the command had been executed.

3.6   Minimalism Is Just Another Word for Job Aids

Some authors have argued that the essence of minimalism is merely an expanded role for job aids. For example, Horn (1992, 9) says, "In one respect Carroll appears to reinvent the wheel: the job aid" (see also

DeWeaver and Bauman 1992; Carlson 1992, 18). Gong and Elkerton (1990) characterize minimalism as producing documentation "whose organization, down to the lowest level procedural step, communicates purely procedural or 'how-to-do-it' information" (p. 102).

There is something to these remarks. Minimalism aims to get users started quickly on real tasks. To a considerable extent, this involves conveying basic procedural information in a very succinct form. Conceptual information is included only when it is necessary for adequate understanding and execution of tasks; the achievement of meaningful tasks is the foundation for subsequent conceptual elaboration.

Some of this is true of job aids. Job aids are succinct procedures. Typically, however, they are used for reference by people who have already received instruction (Rossett and Gautier-Downes 1991). Thus, they are not designed to convey a model of the system or the task domain. From the standpoint of learning operations and tasks, job aids are often an arbitrary set of cards that belong together only because they are packaged together. They are not designed to provoke task-oriented reasoning on the part of the user, but merely to support execution of a set of steps. They are intended merely to help people play back a set of instructions; they do not address errors.

One of the earliest minimalist projects developed and studied in the minimalist approach was also the one most similar in design to job aids. Guided Exploration cards were an early exploration of the amount of information and structure secretaries required when learning to use word processing equipment (Carroll et al. 1985). Each card briefly addressed a particular functional goal that could be understood on the basis of the user's prior knowledge of office tasks (figure 3.7). The cards were deliberately incomplete, often providing only hints, so that users would stay focused on the task. Each card separately addressed one basic task goal without reference to material covered on other cards; the set of cards was delivered as an unbound deck. Finally, each card included specific checkpoint information (to help users detect and diagnose errors) and error recovery information (to help them get back on track).

Another example of minimalist documentation that initially seems much like a job aid comes from Gong and Elkerton's study (1990). Figure 3.8 illustrates a page of their procedural manual.

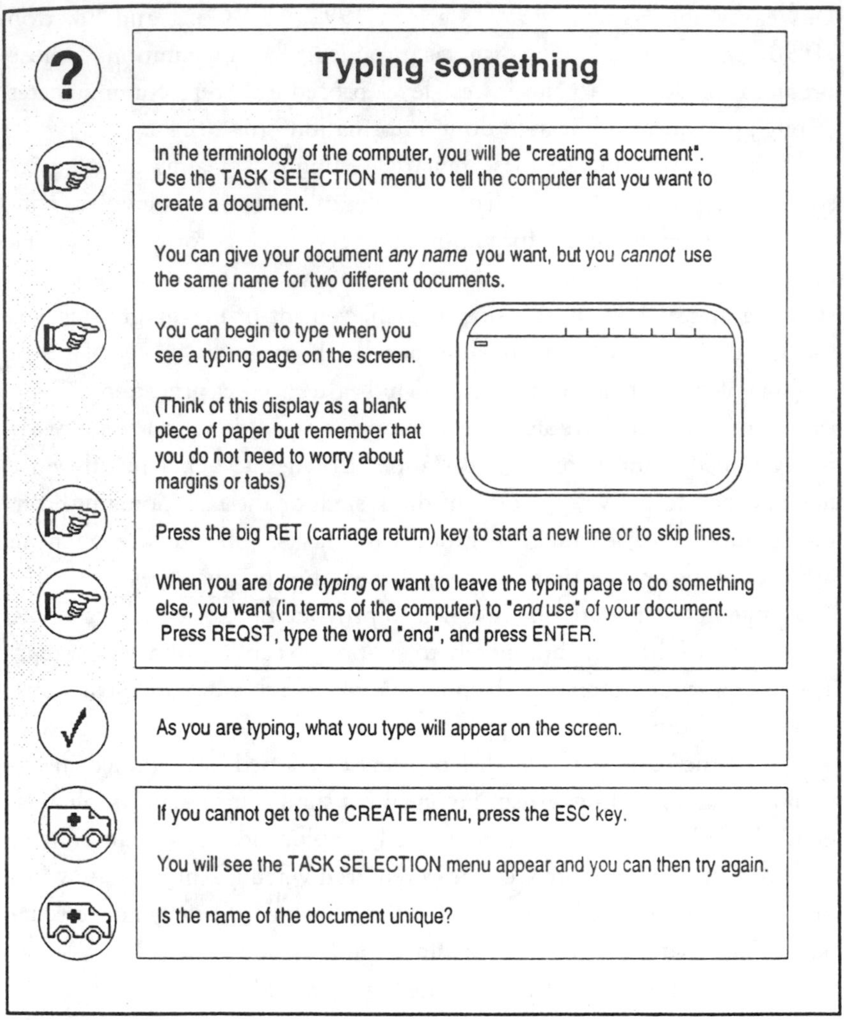

Typing something

In the terminology of the computer, you will be "creating a document". Use the TASK SELECTION menu to tell the computer that you want to create a document.

You can give your document *any name* you want, but you *cannot* use the same name for two different documents.

You can begin to type when you see a typing page on the screen.

(Think of this display as a blank piece of paper but remember that you do not need to worry about margins or tabs)

Press the big RET (carriage return) key to start a new line or to skip lines.

When you are *done typing* or want to leave the typing page to do something else, you want (in terms of the computer) to "*end* use" of your document. Press REQST, type the word "end", and press ENTER.

As you are typing, what you type will appear on the screen.

If you cannot get to the CREATE menu, press the ESC key.

You will see the TASK SELECTION menu appear and you can then try again.

Is the name of the document unique?

Figure 3.7
A Guided Exploration card (Lazonder 1994)

TOPIC 5 - SAVING INFORMATION TO DISK STORAGE

1.   Press the key labeled "Alt" and the "M" key at the same time.

2.   Press the "S" key.

3.   Create a file for the onscreen parameters and calculations:
      A.   Press the "D" key.
      B.   Press the "C" key.
      C.   Verify that the bottom window of the display looks like the following:

Respond to each prompt. <ESC> to delete, <CR> without entry to skip.

Please select the disk drive A, B, C, etc. and press <CR>, [.].
Give subdirectory if any: \........\. Eight letter max then <CR>.
Give filename: [........]. Eight letter max, no extension, then <CR>.

      <CR> for default: (), <C>reate, <D>irectory, ESC quit.

      D.   Decide in which drive you want to save the information. Then type in
            the letter corresponding to that drive. Then press RETURN.
      E.   Decide if the file will be saved in a sub-directory. If so, then type in the
            name of the subdirectory and press RETURN. If not, then just press
            RETURN and proceed to the next step.
      F.   Type in the name of the file in which the information will be saved.
            Then press RETURN.

4.   Decide if all the entered information (drive name, subdirectory name, and
      filename) are all correct. If so, press the "Y" key, and you have finished the
      save procedure. If not, press the "N" key and return to step 3C.

Figure 3.8
A page from a procedural manual (Gong and Elkerton 1990)

These two examples also illustrate several key differences between
minimalist materials and job aids with respect to the type of support
each provides to users. Guided Exploration cards only occasionally offer
explicit prescriptions for procedures. Whenever possible, users are given
instructions that are general enough to support user actions for related
procedures or tasks. Figures 3.7 and 3.8 illustrate this principle well.
Users are not given exact prescriptions on what to do in typing or
saving but are given enabling hints. Job aids, in contrast, succinctly
present the step-by-step minutiae of procedures; as tools for learning

and thinking, these are deskilling characteristics and not at all consistent with minimalism.

The Guided Exploration cards provide frequent feedback; each card includes at least one explicit coordinating anchor between the system state and the instructional material. This feedback conveys to users that they are on the right track; more broadly, it confirms the user's current understanding and helps to build self-confidence. The provision of feedback also helps users coordinate and switch attention among the screen, the manual, and the keyboard. Finally, feedback gives users a point of reference when they do make an error; it indicates a place from which they might have gone wrong.

The mere presence of error information in the Guided Exploration cards does not distinguish them from job aids. Some job aids are designed especially for troubleshooting. What sets the two apart is that the Guided Exploration cards integrate corrective with constructive information. Regular ("constructive") procedural instructions are accompanied by information about what to do if things go wrong. In most job aids, the support for constructive and corrective actions is rarely integrated. In contrast, minimalist instruction puts a high priority on putting the error information where it is likely to be most helpful, which is in the immediate vicinity of error-prone actions (Van der Meij and Carroll 1995).

By taxonomizing the procedures of a domain in terms of the basic task goals that users want to pursue, Guided Exploration cards convey a task-oriented model of the system and the domain of activity. Conveying such a conceptual framework is not an objective of job aids; it is sufficient for job aids merely to lay out the steps for various procedures. This focus on conveying goals and plans, and not just procedural steps, clearly differentiates all minimalist materials from job aids (Draper and Oatley 1990, p. 228). Indeed, subsequent minimalist projects emphasized this more than the Guided Exploration cards (among others, they lack goal descriptions), thereby drawing the distinction even more sharply.

3.7   Minimalism Works Only for Simple Domains

Minimalist instruction developed in relatively simple domains. Most of the early work addressed elementary word processing functions out of a practical convenience and because this domain offered the chance for greater and more rapid practical impact. Some writers have mistakenly concluded from this that minimalism is intended only for simple domains, and that it can work only in such domains (Halgren 1992; Farkas and Williams 1990; Horn 1992). The reasoning seems to be that a simplified, action-oriented approach to elementary skills cannot in principle scale up to complex, integrated system environments. In our opinion, there is no reason to believe that even the most intricate and complex domain cannot be conveyed through an action-oriented approach that focuses on core skills.

Some of the specific principles of minimalism too may have triggered the misconception. For example, the principle of getting started fast (Carroll 1990) could suggest that minimalism is applicable only to the earliest stages of learning. But in fact one can get started fast anywhere along a learning trajectory. And the minimalism claim is that this indeed is what learners prefer to do. Heuristics such as selecting or designing instructional activities that are real tasks, creating components of instruction that reflect the task structure, and providing closure of chapters support these action-oriented preferences (Van der Meij and Carroll 1995). Similarly, the minimalist principle of exploiting prior knowledge (Carroll 1990) could suggest that minimalism is applicable only to domains people are already familiar with. But in fact, adult learners always have relevant prior knowledge and cannot help but draw on it when they try to learn. The issue is not one of whether there is prior knowledge but one of helping the learners to identify what prior knowledge is relevant, and how. Misinterpreting the principles along these lines could entrain the conclusion that minimalism is suitable only for instruction in simple (and known) domains and only for instructing first-time users.

One of our main motivations in undertaking the development of minimalist instruction for Smalltalk and object-oriented design was to challenge the "simple domain" misconception. Our user group in that work was professional programmers in IBM. These highly skilled individuals wanted to continue to develop their skills by learning the object paradigm. We developed special programming environments (Carroll et al. 1990; Rosson, Carroll, and Sweeney 1991) and a minimalist tutorial

(Carroll and Rosson 1995; Rosson, Carroll, and Bellamy 1990). This was an extensive and successful minimalist project, carried out in an extremely complex, technical domain.

Another signal of the applicability of minimalism to a variety of domains and applications comes from the reported studies in the literature. Minimalist instruction has been produced for word processing (Displaywriter, WordPerfect), computer-assisted design, desktop publishing (PageMaker, ViewPoint), a time-registration program, telephony (Hayes Fax-modem, Norstar), an occupational safety application, e-mail (UNIX and VME), programming (CNC and Smalltalk), Hypercard, and database programs (Carroll 1990; Van der Meij and Carroll 1995). And this variety is growing rapidly; we are constantly tracking down new developments.

It is true that most minimalist work has concentrated on instructing first-time users, but this does not indicate an inherent problem in applying it to advanced training or reference documentation applications (as suggested in Horn 1992). In fact, two of the earliest commercial applications of minimalism were in the area of reference documentation: for the Xerox Viewpoint Electronic Publishing system and the Norstar telephone system (both reported in Carroll 1990). In addition, in some of our recent projects, we obtained promising outcomes of minimalist reference materials. We do agree, however, that much work needs to be done on finding out how minimalism can contribute to the development of better reference documentation.

3.8   Minimalism Merely Reflects the Preconceptions of Users

One of the key ideas of minimalism is to leverage the learner's task-oriented motivation and reasoning. People want to accomplish meaningful goals; they want to try things out, to learn by doing. This can be read as merely an injunction to satisfy every preference of the user. And indeed, there is a deep issue here about the appropriate role of the user in the design process (Greenbaum and Kyng 1991). Our intention is far narrower, however. Whether we take the design stance of satisfying every user preference or not, we should at least respect the integrity of the user's activity (Van der Meij and Carroll 1995). This is not a matter of giving the user 256 colors, animated graphics, and full-motion video. It is a matter of designing tools and information so that they do not obstruct and impair the user's task-oriented goals. In this minimal sense, it is a matter of ensuring that a presumed tool is not antithetical to use.

This may seem beyond obvious, but our early work showed that the dominant approaches to designing instructional material in fact did obstruct and impair task-oriented activity. One of the reasons that this situation persisted for quite some time is that people often think that what they are used to is also what is best. From previous schooling and experiences, most people are quite familiar with study books, and so this is what they put up with. They (or managers) may simply voice social inertia ("It worked in the past," "It is too costly to change"). In addition, lacking comparative materials, they may also have been unaware of better alternatives.

Our efforts to improve the situation began by observing scores of users. We carefully documented how initially well-motivated users were successively defeated by repetitive exercises and expansive conceptual sections, ultimately wondering aloud what they were supposed to be doing or learning (e.g., Carroll and Mazur 1986; Carroll and Mack 1984; Mack, Lewis, and Carroll 1983). This substantiated the need for improvement. To convince technical writers (and managers) of the possibilities for improvement, we began to design minimalist instructions and conducted a number of comparative experiments. These studies clearly showed the superiority of minimalist instructions over conventional instructional materials (Carroll 1990; Van der Meij and Carroll 1995; Carroll et al. 1987–1988; Lazonder 1994). In addition, users often indicated their satisfaction with these materials.

In our user-centered approach, it has never been our chief intention "merely" to please learners. Users do not have to love the manual in order to learn from it. They have to accept it to the extent that they use it effectively; people's meta-knowledge about their own information needs is often flawed. Thus, over the years, we have encountered users who voice the desire for more complete manuals, but we have weighed this misfit between their desires with the results we have obtained for learning outcomes: they learned more than their peers who used more complete manuals.

At the same time, we have always found it necessary but difficult to create instructions that work best for the majority of users in a given situation and simultaneously come closest to theoretically ideal instructions—a hard balancing act. For example, users often have different, or conflicting, opinions about the things they would like to see changed in instruction or information. One cannot design to suit user preferences in such cases, because one is pulled in opposing directions. So here theoretical arguments prevail. But while it may be theoretically ideal to have people read in advance or solve problems before they engage in task executions (Charney, Reder, and Kusbit 1990; Sweller and Chandler 1994), this approach does not work for most users. So here practical considerations lead the way.

3.9   Minimalism Offers a Complete Documentation Solution

Minimalism offers a simple but expansive program for the design of documentation and training. From this, one could conclude that minimalism constitutes a comprehensive design model for all documentation—a complete documentation solution. For example, Farkas and Williams (1990) consider the minimal manual (and other single training tools) to be offered as complete solutions. A major point of their discussion is to contend that these minimalist approaches are not complete solutions. They directly contrast them with what they call a "contemporary documentation set (CDS)"—a tutorial, a user's guide, a quick-start manual.

The first point to make is that there are potential downsides to having complete documentation solutions. People can get lost in the training and documentation options, as well as in any particular component. The positive effects of minimal manuals are telling in this respect.

In addition, we believe that a complete documentation solution requires an actively evolving solution rather than a relatively stable and contemporary documentation set. Increased insights into the specific needs and deficiencies of users should prompt designers into creating new solutions. For example, the contemporary documentation set has not been able to solve the problem of unused commands; users still typically use only a very small portion of the options of a program (Rosson 1984; Westendorp 1993). Similarly, the set offers no solution for fixed but inefficient routines of users. For these (new) goals, new solutions are called for (e.g., some programs already offer advice to users about their inefficient routines).

Not only the goals of instruction are changing; the means of instruction are too. For example, the complete documentation solution of today is likely to be a mixture of paper and on-screen support. In our view, one of the most pertinent issues here is that of the interplay between the software product and the user support. We have directed some of our efforts to this issue, such as with the creation of the Smalltalk Guru, MoleHill's intelligent tutoring system, and the training-wheels technology (see Carroll 1990; Alpert, Singley, and Carroll 1995; Rosson et al. 1993; Singley and Carroll 1990). But the topic is surely underanalyzed. For example, we have yet to see the first article outlining the main principles of the interplay between online help and paper support.

An altogether different reason that minimalism does not offer a complete documentation solution resembling the CDS of Farkas and Williams (1990) is that it is an orientation toward design that does not aspire to eventuate in a final cookbook. The relevant theory and practical experience about learning and using information that bear on the design of instruction and documentation are too vast and too diverse to be susceptible to cookbook treatment.

3.10   Minimalism Has No Theoretical Foundation

Because the development of minimalism has been so firmly rooted in the world of design and design evaluation, some writers have come to see it as essentially consisting of rules of thumb, or to put it more grandly, as an "aesthetic" of documentation. They have accordingly complained that minimalism lacks a theoretical foundation—that even if it does work well, we will never know why (Halgren 1992, p. 12).

This is more than merely academic interest: rules of thumb cannot support systematic, technical progress or refinement. Rules of thumb are grounded only vaguely and holistically in standards of practice and are bound together only by being listed together. They do not support deductions or inferences. Basically, one takes them or leaves them. Thus, if minimalism's foundations could not be identified and explicated, in principle it would not be capable of providing a framework for developing new approaches to instruction and documentation.

Two characteristics of minimalism, or more specifically of presentations of minimalism, may have encouraged this misconception. First, statements of the core principles of minimalism have varied over the years (contrast Carroll 1990, Van der Meij and Carroll 1995, Carroll 1984), perhaps leading some readers into worrying that the principles are somewhat arbitrary and therefore do not have a sound foundation. This is entirely mistaken. The content of the principles has in fact changed very little over the years. The varied presentations of minimalism reflect our best guesses as to the most effective way to articulate the essential content of the approach. Beyond this, we have always resisted taking ourselves so seriously as to sanctify a minimalist litany. Our interest has always been in developing and evaluating ideas and techniques, not in mouthing particular words.

A second characteristic that may have encouraged the view that minimalism lacks theoretical foundations is that most developments and presentations of minimalism are strongly empirical. We do not find this problematic, the design of instruction and documentation is fundamentally empirical. Theoretical foundations are significant only if they have strong empirical content, providing specific guidance to designers and being empirically testable. It is unfortunately typical to see information design philosophies justified by relatively vacuous appeals to intuition and assorted theory. For example, Carroll (1990) observed how Gagné & Briggs (1979) was "justified" by broad appeals to behaviorist learning theory, while Gagné, Briggs & Wagner (1988) was "justified" by broad appeals to cognitive learning theory. These were successive editions of the same book, presenting the same design approach; only the foundation had changed. Readers looking for such "foundation" will have been frustrated by minimalism.

Indeed, the empirical nature of the minimalist approach has facilitated many focused empirical studies. Thus, a considerable body of work replicates the results of Carroll et al. (1987–1988) with respect to minimal manuals (Vanderlinden, Cocklin, and McKita 1988; Gong and Elkerton 1990; Lazonder and Van der Meij 1993; Draper and Oatley 1990; Lazonder 1994; Black, Carroll, and McGuigan 1987; Frese et al. 1988;

Olfman and Bostrom 1988; Ramsay and Oatley 1992; Van der Meij 1992; Wendel and Frese 1987). Draper & Oatley (1990) conclude their review with the statement that "minimalist instruction is a robust and reliable method for writing documentation that out performs most conventional manuals" (p. 222). A variety of empirical studies have examined specific aspects of the minimalist approach: task orientation and error information (Gong and Elketon 1990; Lazonder and Van der Meij 1994, 1995; Lazonder 1994), brevity and inferencing (Black, Carroll, and McGuigan 1987), the depiction of screens to facilitate user coordination (Nowaczyk and James 1993), and various kinds of problem-solving practice (Wiedenbeck, Zila, and McConnel 1995).

The third characteristic of presentations of minimalism that may encourage the misconception that the approach lacks foundation is the unwavering incompleteness of these presentations. No definitive set of minimalist guidelines has ever been published; no step-by-step procedure for creating minimalist documentation exists (the closest approximation is Van der Meij and Carroll 1995). Developers new to minimalism frequently complain about this; their expectations have been prefigured by prior experiences with systematic approaches that have the explicit goal of reducing information design to rule following (Halgren 1992; Gong and Elkerton 1990; Lazonder 1994; Van der Meij 1992; Janssen 1994; Nickerson 1991; tripp 1990). Minimalism has always had the goal of opening up documentation design as a process, while focusing it on the objective of supporting the user's sense making:

What is instructional design know-how? Is it merely the ability to follow checklists? Is it merely to have a checklist? Or is it a fundamental commitment to a goal and to the process of discovery and invention that spring from having that goal? The key to minimalist instruction is not, for example, whether the designer blocks error consequences but whether the designer has made the far more fundamental commitment to discover how to support the learner's sense-making efforts. An ironic way to put this is that our goal is to fail to get designers merely to apply our guidelines but in doing so to succeed at getting them to discover minimalism and to invent minimalist approaches far more effective than those discussed here. (Carroll 1990, 304–305)

This misconception, in any case, is a misconception. *The Nurnberg Funnel* cites a foundation of over two hundard books and technical papers drawn from educational psychology, learning theory, cognitive science, human-computer interaction, and information design. The exposition of the basic model (pp. 77–90 of that book) alone contains over eighty technical citations. The theoretical foundation, as we understand it, has three main roots: John Dewey's view (1910) that the realm of the mind includes the situations and tools that comprise problems and are used to solve them, Jean Piaget's view (1963) of the mind as transforming itself by confronting and solving new sorts of problems, and, most directly, Jerome Bruner's view (1966, 1973) that students must be active in their own learning in order to become independent learners. This foundation has indeed become conceptually and empirically stronger through the course of the past decade, for example, in developments of constructivist theories of the mind (Duffy and Jonassen 1992).

At a finer level of articulation, minimalism rests on a broad foundation of specific psychological theories and results (e.g., action theory, attention, relevance, confidence, satisfaction (ARCS)-motivation theory, cognitive load theory, the principle of worked examples, the just-in-time principle, the redundancy effect, and the split attention effect). For example, a fair number of minimalist principles and heuristics are also presented as design suggestions in the ARCS-motivational theory of Keller (1983, 1987). In addition, the task-oriented nature, the usage of real or realistic tasks, the support of coordinative actions, an experience-related deepening of skill, and a striving toward increasing independence of the user all fit within the general framework of action theory (Norman 1986; Rieder and Oesterreich 1994).

3.11   Conceptions of Minimalism

Minimalism necessarily evolves with the context of information technology and information development practice. Action orientation in instruction and documentation, for example, may not yet be standard practice, but it is widely employed, in striking contrast to the context before the minimalism. Task orientation is also widely accepted, but it is more of a frontier for application, particularly in complex domains, for which it is often difficult to create meaningful tasks that are manageable within relatively short spans of time. Support for error handling and problem solving is still not standard practice, but has become accepted as common sense. Use orientation, support for the great variety of user activities and concerns, in many cases has become a team effort of graphic designers, instructional designers, technical communicators, system designers, and users themselves—directed at rich but invisible scaffolding and at helping more by imposing less.

We do not regard misconceptions of minimalism as merely mistakes. Although we have tried to investigate and articulate the minimalist approach clearly and effectively, we are well aware that much remains to be done. Misconceptions about minimalism at the very least embody feedback for those who wish to develop and communicate this approach. They are pointers to issues that have not yet been effectively clarified and resolved. In this sense, each of the ten misconceptions (and there may well be more than ten) can be seen as an implicit need statement for further investigation and analysis.

It is in that spirit that we have tried to identify several of these misconceptions, to indicate why and how we believe they might have arisen, and to address them, based on our own understanding of what minimalism is and of the current state of evidence and practice. Our objective is to stimulate more convergent, more productive discussion and development of minimalism. As we have tried to emphasize and epitomize in this discussion, minimalism cannot be reduced to an operational dictum. It is a program for continuous discovery for both users and developers.

The rate and scope of change in the technology context of both users and developers presents more opportunities for discovering minimalism and more challenges for applying minimalism than ever before. We hope that readers will take these ten misconceptions about minimalism as ten directions for further research and analysis. We look forward to further lively discussion and investigation of minimalism emerging from this context.

References

Alpert, S.R., M.K. Singley, and J.M. Carroll. 1995. "Multiple mutimodal mentors: Delivering computer-based instruction via specialized anthropomorphic advisors." *Behaviour and Information Technology* 14:69–79.

Arnold, B., and R. Roe. 1987. "User errors in human-computer interaction." In M. Frese, E. Ulich, and W. Dzida (eds.), *Psychological issues of human computer interaction in the work place* (pp. 203–222). Amsterdam: Elsevier.

Bailey, R. W. 1983. *Human error in computer systems*. Englewood Cliffs, NJ: Prentice Hall.

Black, J. B., J. M. Carroll, and S. M. McGuigan. 1987. "What kind of minimal instruction manual is the most effective?" In J. M. Carroll and P. P. Tanner (eds.), *Proceedings of CHI+GI'87 Human Factors in Computing Systems and Graphics Interface*. New York: Association for Computing Machinery.

Brockmann, R. J. 1990. *Writing better user documentation: From paper to hypertext* (2nd ed.). New York: Wiley.

Bruner, J. S. 1966. *Toward a theory of instruction*. Cambridge, MA: Harvard University Press.

Bruner, J. S. 1973. *Beyond the information given*. New York: Norton.

Card, S. K., T. P. Moran, and A. Newell. 1983. *The psychology of human-computer interaction*. Hillsdale, NJ: Erlbaum.

Card, S. K., T. P. Moran, and A. Newell. 1990. "The keystroke-level model for user performance time with interactive systems." In J. Preece and L. Keller (eds.), *Human-computer interaction: Selected readings*. Hemel Hempstead: Prentice Hall.

Carlson, P. A. 1992. "From document to knowledge base: Intelligent hypertext as minimalist instruction." *Journal of Computer Documentation* 16, no. 1:17–31.

Carroll, J. M. 1984. "Minimalist training." *Datamation* 30, no. 18:125–136, November 11.

Carroll, J. M. 1990. *The Nurnberg funnel: Designing minimalist instruction for practical computer skill*. Cambridge, MA: MIT Press.

Carroll, J. M. (ed.). 1995. *Scenario-based design: Envisioning work and technology in system development*. New York: Wiley.

Carroll, J. M., and C. Carrithers. 1984. "Blocking learner errors in a training wheels system." *Human Factors* 26, no. 4:377–389.

Carroll, J. M., and R. L. Mack. 1984. "Learning to use a word processor: By doing, by thinking and by knowing." In J. C. Thomas and M. L. Schneider (eds.), *Human factors in computer systems*. Norwood, NJ: Ablex.

Carroll, J. M., R. L. Mack, C. H. Lewis, N. L. Grischkowsky, and S. P. Robertson. 1985. "Exploring exploring a word processor." *Human-Computer Interaction* 1:283–307.

Carroll, J. M., and S. A. Mazur. 1986. "LisaLearning." *IEEE Computer* 19, no. 11:35–49.

Carroll, J. M., and M. B. Rosson. 1995. "Managing evaluation goals for training." *Communications of the ACM* 38, no. 7:40–48.

Carroll, J. M., J. A. Singer, R. K. E. Bellamy and S. R. Alpert. 1990. "A view matcher for learning Smalltalk." In J. C. Chew and J. Whiteside (eds.), *Proceedings of CHI'90 Conference: Human factors in computing systems.* New York: Association for Computing Machinery.

Carroll, J. M., P. S. Smith-Kerker, J. R. Ford, and S. A. Mazur-Rimetz. 1987/1988. "The minimal manual." *Human-Computer Interaction* 3:123–153.

Charney, D. H., L. M. Reder, and G. W. Kusbit. 1990. "Goal setting and procedure selection in acquiring computer skills: A comparison of tutorials, problem solving and learner exploration." *Cognition and Instruction* 4:323–342.

DeWeaver, M. J., and J. M. Bauman. 1992. "The Nurnberg funnel: Designing minimalist instruction for practical computer skill." *Performance and Instruction* (April):25–26.

Dewey, J. 1910. *How we think*. New York: D. C. Heath.

Draper, S. W., and K. Oatley. 1990. "Action centered manuals or minimalist instruction? Alternative theories for Carroll's minimal manuals." In P. Holt and N. Williams (eds.), *Computers and writing: State of the art* (pp. 222–243). Oxford: Intellect Books.

Duffy, T. M., and D. H. Jonassen. 1992. *Constructivism and the technology of instruction: A conversation*. Hillsdale, NJ: Erlbaum.

Farkas, D. K., and T. R. Williams. 1990. "John Carroll's *The Nurnberg Funnel* and minimalist documentation." *IEEE Transactions on Professional Communication* 33, no. 4:182–187.

Frese, M., K. Albrecht, A. Altmann, J. Lang, P. von Papstein, R Peyerl, J. Pruemper, H. Schulte-Goecking, I. Wankmueller, and R. Wendel. 1988. "The effect of an active development of the mental model in the training process: Experimental results in a word processing system." *Behaviour and Information Technology* 7:295–304.

Frese, M., and A. Altmann. 1989. "The treatment of errors in learning and training." In L. Bainbridge and S. A. Ruiz Quintanilla (eds.), *Developing skills with information technology*. Chichester: Wiley.

Frese, M., F. Brodbeck, T. Heinbokel, C. Mooser, E. Schleiffenbaum, and P. Thiemann. 1991. "Errors in training computer skills: On the positive function of errors." *Human Computer Interaction* 6:77–93.

Gagné, R. M., and L. J. Briggs. 1979. *Principles of instructional design*. New York: Holt, Rinehart and Winston.

Gagné, R. M., L. J. Briggs, and W. Wagner. 1988. *Principles of instructional design* (3rd ed.). New York: Holt, Rinehart and Winston.

Glasbeek, H. 1992. *Leerstijlen van computergebruikers* [Learning styles of computer users]. Master's thesis, Utrecht University.

Glasbeek, H. (1994). "Improving the quality of tutorials: Does minimalism really help?" In M. Steehouder, C. Jansen, P. van der Poort, and R. Verheijen (eds.), *Quality of technical documentation* (pp. 77–83). Amsterdam: Rodopi.

Gong, R., and J. Elkerton. 1990. "Designing minimal documentation using a GOMS model: A usability evaluation of an engineering approach." In J. C. Chew and J. Whiteside (eds.), *Proceedings of the CHI'90 Conference: Human factors in computing systems* (pp. 99–106). New York: Association for Computing Machinery.

Graesser, A. C., and K. Murray. 1990. "A question-answering methodology for exploring a user's acquisition and knowledge of a computer environment." In S. P. Robertson, W. Zachary, and J. B. Black (eds.), *Cognition, computing and cooperation* (pp. 237–267). Norwood, NJ: Ablex.

Greenbaum, J., and M. Kyng (eds.). 1991. *Design at work: Cooperative design of computer systems.* Hillsdale, NJ: Erlbaum.

Hallgren, C. 1992. "*The Nurnberg Funnel:* A minimal collection." *Journal of Computer Documentation* 16, no. 1:11–17.

Horn, R. E. 1992. "Commentary on *The Nurnberg Funnel.*" *Journal of Computer Documentation* 16, no. 1:3–11.

Janssen, C. J. M. 1994. "Research in technical documentation in the Netherlands." *Technical Communications* 41, no. 2:234–239.

Jonassen, D. H., W. H. Hannum, and M. Tessmer. 1989. *Handbook of task analysis procedures.* New York: Praeger.

Kamouri, A. L., J. Kamouri, and K. H. Smith. 1986. "Training by exploration: Facilitating the transfer of procedural knowledge through analogical reasoning." *International Journal of Man Machine Studies* 24:171–192.

Keller, J. M. 1983. "Motivational design of instruction." In C. M. Reigeluth (ed.), *Instructional-design theories and models: An overview of their current status.* Hillsdale, NJ: Erlbaum.

Keller, J. M. 1987. "Development and use of the ARCS model of instructional design." *Journal of Instructional Development* 10, no. 3:2–10.

Lazonder, A. W. 1994. "Minimalist computer documentation. A study on constructive and corrective skills development." Ph.D. dissertation, Twente University.

Lazonder, A. W., and H. Van der Meij. 1993. "The minimal manual: Is less really more?" *International Journal of Man Machine Studies* 39:729–752.

Lazonder, A. W., and H. Van der Meij. 1994. "The effect of error-information in tutorial documentation." *Interacting with Computers*, 6, no. 1:23–40.

Lazonder, A. W., and H. Van der Meij. 1995. "Error-information in tutorial documentation: Supporting users' errors to facilitate initial skill learning." *International Journal of Human-Computer Studies* 42:185–206.

Mack, R. L., C. H. Lewis, and J. M. Carroll. 1983. "Learning to use office systems: Problems and prospects." *ACM Transactions on Office Information Systems* vol 1:254–271.

Merrill, P. F. 1987. "Job and task analysis." In R. M. Gagné (ed.), *Instructional technology: Foundations.* Hillsdale, NJ: Erlbaum.

Mirel, B., S. Feinberg, and L. Allmendinger. 1991. "Designing manuals for active learning styles." *Technical Communication* 38, no. 1:75–87.

Nickerson, R. S. 1991. "A minimalist approach to the 'paradox of sense making.'" *Educational Researcher* 20, no. 9:24–26.

Norman, D. A. 1986. "Cognitive engineering." In D. A. Norman and S. W. Draper (eds.), *User centered system design: New perspectives on human-computer interaction.* Hillsdale, NJ: Erlbaum.

Nowaczyk, R. H., and E. C. James. 1993. "Applying minimal manual principles for documentation of graphical user interfaces." *Journal of Technical Writing and Communication* 23, no. 4:379–388.

Olfman, L., and R. P. Bostrom. 1988. "The influence of training on use of end-user software." *Proceedings of the Conference on Office Information Systems.* New York: Association for Computing Machinery.

Piaget, J. 1963. *The origins of intelligence in children.* New York: Norton.

Prümper, J., D. Zapf, F. C. Brodbeck, and M. Frese. 1992. "Some surprising differences between novice and expert errors in computerized office work." *Behavior and Information Technology* 11, no. 6:319–328.

Ramsay, R. E., and K. Oatley. 1992. "Designing minimalist tutorials from scratch." *Instructional Science* 21:85–99.

Rieder, K., and R. Oesterreich. 1994. "The task-oriented training methodology for training software packages." In J. M. M. van der Sanden and F. J. J. van Bussel (eds.), *Atrium in Europe: The development of learning abilities in youth training.* Tilburg University.

Rossett, A., and J. Gautier-Downes. 1991. *A handbook of job aids.* San Diego: Pfeiffer & Co.

Rosson, M. B. 1984. "Effects of experience on learning, using, and evaluating a text-editor". *Human Factors* 26:463–475.

Rosson, M. B., J. M. Carroll, and R. K. E. Bellamy. 1990. "Smalltalk scaffolding: A minimalist curriculum." In J. C. Chew and J. Whiteside (eds), *Proceedings of CHI'90 Conference: Human factors in computing systems.* New York: Association for Computing Machinery. pp. 423–429.

Rosson, M. B., J. M. Carroll, R. K. E. Bellamy, S. R. Alpert, and J. A. Singer. 1993. MiTTS: Minimalist tutorial and tools for Smalltalk/V. Yorktown Heights, NY: Computer Science Department, IBM T. J. Watson Research Center.

Rosson, M. B., J. M. Carroll, and C. Sweeney. 1991. "A view matcher for reusing Smalltalk classes." In S. P. Robertson, G. M. Olson and J. S. Olson (eds.), *Proceedings of CHI'91 Conference: Human factors in computing systems.* New York: Association for Computing Machinery.

Singley, M. K., and J. M. Carroll. 1990. "Minimalist planning tools in an instructional system for Smalltalk." In D. Diaper, D. Gilmore, G. Cockton, and B. Shackel (eds.), *Proceedings of Third IFIP Conference on Human-Computer Interaction.* Amsterdam: North-Holland.

Sweller, J., and P. Chandler. 1994. "Why some material is difficult to learn." *Cognition and Instruction* 12, no. 3:185–233.

Thing, L. 1984. "What the well-dressed manual is wearing today." *Technical Communication* 31, no. 3:8–12.

Tripp, S.D. 1990. "Book review of *The Nurnberg Funnel*." *Educational Technology Research and Development* vol. 38, no. 3:87–90.

Van der Linden, G., T.G. Cocklin, and M. McKita. 1988. "Testing and developing minimalist tutorials: A case history." In *Proceedings of the 35th International Technical Communications Conference* (pp. RET 196–199). Washington, DC: Society for Technical Communication.

Van der Meij, H. 1992. "A critical assessment of the minimalist approach to documentation." In *Proceedings of the 10th Annual International Conference on Systems Documentation* (SIGDOC '92). New York: Association for Computing Machinery.

Van der Meij, H. 1994. "Catching the user in the act." In P. van der Poort, M. Verheyen, M.W. Steehouder and C. Jansen (eds.), *Quality of technical documentation*. Amsterdam: Rodopi.

Van der Meij, H. 1995. Helpt de handleiding? [Does the manual help?]. *Tijdschrift voor Taalbeheersing* 17, no. 4:267–288.

Van der Meij, H., and J.M. Carroll. 1995. "Principles and heuristics for designing minimalist instruction." *Technical Communication* 42, no. 2:243–261.

Van der Meij, H., and A.W. Lazonder. 1993. "An assessment of the minimalist approach to computer user documentation." *Interacting with Computers* 5, no. 4:355–370.

Wendel, R. and M. Frese. (1987). "Developing exploratory strategies in training: The general approach and a specific example for manual use." In H. J. Bullinger, B. Shackel, and K. Kornwachs (eds.), *Proceedings of the Second IFIP Conference on Human-Computer Interaction*, pp. 943–948. Amsterdam: Elsevier.

Westendorp, P. 1993. *Gebruiksaanwijzingen*. [User manual] Instituut Vervolgopleidingen, Technische Universiteit Eindhoven.

Wiedenbeck, S., P.L. Zila, and D.S. McConnell. 1995. "End-user training: An empirical study comparing on-line practice methods." *Proceedings of CHI'95 Conference: Human factors in computing systems*. New York: Association for Computing Machinery.

Williams, T.R., and D.K. Farkas. 1992. "Minimalism reconsidered: Should we design documentation for exploratory learning?" *SIGCHI Bulletin* 24, no. 2:41–50.

Wright, P. 1988. "Issues of content and presentation in document design." In M. Helander (ed.), *Handbook of human-computer interaction*. Amsterdam: Elsevier.

Wright, P. 1994. "Quality or usability? Quality writing provokes quality reading." In P. van der Poort, M. Verheyen, M.W. Steehouder, and C. Jansen (eds.), *Quality of technical documentation*. Amsterdam: Rodopi.

4

Exploring Minimalistic Technical Documentation Design Today: A View from the Practitioner's Window

Patricia A. H. Anson

When desktop computers began to appear in the workplace in the early 1980s, novice users had several avenues for finding information about using these innovative office resources: take a class and then practice what they learned, enlist the help of the computer guru in the office, or learn from the documentation provided with the computer hardware or software application. Unfortunately for the user, the documentation distributed at that time was developed by the technical wizards who had programmed the code or engineered the technology. As a result, the documentation was typically quite lengthy and written in a technically oriented style. Naive users had to sort through pages and pages of text and be able to decipher programmer jargon to find out how to accomplish even a simple task.

Computer documentation has improved since those early days—document size has drastically reduced, less technical language is used, more illustrations with visual cues are added as a convenient reference to increase ease of use—but users continue to loath documentation as something of a necessary evil and used only as a last resort (Young 1989; Deterline 1988; Martin 1986; Wilton 1985; Knowles 1983). Even with this attitude, documentation has become a security blanket that most users, including those who are highly knowledgeable technically, are not willing to do without. Users want good documentation to be available when problems occur, but at the same time they perceive it as not helpful because it is so difficult and time-consuming to find the right information to troubleshoot, solve the problem, and complete the task.

The minimalist approach is beginning to change this attitude. Users are beginning to notice that technical documents are not as intimidating, even if the information remains difficult to locate. The full potential of minimalism will be realized when technical writers take an approach to developing documentation (online and on paper) that models the natural cognitive processes of users who are seeking to fill knowledge gaps through the right information, presented at the right time, and in the right place to meet task goals.

4.1   Why Now? What Is Driving the Minimalist Initiative?

The academic literature has discussed minimalism for over fifteen years, and field training has presented the principles of minimalism for at least half as many. Yet minimalism is only slowly gaining visibility and acceptance as it infiltrates the computer and hardware industry.

Adoption is happening now for a variety of reasons. The original context of minimalism has changed. The changing workplace has proliferated the minimalist initiative. The basic requirement for technical documentation to transfer new knowledge to user-learners has not shifted. There is an even greater need for well-developed documentation because the complexity and number of software and hardware applications that a user must learn to complete tasks has increased, even though the human-computer interface has become more intuitive to experienced computer users. Technical communicators are embracing minimalism because of three trends:

1. The business need to reduce production and distribution costs of documentation.
2. A transformation in the technology industry that focuses on user- and learner-driven development rather than designer driven.
3. The demanding response of savvy computer users who expect "smart" documentation immediately at their disposal from innovative technology that can deliver it.

The business need is probably the main reason that minimalism is resurging as a viable option for documentation development: it makes practical and economic sense to change the way user information is disseminated. The increased cost of producing documentation is one factor. User documentation typically consists of a large set of thick books, which results in significant paper and printing costs, on top of rising development and translation costs, to meet the needs of a global market. Similarly, product development time has been cut drastically in a very competitive market. Because the end product itself does not vary much from one manufacturer to another, the product that meets the market first has an advantage. The pressure of meeting market introductions bears down on documentation developers daily. Traditionally, documentation has been the last part of the total product solution, finished after the product itself reaches final design, development, and testing. Today the document life cycle is on the critical fast path, simultaneously with product development, to meet introduction goals. Manufacturers are looking for ways to reduce costs and time to market while meeting tough customer satisfaction criteria.

The second trend, user- and learner-driven development, has always been a consideration, although perhaps not in the forefront as much as it is today. Not unlike technology designers, technical communicators have finally become more focused on satisfying customer needs and designing usability into information products. A recent article (Soloway and Pryor 1996) presented the evolution of human-computer interaction over the past forty years and predicted into the year 2000. The industry has shifted from the technology (product)-centered design of early computers —those produced from 1950 to 1980—to a user-centered design today and has evolved to a learner-centered design focus. From investigations targeted at gathering data about users, technical communicators are realizing that the product-oriented approach of documenting with the sole purpose of describing the product's functionality does not generally align with the needs of the typical adult who is learning to use a new product. Technical communicators are discovering that a user- or learner-centered approach is more likely to align with actual user behavior and thus provide efficient and effective learning. The focus of development becomes to provide an instructional framework from which users can gather new information or alternative approaches to complete tasks. By focusing on the user who has an immediate learning need, documents are more likely to provide information to complete real tasks quickly. For example, typical users do not care about learning the mechanics behind the printer's operation. They *do* want to know how loading paper in the new machine differs from that of a previously used one, when a procedure is unique, and how to recover from errors. Users go to documentation when they cannot get help elsewhere (Anson 1995). They expect to find it readily available and accurate so they can finish the job.

The third trend driving the increased need to apply minimalism is that the complexion of the workplace and the user has changed. Using technology to support tasks and productivity rarely produces anxiety anymore; rather, technology has become a familiar and expected work tool, found on every desktop. As such, users do not have time to waste looking for answers to resolve problems that occur with machines that are supposed to be adding efficiency to their work. With the increased ease of using technology have come innovative methods for delivering information about it use. More and more adults are receiving just-in-time, self-identified, on-the-job documentation as the key support system to help them use new technology.

4.2   Applying Minimalism to Meet Industry Trends

Although more and more technical communicators are embracing minimalism, it is uncertain whether they understand the minimalist concept and how it is taken from theory to practice. For example, they seem to be implementing minimalism using the traditional approach to technical writing: reduce the size of documentation by writing clear and concise text, and include more visual presentations and less redundant information. Is this all there is to incorporating minimalism: cutting words and adding pictures? Is minimalism only an approach to writing? Taking a product-focused approach to design documents does not meet user needs. Technical communicators must take a more discriminate look from the user's perspective. The user is a learner as well, and the challenge for technical communicators is to discover an approach that identifies user-learner characteristics, gathers user content requirements, captures models of user behavior when searching for information, and then couples this approach with that of solid technical writing skills.

A case example to demonstrate that perhaps the accepted approach to implementing minimalism is incomplete is a recent documentation evaluation initiated by the Information Engineering group at Hewlett-Packard

Company (HP), Boise LaserJet Group. A third-party contractor was asked to analyze and evaluate one of the HP LaserJet's documentation set. HP requested that one criterion in particular be emphasized in the analysis: critiquing the documents' representation of minimalism. In a presentation summarizing the results of the study, the subcontractor addressed minimalism as a checklist:

- Reduce passive voice.
- Be concise.
- Write task-oriented procedures.
- Say it once.

Generally this checklist validated the approach taken to develop the documentation: "If the writing is good, then the user will be satisfied." This list nevertheless left several of the developers puzzled. Is the checklist all there is to applying minimalism? Is minimalism only a checklist? If so, shouldn't we be doing these things already if we are good technical writers? Why bother attaching the label of minimalism to a set of already established literary guidelines? Although this checklist attempted to provide some guidelines for developing minimalistically, it does not nearly align with the original minimalist principles.

Carroll identified nine principles that provide guidelines for developing minimalist-based documentation (Carroll 1990, 1992; Farkas and Williams 1990). Documentation must:

- Help users get started fast.
- Train users on real tasks.
- Allow for reading in any order by providing modular units of information.
- Exploit the user's prior knowledge and experience.
- Coordinate the system they are trying to learn with the actual training material.
- Support error recognition and recovery.
- Use the situation to provide opportunities to learn about how the system works.
- Be developed using optimal training designs.
- Promote reasoning and improvising that increases comprehension, retention, and active involvement in the learning process.

Carroll's principles more accurately describe the outcomes for a minimalist document and more aptly allude to a design process for achieving minimalism. These nine principles describe what minimalist documentation is, not necessarily how to design it. The minimalist principles assume that the document designer has an in-depth understanding of how users' needs translate into an instructional design based on predictable behaviors and the mental processing of information. The focus of minimalism in the field currently takes place during development rather than during the design stage of the project life cycle. Perhaps it is necessary to examine minimalism as a part of the larger design process that stresses the importance of analyzing user characteristics and information needs prior to architecting the product.

4.3 Minimalist Methodology for Facilitating Content and Delivery System Definition

A methodology for creating minimalist documents begins with a user requirements analysis. This analysis must align with understanding what we know about users as learners so as to identify the map for delivering information that ultimately guides the technical writing process (figure 4.1).

The details of each aspect of the proposed minimalist methodology are as follows:

1. Define the *information context* of the task to be performed so that the type of information required by users—conceptual, procedural, or problem solving—can be determined.

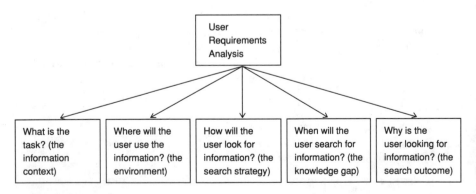

Figure 4.1
The beginning of a minimalist methodology

2. Identify the *environment* in which the information will be utilized to determine where the information must be available (online or in a paper document, or read simultaneously to completing the task).

3. Determine the modality of user *search strategies* for the information sought (key-word or context-sensitive indexes, topically organized table of contents, graphics or text to represent concepts and procedures, scanning pictures and text versus reading word for word and line by line).

4. Identify a user profile that details the user's past experience or prior knowledge of a topic, to drill down to the *knowledge gap* the user is trying to fill.

5. Verify the *search outcome* to that of reading to learn to do or merely to complete a task without necessarily retaining the information for later recall.

4.4   The Alignment Between Minimalist Methodology and Minimalist Document Design

User Requirements Analysis

User requirements analysis is conducted to identify the users' current knowledge of product features, the types of tasks to be performed with the product, the extent that processes and procedures must actually be learned by the users versus those that require only a reference to aid performance, and the environment in which the user will use the product. In industry, information is gathered from customer visits, focus groups, survey research, and usability studies. Each of these investigations provides opportunities to gain insight into the users and their work environments. The data that are gathered about the user help narrow the scope of information required for documentation. The analysis is a precursor to achieving the nine principles originally described as minimalism (Nowaczyk and James 1993; Carroll, Olson, and Anderson 1987; Farkas and Williams 1990; Vanderlinden, Cocklin, and McKita 1988).

Although user profiles are constructed from user-specific information gathering and principles about adult learners, the practices of users within computer environments underlie the final identification of user profiles. Adult computer users bring their own mental models and behaviors to a task. Adults approach tasks with a reservoir of past experiences and a self-directed, goal-oriented approach directed toward gaining only information relevant to the situation at hand (Knowles 1984).

The extent to which the average user of a product has gained prior knowledge and experience and the nature of the task determine the content of information required in documentation. Users process new information and organize it according to its relationship with their existing cognitive structures (Litteri 1982). They integrate past experience, current knowledge, and skills with new information before it is stored in long-term memory. The mental model is accessible to the user as an internal resource when learning is required. Users draw on these developed mental models—conceptual as representations of how they should interact with a system—to learn new technologies. Familiar mental models provide users with predictive and explanatory powers that guide learning (Schumacher and Czerwinski 1992; Carroll, Olson, and Anderson 1987; Owen 1986; Young 1983; Moran 1981). Researchers have identified that as users gain knowledge and experience, they evolve from novices to experts based on the development of accurate and consistently applied mental models.

When user-learners of technology are exposed to a situation with a new product, they access their current mental model to identify what they already know about using the product and then employ search strategies (such as making inferences, seeking associations, practicing, and employing trial and error) to fill in the information they do not know, undergoing an internal knowledge modeling process (figure 4.2). Expert users have developed mental models, an internal information resource, that help with learning new tasks using technology, compared to novice users who have not likely gained experience or knowledge to draw on. For instance, we generally do not have to explain to the expert user how to set up the standard printer, install software, or use every feature of the software. We will likely have to explain these things in detail to the novice user. The level of expertise influences whether a user needs to access documentation, the type of information sought, the length of time needed to use the documentation, and thus the length of time it takes to accomplish a task.

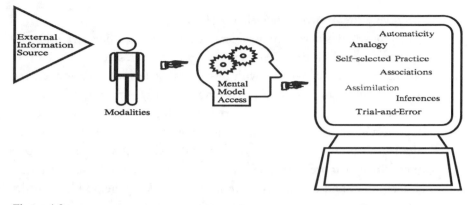

Figure 4.2
Internal knowledge modeling process

Many studies have examined the user as a learner—someone who is processing new information to internalize its meaning for later application. Documentation designers struggle with presenting information that is not too basic or detailed for the expert user, yet conceptually appropriate for the novice user who lacks the experience or knowledge to understand how a new product works or how it can be used. Typically technical document developers do not analyze their audience to understand their ability to assimilate new information with that they have previously learned or what is intuitively accessible. Therefore, designers consider their job successful when they have provided complete, step-by-step information for the user, targeting the novice but with an attempt to satisfy the expert user by assuming "the more information, the better." Unfortunately, with this approach, the expert user must sort through vast amounts of information to find the one or two steps that vary from a past experience. And perhaps the novice user finds the information difficult and unwieldy.

A minimalist strategy applied during the design phase could possibly work to resolve this dilemma for the user. For instance, if HP designers can understand the expert user's knowledge and experience base using printers, information requirements change to providing only those that explain unique procedures or processes. Carefully analyzing user needs and addressing to a degree the differences between novice and expert information needs would lead to more appropriate content specifications.

Identifying the Appropriate Delivery System

If they have considered the problem at all, designers have traditionally taken the approach that user expertise can be addressed merely by presenting information written with less or more technical jargon. In the past, the delivery of information has not typically varied whether a user is a novice or an expert. A different title for the book—for instance "operator's guide" as opposed to "user's guide"—is often used to indicate to the users which book they should pick up. And online help is often directed more at the expert user because this user is not afraid of computers and thereby is more likely to look for help online. In the defense of designers, until recently technology was not capable of providing real ease of use for information delivery, nor were many users technologically savvy. Because technology is more pervasive today, the natural evolution of a more sophisticated user has produced expertise with two critical impacts on minimalist documentation design. First, expertise has an impact on the task instructions that need to be given. Second, the intended users' expertise influences the decision about how best to deliver the information. Designers no longer have the luxury of simply placing all information online and/or on paper without some thought as to the type of information they are presenting in these locations.

Documentation designers cannot expect users to search all the documentation for their answers. Time is valuable. In fact, we know that users go to documentation as a last resort, first seeking information from their immediate environment. This user strategy effects the designer's decision about an information delivery system. In a study conducted by Anson (1995), novice and expert users followed a consistent pattern of behaviors to locate a procedure, solve a problem, or seek conceptual information. They begin by looking on-screen, scanning the user interface for familiar or perceived relevant information. They go to Help depending on the type of task (conceptual, procedural, or problem solving) and their own knowledge and skill (novice versus expert). Novices are more likely to turn to paper documentation, and experts seek online help. This behavior pattern occurs if there is no acknowledged expert close by to answer quick questions. The local expert may be asked to help first if time constraints are pressing the user. This research strongly indicates that users take what they perceive to be the easiest, fastest, and most convenient path to find information first.

It is ironic that users almost practice minimalism as they apply a structure or strategy to accomplish their learning task. They rely on their prior knowledge and past experiences before going for assistance, seeking help only after they have exhausted all personal resources. When they go to documented help, they search for the desired information by skimming pages and scanning the content presented to locate key words or phrases that describe what they want to do or what they have not already tried. Users are active explorers in learning situations, not passive receptors of information; they take the path that is most efficient for them, not the logically sound one identified by the documentation designer. "The right information, in the right place, at the right time" demands careful design of information delivery systems based on user search strategies. With this information about the user, document designers are required to model a user's minimalist approach in the design of documents to match the user's strategy for searching information.

4.5   How Hewlett-Packard Incorporates Minimalist Methodology with Minimalist Document Design

Minimalist Applications at Hewlett-Packard

Hewlett-Packard has initiated two broad-scope efforts specifically to incorporate minimalism into the design and development of user education products. One case, with the Electronic Design Division's Learning Products group in Fort Collins, Colorado, was to design and write tutorials for an HP printed circuit design system. The second application took place in the spring of 1994 at HP's LaserJet Operation in Boise, Idaho, to produce the end-user documentation shipped with a personal desktop laser printer.

After identifying product content requirements, the Fort Collins product team began with the development of a prototype that was subsequently tested at the usability lab. For the test, the group developed a guided-exploration prototype (based on the guided-exploration model developed by John Carroll and associates at the IBM Watson Research Center) and compared it with a self-study (SS) tutorial, the model used for similar products. The guided-exploration model was modified to include some procedural information (GE+P). Although the product was never released, the findings of the prototype usability test offered direction for future products. The results of the test identified that the GE+P approach was an effective learning tool for complex applications. Novice-level subjects with little computer experience were better able to learn how to interact with the system. The addition of procedural information did not have an impact on learnability. Although GE+P subjects spent 10 percent more time working through the tutorials, they had fewer problems and completed a posttutorial test more quickly and more accurately than the SS subjects, who had to refer back to the tutorial four times more often to complete the posttutorial test.

With the release of the spring 1994 printers and its software applications, the Boise developers of LaserJet documentation had applied the basics of minimalism—the style guide checklist mentioned earlier. Designers and developers initially were skeptical, fearing that the minimalist trend would increase user complaints because information would not be available to the user in multiple locations throughout the document set. They also feared the change in writing style would eliminate information that the user needed.

Prior to the spring 1994 release, the design approach began with generating a content outline. A document designer analyzed the printer to identify document topics and then brainstormed all the possible locations a user would likely look to find information about a topic. The same information was documented in each of these places. For example, when using a network printer, a user could find the procedures for loading a toner cartridge in the getting-started guide, the user guide, through online help, and on the installation guide shipped in the box with the toner, as well as through control panel messages. The same procedure was listed in five separate locations. Instead of presenting the information in the most likely place of first contact—through the in-box installation guide, for instance—the cover-it-everywhere approach was justified because it increased the likelihood that the users would find the information, no matter where they looked.

Since 1994, the original approach for applying minimalism has changed. To help users find the information they want quickly, the current focus is to place it in the most likely, first-sought-out location. The primary focus of the information group is to place "the right information, in the right place, at the right time" for customers. With this focus and a revised strategic approach for producing documentation, the Boise group has also changed its name from Learning Products to Information Engineering. The basic premise underlying the name change is that the group now takes a more critical approach to the design and scope of information (rather than a product-focused approach), as the architect that plans the structure of the information before moving to its development.

The most dramatic example of the change in approach at HP is signified by two similar products: the network printer documents that were introduced in the fall of 1993 with six separate documents totaling 650 pages and those introduced with the spring 1994 product containing two separate documents totaling 270 pages. The 1993 document set contained a getting-started guide, an operator's guide, network notes, software application notes, a user reference manual, and a quick reference guide. It did not include the information delivered through online help to support the software drivers and or the installation guides shipped separately with consumable and accessory products. Truly a signature of an industry-wide documentation standard at that time, users had access to all the information they could possibly ask for, in multiple locations, and sometimes with the same information written in many different ways.

The 1994 document set was one of the first real attempts at the Boise site to minimize documentation. The printer was introduced with two documents: a comic book–like getting-started guide and a user's guide. The document set provided task-oriented text and included many visuals to help users complete procedural tasks. Text was used sparingly throughout the documents, primarily to support visual communication, except when conceptual information was presented in six- to eight-sentence paragraphs. Minimalism was applied using three criteria: a brief and concise writing approach, task-oriented procedures, and information placed in only one location, unless the information was required in various places to caution or warn the user. Information was still segmented by topic areas describing product features or functionality (the printer's paper handling features, its control panel, and software), task procedures, troubleshooting and problem solving, and maintenance information.

Usability testing of the documentation confirmed that users liked the smaller task-oriented documentation. Nevertheless, the tests also found that it was still difficult for users to locate information quickly and easily. What we had missed in the design was an understanding of user search strategies. The minimalist approach used did not accommodate user behavior. The user investigation, based on information gathered from product-focused assessments, led to information designed around the product's topic requirements, not the user's need for specific information. A broader definition of minimalism and a working strategy to achieve it were required.

The Product Life Cycle Process

The HP Information Engineering (IE) product life cycle process is synchronized with the product's design and development. The primary milestone phases of the life cycle are investigation, product definition, prototype, development, and introduction. The IE group also aligns its product development life cycle process with processes used by instructional designers and technical communicators in other companies. The life cycle stages are (1) user analysis, (2) design, (3) development, (4) evaluation, and (5) implementation.

In the recent past, the first stage of the process, *user analysis*, consisted of identifying the tasks users perform, the size of their organization, and their access to a particular operating system environment. Essentially this information described the profile of the targeted user: the customer using the product. For instance, the size of the user's organization indicated whether the user had support on-site to help with problems. A personal printer user does not always have support nearby, while a mid- to high-end user may have access to a PC help desk for assistance as needed. This profile did not influence the content and structure of the documents or the delivery system. The content and structure of the documentation were designed to explain product features and functionality. The same set of information was developed for each of these two user profiles, except that the documents written for the personal printer user were designed using simpler, easier-to-understand language and a friendlier tone. Additionally, the documents were titled to indicate a user versus network manager audience.

During the *documentation design* stage, the product manager established design specifications by organizing information into an outline for each delivery system: a printed document or online help.

The *Development* stage produced the documentation. Often *design* and *development* were used synonymously to mean the stage at which a technical communicator began creating text and graphics to explain information to the user. Minimalism evolved during development, as the technical communicator actually created the document, writing the words and identifying accompanying illustrations—again an indication that minimalism was typically applied as a writing style by professionals in the field.

The *evaluation* stage overlapped that of development since documentation was tested with the product. Usability tests of the documentation were haphazardly aligned with the developmental phases of the product. These tests were targeted to test the unique features and functionality of the printer. The development schedule for the documentation did not necessarily allow for the testing of the content and structure of the documents. For instance, the first usability test of the product tested procedures for using an innovative paper tray design. In the writing group, the documents to support this test were produced in a mad scramble to find a writer-illustrator who could track down the product, scratch some notes and drawings, and then quickly transfer them electronically through a word processor. The focus of the test was not to validate document design concepts but to support the product if the test subject had a problem. A document-specific test plan was not developed. As the product's design solidified, so did the documentation. Further drafts of the documentation were made available during tests conducted for the product. The tests confirmed the user's need for information support and the flaws in the document design that keep the user from finding information quickly.

The Evolution of a New Practice of Minimalism

By embracing minimalist principles, the IE group is developing a different approach to document design and development. The focus to provide information using proved methodologies that increase user performance is the primary reason for analyzing the application of minimalism.

However, another, albeit fundamental, reason is how minimalism affords the opportunity to meet changing trends in the technology industry through innovative operational strategies. The shift in IE's operational strategies has evolved for a number of reasons.

Increase in Business Partners   The IE group provides information, product design, development, localization, and integration for seven different HP organizations. The organizations produce similar types of products (printers and scanners) that ship to different markets or, in some cases, the same market (for instance, the high-end network printers and personal desktop printers are found in both mid- and large-size businesses). Because the HP LaserJet business sources information product development to one group, they gain the following advantages:

• A consistent look and feel for the documents of similar products that may be used by the same audience (which can increase customers' ability to locate reference information quickly because of their familiarity with the format of an HP document).
• Cost efficiencies because they do not have to fund a separate technical communication group for each organization.
• The opportunity to leverage information across each of the organizations because they serve on multiple product teams and can view the big picture, the common and unique features, and functionality across the product lines.

Industry Downsizing   Downsizing, or rightsizing, is the industry trend today: How can we do more with less in a competitive world? In the past two years, the IE group has lost one-third of its original forty-five members. Fewer people without a reduction in workload leads to a necessary redefinition of job roles and responsibilities, as well as the identification of strategies that help the group work smarter.

Outsourcing Document Development   Another industry trend is outsourcing. Manufacturing companies are outsourcing everything from the initial product concept and design to the entire manufacturing and distribution process. The IE group is outsourcing the development of documentation products to subcontractors. This shift from internal to external development has increased the need for the group to evaluate products and processes more critically. Communication is the critical link. The development of documentation for each product is awarded to a different contractor, so the leverage of information and the effort to maintain consistency among products are challenges. The IE group has had to develop processes to increase communication among various internal project teams across product lines, as well as between internal and external project teams.

Shift in Technology Trends for Delivering Information   The access to vast amounts of information is perhaps the greatest contribution to today's technology. More and more information is available from electronic delivery mediums, such as CD-ROM and the worldwide communication network, facilitated by hypertext and multimedia presentation. With the speed and ease of use of the new technology, it is now possible to access most types of information from the computer quickly. Within the communication industry, technological advancements have opened new opportunities for design and development as systems have become more capable and flexible in creating text, graphics, animation, sound, and motion. Innovative technology has had an impact on the design and delivery of IE products. Along with other technical communicators in the field, IE is evaluating the strengths and weaknesses of delivering traditional paper documents in an online format.

Shift to User and Learner-Centered Information Product Design   Documentation has always been a by-product of the lab teams and marketing at HP. With a technology-centered approach, the lab team mandates information for documentation that describes and explains the features and functionality of the product in great detail and in multiple locations throughout the documentation. Marketing teams have tried to use the documentation as another vehicle to sell the product. In addition, the customer support center wants to include information in the documentation so they can send it to users who call for help rather than look through the document first; the product designers want to explain design flaws or nonintuitive features and functionality.

The IE group is changing these attitudes about the design of documentation very slowly, in part because of the fiscal need to identify ways to reduce documentation costs. Field studies of users show that they do not want a large set of documents; rather, they want to find complete information in the place they look first. The group has increased investigation efforts dramatically in order to identify the content and delivery system most appropriate for HP printer users. Users want information accessible and ready at the site of the problem; the source of the information must be close to the origin of need.

The Paradigm Shift

The IE group needed a different organizational structure to address all of the trends noted. Originally the department was divided into groups according to a particular market segment. One team would be assigned to personal printer products (desktop printers), another to mid-range (small work-group printers), and a third to high-end networking printer (large work-group printers) products. IE management decided to restructure the organization to maximize the resources needed to meet business needs and to meet the emerging challenge of designing information for different delivery systems. Department staff are now segmented into three functional areas: project architects (planners), project managers, and localization and integration specialists.

The *project planners* attend multifunctional team meetings during the early design stage of the project. Their primary job is to define information products by developing a strategic plan that includes needs analysis investigation activities, identifying critical business partners, milestone schedules, the localization strategy, and information product specifications. Each planner has additional roles as divisional liaisons, investigating new communication technologies, conducting market research, designing and testing prototypes, and contributing to the identification of internal departmental process improvements.

The *project managers* become involved in the project just prior to the beginning of documentation development. Their primary job is to manage the outsourced subcontractors throughout the development and localization phases of the project. They are responsible for maintaining the integrity of the initial product specifications (unless a change in strategy is required because the scope of the product has changed) and the quality of the final product. The project managers must continually refine their strategic tactics as they work with different outsourced teams, different products, and different internal business partners. The project managers retain project contact until product introduction, and then they monitor any succeeding changes.

The *localization and integration team* is responsible for managing global translation activities, including scoping and monitoring the costs of localization and working with manufacturing schedules to align printing and duplication with product shipping schedules.

The greatest change created by the revised organizational model is the emphasis now placed on the user needs analysis stage of the information product life cycle. Project planners are moving out into all aspects of the business, collecting information and studying the processes of other groups, the tools used to design and implement products, and other team investigations of user needs. The planners have also increased the amount of research conducted specific to documentation design (as opposed to product-specific needs). Research is focused on collecting data from secondary and primary research activities. Secondary research findings are gathered from research firms such as InfoTek and DataQuest, as well as from trade publication reviews. Primary research consists of collecting information by means of usability tests, customer visits, focus groups, telephone and disk-by-mail surveys, as well as postproduct introduction follow-up studies and competitive analysis. The planners work as a collective, tightly communicating group to interpret the findings of these studies and mobilize findings into actions to improve document design and development.

In the past, IE staff limited user investigations to those conducted by members of product teams. Although IE shares the same customer base as the product teams and will continue investigating product needs along with these teams, there is a specific need to identify the ways users access information resources. IE project planners are increasing their own investigations, specific to documentation.

With this focus on front-end analysis, the IE planning team will be able to get to know the users and their specific information needs, and identify additional ways to streamline and leverage information across all the market segments. By separating the user information investigation from the product investigation, the planning team will better identify the two primary user audiences, in addition to those identified according to the printer segment. The planning team has identified novice-level users, who typically have little prior experience or knowledge base about printer products, and more advanced expert-level users, who know a lot about technology and use prior experience and knowledge as a personal resource to learn about new products. The team will discover how the information requirements of each of these audiences differ.

The IE team is also modifying its use of the usability test process so that it parallels the product life cycle tests. As product features are tested with user subjects, the documentation design will be prototyped and tested. As the product design moves toward testing intuitive use and operational functionality, the content of the information will be tested to determine its adequacy in meeting user needs. Usability test findings will influence the design of current product documentation and affect future design.

Minimalism Applied

The information a user needs to operate a printer is slightly different from other technology. The printer, as a peripheral device, is treated much like an appliance. It sits in the background of the user's workstation and is expected to work as requested. When it fails to work as required, troubleshooting and a problem-solving procedure must be immediately available to the user. Printer failures occur in the hardware or with the software. As such, failures can be corrected through multiple avenues, at the printer or at the computer. In the high-end network environment, two user types require different types of documents, in three different environments, at two different computer workstations and at the printer. The network managers may require information at their computer workstation and at the printer to help them solve complex technical problems. The work-group end users may require information at their personal workstation and at the printer to resolve the most common simple-to-solve problems

Designing information products for the high-end network printer environment provides a prime example of how minimalism should be applied in the field today. In this example, the focus of the user analysis at HP is to uncover the information requirements for each of the user groups and the content required to explain the features, functionality, and potential problem areas for the user. The IE group has identified two separate user expertise levels in the high-end environment: the work-group end user and the network manager. The end users are experts in their particular domain of work and have some experience using a printer product, but their technical expertise is limited. Thus, they approach the task of learning how to use a new printer product to perform known tasks at a novice level. They rely heavily on other resources to help with unique problems. When other human resources are absent, they more often than not turn to paper documentation, if it is available. The documentation is likely stored with the network manager, who is an expert-level user, very comfortable with his or her knowledge and skill with technology. This user typically initiates learning new products. Like the work-group end users, a network manager who has exhausted all internal resources of information will first go online for help and to a paper document for more in-depth assistance (Anson 1995).

The IE team has also identified two different types of information based on the task needs of the network manager and the work-group end user. The network manager needs information to install the printer and its associated software and also information that can be passed on to the end user that describes the features and how each is operated. This user needs to be able to troubleshoot and solve problems that arise and maintain the printer. The end user, in contrast, needs to be able to identify the features and functions for performing work tasks. These users need common troubleshooting and problem-solving information, such as how to select the appropriate paper tray from the software application or how to access the size of paper they wish to print on. At the printer, these users need to know how to change the toner cartridge or clear paper jams, information that will help expedite error recovery to resume their work.

In this example, a document solution must meet the diverse access and content needs of multiple users. Some of the information required is similar across the two user types. With a minimalist approach, the information will be presented using task-oriented procedures and clear and concise descriptions, and it will also be scoped across multiple paths of entry, targeted at the first place a user will look for the information—the right information, in the right place, at the right time.

The primary user of a printer's installation information in the high-end networking environment is the network manager. A computer is not readily available in the area where the hardware setup of a printer takes place, so a paper document is needed that describes setup and installation procedures. Software installation is another aspect of printer setup. Software naturally must be installed on the computer. The paper-based installation guide should include directions that take the network manager to the computer for this next set of procedures. The procedures for installing software should be located online, as part of the software installation procedure or supplemented in a help system, at the point of ready access.

The network manager often keeps all technology documentation out of the hands of dangerous users (those who like to fix things themselves and by doing so often create more work for the network manager). Thus, work-group end users do not usually have access to basic feature and how-to information, or to troubleshooting information. Perhaps the document delivered to the end users should take advantage of the latest online book technology and provide information online for the network manager to access, while providing a means to provide discretionary information in print to the end user. For instance, the network manager could print only the information that describes the basics of the printer written at the novice level—enough information to get the end users started with the printer. In addition, this information could also be stored at the printer for ease of end user access.

Work-group end users also need problem-solving information, at both the printer and their personal computer workstation. At the printer, paper-based reference consists of troubleshooting advice and solutions documented to be used near the printer. At the computer, the user needs access to online help, a click away from the physical location of paper trays, setting size, and so forth.

This solution suggests two basic constructs of an expanded definition of minimalism:

1. A definition that incorporates particular learning styles of two different user groups, novice and experts.

2. A content map that identifies the type of information and the most appropriate location for the user to find and use it.

The solution described incorporates search strategies enlisted by the two user levels and matches information to the component of a solution that reaches across multiple work environments (two separate computer workstations and job responsibilities), as well as in the users' shared environment (at the printer).

4.6   What Is the Future of Minimalism?

A continually increasing amount of information is available to people from more resources, paper and online. The more information available, the more information people need to access, and the more critical it is to communicate effectively. If we do not use the technology to distribute and access information, we risk information's aging during the distribution process. Technical communicators must increase their effectiveness and efficiency in delivering information that is timely and easy to access and use by improving development and dissemination processes. They must become more than expert writers or designers of documents. To remain competitive in the field and to meet user expectations, they must learn more about the users and their actual learning and usage needs. To become more learner centered in the approach to document design and to refocus minimalism from a writing style to a way of communicating information, they must also incorporate minimalist principles, instructional methodologies, and the basic principles of adult learning theory.

Users seek documentation when they have a problem to solve. They go to a document because they do not know something and need to learn it to be able to complete a task. The definition of technical documentation prior to the 1990s stemmed from technology-centered design and development, technical information that explains the form, feature, and functionality of a product. The responsibility of the document designer at that time was primarily to support the product's needs.

The user has now come to the forefront of the technology age. Where earlier it seemed the technology was developed purely for the advancement of mechanization, now users are demanding that technology be an unobtrusive and fully functional support system for their work. If the user cannot use it easily and in most cases intuitively, then the machine is not valuable. While the content of documentation continues to support the product's user-centered design, the design and development of documentation are converging on user- and learner-centered design.

Technical communicators have a basic grasp of the principles of minimalism; however, they still tend to focus narrowly on minimalism as writing style. The view of minimalism must expand to include a formal methodology that emphasizes the analysis of user needs and search strategies as the underpinning to higher-quality documentation over simply reduced quantity. A number of questions still need to be addressed to move document designers in this direction.

What information about users is required to design minimalist documentation? Four types of information are key: the tasks performed, learning styles, expertise, and information search strategies. Undoubtedly there are many more. Research is needed to determine the areas with the most leverage for improving documentation design.

Once we collect better information, tools or techniques are needed to help organize or model it and target the appropriate delivery resource. Information mapping, cognitive modeling, and simple flowcharting are examples of some generic techniques. Here the question is, *How do we apply modeling techniques to achieve minimalist principles?*

Another question arises after we understand minimalism and know how to deliver it: *How do we justify the approach to our business team?* Technical communicators need to push the envelope of how to apply their knowledge of document design. Team members outside of Information Engineering tell us during document reviews that we must include all levels of detail, to the point that we are covering the most extreme cornercase situations by placing information in multiple places, more often than not to explain product deficiencies. Our traditional role was to provide structure for these demands. Our future role must include explaining how the minimalist approach provides what the customer really wants.

How do new delivery systems affect the minimalist model? Sophisticated online development systems, based on hypertext and multimedia, will provide a potpourri of delivery methods, opening up opportunities for more appropriate information delivery. The prescriptions we have identified for the most usable paper documentation, such as format and type, will change with the new delivery systems. The constraints placed on designers by the online systems, such as size of screen and readable text size limitations, will have an impact on the design of information. These systems will naturally force developers to refine and structure information using minimalist design principles. With these new systems, the minimalist principles will remain the same, but perhaps the specifics of the principles may change.

How do we gain a better understanding of how to apply the minimalist approach to document design? Although our challenge will be to identify the appropriate delivery system for information, our opportunities for meeting individual learning needs will increase. A strategy with specific guidelines for processing information will help designers meet user needs.

Hewlett-Packard has realized cost savings and user satisfaction with the direction our documentation has taken using minimalism thus far. However, there do appear to be gaps in our understanding, which limit our full adoption of the minimalist principles. We may be closing the gaps by focusing on user analysis in the life cycle process, assessing the user as a learner as well as the user of the product who has specialized tasks to perform, assessing the user's total work environment to ascertain the most appropriate delivery system, detecting the right place for information, and delivering it in a more timely manner to the user. These efforts are not officially stated as part of the minimalist principles as defined by Carroll, but they may be the underpinning of minimalism in practice. Perhaps the technical communication field is ready for a broader definition of minimalism that includes a strategy for applying the principles. If HP is representative of other industries, then addressing these issues may spread the adoption of minimalism in the field.

References

Anderson, R. C. 1984. Some reflections on the acquisition of knowledge. *Educational Researcher*, 13(9), 5–10.

Anson, P. A. H. 1995. A comparative analysis of paper versus online documentation search strategies accessed by novice and expert adult computer users to achieve learning and performance goals. Ph.D. dissertation, University of Idaho.

Beasley, R. E., and J. A. Vila. 1992. The identification of navigation patterns in a multimedia environment: A case study. *Journal of Educational Multimedia and Hypermedia, 1*, 209–222.

Carroll, J. M. 1990. *The Nurnberg funnel: Designing minimalist instruction for practical computer skill* (pp. 73–102). Cambridge, MA: MIT Press.

Carroll, J. M. 1992. Minimalist documentation. In H. D. Stolovitch and E. J. Keeps (Eds.), *Handbook of human performance technology* (pp. 331–351). San Francisco: Jossey-Bass.

Carroll, J. M., Olson, J. R., and Anderson, N. 1987. *Mental models in human-computer interaction: Research issues about what the user of software knows* (Technical Report 12). Ann Arbor: Cognitive Science and Machine Intelligence Laboratory, University of Michigan.

Deterline, W. A. 1988. User-friendly ... or what? *Journal of Performance and Instruction, 1,* 1–4.

Farkas, D. K., and T. R. Williams. 1990. Carroll's *The Nurnberg Funnel* and minimalist documentation. *IEEE Transactions on Professional Communication, 33*(4), 182–187.

Knowles, M. S. 1983. Malcolm Knowles finds a worm in his apple. *Training and Development Journal, 5,* 12–15.

Knowles, M. S. 1984. *The adult learner: A neglected species* (3rd ed.). Houston, TX: Gulf Publishing Company.

Litteri, C. A. 1982. Cognitive profiles: Relationship to achievement and academic success. In *Student learning styles and brain behavior: Programs, instruments, research* (pp. 22–34). Reston, VA: NASSP.

Martin, P. 1986. Computer user documentation problems: Their cause and solutions. *IEEE Transactions on Professional Communications, 29*(4), 19–20.

Moran, T. P. 1981. An applied psychology of the user. *Computing Surveys, 13,* 1–11.

Nowaczyk, R. H., and E. C. James. 1993. Applying minimal manual principles for documentation of graphical user interfaces. *Journal of Technical Writing and Communication, 23*(4), 379–388.

Owen, D. 1986. Naive theories of computation. In D. A. Norman and S. W. Draper (Eds.), *User centered system design: New perspectives on human-computer interaction*. Hillsdale, NJ: Erlbaum.

Schumacher, R. M., and M. P. Czerwinski. 1992. Mental models and the acquisition of expert knowledge. In R. R. Hoffman (Ed.), *The psychology of expertise: Cognitive research and empirical AI,* (pp. 61–79). New York: Springer-Verlag.

Soloway, E., A. Pryor. 1996. The next generation in human-computer interaction. *Communication of the ACM 39*(4) p. 16.

Vanderlinden, G., T. G. Cocklin, and M. McKita. 1988. Testing and developing minimalist tutorials: A case history. *Proceedings of the International Technical Communication Conference,* RET196–199.

van der Meij, H., and J. M. Carroll. 1995. Principles and heuristics for designing minimalist instruction. *Technical Communication,* Second Quarter, 243–261.

Wilton, J. A. 1985. What PC users say about documentation. *Proceedings of the 32nd International Technical Communication Conference*, RET10–12.

Young, A. R. 1983. Surrogates and mappings: Two kinds of conceptual models for interactive devices. In D. Gentner and A. L. Stevens (Eds.), *Mental models* (pp. 35–52). Hillsdale, NJ: Erlbaum.

Young, A. R. 1989. Good documentation isn't good enough. *Technical Communication*, Third Quarter, 196–200.

5

Follow-up on Training in Minimalism: How Are Technical Communicators Using Minimalism?

Stephanie Rosenbaum

For the past few years, I have taught a course titled "Minimalist Design for Documentation" at the University of California Santa Cruz Extension. The attendees have been primarily experienced technical writers working in the documentation field, taking the course for professional development. This chapter discusses how these professional communicators responded in class to the minimalist approach, then reports how some of the students have been able (or unable) to apply minimalism within their own organizations.

I conducted the follow-up study described in this chapter for the same reasons I designed and taught the minimalist course itself. I believe that documentation for business and personal products will better support the needs and goals of its users if authors and editors learn and apply the principles of minimalism. Thus, I am interested in exploring how and why people have problems applying minimalist principles, so we can more effectively promulgate their use.

Some of the issues that arose, both during the class and in students' later attempts to apply minimalism, included problems with defining appropriate tasks to cover in minimalist modules and resistance from both writers and subject-matter experts to providing "incomplete" information. In the follow-up study, participants also described concerns about integrating minimal manuals with other kinds of user support such as online help and training classes.

Considering the impact that the minimalist model has had on documentation design theory over the past ten years, I was surprised and somewhat disappointed by its limited penetration into commercial documentation practices. Even a group of technical writers who were motivated to take a day-long course in minimalist design seemed only to scratch the surface of the usability gains possible from a minimalist approach.

The responses of the follow-up study participants, both in the survey questionnaires and in interviews, give considerable insight into the obstacles these people encountered when they tried to apply minimalism. Using the follow-up study data, I suggest some approaches to help improve the acceptance of minimalism in current documentation practices.

5.1   Description of the Minimalist Design Course

I taught the one-day minimalist design course six times between 1993 and the end of 1996. Until the 1995 van der Meij and Carroll article, the course content followed quite strictly the principles and examples of minimalism described in *The Nurnberg Funnel* and Carroll's earlier work. Even after that article appeared, I stayed with a fairly strict interpretation of minimalist principles, assuming that dilution always occurs as principles are put into practice.

Topics Covered in the Course
The lecture and discussion portions of the course covered the following topics (for details of the content of each module, see the appendix to this chapter):

Module 1: Problems with Documentation and Training Materials
Module 2: What Is the Minimalist Instructional Approach?
Module 3: Why Do We Believe Minimalism Works?
Module 4: Identifying Real Tasks for Real Users
Module 5: Writing Minimalist Instruction for a Task
Module 6: Editing Minimalist Instruction
Module 7: Using the Minimalist Model in Online Support

A key element of the course was hands-on experience in identifying problems with conventional documentation and attempting to solve the problems using minimalism. The students chose sample manuals for actual products, and as the day progressed, they first identified usability problems with their samples, then rewrote portions of the samples using the minimalist approach.

In the first exercise, students were asked to skim their sample manuals and identify three things described there that users might want to do right away. (For example, in a database management system sample, a user might want to catalog her videotape library.) Then I asked the students to choose one of these three tasks and analyze how much explanatory text precedes the actual task information, as well as what errors users will make if they start the task without reading the explanatory text.

After a group exercise in which the students created user profiles and usage scenarios for target users of the sample product and documentation, I asked them to identify a user task that might be a suitable minimalist instruction module and to list its subtasks. Then each group wrote either a minimalist card or a topic chapter about the task.

Finally, each group exchanged its minimalist card or chapter with another group; that group became the editor for the card or chapter it received. Using a series of probing questions, I asked the groups to consider how well they would be able to do the tasks with the instructions provided. The "editor" groups revised the cards and chapters, then explained to the class how and why the revisions would improve each card or chapter.

Variations from Minimalist Literature

The course that I taught differed in two ways from published descriptions of the minimalist model. First, we spent an entire module (Module 4) on user profiling and usage (task) scenarios. I viewed this addition as necessary for audiences largely without formal training in psychology, human factors, or usability engineering.

Second, we added a module on editing minimalist instruction (Module 6), which treats the editor as heuristic evaluator (Rosenbaum 1989). The parallel between the documentation editor and the usability evaluator has not been well recognized, but editors and usability engineers can both benefit from studying the techniques of the other profession. The particular value of an editing module is that a one-day course cannot include usability testing of the minimalist modules created during the exercises, but the editing process provides heuristic evaluation.

5.2   Problems People Encountered Studying Minimalism

The students in this course were mostly experienced technical communicators, with backgrounds similar to those of writers at my usability and documentation firm, Tec-Ed. Therefore, it is not surprising that the questions that arose during the course—and the difficulties the students encountered—were similar to those my colleagues and I at Tec-Ed faced when we began designing and implementing minimalist documentation.

The majority of problems that occurred during the day-long course fell into two areas: specifying information incompletely (that is, encouraging users to learn by exploration) and deciding what kind and size of tasks should constitute a topic chapter or "chunk" of a minimal manual. The first problem arose during the lecture and discussion modules and the second during the exercises.

Concerns About Completeness

Students were concerned about how much information could be left for users to learn by exploration, rather than being presented explicitly. They worried about users' success with "incomplete" documentation that would, at least eventually, be used for reference purposes.

Interestingly, they accepted that the cognitive effort of exploration would improve learning (as evidenced by the faster learning and faster performance of realistic tasks by users of the "inferential manual" group in Carroll's study [1990]). However, they were not reassured by *The Nurnberg Funnel* data about more successful reference use of minimal manuals.

Their primary design question was, "How will we know how much exploration is enough?" They pointed out that the pressures of product development in their commercial environments did not permit iterative testing of documentation before product release, even if budget were available.

Many students' companies did no usability testing at all; some did product testing with only incidental documentation use, not task-based documentation testing (Rosenbaum and Anschuetz 1994). Even the few whose companies explicitly tested documentation said they did not test any document more than once. Thus, the students doubted their ability to make data-driven decisions about how much to rely on user exploration.

Interestingly, in the questionnaires and interviews that constituted the follow-up study, I found that two people (Participants 4 and 13) did perform iterative documentation testing—in one case, between product releases. Both were more confident about the effectiveness of their document design decisions than were other participants, and both had taken quite innovative approaches to document design.

In addition, the students anticipated resistance from engineers and other development staff to any lack of completeness ("leaving out information"). The data collected during the follow-up study, and described later in the chapter, show that this concern was accurate.

Problems with Task Definition

During the exercises in which students wrote (and then critiqued and edited) minimalist chapters, they struggled extensively with decisions about what should constitute a topic chapter. The students had two kinds of problems:

• Distinguishing user tasks from product features, and then choosing topics that were user tasks.
• Deciding how large a task (or subtask) should be covered in one minimal "chunk" (card or topic chapter).

In the lectures, I had emphasized the importance of meaningful, realistic tasks. But when the time came to turn existing documentation into minimalist documentation, the students had great difficulty identifying and separating real-world user tasks or activities from "tasks" that were simply exercising software features.

Their real-world tasks tended to be too large for a minimal topic chapter; they were things like cataloging a video library for the database management program or publishing a newsletter for the word processing software. But the "tasks" that would fit on a stand-alone minimalist card or topic chapter were procedures such as saving a file or defining a formula in a spreadsheet—necessary to use the software successfully but not always meaningful goals.

The two problems were clearly related. Many realistic tasks did not lend themselves to short topic chapters, and the students also had difficulty deciding when to include a subtask or procedure in a chapter and when simply to say, "Do X" and include a cross-reference to the correct chapter.

The students who picked a small, feature-related task had little or no trouble with their minimalist chapters. Those who picked realistic tasks had many problems. Some of their problems related to a lack of domain knowledge and poor source information, because we offered a small selection of sample manuals to rewrite. The students who succeeded in writing minimalist documentation about realistic tasks were those who already knew the product (or a similar one) and could clearly imagine not only what someone would want to do but also how they would do it.

In the real world, product users do indeed have large domain goals, such as cataloging a video library. Creating documentation that addresses real-world goals with tasks that are small enough to be tractable may be an impossible challenge, especially for complex products.

Successful minimalism may consist of believable approximations. Just as theatergoers suspend disbelief, learners may be willing to accept realistic rather than real tasks. For example, a minimal topic chapter might describe how to add a new entry or a new subject category to a video library catalog, or even how to set up the catalog structure. The shortcoming of nonminimalist documentation is that users see no connection at all with their real work, not that the connection must be complete; this is comparable to the issue of realism in fiction (Draper, personal communication).

The balance between real goals and tractable tasks is central to the design of minimalist documentation, and indeed to all documentation design. The practice of minimalism requires writers to address the trade-offs explicitly. My follow-up study indicates that domain knowledge and its application continued to be important when the students tried to incorporate minimalism into their work practices.

5.3   The Follow-up Study

In the follow-up study, I sent questionnaires to the people who had attended the course. The questionnaires consisted of Likert-scale questions, followed by requests for "why or why not?" explanations, plus a few requests for specific information items. I received thirteen completed questionnaires and conducted thirty-minute telephone interviews with five people (selected at random from the respondents who were willing to be interviewed).

Participants

The participants were mostly technical writers, although three were managers of five to ten people. Their titles were as follows:

Participant 1: Senior editor
Participant 2: Documentation specialist
Participant 3: Principal technical writer
Participant 4: Technical writer 3 (lead)
Participant 5: Components cost training manager
Participant 6: Systems and program supervisor
Participant 7: Documentation systems analyst
Participant 8: Manager, online technologies
Participant 9: Technical writer
Participant 10: Training development and communications specialist
Participant 11: Senior technical writer
Participant 12: Senior writer
Participant 13: Technical writer

Three participants had been in their current positions less than one year, three for one to two years, and seven for more than two years. Three participants had used the minimalist approach before attending the course; the others had not, although five started using minimalism to some extent after the course. The amount of minimalist documentation participants or their groups had created ranged from none to 2,500 pages:

Participant 1: One product, 2 chapters, 20 total pages
Participant 2: None wholly minimalist
Participant 3: Two products, 3 total documents, about 850 total pages
Participant 4: One beta product, no pages yet
Participant 5: Three related products, 23 total documents, about 70 total pages

Participant 7:   Four products, 120 to 200 total documents, 2,500 total pages

Participant 8:   Four products, 4 total documents, about 75 total pages

Participant 10:   Five products, 30 total documents, 140 total pages

Participant 13:   One product line, 2 total documents, 15 total pages

Participants 6, 9, 11, and 12 did not respond to this question; they were not using minimalism.

Use of Minimalism

I asked the participants if their groups had begun using minimalism after they took the course, and if not, why not. Participants 7, 8, and 10, whose groups had already been using minimalism before they took the course, did not answer this question.

Of the ten respondents, half said they began using minimalism after the course, and half said they did not. However, of the five who answered yes, three strongly qualified their answers, saying they used minimalism sparingly, only in some documents, or only in online help.

The people who said they did not apply minimalism after the course had several explanations. Two were in organizations that had adopted some minimalist techniques but not others. Two were in organizations that do not have a defined approach to documentation design, although one was working on processes that would include several minimalist principles. One respondent felt that minimalism is only for novices.

Thus the participants' explanations are more revealing than their yes/ no responses; some explanations by those who answered no describe more use (or intended use) of minimalism than several of the yes answers. The answers were as follows:

Participant 1:   "Yes, sparingly."

Participant 2:   "No. Some sections do follow the minimalist model, but the docs as a whole do not. We are not fully confident it [minimalism] is what our users want (which is not necessarily what works best)."

Participant 3:   "Yes, in some docs."

Participant 4:   "Yes, for online WinHelp (paper docs provide conceptual [information] and are not minimalist)."

Participant 5:   "Yes, applied some new ideas to my own version of minimalism."

Participant 6: "No. We have not established a written standard for documentation."

Participant 9: "No. My current department doesn't call its work minimalist, but uses some features of minimalism. Our work is modular by nature: technotes, tech news, troubleshooting guides; the style is generally spare."

Participant 11: "No. Minimalism is primarily of use with novice users. Our products target professionals who require as complete an information set as possible."

Participant 12: "No. I took the class partly to confirm for myself that I knew what minimalism is really about. Since that time, the pubs group at [company name] has been going through the process of reinventing our processes and our approach to documentation structure. It's a slow process because we also have to continue to get out books as required.

"Of the minimalist concepts, we plan to incorporate task analysis, chunking, shorter chapters, and describing information once only.

"Last spring I also took a class ... on writing for reusability, which stressed many of the same things. I'm now in the process of analyzing our current documentation set to come up with new structures that will communicate our information more successfully.

"I expect that we will never have the testing resources to allow us to feel comfortable taking a strictly minimalist approach (cutting out all intros, overviews, etc.), especially since our product is highly technical and requires significant conceptual explanations."

Participant 13: "Yes."

Of the eight participants who responded to a question about the process of creating minimalist documentation, five said that minimalist documentation required the same amount of staff resources to produce as their earlier, more comprehensive documentation. One participant said it took fewer staff resources, one said somewhat more staff resources, and two said a lot more staff resources. However, two of the explanatory comments indicated that available resources were a constant, unaffected by the documentation approach:

Participant 1: "For our traditional documentation, writers massage engineering input. The minimalist approach requires much more writer input and evaluation."

Participant 2: "We have been understaffed, and still needed 100 percent of our available resources."

Participant 3:   "There's less to write."

Participant 4:   "We are new at it, it takes more testing and more revisions."

Participant 5:   "Based on project deadlines, budget, etc. I have the same resources regardless of what is produced."

Participant 7:   "By using minimalist design, we have freed more time, thus completing more work."

Participant 10:   "We can document more tasks, so [still] need same people [amount of staff resources]."

Participant 13:   "We test it. It's not *easier*—only better."

Support for Minimalism

When I asked what support people had received from their management and coworkers in applying minimalism to their documentation, most reported strong or moderate support. Participants answered as follows:

Participant 1:   Strong support, minimal support, strong opposition [participant circled all three to indicate different levels of support from different individuals]

Participant 2:   Strong support

Participant 3:   Moderate support

Participant 4:   Moderate support

Participant 5:   Strong support

Participant 6:   [Did not answer]

Participant 7:   Moderate support

Participant 8:   Strong support

Participant 9:   [Did not answer]

Participant 10:   Strong support

Participant 11:   Neutral

Participant 12:   [Did not answer]

Participant 13:   Strong support

The question, "Who were the hardest people to convince, and why?" received the following responses:

Participant 1:   "I encountered strong opposition from writers who were unsure of their subject material and audience. I had minimal support from the pubs manager. I had strong support from writers who knew the material and the audience."

Participant 2:   "Marketing, who thinks every feature needs to be spelled out."

Participant 3:   "Marketing product manager for a complex application and an editor. Tech Support didn't fight it, but they hate the minimal documents."

Participant 4:   "Our usability analyst is not a proponent or opponent but feels minimalist docs must be well tested."

Participant 5:   "No one—I fortunately am able to use what I believe is most effective."

Participant 7:   "Convincing the users was most difficult. They thought 'more' was obviously 'better.'"

Participant 11:   "Nobody was especially keen on it. We consider well-organized, concise, complete information to be of more use to our customers."

Participant 13:   "One coworker, who wanted to do usability testing (which she did on ten subjects). We have gotten user feedback from thirty-five customers, all positive."

From these comments and others during the interviews, resistance to minimalism falls into four categories: objection to the additional effort required to understand the domain and the users, a belief that product value is tied to the number of features (rather than their usefulness or relevance to the user community), a probably related desire for quantity or completeness of documentation, and an admirable desire to confirm any theory with user-testing data.

Success and Effectiveness of Minimalism

When asked to comment on the statement, "Implementing minimalist documentation has been successful within my organization," four participants strongly agreed, two agreed, and two somewhat agreed. One participant, whose organization uses some minimalist techniques but has not prepared minimalist documentation, was neutral. Participants responded as follows:

Participant 1:   Strongly agree
Participant 2:   Neutral
Participant 3:   Somewhat agree
Participant 4:   Somewhat agree
Participant 5:   Strongly agree

Participant 6:   [Did not answer]
Participant 7:   Strongly agree
Participant 8:   Agree
Participant 9:   [Did not answer]
Participant 10:   Agree
Participant 11:   [Did not answer]
Participant 12:   [Did not answer]
Participant 13:   Strongly agree

Of the four participants who strongly agreed, only one had used minimalism before the course, an indication that formal training in minimalist design can help it succeed. (Participants 7, 8, and 10 had used minimalism prior to the course.)

Feedback from the user community was strongly positive for three participants and positive for two. The participant whose organization uses some minimalist techniques but has not prepared minimalist documentation reported neutral feedback. Finally, the participant who noted that "Tech Support ... hate[s] the minimal documents" said feedback was negative. (Six participants did not answer.)

When I asked how participants learned the feedback, responses included the following (the words in square brackets are the participants' answers to the original multiple-choice question about feedback from the user community):

Participant 2:   "No comments addressing minimalism specifically. Most comments on docs are negative (who tries to call customer service when things work right?)" [Neutral]

Participant 3:   "From Technical Support. Press reviews have been neutral to somewhat positive." [Negative]

Participant 4:   "Usability testing on prototype help systems." [Positive]

Participant 5:   "Multiple ways" [Strongly positive]:
  A. Conducted usability testing prior to release.
  B. With implementation (internal product) went to each site/user, observed their needs and solicited feedback.
  C. Solicited list of requested titles for delivery of documents.
  D. Ran drafts by users to get the appropriate level of detail, etc.

Participant 10:   "Talked to them [users] before and after instituted minimalist documentation." [Positive]

Participant 13: "Sent out 100 user surveys, got back about 35." [Strongly positive]

What Makes Minimalist Documentation Successful?

Although the survey questionnaire did not ask explicitly about the domain or complexity of the products documented, several participants volunteered such information. Most participants agreed that some documents are more successful than others when prepared using the minimalist approach. Of the four participants who were neutral (none disagreed), two had not yet prepared minimalist documents, but two had been using minimalism since before taking the course.

When asked which documents were more successful and why, participants answered as follows:

Participant 1: "Installation guides are good candidates for the minimalist approach."

Participant 3: "Onscreen help and user's guides for applications for which there is a relatively simple metaphor (for example, a word processor or address-book software)."

Participant 4: "WinHelp systems must be minimalist, our users just give up if the screen contains too much text. They decide it is easier to go back to the screen to figure it out."

Participant 5: "I do both conceptual and task-oriented documentation. Task-oriented works very well. Users prefer the conceptual documentation to be more 'textbook' in detail and layout. I would really like to find a successful minimalist format for the concepts, but haven't met with any degree of success."

Participant 6: "User manuals—difficult to get users to read manuals."

Participant 9: "Docs giving instructions for tasks, especially urgent tasks, requiring few design decisions; for example, installation and troubleshooting."

Participant 10: "Less technical ones, although charts, graphs, and tables are helping to get technical information to technical users faster."

Participant 11: "Training manuals and tutorials targeting novice and intermediate users, who are confused by superfluous information."

Participant 12: "I would expect that most documents would benefit by applying the basic principles of minimalism."

Participant 13: "We are working on a similar approach [to a sample minimalist document the participant supplied]: with a new product line. It's pretty intricate—many flavors of the product. A lot of work to design."

These comments were consistent with the more detailed remarks obtained during the interviews. Overall, participants thought minimalism worked well for procedural information in relatively simple domains. They had reservations when the topics were technically complex or conceptual information was critical.

The participants were quite diverse in their response to my final, summing-up question. To the statement, "I believe that well-designed and implemented minimal manuals support users better than comprehensive manuals do," two participants strongly agreed, four agreed, two somewhat agreed, three were neutral, one somewhat disagreed, and one disagreed.

Of the three neutral participants, only one was using minimalism, and for online help rather than for manuals. The participant who somewhat disagreed with the statement had started using minimalism to the dismay of internal (technical support) users. Finally, the participant who disagreed with the statement thought minimalism was appropriate only for novice users, not her audience of "professionals." Participant comments included:

Participant 1:   "I believe that a minimalist manual with a good reference volume (where necessary) is the best combination." [Agree]

Participant 2:   "People learn in different ways. Computers intimidate some people and make them fear the exploration that minimalist docs require. They are uncomfortable and dissatisfied with the docs and therefore the product. People willing to explore will be served better by minimalist docs but, ironically, they are the least likely people to need/read the docs." [Somewhat agree]

Participant 3:   "When *I* really need help with an involved procedure, I still use the two-year-old comprehensive manual!" [Somewhat disagree]

Participant 4:   "Our manual will be conceptual and will not be minimalist on the first edition." [Neutral]

Participant 6:   "Typically, there are [a] few common problems encountered by the majority of users." [Strongly agree]

Participant 7:   "Designing a manual correctly will have users going to the correct location on the first try." [Agree]

Participant 8:   "Easier to use." [Agree]

Participant 9:   "Depends on the application. Comprehensive materials may offer ways of thinking about work that may be faster than the minimalist learning curve." [Neutral]

Participant 10:   "Technical information sometimes needs to be more detailed." [Somewhat agree]

Participant 12:   "I don't know the answer to that for our industry. I'd like to see a lot more testing results for the kind of highly technical products that come out of the Electronic Design Assistance (EDA) industry." [Neutral]

Participant 13:   "Nobody wants to read manuals, especially the more advanced users. They like to figure it out and play with products." [Strongly agree]

Because the question directly compared minimal manuals with comprehensive manuals, several of these answers addressed the issues of completeness, especially with respect to reference or conceptual information. Again we see the trend that minimalism is acceptable for training but not for reference, an opinion I believe is superficial.

My colleagues and I at Tec-Ed were fortunate to encounter early enthusiasm for minimalism at Xerox Corporation, for whom we designed a large set of minimalist reference documentation, described under "Some Recent Applications" in *The Nurnberg Funnel* (1990). It was not easy to implement minimalism in reference manuals, nor were we completely successful, but we learned that applying most minimalist principles greatly improved the results. The minimalist focus helped writers to maintain a user-centered point of view and, especially, to distinguish information related to system use from developers' archival information.

Questionnaire Data as Case Studies

Although I conducted in-depth interviews with only Participants 1 through 5, the responses and explanations provided by all the participants give considerable insight into their situations.

Participant 2's organization is using minimalism in only a limited way. They are understaffed, and marketing has been hard to convince ("thinks every feature needs to be spelled out"). He's concerned that computerphobic users will resist "the exploration that minimalist docs require." It is not surprising that he gave a neutral response (the most negative of eight responses) to the statement that implementing minimalist documentation has been successful in his organization. However, the interview with this participant revealed that the research described in the course helped his group justify their new document design decisions.

Participant 6, although saying her organization had not begun using minimalism, felt that user manuals were good candidates for successful minimalist documents. This participant was one of only two respondents who strongly agreed with the statement, "I believe that well-designed and implemented minimal manuals support users better than comprehensive manuals do," saying, "Typically, there are [a] few common problems encountered by the majority of users." Her comment ties closely to the issue of realistic tasks; if real-world problems with product use can be addressed by documentation, then her minimal manuals are likely to be successful—if she can get permission to produce them.

Participant 7's comments related to users' behavior and responses rather than to her organization's. However, she also was unusual in commenting that minimalist design freed time to do more work, so it is not surprising that organizational resistance was not an issue. For this participant, a successful minimalist manual "will have users going to the correct location on the first try." Again, goal and task knowledge is an underlying issue. Providing the "correct" information will obviate the need to provide large volumes of information, yet knowing what that is implies extensive domain understanding.

Participant 11 clearly believed lack of completeness to be a major shortcoming of minimalism. All her comments were consistent, stating that minimalist tutorials for novices might be successful, but her organization's customers were "professionals who require as complete an information set as possible." It was no surprise that her organization did not use minimalism. However, there was no indication that this organization has obtained any user feedback about documentation, and our questionnaire did not specifically address domain complexity, so we do not know what data underlie this opinion.

Although Participant 12 answered no to the question about using minimalism, her extensive comments make it clear that her organization's new work processes, being developed at the time of the survey, will in fact incorporate many minimalist principles, which she states would benefit "most documents." However, she was neutral about whether minimal manuals support users better than comprehensive ones, hoping to see "a lot more testing results" for their kind of "highly technical products." Her comments showed a concern for communicating domain-specific conceptual explanations.

Participant 13 was a strong proponent of minimalism, although her group had not used it before she attended the course. In every survey question, she strongly agreed with statements about the value and success of minimalism, although she responded that minimalist documentation required "a lot more" resources. Hers was the only group that performed user surveys and usability testing, both with positive results. Her responses support my conclusion that organizations that collect user data are more likely to apply minimalism and to use it successfully.

5.4   In-Depth Interviews with Participants

After reviewing the questionnaires, I conducted telephone interviews with five of the participants to explore the subject matter they were documenting, its target audience, and more details about the structure, content, and work process used to create their minimalist documentation. Although the minimalist applications varied greatly, several trends did appear.

Participant 1: Software Engineering Tools

Participant 1 is a senior editor for a company that designs debuggers, simulators, and compilers for software engineers and programmers. The manuals for this software have two audiences: one of highly sophisticated, experienced programmers and the other of well-educated programmers who do not yet have much hands-on industry experience.

Experienced users tend to like the company's comprehensive reference manuals, but new programmers do not know when and how to apply the various features. The company offers two- to five-day introductory training classes about the debugger that give programmers the highlights (for example, show them how to set break points and examine code). The marketing staff have also created a short "demo manual" that is minimalist in approach.

In the current work process, writers receive draft manuals from engineering and rework them ("massage engineering input"). The average manual is 150 to 200 pages long and takes two to six weeks of a writer's time. The documentation group is considering using the minimalist approach to create some getting-started and procedural chapters aimed at the second, less experienced audience.

Participant 1 encountered considerable resistance among the writers when she proposed this plan. As stated in her questionnaire responses, minimalist manuals would require the writers to understand their subject matter better, apply more critical and evaluative thinking, and add more of their own input. Minimalist manuals would require more work and more time ("in six weeks they can't do it"), and most of the writing staff are comfortable with the existing situation.

The group's first attempt at applying the minimalist model was not used because it highlighted the extent to which the document duplicated existing online help. Nevertheless, the group is still planning on trying minimalism for future manuals, because of the need to support their second audience with task-oriented documentation. In the current plans for implementing minimalism, the information removed to create the new procedural chapters or manuals would still be retained in reference chapters.

The company is also debating how much domain information to provide in the documentation. Some people say that the company will lose business if documentation does not explain why to do things (for example, why and under what circumstances to set break points). Management staff responsible for profitability say this is not the responsibility of documentation; users needing this kind of support should attend the training classes offered by the company. Participant 1 thinks this issue will resurface as they draft minimalist procedures, which will not include such explanations.

Participant 2: Small Business and Home Office Software

Participant 2 is a documentation specialist for a company producing invoicing, labeling, and mailing list management software for businesses with fewer than ten employees. The audiences range from complete novices (for whom this product was the first they installed that did not come installed on their computer) to small business people who are also computer hobbyists. Participant 2 worked in technical support for the company prior to his documentation position.

When this company started, its management believed that needing a manual at all meant the software was not designed well, so the documentation was short. However, the company's initial, very narrowly focused products have grown to include more features that satisfy greater customer expectations.

Now, each product comes with a manual, a getting-started card, and online help. The manuals range from 64 to 120 pages in length, and the cards are actually three-panel, two-sided sheets. The online help covers the same topics as do the manuals. Participant 2 thinks "the current documentation is doing as well for the more complex software as the previous documentation did for the simpler software."

Feedback on the documentation has been mixed. Some technical support feedback says that users want things made simpler, with more steps and explanations. One customer said that the manual did not cover everything in the program; when asked what was missing, he confessed that he had never opened the manual, but obviously such a thin manual could not describe the whole program.

Some sections of the current documentation follow the minimalist model, but not all of it. The writers think that not all their users want minimalist documentation and that even users who do like minimalism may sometimes want more information. However, the writers hope to learn more from a forthcoming survey on documentation that will include questions about users' expectations for documentation, their satisfaction with the current documentation, and their frequency of use for various document types.

The company gives its writers a great deal of freedom with respect to document design; if they can justify an approach, they are usually allowed to do it. They have used the research described in the course as justification to concentrate their limited resources on user's guides, rather than providing separate tutorials that marketing has requested. Although tutorials would help some people, they now believe that better user's guides will be more helpful to more people.

Participant 3: Desktop Tools and Database Software
Participant 3 is a technical writer for a personal computer software firm that targets home and small business users. Her group has created minimalist documentation for two products: a desktop tools product for novice users and a database system.

The greatest application of minimalism was for the user's guide for the desktop tools product. The group had a strong directive from corporate management to reduce the product's cost of goods and therefore to shorten the documentation. The database system documentation had a similar objective.

The group implemented minimalism in several ways. First, writers slashed the verbiage by reducing repetition ("it cut out a lot of 'tell them what you're going to tell them/tell them what you told them' blather") and doing less stating of the obvious (such as "Choose Close. The document closes"). They also replaced redundant information with cross-references, expository text with tables, and expository text with callouts to illustrations.

Second, although the user's guides tell how to use the products' capabilities, they describe only one way to use each feature ("what we've left out is the fifteen different ways you can do anything"). The desktop tools product user's guide also omitted a few especially sophisticated product features entirely. When deciding which method to describe, the writers favored the easiest ones for users to perform or the easiest ones to document. Participant 3 commented, "You can make [the product] go with just the user's guide."

However, although the user's guides now follow minimalist principles, the other information—alternative methods, complicated procedures, conceptual explanations, other reference material—did not vanish from the products' documentation. Rather, this information is now supplied in online help. Thus we see the following comparison:

Desktop tools product, old version: 585-page user's guide, 250 help topics

Desktop tools product, new version: 184-page user's guide, 1060 help topics

Database system, old user's guide: Mac edition, 448 pages; Windows edition, 415 pages

Database system, new user's guide: Mac edition, 341 pages; Windows edition, 329 pages

Between the two documentation versions, about 30 percent new features were added to each of the products. The reduction in size is even more dramatic, considering the increased amount of information to be documented.

Participant 3 said that no one in the company outside the writing group viewed this size reduction as a quality improvement effort. However, when she observed product usability testing, people using nonminimalist manuals for other products "got tangled up in too many choices and steps." (Usability testing did not specifically address documentation.) She also noted some management surprise that writers were spending a lot of time creating online help.

Participant 4: Library Automation Software
Participant 4 is a technical writer whose company was preparing to release its first Windows version of a library automation product that previously ran only under DOS. The product has three distinct audience groups: a broad general audience that uses online public access catalogs, technical users such as catalogers who create the database records, and system administrators.

The documentation group's first minimalist project is a Windows help system of procedural, reference, and system administration information for the new product. Procedures provide how-to information for library users, and the reference information consists of field definitions and conceptual explanations (such as how the system calculates dates). The system administration help is also procedural, with topics for that audience. The total help system will cover about three hundred topics.

The company will also provide the reference information as printed documentation. In addition, writers are reworking the manuals for the DOS product, separating procedures from conceptual information. However, the company is not currently using minimalism for the printed documentation; when conceptual or reference information is lengthy, it will be supplied in the printed manuals but not in the help system.

Many of the documentation changes in progress are based on the work of a staff usability analyst, who has done three rounds of iterative usability testing on the procedures. After each round of testing, the writers implemented greater minimalism. Based on conversations during the course sessions, as well as other participant responses, this much documentation usability testing is very unusual.

The group's first draft of help procedures contained introductions, detailed instructions with many steps, and extensive feedback information saying what the system would do when the user did something. The text was also crowded and dense on the screen. Participants in the first usability test "didn't even want to read it" and tended to skip steps.

After the first usability test, the group reduced the amount of explanation and removed "locators" that said where on the screen to click various buttons. After the second test, they removed all but the most critical feedback statements.

During the interview, Participant 4 said that when she took the course, minimalism was completely new and "energizing" to her. But their usability analyst pointed out that successful minimalism requires both knowing the audience and being able to do extensive testing.

Participant 4 described the usability analyst as being neither for nor against minimalism, but rather supporting what testing showed to be usable. Her description of the test results seems mostly consistent with minimalist principles.

Participant 5: Microcomputer Components Cost Analysis

Participant 5 is the training manager for the components cost group of a large semiconductor manufacturer. Her responsibility is to provide cost training for financial analysts; company policy calls for job rotation among finance assignments approximately every two years, resulting in "new" financial analysts in the components cost group.

These financial analysts receive two days of classroom training after they begin their new assignment. However, from a practical standpoint, new analysts cannot always take classes as soon as they join the group, and they need very task-oriented information to be successful at all during their first few weeks on the job.

The company recently changed to a new financial system that needed new training materials and documentation. To help support the new system, Participant 5 developed a series of two-page quick-reference guides (QRGs). Each QRG contains the procedures for a particular cost calculation process. There are twenty-five QRGs, all using minimalist design, color coded and punched to fit in a three-ring binder. New financial analysts can begin work immediately using the QRGs. The topics were suggested by users, and Participant 5 revised the guides after observing the financial analysts use them.

In addition, the new analysts receive two nonminimalist documents: a conceptual manual (called a user's guide) and a window reference manual. The conceptual manual includes about 70 pages of explanations and 150 pages of sample reports. The window references consist of about 5 pages of description for each of twenty-four windows. There is also a computer-based training (CBT) module covering the conceptual information.

The classroom training, the minimalist documentation, the traditional documentation, and the CBT are all integrated into a training program that is used during financial analysts' first months on the job. When possible, new financial analysts spend a little time with their predecessors, but then they must function on their own using the minimalist QRGs.

Taking the conceptual CBT is a prerequisite for attending the two-day classroom training. After a month or two on the job using the minimalist QRGs for the basics of their workday tasks, the financial analysts are better able to understand and appreciate both the conceptual CBT and the classroom training.

Participant 5 commented that if classroom training is provided too early, people remember only the specific things they need to do their job tomorrow, rather than learning the larger perspective and decision-making trade-offs they need to do a better job for their entire two-year assignment. She commented, "If I train them too early, I've wasted everyone's time."

5.5 Conclusions and Recommendations

The follow-up study of attendees at the minimalist course showed some interesting themes. Each person I interviewed (or whose questionnaire

I received) had a different situation: different products, different audiences, different objectives and priorities. Nevertheless, some trends were apparent.

Conclusions from the Follow-up Study

Most participants divided support information into three types: procedural and how-to information, usually presented in steps; definition-type reference information, such as acceptable field formats and values; and conceptual explanations. Conceptual information was closely related to domain knowledge and was presented in training classes (as well as in documentation) by two companies.

The participants were clear about what constitutes procedural or how-to information, and they believed that such information is a good candidate for the minimalist approach. Reference information was more of a catch-all, being the repository for definitions of terms, fields, valid parameters, and so forth, as well as for conceptual explanations. Participants' ideas about implementing minimalism in reference documentation were much less developed, a finding consistent with the published research information.

None of the participants applied minimalism throughout their documentation library. Most applied it only to procedural or how-to documentation (mentioning such topics as installation and troubleshooting), although a few had attempted to "slash the verbiage" on reference information. No one had applied minimalism to conceptual explanations, although several wanted to do so and wondered how they could go about it.

No one applied minimalism equally to both online and print documentation. Rather, they tended to use one medium as a repository for the information they took out of the medium that was their target for the minimalism effort.

Participants noted pressure for completeness in documentation from several sources: marketing and engineering staff who wanted to talk about every feature, customers who wanted to be sure they had everything, and writers who did not want to think about user tasks. On the other hand, there was also financial pressure to shorten documents.

Several participants took advantage of graphics to assist in their implementation of minimalism, using charts, graphs, tables, and illustration callouts to minimize the amount of text. One participant reduced a manual to a large, maplike chart.

Only one of the participants interviewed had created "inferential" minimalist documentation, and that company did so for only one of two products for which it created minimalist documentation. This participant was also the only one who mentioned describing just one of the several possible ways to perform a function, a technique that was mentioned in some of the course discussion.

When participants commented on why minimal manuals did or did not support users better than comprehensive ones, the concerns about minimalism centered on complicated procedures and highly technical information, although fear of exploration and need for conceptual information were also mentioned.

Although all participants interviewed (as well as virtually all course attendees) recognized the value of usability testing to confirm and validate documentation, especially minimalist documentation, only a minority currently perform such testing. Of the thirteen questionnaire respondents, three mentioned conducting documentation usability testing; a fourth observed some documentation issues during product usability testing. These four also had made the most progress toward successful minimalist documentation.

How Can We Increase Minimalism in Documentation Practice?
Both my experiences in teaching the course and the data collected during the follow-up study indicate that the documentation community is not yet taking advantage of the potential usability improvements minimalism offers. Successful minimalist documentation requires knowledge of the user audience and the domain, both of which may be difficult or expensive to gain. However, successful documentation of any design has the same requirements; minimalism simply makes it harder to dodge them.

Those responsible for documentation can increase minimalism in documentation practices in several immediate ways:

• Apply to all documentation those minimalist principles that are less affected by concerns for completeness or technical complexity: slashing verbiage, omitting repetition, and limiting expository text. Do not just move wordy, poorly organized text to another medium.

• Probe or critically explore the context of requests for completeness; what constitutes complete documentation depends on its audience. For example, many kinds of information are important for maintaining products rather than for using them, and can be separated into internal documents less costly to produce.

• Always choose a user-centered orientation rather than a system-centered one. Even when you are documenting every feature or capability of a product, employing users' concepts and terminology will enable them to draw on their prior experience. Users will be able to find the information they need more quickly, and explanations can be shorter when writers use language familiar to readers.

Other approaches to increasing the penetration of minimalism depend on long-term planning and research:

• Collect user data early and often. In the follow-up study, the organizations that performed usability testing or conducted user surveys tended to apply minimalism. Those who "knew" what their customers needed were less minimalist in approach.

• Support research in less-studied areas of minimalism. What is the relationship between users' understanding of the conceptual framework or the domain context of a product and their success with it? The initial minimalism research was conducted with products of limited complexity, but Participant 5 found that task experience helped users of fairly complex systems to benefit from conceptual training. The role of conceptual information in the minimalist model needs more investigation, as does the use of minimalism in highly technical or complex systems.

• Continue monitoring the practice of minimalism with longitudinal studies. I will be glad to share the questionnaire used in my follow-up study with any researchers who want to collect comparative data in the future.

Minimalism has not gained the penetration I expected in commercial documentation practice, and the study described in this chapter gives us some insight into the reasons. The existing body of traditional comprehensive documentation and those responsible for it (authors, product developers, and marketers) supply a great deal of inertia.

Researchers and practitioners concerned with promoting more usable documentation will need to publish—and publicize—the value added by following the minimalist approach. The more we can measure and communicate the gains in user performance and customer satisfaction achieved by research-based methodology such as minimalism, the easier writers in industry will find it to apply these methods.

Acknowledgments

I am grateful to all the students in my University of California Santa Cruz Extension course who participated in this study, especially the five interview participants. Participant 2 was Jon Baron of MySoftware Company in Palo Alto, California; Participant 3 was Chris Panero from Claris Corporation in Santa Clara, California; the remaining participants did not release their affiliations for publication. I received valuable review and editing from Tec-Ed staff member Lori Anschuetz, as well as helpful suggestions from authors of other chapters in this book.

References

Carroll, J. M. 1994. *The Nurnberg Funnel: Designing Minimalist Instruction for Practical Computer Skill.* Cambridge, MA: MIT Press.

Draper, Steve. Personal communication.

Rosenbaum, S. 1989. "Usability Evaluations Versus Usability Testing: When and Why." *IEEE Transactions on Professional Communication* 32, no. 4:210–216.

Rosenbaum, S., and L. Anschuetz. 1994. "Whole-Product Usability: Integrating Documentation and Rest-of-Product Usability Testing." *Conference Record IPCC 94: Scaling New Heights in Technical Communication*, pp. 127–133. IEEE Professional Communication Society.

Van der Meij, H., and J. M. Carroll. 1995. "Principles and heuristics for designing minimalist instruction." *Journal of the Society for Technical Communication* 42, no. 2:243–261.

Appendix: Details of Course Topics

The lecture and discussion portions of the one-day "Minimalist Design for Documentation" course covered the following topics:

Module 1:   Problems with Documentation and Training Materials
• Traditional systems approach to documentation and training

- What traditional training materials expect
- What learners actually do
- Results of inconsistencies between traditional documentation and user behaviors

Module 2:   What Is the Minimalist Instructional Approach?

- Learners start immediately on meaningful, realistic tasks
- Results of direct activities toward meaningful goals
- Reduced reading and other passive training activity
- Real readers use their initiative
- Minimalism encourages self-directed reasoning and improvising
- Ability to read in any order
- More links between system and training
- Explicit support of error recognition and recovery
- Some types of user errors
- Prior knowledge: Adult learners are never novices
- Take advantage of real work contexts and situations
- Summary: Guidelines for designing minimalist training

Module 3:   Why Do We Believe Minimalism Works?

- Faster and more successful learning
- Error recognition and recovery
- Reference after training
- Targeted errors and skills
- Subjective measures
- Another study: Four versions of the minimal manual
- Summary: Minimal manual users performed better and more efficiently
- Some concerns still remain

Module 4:   Identifying Real Tasks for Real Users

- Work process for identifying appropriate tasks
- Audience groups to consider
- User profile data to collect
- Usage scenarios to consider
- Computer industry example of user-task pairings
- Medical example of user-task pairings

Module 5:   Writing Minimalist Instruction for a Task

- Minimalist instruction cards: Carroll's first approach
- Contents of each card

- Cards in Carroll's study
- Examples of cards
- Designing the minimal manual
- Example of a chapter of the manual: Typing something
- Only testing confirms minimal content and organization
- Guidelines for writing minimal manuals

Module 6:   Editing Minimalist Instruction

- The editor emulates the test process
- Goals for effective editing of minimal manuals
- The editing process for minimalism

Module 7:   Using the Minimalist Model in Online Support

- Nurnberg Funnel: The training-wheels interface
- Results of testing the training-wheels approach
- Nurnberg Funnel: Systems with task intelligence
- Problems with "mere advice"
- After 1990: Progress in minimalism for online support
- Summary of minimalist principles in 1995
- Related principles in online guidelines
- Successes and failures of minimalism in online support depend on the implementation

6

Choosing a Minimalist Approach for Expert Users

JoAnn T. Hackos

In the late 1980s, my consulting group, Comtech Services, was engaged by a company to provide a new type of software documentation for potential customers. The documentation would serve both a marketing and an instructional purpose. It would introduce the benefits of the software to a new group of customers, and it would provide a brief getting-started instruction for all users of the new version of the software being released. The project appeared to provide an excellent opportunity to pursue a minimalist approach for a new group of users, technical experts who would use the software to analyze large volumes of data.

I first encountered John Carroll and colleagues' views of minimalist instruction in their 1984 article in *Datamation* and was immediately convinced that the direction I had been pursuing at Comtech to create highly task- and user-focused manuals was moving in the right direction. From the first (I founded Comtech in the late 1970s), we had taken an instructional-design perspective rather than a systems-documentation perspective in the design of user documentation. Carroll's minimalist research strongly supported our practice of analyzing and supporting specific user learning needs.

Carroll's discussion of a minimalist approach also introduced several new concepts, such as guided exploration and a focus on error recovery, that we were eager to try. However, most of our clients at the time were barely able to accept a task-based structure rather than a menu-based structure for software manuals. A minimalist approach would require an unusual case and a client willing to try something new. Precision Visuals, Inc. (PVI), of Boulder, Colorado, became that client because they were willing to innovate and had a special project, directed by marketing rather than engineering, that required a radical approach to be successful.

The challenge of the project was to create an introductory document for a group of potential users who were experts in analyzing very large data sets. Many of them had mainframe computer experience using statistical software, including PVI's mainframe product. By the mid-1980s, most of the users also had PC experience in a DOS environment. The new software, called PV-WAVE, translated the mainframe application to the PC. We knew that Carroll's approach to minimalism could work with novice users. Could we also apply it effectively to expert users? Would the approach need to be modified for expert users?

To decide upon a minimalist approach, we asked the following questions:

• What characteristics of the users would help us identify the nature of their expertise? Were they experts in their domain, capable of formulating and articulating their own goals for using a software application and capable of translating their goals into system choices? Were they also experienced users of software, capable of navigating through menus and dialogue boxes with little assistance from documentation?

• What characteristics of the software would promote a minimalist approach? Was the software sufficiently consistent to allow the user to quickly build an adequate mental model of its functionality? Was the software sufficiently revealing of the work flow that users could make good guesses about how to proceed with little external assistance?

• What kind of information did the expert users want from the documentation? Did they need support in performing tasks? Were they interested in how the software was designed or in how its functionality related to their task goals?

The answers to these questions would enable us to decide if and how to use a minimalist approach. Since minimalism had chiefly been tested with novice users, we were concerned that perhaps experts would want more information about the software rather than less, that they would be impatient with suggestions to explore on their own, and that incomplete information and a focus on errors would be unwelcome to users who wanted quickly to reach their goals.

6.1   Characteristics of Expert Users in the Light of Minimalist Design

Providing informational (conceptual, procedural, and instructional) text for expert users presents a number of dilemmas for the designer. Experts in the knowledge domain (those who know the professional content area or subject matter of the information very well) need to understand how the application software will assist them in accomplishing tasks that are already well defined by their experience. These experts know what they want to do but not how to do it with the software tool provided:

• They want conceptual information that helps them relate their goals to the functions designed into the application.

• They want to know what the application can do for them, not in terms of software design, but in terms of the knowledge domain in which they work.

• They may need procedural information that assists them in selecting the appropriate actions to accomplish their goals: which selections to make, what paths to take through the application software, or what responses to make to the fields in dialog boxes.

• They may welcome instructional information in the form of extended examples (narrative or implied narrative) of how a particular problem was solved using the application software.

If these same domain experts also have experience using software applications in general, they have little need for detailed step-by-step instructions for manipulating the interface objects and navigating through the interface. They already know how to use the screen objects and how user interfaces operate in general. They have achieved an adequate conceptual model of the function of interface objects that allows them to navigate the interface easily. They know how pull-down menus work, what scroll boxes are, how to respond to check boxes and radio buttons, and so on. If the screen objects are labeled correctly (the interface designer has used the commonly known terminology in the domain), they do not need information about how to interpret the minimalist text on the screen. The labels on buttons and field names should provide sufficient information to support their needs.

Experienced software users, as I have defined them, may need some suggestions that help them increase efficiency and decrease learning time, but they do not need to learn how to react to the on-screen stimuli provided by the language, icons, and layout of the graphic user interface. Simply put, they know what the buttons, pull-down lists, and other widgets are for and how to use them. And if the interface designers used common terminology and well-understood visual symbols, they should immediately recognize the significance of the minimalist text and images on the screen.

These double experts—experts in the knowledge domain of their profession and experienced in using standard software applications—are strong candidates for a minimalist approach to informational text. They need just enough information to get them started in the right direction with a new software application. They need to know where to begin, where to go next, what the possibilities are, and how to get out of trouble. They do not need detailed task-oriented instructions to manipulate the interface objectives, nor do they need to consult instructional information to understand the primary purposes served by the software application. They already know the subject matter and have clearly defined what they want to accomplish. They simply do not know how to accomplish their goals with the software.

Adapting Minimalism for Expert Users

By using a minimalist approach with expert users, we are able to minimize text by assuming prior knowledge and experience, take advantage of the experts' ability to skim for salient information, and emphasize instruction on more difficult tasks while assuming that the simpler ones will take care of themselves. By adapting minimalism for experts, we insist that the information designer identify and analyze the users' learning styles and information needs. We avoid the common excuse of technical communicators who claim that they must include everything because they do not understand how much the users already know.

Through interviews and participative design sessions with expert users, we have learned that they already use a combination of techniques to become acquainted with software that supports their special domain requirements. They feel confident enough to experiment with the software directly, navigating through menu choices and dialog boxes to learn what is available. They are often willing to supplement their hands-on approach with references to online help. In fact, we have found that expert users are the most enthusiastic and frequent users of online help systems. When they think of a function they want to perform and cannot immediately see how to perform it from the minimalist text on the interface, they consult online help for a quick look at the actions to take to achieve their ends. The online help thus becomes the means to the end for expert users—at least, that is, if they can find the task they want to perform in the help. Their ability to locate the information they need depends on the extent of the technical communicator's knowledge of the functions that expert users want to be able to perform and their ability to label the functions correctly.

In addition to manipulating the interface objects directly to learn about the application software, expert users often admit to skimming the paper documentation provided by the software development organization. For the most part, they orient themselves, attempting to understand what functions are available to them and if and how those functions relate to the goals they want to achieve and the tasks they would like to perform. These expert users may flip quickly through the pages of task-oriented or system-oriented documentation, trying to obtain an overview of the application. They will stop to read more detailed procedural or conceptual text when the function appears to be something they would like to use.

Unfortunately, expert users often find procedural text to contain inadequate information for them. Since they can often figure out how to perform the function using the interface objects, they find that procedural text with its step-by-step list of actions does not satisfy their needs for information about the function. They might prefer text that is more conceptual, with a brief but complete conceptual overview of how the function works. However, they do not want to know about how the function was programmed, which is usually the type of conceptual information provided by software developers and technical communicators whose only information source is software developers. They need to know how the function was conceived to support the needs of users like them, something that the software developers often do not know and cannot provide to the technical communication professionals. That means that most documentation fails to meet the expert users' need for information about the software.

Once they find an interesting or useful function, experts tend to skim the text to get a sense of the whole task from beginning to end, rather than concentrating on a single step at a time before moving to the next step. They appear to want to know what the whole is like before focusing on the parts. Expert users in participative-design sessions tell us that they are particularly annoyed by interruptions in the flow of action steps. They seem to prefer instructions that are uninterrupted by asides dealing with exceptions or by warnings and cautions. They appreciate that the exceptions may be important and the warnings and cautions noteworthy, but they object to anything that interrupts their ability to skim for the highlights of the task. It is as if they want to be certain they can interpret the main flow of the task on their own. They appear to be looking for details that depart from their expectations of the way a task should work within the software. They stop their rapid skimming only when something attracts their attention: an unexpected detail, a new direction, or a task they have never performed or did not know was possible.

Most traditional documentation published by the software manufacturer does not accommodate these needs of expert users. Even when information is task oriented, the tasks described are often from the perspective of the system (system oriented) rather than the user (user purpose oriented). The typical procedural text frequently includes lengthy asides, exceptional cases, alternative approaches, and warnings of dire consequences should the user do something incorrectly. These exceptions are often integrated into the main task instructions, further complicating finding the main route through the information, as well as obscuring potentially interesting information in the asides.

Experts say that all of this extra verbiage gets in the way of a skimming strategy and their attempts to read to learn to perform the tasks they have already defined for themselves (Redish 1988). They do not want to know what the system does (system description), which is often the content of much additional explanation. Rather, they want minimal task information but more information that enables them to learn how the software supports their goals. They appear to ask how the software is designed to support their specific purposes. In fact, they want to know if the developers knew when they designed the software what expert users are trying to do.

Much of the conceptual information discussing the nuances of using the application effectively—information that the expert users would like to know—does not exist in most task-oriented documentation. Its absence often stems from the nature of the software organization that produces the manufacturer's documentation. In these organizations, technical communicators who create the software manuals have little or no access to actual users of the software. Because they know little about their audiences, the communicators are forced to rely on the software developers for the sources of their information. Unfortunately, the software developers know only about how the application software was developed. They often admit to knowing little about how anyone will use the application. Their interests focus, appropriately perhaps, on how they have put the underlying structure of the software together, not on how it will be used. Thus, the exchange of information between the software developer and the technical communicator often leads to either systems-oriented documentation or task-oriented documentation that focuses on the tasks that the application software is designed to support, such as the navigation among and manipulation of the interface objects.

Expert users correctly consider documentation that is systems oriented or oriented around system tasks to be virtually useless to them in their initial approach to the software or for learning new tasks. They are experienced users of software and are already able to find their way around most logically designed interfaces; they are only peripherally interested in the underlying structure of the software if it does not affect the way they use the application or tool. Thus, the information that can be provided most easily by the software developers and the technical communicators does little to assist the goal-oriented performance of the experts.

In order to illustrate how we might better approach the needs of expert users in software documentation, I introduce the PVI case study, explain why we chose a minimalist approach, and describe how the resulting manual was organized and written. Finally, I draw conclusions from the design approach that might serve as guidelines for others engaged in meeting the needs of expert users.

6.2   The PVI Case Study

When PVI approached us to provide a procedural manual for their new visually oriented trends analysis software, we recommended a minimalist approach. Some of the impetus came from PVI's desire to reduce costs in producing the manual. More important was the assessment by the PVI marketing organization that the users of the new product were more likely to appreciate minimal information.

The company's intent was to attract a new group of users to their visual trends analysis software. The software had experienced strong user acceptance among scientists, especially those with university affiliations. However, a larger potential market existed among corporate engineers who, like the scientists, needed to analyze large volumes of data. The marketing organization was intent on attracting this new group of corporate users, but it was concerned that they would not be willing to use the traditional manuals produced by PVI. These manuals offered detailed step-by-step information on the tasks that could be performed by the application (and indirectly, the users). The user's manual was voluminous, easily totaling four to five hundred pages.

Rationale for a Minimalist Approach

In the PVI case, organizational issues nearly subverted the development of a useful document for expert users. In the organization, the tradition of producing system- and task-oriented documentation that focused on system tasks nearly kept us from addressing the needs of the expert users. However, we were able to convince PVI that a minimalist approach would work by focusing on marketing's request for a small manual.

Throughout the negotiations with PVI executives, marketing, and developers about the project, one primary concern about our recommendation of a minimalist approach predominated. The developers believed strongly that their customers wanted more, not less, information about the software and would find a minimalist approach to be condescending. Developers were concerned that a minimalist approach would not meet the needs of their expert users and would leave out important and necessary information.

The development organization had, in fact, also decided to prepare a detailed reference and task-oriented manual to supplement the minimalist approach, a manual that was determinedly systems-task oriented. This manual described all the screens and all the menu choices, fields, icon buttons, and choices on dialog boxes and was organized according to the structure of the interface. In short, this was yet another menu-oriented, screen-oriented reference manual that is still being produced in great numbers by many technical communicators. The manual appeared task oriented on the surface but was actually organized around the actions that the software enables the users to perform, not on the tasks that the users want to perform to reach their goals.

Marketing, on the other hand, was convinced that a new approach was needed. The documentation that the company had been producing for their visually oriented trend-analysis software was designed originally for users of a mainframe. Information from sales engineering and customer services had led marketing executives to believe that the new users they wanted to reach would not be accommodated by the traditional approach designed for mainframe users. They needed a different sort of documentation that would encourage a new mini- and microcomputer user to adopt the software product to meet their analytical needs and to accomplish their goals quickly with only minimal references to the documentation.

Marketing believed that the new engineering users would find more acceptable and useful a manual of approximately fifty pages that addressed the primary tasks they could perform using the system. The longer reference manual would be available to them for comprehensive explanations and more advanced uses of the software, or so the theory went among the marketing professionals.

The interest in smallness gave us the political support to use a minimalist approach to producing information that would better meet the needs of the expert users than a traditional systems- and task-oriented approach. Even after the drafts were completed and we had succeeded in staying within the page count requirements, we encountered considerable argument from software developers and senior management who wanted the systems-oriented information rewritten into the minimalist manual.

Only because this information would have made the manual much larger were we successful in resisting the pressure.

The strength of the view that more is better led to a design change in the next version of the manual, produced by the in-house writers. In the new chapter added for the version 2.0 manual, the writers reverted to the systems-oriented and system-task-oriented style that the company's developers and management found more amenable to their notions of what user documentation ought to contain. The technical communicators told us that they tried to follow our template for a minimalist manual. But without grounding in the approach we used to design the minimalist information in the first place, they were heavily pressured by their development and senior management to add more and more systems-oriented detail and to include step-by-step procedures in the traditional task-oriented format that Carroll so aptly describes in *The Nurnberg Funnel* (1990).

Needs Analysis

The first step in our process of identifying the information needs of the expert users was a needs analysis to corroborate or contradict marketing's notions about the users and to decide if a minimalist approach was indeed viable. This marketing organization had focused on an analysis of the potential corporate buyer but had only peripherally looked at the characteristics of the user. Our needs analysis found two key characteristics that recommended a minimalist approach to the information: a user expert in trends analysis and the manipulation of data (expert in the domain) and a computer-literate user (experienced user of software).

The expert users, we learned, were primarily research scientists and engineers in fields such as test engineering (analyzing data from cryogenics and materials testing), space exploration and astrophysics (analyzing solar seismology and simulating astronomical events), computational fluid dynamics (identifying flow patterns such as shock waves, vortices, shear layers, and wakes), medical imaging and remote sensing (postprocessing remote-sensing data and displaying and analyzing bioscience imagery), and earth sciences (interpreting seismic data and simulating meteorological conditions). These users were especially interested in analyzing the trends of enormous data sets, data too numerous to be analyzed by eyeballing. Trends-analysis software permits them to create visual images of the data and more quickly and easily identify trends.

We were also concerned in examining this user group in the light of seemingly contradictory information that we had obtained in focus groups with expert users on previous projects and through observations of product-specific usability assessments. Although experts we interviewed and observed appeared willing to experiment and tended to skim the procedural text they did consult, we also knew that in many instances, experts believed that the manufacturers failed to provide sufficient detailed information about how they might use the software effectively. The missing information appeared to be conceptual rather than procedural.

For example, in work done for a software developer on a statistical analysis tool, we learned from user investigations that expert statisticians wanted detailed information about exactly what algorithms were used in each statistical routine and how the software handled their data. They wanted to know a great deal about the mathematical structures used in the application software, especially if they affected the way the statistical calculations were handled, a requirement drastically different from the average user of application software, who simply wants to reach a goal. The expert users were not interested in the details about the software's behavior but in how the developers had implemented a characteristic that was very important to their work. They needed to know if any problems might occur in their interpretation of results depending on how the calculations were implemented.

PVI expert users appeared to have similar concerns. They wanted to know how the software handled their data so that they could be assured that the results they obtained were accurate and represented the actual shape of their data.

We were aware that a thorough understanding of how the software functioned in relationship to the users' goals was best achieved through experimentation and feedback in observing how different interface options (picks among choices in dialog boxes) influenced how the resulting calculations changed. Thus, the requirement for detailed conceptual information was not necessarily contradictory to the users' desire to experiment and skim information. If we could facilitate a quick reading and confident experimentation, we might be able to hook the experts sufficiently to try the software and test its correspondence with their technical requirements.

Second, we noted that a very high percentage of the potential PVI audience were experienced computer users. Most of their experience, however, was with data analysis tools run on the mainframe rather than the PC. In fact, PVI's legacy products were all mainframe based. The new application software was their first PC-based solution. Would the transference of mainframe to PC affect the users' ability to manipulate the software and navigate quickly to the activities in support of their goals?

We also noted that the professional training of the users strongly suggested a willingness, even eagerness, to experiment. Because they exhibited a strong conceptual understanding of how computer software works in general, they would also be comfortable working with minimal information that encouraged exploration.

At the same time we conducted the needs analysis of the new and existing user communities, we also analyzed the product to decide if it would support a minimalist approach. We felt that the software had to be reasonably well designed to allow us to pursue a minimalist course. Badly designed software that presents an inconsistent interface in which similar actions are performed differently at different places in the software does not lend itself well to a minimalist approach. An inconsistent interface with an inconsistent underlying metaphor requires that the user change tactics depending on the part of the interface being used. What the user learns to do in one part of the application cannot be applied consistently to other parts of the application interface. As a result, procedural material must lead the user through the confusion and provide the learning cues absent from the interface.

In this case, the core application presented in the interface appeared to be reasonably consistent. The users could change the views of their data easily by selecting different configurations from the choices presented in the dialog boxes. As a result, we decided that the core application would support a minimalist approach. The consistency and ease of use built into the product would allow us to suggest experimentation to the users without concern that their "learning to do" would lack continued support (Redish 1988).

One significant part of the interface presented a problem for the designers: the data import function. The process of importing data into the application was not consistent with the core application. After our analysis, we felt that a minimalist approach would not be appropriate for this function. In order to handle data import, we settled on a task-oriented step-by-step approach that would carefully lead the users through the process and minimize errors. Once they had succeeded in importing their data, we would pursue a minimalist approach through the rest of the core application.

Because of the complexity of the data-import process, we also provided users with an opportunity to practice using the core application without having to go through a difficult and possibly time-consuming data preparation step. Consequently, we provided sample data that could be imported and used in practicing with the application. This sample data was specifically designed to be easy to import, a design that supported the principle of a training-wheels interface introduced by Carroll. Although we understood that users might conclude that the import process was simpler to use than it actually was, we determined that a successful import and the subsequent practice with the core application would contribute more to the learning process than a disastrous experience with importing difficult data. However, we informed the users that they certainly might decide to import their own data and could do so following the step-by-step instructions carefully. We noted, because of our minimalist focus on error recovery, that they might experience difficulty in using the import function. Unfortunately, no one in the development organization could tell us what the difficulties might be or how to correct them. Remember that this was version 1.0 software.

To summarize the results of the needs analysis, we concluded that a minimalist approach was indeed appropriate to the PVI users:

• Their interest in experimentation would support an exploratory approach.

• Their domain expertise meant that they would want to experiment to discover if the software could give them the results they needed in their analysis of large, complex data sets.

• Their domain expertise would allow us to focus on using the software effectively in support of their goals without having to explain in detail the relationship between user goals and the software functions.

• Their familiarity with computers would minimize their need for instruction in using the interface objects.

• The software was sufficiently consistent not to require detailed task-oriented instruction to use it correctly.

• Only one part of the software appeared difficult to understand and use, requiring detailed task-oriented instructions for importing data.

• Importing data was sufficiently trouble fraught that a test database seemed to be appropriate to encourage experimentation while avoiding potential problems with data sets that would be time-consuming to import. We wanted the users to experience immediate success at using the software to analyze data trends without spending considerable time on the import function.

Document Design

Based on the results of the needs analysis, we focused on several significant user characteristics to design a minimalist approach to the information.

• First, we knew that the users were anxious to experiment on their own. A minimalist approach encouraging experimentation would support their preferred learning style.

• Second, the users' familiarity with software applications meant that they were unlikely to make many errors that could not easily be corrected, except for the data import function. This function would have to be carefully explained to focus on error correction and problem solving.

• Third, the users' preference for skimming and skipping information and focusing on accomplishing tasks meant that verbiage would need to be reduced to the minimum needed and that sections of text must be carefully labeled to assist in skimming.

• Fourth, a data set that is easy to import should be provided so that users could experiment with the software without becoming entangled in a difficult importing activity.

Although the primary goal of the document design was to produce a minimalist procedural manual that would serve the needs of the users, another goal for the manual also influenced the document design: the company's marketing organization wished to use the procedural manual as a marketing tool, as well as a tool to assist users. They hoped to provide the small manual to prospective users, along with a data tape, and let them experience the software's capabilities for themselves. As a result, we had to include information at the beginning of the manual that described the product's purpose rather than moving directly into the task-oriented instruction.

Despite the marketing purpose included among the design criteria, the descriptive sections occupied only six and a half of the final fifty-six pages of the minimalist user's guide. These descriptive pages emphasize the benefits that the product might provide the user in visually analyzing large volumes of data through multidimensional graphics, animation, and color. By the ninth page, the user is invited to begin using the software.

Experimentation

The core element of our minimalist approach in the document design is on experimentation: learning by doing. We applied the following minimalist guideline, interpreted for expert users, in the PV-WAVE documentation.

Guideline

Emphasize experimentation rather than exhaustive task-oriented step-by-step procedures or system-oriented descriptions of interface objects.

Although this guideline also applies to minimalist information designed for novice users, we believe that experts are more likely than novices to experiment and infrequently consult task-oriented information that focuses on system tasks. We assume that expert users know how to interpret dialog boxes, pull-down menus, and other on-screen tools that can be used without data-destroying consequences. We also assume that expert users prefer to experiment with options, especially when the results of their actions are immediately displayed on the screen (feedback) and no damage to data results.

Discussion   The emphasis on experimentation in the PV-WAVE manual begins on the first page of procedural text, following the marketing-oriented introduction. Chapter 2 begins with the exhortation shown in figure 6.1.

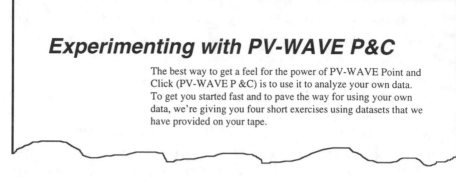

Experimenting with PV-WAVE P&C

The best way to get a feel for the power of PV-WAVE Point and Click (PV-WAVE P &C) is to use it to analyze your own data. To get you started fast and to pave the way for using your own data, we're giving you four short exercises using datasets that we have provided on your tape.

Figure 6.1
The PV-WAVE minimalist documentation begins with the suggestions that users experiment with their data and the data set included with the software.

Throughout the text, we recommend that the users try using parts of the application on their own and with their own data. One of the first tasks presented to the users involves using the online Help cards. The Help cards allow them to learn how to perform tasks that are not mentioned in the getting-started text. This application was created before Microsoft had developed Windows, and the help application had to be designed from scratch as part of the application software. The help text was written by the PVI technical communicators and did not necessarily directly support the minimalist approach.

To encourage experimentation and independent use from the beginning, we chose immediately to suggest that users work with the Help cards (figure 6.2).

Our recommended best practice in all the manuals we design, and especially in a minimalist manual, is to tell users how to get out of a situation before we tell them anything about it. Users are often frustrated when they get stuck in part of an application and have no idea how to extricate themselves. We try to help them avoid that difficulty by quickly providing them with exit instructions.

The passage in figure 6.3 illustrates the experimenting style we chose for the text, suggesting that the users explore the Help cards before continuing with their exploration of the application. At the time that this software was released, in the mid-1980s, online help systems were not

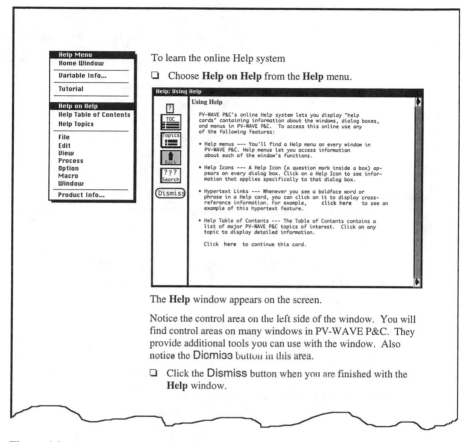

Figure 6.2
The suggestion to use the help cards points users toward information that will support task performance should they need such support.

common. Today, the suggestion of looking at help may not be needed for a class of expert users.

Thus, the first task presented suggests to the users that they begin to explore the system and its capabilities. We know that this suggestion does not, in this context, appear to be a radical one. Many documentation developers unfamiliar with the minimalist approach of guided exploration would still be comfortable with our recommendation that users be encouraged to explore the help system. The recommendation becomes more problematic when primary user tasks are addressed.

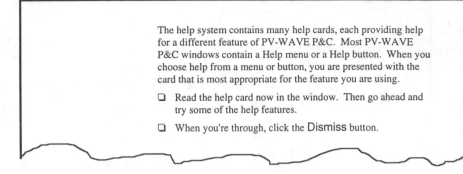

The help system contains many help cards, each providing help for a different feature of PV-WAVE P&C. Most PV-WAVE P&C windows contain a Help menu or a Help button. When you choose help from a menu or button, you are presented with the card that is most appropriate for the feature you are using.

❑   Read the help card now in the window. Then go ahead and try some of the help features.

❑   When you're through, click the Dismiss button.

Figure 6.3
The exploratory focus of minimalist documentation is reinforced in the language used to introduce the help system.

In the PV-WAVE manual, the help exploration suggestion is only a beginning, establishing the tone for the rest of the procedural text. Because we strongly affirm the discussion in Redish (1988) that users "read to learn to do," we have kept the explanations brief, the instructions simple, and the encouraging tone strong throughout the brief guide. We continue to suggest that the users explore the software, but that they do so in a particular sequence suggested by the overall work flow implied in the application design. Once they have imported their data, they can begin to analyze the data by plotting and viewing the data, as described in figure 6.4.

We continue making suggestions for exploration in the primary tasks supported by the minimalist manual. The text that occurs after the users have displayed a plot in the View Window is shown in figure 6.4.

At this point, we hope that the users will try modifying their initial plot by using the menus and the control area. Since the users are familiar with application software, and since they can do little damage by choosing different views and modifying their graphs, we encourage them to experiment. We also use the phrase, "We'll explain more about this later," to let them know that more information about this task is coming but they really do not need to know much more in order to experiment with the view function at this point.

This minimalist style of guided exploration, encouraging user experimentation with the software and the sample data set, continues into the

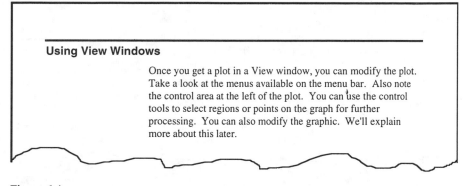

Using View Windows

Once you get a plot in a View window, you can modify the plot. Take a look at the menus available on the menu bar. Also note the control area at the left of the plot. You can use the control tools to select regions or points on the graph for further processing. You can also modify the graphic. We'll explain more about this later.

Figure 6.4
Exploratory suggestions that the user try to modify the plot using the view menu. No details are provided; rather, the user is encouraged to try the additional menu options available.

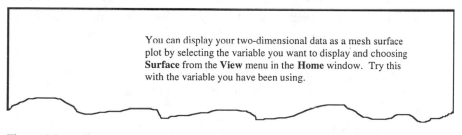

You can display your two-dimensional data as a mesh surface plot by selecting the variable you want to display and choosing **Surface** from the **View** menu in the **Home** window. Try this with the variable you have been using.

Figure 6.5
Exploration hints continue to encourage the user to act independently and experiment with the software using the sample data set.

discussion of mesh surface plots (figure 6.5). Finally, throughout the text, we include subsections recommending that the users experiment on their own with their own data sets (figure 6.6).

Because the users are experts in the domain and already know what they want to achieve, the writer has taken the position that encouraging the users to work on their own is more important than providing step-by-step instructions. The functions are relatively simple to change, and the visual images can be varied extensively through menu choices. And the expert users are comfortable experimenting with software.

A novice user might not be comfortable with the suggestion to experiment. A novice user of PV-WAVE would both be unfamiliar with

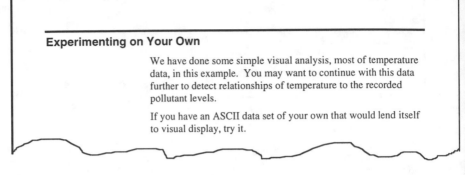

Experimenting on Your Own

We have done some simple visual analysis, most of temperature data, in this example. You may want to continue with this data further to detect relationships of temperature to the recorded pollutant levels.

If you have an ASCII data set of your own that would lend itself to visual display, try it.

Figure 6.6
The text continually suggests that users experiment with their own data or with the data provided by running additional analyses.

trends-analysis software and would be new to the field of visual trends analysis. In that case, we would envision providing much more information about how to use the application and how to apply it to more general data analysis goals. The additional explanation and the use of step-by-step task instruction would, we believe, be needed for a novice user to get started with a difficult application program.

Information Selection
From our needs analysis, we know that expert users prefer to skim and skip text looking for something that they can immediately use to reach their goal. Since their goals are well defined, they want to spend little time reading procedural information and more time working with the software. The following minimalist guideline allows experts to avoid excessive reading.

Guideline

Encourage exploration and minimize the time spent reading.

We assume that expert users know what they are looking for in the product documentation and can use that information effectively once, or if, they find it. They wish to avoid excessive reading. We know that their strategy is to skim and skip sections they do not find immediately relevant.

If we limit chunks of information to a few short paragraphs at the most and label each chunk clearly, the users can decide how they will

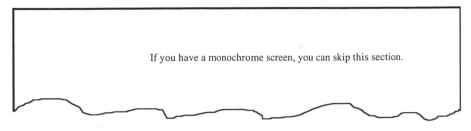

If you have a monochrome screen, you can skip this section.

Figure 6.7
A label suggests that users avoid reading a particular section that may not apply
to their work environment.

limit the amount of time they spend reading instructions rather than
experimenting with the application software.

Giving expert users hints about directions they can pursue rather than
step-by-step instructions takes advantage of their interest in exploratory
learning. Novice users may need more guidance than experts in pursuing
an interesting path of action.

Discussion   We have noted that while attempting to use traditional
comprehensive manuals rather than minimalist manuals, many users
complain that they do not know how to avoid reading information that
does not pertain to solving their problem. They read passages that appear
useful, but in fact focus on special problems that apply to some, but not
all, users. In the PV-WAVE manual, we tried to label information so that
users might avoid reading information that did not apply to them. (See
figure 6.7.) Labeling information in this way decreases misreading and
helps the users find what they really need to know.

Another way we found to help expert users avoid reading something
they did not need to know was to keep the information chunks small. No
section in the PV-WAVE document exceeds two pages, including illustrations of software screens. Short sections and frequent headings rein-
force the design goal of less reading and more experimentation.

Error Correction
Like all other users, expert users want to find in the documentation quick
ways to troubleshoot and correct problems. Expert users, however, make

different kinds of errors from novices and encounter different problems. They rarely experience problems that involve misinterpreting the purpose of a function, especially if that function has been well designed. They are also able to recover more quickly than novices can from typing and interface selection errors. However, they do make errors involving making choices from menus and on dialog boxes that are not exactly what they intended. Such errors can be pointed out with suggestions to try the options that will not affect the original data set.

Guideline

Point out potential problems and suggest ways to avoid them.

The problem-recovery information provided for expert users is different from the recovery information usually needed by novices. Novices need to know how to recover from mistakes in choosing options on menus or dialog boxes. Expert users, we might assume, make fewer errors from which they cannot recover than do novice users.

Expert users are better able to interpret the choices provided them in a menu or dialog box. They are also more likely to know when they have made an incorrect choice and can more quickly identify a wrong path and recover. They can get back to their starting point more quickly and try again than novices are likely to do. They are also likely to be willing to try something that may not work or may affect their data. Such potential problems may be anticipated with suggestions about what may happen, how to avoid the problems, and how to correct them after they occur. Such error recovery information must be based on a thorough knowledge of the paths that expert users might be expected to take if they misinterpret the software in particular ways.

Discussion   Although the PV-WAVE manual does not include as much error correction information as we would have wished, we were able to make suggestions to help users anticipate problems and avoid reacting incorrectly.

Because our users were experienced at using software on mainframes and on the PC, we believed that we might provide some key warnings and cautions about software problems without overemphasizing error correction. All users make errors, but experienced users are more likely

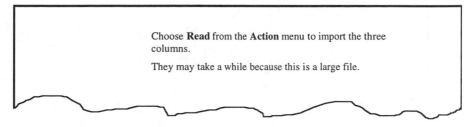

Choose **Read** from the **Action** menu to import the three columns.

They may take a while because this is a large file.

Figure 6.8
A brief statement anticipates a delay that users are likely to encounter with the software import function.

to recover from errors on their own than are novice users. They need to be aware, however, of instances in which problems are most likely to occur and further errors are predictable.

For example, we suggest that users may encounter problems and delays in importing their data sets (figure 6.8).

By anticipating a slow import, we hope that users will not fill up a buffer with unnecessary keystrokes because they fear that nothing is happening. Unfortunately, no visual or textual feedback was provided on the screen to let the users know that the file was loading. Such feedback would have made the warning in the text less necessary. As is often the case, we placed the warning in the text hoping that the user would see it when the problem occurred. We know, however, that most users will be troubled by the lack of feedback on the computer screen because they often do not consult the manuals until they have experienced a problem and tried to recover on their own. The software deficiencies often mean that even well-designed documentation will be unsuccessful in preventing user errors in the absence of strong support from on-screen messages that provide minimalist text and feedback information as an integral part of the interface.

In another instance, illustrated in figure 6.9, we hoped to help users to take the right path to detect and correct problems when we advised them that they may experience printing problems. There is not much real help here because we could not know how their local site might be configured, but we hoped that our suggestion of an action might lead the users in the right direction to obtain assistance in their own organizations.

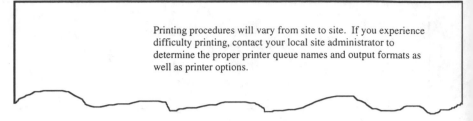

Figure 6.9
A note that printing problems might occur leads to suggestions to discuss the problem with a local site administrator.

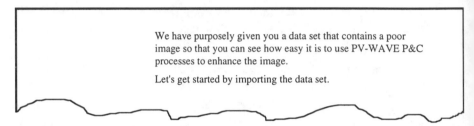

Figure 6.10
A note anticipates a poor image before providing information on correcting the image.

In still another instance, illustrated in figure 6.10, we tried to work with the users to anticipate and respond to problems with the display of certain data sets. At another problem point, illustrated in figure 6.11, we explain that they may still not be able to display a problematic image. Then, in figure 6.12, the image can be corrected.

Throughout these warning statements, we provide information about the potential consequences of user actions that will, we hope, help them diagnose problems and find ways to improve their results. In each case we emphasize solutions to what van der Meij calls semantic problems: problems in understanding how to reach a goal using the tools provided in the application. We are less concerned with helping this class of users avoid syntactic problems based on mistakes in executing input instructions (Lazonder and Van der Meij 1995).

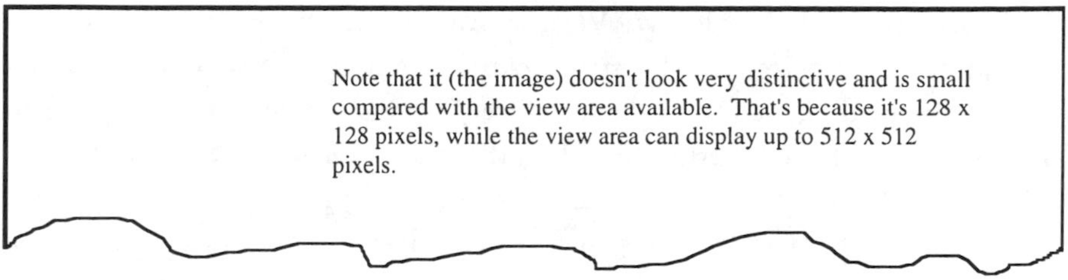

Note that it (the image) doesn't look very distinctive and is small compared with the view area available. That's because it's 128 x 128 pixels, while the view area can display up to 512 x 512 pixels.

Figure 6.11
A note anticipates a poor image on a screen with higher resolution.

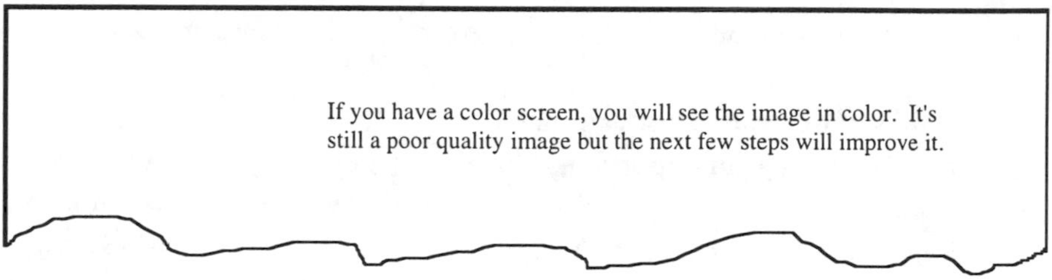

If you have a color screen, you will see the image in color. It's still a poor quality image but the next few steps will improve it.

Figure 6.12
Another note on a possible poor image that can be corrected.

Task-Oriented Instructions for Poorly Designed Software
Some software is so difficult to use because of design problems that a minimalist approach is not advisable. If users attempt to explore the software, they are likely to become confused about the purpose of the application and be unable to proceed. Sometimes the path of action is so obscure and the required input so unintuitive that a minimalist approach will not provide sufficient information for the user to succeed.

Guideline

Provide more instructionally supportive information where necessary to assist in user learning.

Under certain circumstances, users sometimes need more instruction to support their performance of awkwardly designed tasks. Such instructional information (text, graphics, interactivity) must lead them step by step through the performance of tasks.

Discussion In the PV-WAVE application, the import data function is difficult to perform. The steps to achieve a successful import cannot easily be discerned from the interface. For this function, we chose not to use the style of experimentation that we used for the rest of the application but instead employ a detailed step-by-step approach.

When the designer finds that certain tasks are awkward to perform, with insufficient cues in the interface to support decision making, it may be best to use a thorough step-by-step, task-oriented approach rather than a minimalist approach. The users are likely to need supporting explanations of how the tasks are supposed to work and how their underlying structure will allow them to complete the functions.

Results of the Minimalist Approach

We did not have an opportunity to perform a usability assessment on the PV-WAVE P&C manual and have only anecdotal information to assess user response to the minimalist approach used in the information design. We learned from the marketing organization that the getting-started manual for the product met the intended goals of attracting a new audience to the product and giving users the introduction they needed to experiment with the product confidently. The manual helped users trust the interface and move ahead more quickly, without having to face the voluminous reference material also included in the information package.

During the design and development process, the only problems we encountered were from developers and senior managers who argued for comprehensive coverage of everything the product could do. Although our initial direction from marketing was to keep the manual to fifty pages, we experienced continual pressure from these groups to include more options, explain more functionality, and impress the users with more and more words. We successfully argued that all of these suggestions were likely to result in unappreciated volumes of information and users who would not use the manual at all. A user who avoided the getting-started manual might also decide to avoid the product altogether as too cumbersome and difficult to learn. These arguments continued to convince the marketing organization that they were on the right track in their insistence on a short manual and garnered their tacit, although uninformed, support for our minimalist approach. That support resulted, we believe, in a significant breakthrough for the PV-WAVE documentation.

6.3   A Minimalist Approach to Software Design

In addition to the guidelines associated with the information design, two other points are significant to the successful implementation of a minimalist approach for both novice and expert users of software applications.

The design team (developers of the software interface, as well as the documentation) must focus on the learning needs of the users during the entire design process. Front-end analysis to identify user profiles, their prior knowledge and experience with the knowledge domain and the interface, and their goals for the use of the software is essential if a minimalist approach to information is to be successful.

The enterprise of creating information for the users should occur among a team of people who have gained an understanding of the users and their needs. That understanding is the most responsible starting point for information design. The team needs a variety of skills: the ability to use language effectively, to use images effectively, to take advantage of the limitations of the small space of the computer screen for communicating value to the user, and to understand the use of video and other dynamic forms, such as computer animation, effectively.

To produce a true minimalist learning environment, I recommend that people with skills in human factors, communication, graphics, screen layout, and instructional design work together on interface design teams. They should be able to extend the minimalist text of the interface into more varied and comprehensive information for a variety of learners. In our research and observations, we have found that expert users who are sophisticated enough might prefer brief conceptual discussions of the underlying rationale of the application or even comprehensive explanations about the manner in which the software supports their knowledge domain or business practices.

Some users need a lot of information about what's going on in the software and need it in the form of extended narrative text. Other users simply need procedural, user-task-oriented information. To produce such information, technical communicators and other members of the minimalist design team need to obtain a rich picture of the users in their real working environment.

6.4   Categories of Minimalist Information Design

At present, we might want to consider that graphical user interfaces are an exercise in minimalist information design. By using a few words, a few graphics, and an effective use of two-dimensional space, a well-designed interface should function as a minimalist text, providing just enough information so that a skilled user of interfaces and an expert in the knowledge domain knows how to perform the functions that he or she wants to perform. Many simple interfaces created for well-understood applications (accounting transactions, customer service, and so on) are perfectly adequate for use by people already trained in the knowledge domain. Users who are adding information to electronic forms should rarely need any other information besides the words on the screen to perform a task—certainly not the voluminous manuals that tell them over and over again how to "enter a customer's name and address."

Unfortunately, we're not that good at designing interfaces or informed enough about the connection of the information that must be learned through instruction versus information that can be learned through experience. Even experienced users often cannot figure out how to do what they want to do just by looking at the interface objects.

Under such circumstances, we need to consider a minimalist approach to providing additional information. To create user-centered information, we need to know what users do not know and what they need to know about the tasks that the interface supports. As designers of procedural information, we need to address the users' ways of articulating their goals. Then we need to implement a minimal set of words to communicate to the users how to achieve their goals, perform tasks, and understand what they are doing with the software application itself.

References

Carroll, J. M. 1984. "Minimalist Training." *Datamation* 30:129–136.

Carroll, J. M. 1990. *The Nurnberg Funnel: Designing Minimalist Instruction for Practical Computer Skill.* Cambridge, MA: MIT Press.

Lazonder, A. W., and H. Van der Meij. 1995. "Error-Information in Tutorial Documentation: Supporting Users' Errors to Facilitate Initial Skill Learning." *International Journal of Human-Computer Studies* 42:185–206.

Redish, J. M. 1988. "Reading to Learn to Do." *Technical Writing Teacher* 14, no. 3:223–233.

7

Minimalism for Complex Tasks

Barbara Mirel

According to numerous studies, people in business sorely underuse their information-processing technologies (Bikson and Eveland 1987; Strassman 1990; Standard and Poor's 1994). They use these programs mainly for routine tasks such as entering data, calculating profit-loss statements, and maintaining customer lists and rarely use them for more strategic tasks or open-ended problems. As surveys show, despite the data being available, almost four-fifths of business users never use their software to determine staffing needs, decide on profitable investments, or reallocate resources (Standard and Poor's 1994). In part, people do not employ computer support for such problem-solving tasks because they lack adequate instruction in manipulating and customizing programs to serve their job-related purposes (Bikson and Eveland 1987).

Conventional documentation does not teach problem-solving computing so that users may become proficient in tailoring and adapting their programs to the specific demands of their complex tasks and problems. Complex tasks differ from routines such as data entry or standard accounting calculations because they are not performed the same way every time. For instance, deciding on the most advantageous investment is not formulaic; it depends on time, place, and circumstance. Such complex tasks involve many decision points and relationships among factors that are governed largely by surrounding conditions—for example, economic conditions, the politics of a situation, and hierarchical relationships. In addition, part of a problem-solving task is defining the problem itself, the outcomes of which can make or break users' success in reaching goals.

Businesses thrive on people's successful handling of complex tasks, and software capabilities unquestionably offer valuable ways to support and enhance such tasks. Unfortunately, proportionately few users are as competent and as facile as they could be in problem-solving computing. They might become more competent if documentation taught them to adapt software to the demands of complex tasks.

Typically, documentation instructs users in operating the functions and features of a program, assuming that these operations directly map onto users' tasks. Common documentation sections are "Deleting text," "Moving spreadsheet cells," "Inserting borders," and "Creating queries." By making program functions the topics and chapter titles of the instructional text, documentation writers represent users' work as synonymous with the tasks that programmers design into the software. In mapping program functions onto instructed tasks, documentation writers often convey, intentionally or not, the formal modeling bias of software engineering. Writers accept and communicate a vision of users' work as the sum of logically decomposed parts. They focus, as programmers do, on the components that are detailed enough to satisfy the demands and constraints of coding. In doing so, they conflate coding and instructing.

One effect of this formal modeling bias in instructional texts is a vision of intended readers as beginner users who have simple, discrete tasks to perform. The documentation presents tasks as routine steps and routine cognitive processes. These tasks are generic—performed the same way regardless of circumstance, priorities, or situation, and if users perform operations correctly, according to "formula," they are foolproof (Green, Schiele, and Payne 1986).

Minimalism stands as an alternate to the formal modeling bias so often embedded in conventional documentation. Like conventional documentation, most minimalist instructions focus on program-defined tasks and new users. Unlike formal modeling, however, minimalist documentation assumes that effective performance cannot be separated from what users bring to a task. Users bring their motivation, prior knowledge, experience, and exploratory approaches to learning. Given this assumption, minimalists believe that universal and foolproof performance is illusory because tasks involve serendipity, individualized inference, and unavoidable and often tangled errors. For minimalists, the basis for representing tasks is not formal logic but empirical evidence and realistic scenarios.

Minimalist manuals and documentation inspired by formal modeling both highlight program functions, or what I call throughout this chapter unit tasks, using it interchangeably with program-defined tasks. (I use the term *unit task* more loosely than software engineers do to mean the level of detail at which a task is context free, involves no open-ended problem solving, and is codable—for example, "edit text" and not only, as unit tasks are conceived in software engineering, "highlight text"). But the similarity ends at this shared emphasis on unit tasks. In sharp contrast to formal modeling, minimalist assumptions have the potential to lead writers to the core changes in attitude and belief that they need to adopt if they are to move from documenting routine tasks to instructing users in real-world complex tasks and problems.

Minimalism provides documentation writers with one of the best bridges that they have for moving from the familiar terrain of routine tasks to the uncharted territory of computing for complex tasks and problem solving. But minimalism does not address some of the important instructional issues related to learning and doing complex work. It does not, for example, focus explicitly on higher-level views of tasks than unit tasks and consequently neglects the social and contextual nature of complex work.

In this chapter, I analyze the strong contribution that minimalism has to make to the unexplored area of documenting complex tasks and problems. I argue that for complex tasks, documentation needs to represent tasks at a new level of generality. It must shift from a formal mapping perspective and unit task orientation to representations that accord with users' actual visions of their nonroutine work. Users conceptualize their complex tasks at a higher level of activity, a level at which tasks are contingent and shaped by context rather than generic and rule driven. Given the need to document tasks at this higher level, I examine three areas of design specifically relevant to instructions for complex tasks and problems: commonsense knowledge and pragmatic reasoning, cognitive flexibility, and advanced learning objectives. For each of these areas, I analyze what minimalism contributes and omits. I conclude by speculating on new documentation forms and content that are supported by minimalist ideas, approaches that I believe will be more appropriate for complex tasks and experienced users than current conventions, acknowledging as well potential problems for implementing them.

7.1   Representing Complex Tasks at the Appropriate Instructional Level

Documentation that is oriented to program-defined tasks may be crucial for getting new users up to speed on a program. But after as little as three months' experience, users often are ready to adapt their programs to the demands of their more unstructured and context-specific tasks and goals (Mirel 1992). These experienced users know their programs and electronic resources and realize that if they only knew how, they could do things they have never done before. They could facilitate employee reviews by retrieving employee data from multiple sources across their company. Or they could compare customer service records with quality assurance data to see if customer perceptions agree with test results. When users perform these complex tasks—complex in cognitive demands on and off the computer—they are driven, on the one hand, by the interpretive frameworks, priorities, and contextual conditions that shape their work and, on the other hand, by the abilities to read the state of the program in relation to their work goals. Seen in this way, documented tasks ought to be named "analyzing data for performance reviews" rather than "querying a database." But documentation rarely represents this higher-level task at which the messiness and unstructured nature of users' goals, plans, and actions become evident.

One example of a complex task comes from a project manager I interviewed. Her task was to persuade her division head to reallocate resources to the benefit of her project. She turned to the documentation of her database program for help in figuring out how to gather and analyze the data she needed in order to develop support for her proposed reallocation. The unit task orientation of her database documentation told her how to create and run queries and how to format reports. But for this user—and for most other experienced users performing open-ended problem-solving tasks—the actions of this task were greater than the sum of the composite program operations.

She had to decide which data to retrieve, in what order, with what relationships, and with what report formats. She changed her emphasis and direction as she worked, with results from one query prompting her to pursue a different line of reasoning to effect her purposes of persuasion. She wanted but could not find instruction for choosing the best way to set up multiple, interdependent queries, for changing search strategies based on particular factors, and for experimenting with different report formats, sort orders, and levels for persuasive effect. Basically, such complex computer-supported tasks involve problems that may be defined in a number of ways. They also have uncertain or changing goals, approaches that depend on situational variables, and choices between legitimate, contending options. For this user, the documentation thwarted her efforts: it implied a simpler (context-free) course of action than she needed to take.

Perhaps the strongest case against a unit task and formal modeling orientation in documentation for complex tasks is that this orientation is likely to hinder users from learning what they need to know in order to perform nonroutine, context-dependent tasks (Feltovich, Spiro, and Coulson 1993). As empirical findings from studies in instructional design reveal, when people who are ready for advanced learning receive instruction only in discrete, context-free parts of an activity or problem, this instruction actually impedes them from developing the situated knowing and reasoning that they need for solving complex problems.

Complexity admittedly is a relative concept. Users' perceptions of complexity and their corresponding mindfulness or automaticity in performing tasks change with experience and knowledge. Yet for the purposes of analyzing computer-supported work and designing documentation, it is possible to specify concrete qualities that distinguish complex from routine tasks. From empirical studies, researchers have found that the following qualities make complex tasks complex (Feltovich et al. 1993; Frese, 1987; Norman 1986; Nielsen et al. 1986; Pea, 1989; Anderson et al. 1993; Brown, Collins, and Duguid 1989, Ehn 1992):[1]

• Indeterminacy in goals and methods. Goals, plans, and methods vary with circumstances, contingencies, and evolving results. Goals are uncertain or fluid, with several possible ways to achieve them.

• Higher-order cognitive skill. Users coordinate their work in more than one problem space, for example, figuring out whether retrieved data are relevant and whether to change methods midstream. They construct knowledge by drawing on data from diverse sources, for example, from databases across functional units in an organization. Their tasks involve making many decisions between legitimate options based on contextual considerations. Finally, users do not simply accumulate knowledge; they integrate task and pragmatic knowledge in new ways, for instance, looking at data from different angles to argue for reallocating resources.

• Advanced learning and instruction. Users need to view tasks from different angles based on shifting priorities and contingencies, to examine the significance of slight variations in seemingly similar cases, and to apply ideas and dependencies flexibly based on the particulars of a situation. They learn by experiencing "cognitive disequilibrium," that is, by recognizing their own misconceptions, for example, misconceiving that changes in one file have no effect on data configurations in other files.

As both Hackos and Redish (this volume, chapters 6 and 8, respectively) aptly stress, even if a task such as creating a distribution list in e-mail is difficult for a new user, it is still routine (see Farkas, this volume, chapter 9) as well for a discussion of distribution lists). This task requires users to work only in a simple problem domain amid limited possibilities—possibilities that are defined largely by preset sequences of actions designed into the e-mail program. Users face few if any decisions or situationally determined choices. Nor do they need to coordinate cognitive resources. rearrange their pragmatic knowledge, or integrate what they know about sending messages in new ways. Even tasks that are difficult for users may still be routine.[2]

The issue of what level of detail writers use to analyze and describe tasks is vital for understanding the difference between documenting routine and complex tasks. Conventionally, print and online documentation organizes instruction around unit-level tasks, which are equivalent to routines. A higher-level orientation would categorize and name tasks by types of job activities or problems. Each type of activity or problem would consist of repertoires of actions for prototypical and exceptional approaches. As Redish argues, users have goals related to workplace responsibilities, and a unit-level operation is only one of many interdependent and conditional actions and strategies. Researchers have begun to typify some computer-supported complex tasks and problems, revealing that it is feasible to document these tasks at a higher level than unit tasks (Brooks 1991). By representing tasks as classes of job activities or problems, writers can address the contextual and technological factors that shape users' work.

This new area of developing documentation for complex tasks involves an audience that as Hackos notes (this volume, chapter 6) has been neglected by most documentation. This audience comprises users who are more than beginners but less than experts. They are ready for advanced learning and for gaining control over their programs for their own purposes. Instructional designers know less about this group of learners than about novices or experts, yet findings from recent studies reveal that the learning needed for complex and routine tasks is different in kind, not only degree. Training for complexity requires new instructional forms and content, with writers needing to redefine the boundaries of documentation to accommodate this new audience, these users' adaptive computing needs, and their tendency to represent their work as types of job activities or problems (Anderson 1994). The following example, based on findings from a longitudinal field study that I am conducting, describes some of these prototypical traits of a common complex business task: managing and accounting for program costs.

Case Example: Analyzing Financial Statements

Analyzing financial statements, a fundamental activity in most businesses, involves retrieving and interpreting financial data in order to identify the extent to which project costs are running under, over, or at budget at any given time. This activity also involves responding to problems or red flags by tracing them to their sources and preventing problems by taking a big-picture view and discovering opportunities for creative readjustments. Complex to begin with because of multiple decisions, problem spaces, and contextual considerations, these tasks can be even more confounding when managers are in charge of program budgets that split costs and share personnel across functions and cost centers.

My observations and interviews with the program managers of fifteen programs in a research and development laboratory reveal that all managers across functions and programs conduct certain prototypical tasks when analyzing financial reports:

- Look at the costs to date at a summary and detail level.
- Compare year-to-date costs to budgeted costs.
- Identify overruns and underruns.
- Identify aberrations and trends.
- Drill down to more detail for problem areas and potential causes.
- Solve problems by looking at numerous organization-wide possibilities.

Although managers universally conduct these tasks, they do not all do so in the same way. At every turn, managers face choices. They need to decide which data to select at what level of detail and how to relate and display the numbers for the multipronged analysis that they need to conduct. These choices hinge on many external issues: managers' immediate purposes and situational demands, the practices and conventions of their program teams areas, the structures of their functional areas, their insight into their own organization, and their skills and knowledge in designing data tables for multipurpose uses.

Managers' choices also involve technical considerations. Software supports analyzing financial reports and looking more closely at key data through querying, sorting, and reporting functions. My observations and interviews suggest that this activity is synergistic. No formulaic or universal set of operators, methods, or selection rules will adequately instruct users in this task. The use of the technology is intricately intertwined with contextual factors. Users must understand program capabilities in relation to their purposes. They need to know the effects of their actions on program states and the screen cues to look for as they shift to new search strategies when old ones do not produce the results they need.

It may seem that so many variables make this level of task too confounding to document, yet it is possible to analyze and represent prototypical tasks in order to help users learn based on how they represent their work. In interviews, managers stated that they wished documentation represented this job-level view, noting that otherwise (in documentation oriented to program-defined tasks) too many of the issues that help them determine which program interactions to undertake are omitted.

Task Purposes	Why are my monthly costs higher than my budgeted costs?
Analytical Strategies	Look at different likely sources of the problem, guided by: • Precedent • A knowledge of the program • A knowledge of company purchase and charging practices • A knowledge of effort distribution policies
Task Actions	1. Search problems to their likely sources: • Errors in purchasing or inventory data • Complications in effort charged to more than1 cost center • Unanticipated needs for program resources 2. Access the appropriate databases and construct the right questions to "drill down" into sources of the problem.
Knowledge Needed for Relating Tasks to Programs	Need to know company data, how to access it, how to relate data across departments, and how to improvise when no direct operations exist. Need to move repeatedly between analyzing retrieved data and drilling down or between expanding into a new query and analyzing its direction based on results.

Figure 7.1
Finding the cause of a cost overrun

Figure 7.1 presents one prototypical task that is part of the activity of analyzing financial statements: finding the cause of a cost overrun. Detailed are users' purposes, their task choices and program operations, and the instruction that they seek in order to match the situational aspects of their choices to the uses of program capabilities.

As this example shows, problem solving and computer interactions do not occur independent of each other. Knowing their data and their businesses, users anticipate that they will pursue many searches and lines of inquiry. With future queries in mind, they try to set up early program operations and search results to accommodate later pursuits and possible changes in direction. In addition, users gather data from diverse sources and need to learn how to suspend a search temporarily, conduct concurrent searches into other sources, and add the results to the first search. Finally, users look at the same cost data from various angles and want to learn how to activate and compare many displays of the same data at once. None of the strategies, explanations, and integrated procedures that tie together program uses and situational factors is represented in current unit task–oriented documentation. In the next section, I explore how minimalist design principles help to address many of the integrative issues that users need to learn in order to conduct their complex, computer-supported tasks and problems.

Elements of Complex Task Performance in Relation to Minimalist Principles

Many advocates of minimalism have asked whether minimalist principles are robust enough for complex tasks. Van der Meij (1992) poses the question outright, asking, "What about advanced skill development? ... There is the question how the minimal manual can be made suitable for advanced skills development if, indeed, such *adaptations are possible without compromising the approach*"(emphasis added, p. 15). To answer this question, writers may interpret what van der Meij means by "the minimalist approach" in two ways: (1) the traits of actual minimalist texts as reflections of minimalist principles and strategies or (2) the minimalist principles and strategies themselves. Drawing this fine distinction is important because each interpretation leads to contrary answers to van der Meij's question.

If the minimalist approach means the first way, the traits of actual minimalist texts, then adapting it to the instructional demands of complex tasks will be difficult. At present, with few exceptions, minimalist texts are oriented to program-defined tasks and new users; the content, organizing logic, and textual design are insufficient for complex tasks and experienced users, and they probably require wholesale revamping, not just adaptations. If, by contrast, writers define the minimalist approach by the second way, its principles, strategies, and design rationales, then minimalism offers valuable insights for documenting complex tasks and fostering advanced learning. In many ways, minimalist assumptions about users, task performance, and instructional design target the same issues that researchers argue should direct training for advanced skill development and open-ended problem solving. My analysis of minimalism focuses on this view of minimalism as principles and strategies, not actual textual traits.

Fundamental tenets of minimalism—what Carroll (1990) calls a design-based theory—reflect ideas vital for instruction in complex tasks: that no "one best system" of knowledge and performance exists because each user brings to a task different prior knowledge and experiences, so that any initial design for documentation is bound to be mismatched to actual users' instructional expectations and in need of revision. Minimalists expect procedures to vary according to individuals and situations. They design for plan-as-you-go, opportunistic performances in contrast to formal mapping notions of users engaging in plan-in-advance and rule-based activity. These notions of learning and doing coincide with users' needs for complex tasks. But documentation developers still need to know more about this world of complex tasks and the designs for instruction that may adequately support problem-solving computing. Insights are available from recent work by learning theorists (especially situated cognition and activity theorists), instructional designers, and interface developers.

Studies in these areas indicate that documentation developers must shift their conception of what constitutes a task from program functions to job-related work in context. For this higher-level perspective on tasks, users' actions and interpretations depend on the social context. Some of the know-how included in this higher-level view of tasks is difficult to articulate into rules (for example, "drawing to scale"). Rules satisfy unit tasks—for instance, the drawing of a straight line. But for drawing to scale, this straight line action represents only "the cruder part of the expert's skill" (Schön 1983; Bereiter 1991).

Moreover, in documenting a higher-level (complex) view of tasks, writers need to attend to more than the ways in which program operations support task performance. Programs also may enhance performance (Carroll 1990; Brooks 1991). Writers take on serious responsibilities when they select content and design to instruct people in the uses of software. Their choices help construct users' approaches to their work, the direction that it takes, and the extent to which users understand how to control their software for complex purposes.

In shifting from a unit task perspective to one focused on types of job activities, writers reorient their own conceptions of tasks, learning, and instruction. Researchers in instructional design, situated learning, and interface design have analyzed these reorienting demands of complex tasks and the instructional strategies that are effective for them. Characteristically, performing complex tasks involves three elements: (1) commonsense or pragmatic knowledge, (2) cognitive flexibility, and (3) advanced learning. Minimalism, with its strong emphasis on learning and doing, has something to say about many aspects of these elements, and it complements and enriches instructional strategies proposed by researchers who adhere to different schools of thought. The following discussion presents the relevance of minimalism to these elements of complex task performance, identifying aspects of complex tasks that minimalism does not address, as well.

7.2   Addressing Commonsense or Pragmatic Knowledge

Elements of Complex Task Performance

The first element is that decisions and practices in complex tasks depend on social and cultural context; therefore, commonsense or pragmatic knowledge is vital to performance.

According to conventional wisdom, routine tasks require people to know only the logical parts of their task and the standardized steps for interacting with a program to carry it out. This understanding—what documentation traditionally strives to impart—rests on propositional and procedural knowledge or respectively, the semantics and syntax of a task (Ehn 1992; Rheinfrank, Hartman, and Wasserman 1992). The semantics of a task are the context-free properties and events that comprise its "objective" meaning, a meaning that is modeled in the program—for example, the structures and symbols of querying and the corresponding program structures, arrangements, functions, states, and commands enabled in each state. In finding the causes of cost overruns, the semantics of the querying task include the relational tables that users see and the search logic that the program requires for processing. By instructing users in task semantics, documentation developers intend to help them construct adequate mental models of their task as it connects to the program. Task syntax goes hand in hand with semantics. Equally formalizable, it includes procedures and command syntax, as well as deep grammars and production rules of task activities and program processing—for instance, the "rules" for writing search statements.

Whether knowing task semantics and syntax alone is sufficient for routine tasks and in what proportions have been heatedly debated (Winograd and Flores 1986; Kieras 1990; Wright 1990; Briggs 1990; Human-Computer Interaction 1994). The terms of this debate shift, however, once the focus turns to complex tasks. For complex tasks, specialists in cognition, learning, and human-computer interaction largely agree that people unquestionably need more than semantic and syntactic knowledge. They also need pragmatic knowledge. Pragmatics involve knowing the conditions under which certain meanings, methods, and actions are (and are not) useful and appropriate (Jacobsen and Spiro in press; Spiro et al. 1992; Rheinfrank, Hartman, and Wasserman 1992; Anderson et al. 1993). Pragmatics are the nonformal aspects of work that cannot be formulated semantically or syntactically.

Pragmatic knowledge involves knowing one's way around in a situation—knowing, from a rich store of practical, social, and cultural knowledge, conditions for interpreting, approaching, and conducting a task in one way rather than another. Pragmatic knowledge is tied to a genuine contextual problem or purpose at hand. For complex, computer-supported tasks, task pragmatics involve the program capabilities that are advantageous for specific contextual purposes. To find the cause of a cost overrun, users decide how extensively to search database files across divisions by assessing pragmatically if the overhead of learning is worth it, given the likelihood that another division is causing the problem. In debates about complex tasks, arguments often center on issues related to pragmatic knowledge. Specialists argue about what parts of a task may be framed objectively (formally) and what parts have meaning only in relation to individuals' situated purposes and actions. They also debate whether pragmatic or tacit knowledge can be taught or if it changes once texts articulate and frame it as "teachable" heuristic strategies.

Analysts variously have discussed the pragmatic dimension of complex tasks as commonsense knowledge, tacit knowledge, supplemental knowledge, background know-how, experiential semantics, enactive cognition, pragmatic reasoning, and practical reasoning (Collins 1987; Rheinfrank, Hartman, and Wasserman 1992; Varela, Thompson, and Rosch 1991;

Anderson et al. 1993; Woods and Hollnagel 1988). Although nuances of difference distinguish these concepts, broadly they all communicate the notion that for complex tasks, meaning does not inhere in program and task objects but in how people use them. People's uses—and, by extension, task meanings—are shaped by a network of pragmatic factors, such as organizational and technological constraints; conventional practices in one's work group and workplace; shared, taken-for-granted realities; interpersonal relations; the distribution of labor and authority; and priorities about time, money, and other resources (Rheinfrank, Hartman, and Wasserman 1992; Anderson et al. 1993).

This tacit understanding of how to perform and how to weigh choices in various circumstances is commonsense or everyday knowledge. Commonsense knowledge involves knowing a situation and its limits and understanding the information and activities that are relevant to specific social relations and why. This knowledge is largely inexplicable but encompasses the vast, culturally encoded abilities that people use to recognize patterns and discrepancies and "to use facts, rules, and heuristics in different ways and toward different ends based on their situations and groups" (Collins 1987, p. 357). For example, users' choices for tracing cost overruns may be influenced by an array of situations and social relations beyond the overhead of learning. Program managers may just as likely decide that it is not worth searching across divisions for data if they do not want to jeopardize relations between divisions once a searched division feels "accused."

For computer-supported, complex tasks, users are guided pragmatically by local experience, socially accepted norms, and the negotiated meanings and patterns of their everyday worklives. Pragmatically, they ask, for instance: "What difference does it make to my work group, to the competitive standing of my organization, or to my own intellectual engagement if I frame the problem this way rather than that way?" "Suppose I analyze information in this new way. Will my organization actually do something with it?" And, "Is this approach worth the time, effort, and learning that I have to invest in it?" (Ehn 1988). They reason practically about the results of program interactions and the merits of projected actions, concentrating more on the significance and relevance of output than on the "truth" of the inner processes and structures that generate it. Pragmatically, users are concerned with expressing social and organizational interests more than with finding one true answer or one right course of action.

Pragmatic knowledge largely goes unnoticed. It is fairly intuitive (beneath the surface) as long as people experience no conflict or problem in their work activities (Berger and Luckmann 1967, p. 43). When conflict occurs, pragmatic considerations rise to the surface, and all task knowledge becomes negotiable. In the cost overrun example, if managers believe that another division is the culprit causing the overrun problem, they face a conflict that makes their rationales and motives explicit. They want to retrieve the cross-divisional data yet are reluctant to jeopardize relations. In grappling with this conflict, managers may resolve to search for data across divisions inventively, perhaps inferring the information from other sources. Because these managers' methods are tied to contextual issues, instruction in the formalizable mechanisms of data searching will not answer their needs. They need instruction that helps them put together circuitous routes to search for data.

From this vantage point, propositional and procedural knowledge are posits rather than truths. They provide probable knowledge that users should manipulate as they shape their actions around contextual opportunities and constraints. These posits also provide a reasonable basis for choosing goals and methods and for predicting if they will succeed. But from a pragmatic point of view, predictions of success hinge on the experience of trial and error and correction.

Trial and error is pragmatic because users are likely to make practically based best guesses about the current state of a task based more on their immediate impression of screen information than on some formal, preconceived, mental model of their goal structure and methods (Mayes et al. 1988; Payne 1991; Kitajima and Polson 1992). During trial and error, users are likely to make trade-offs in one place for gains in another, needing to juggle many different factors related to a whole task process (Russell et al. 1993). This pragmatic reasoning is difficult to address in instructions because writers have to deal with users' complicated, conditional web of considerations.

Research shows that instructional designers are mistaken if they presume that the best approach for dealing with users who face numerous, entangled factors—pragmatic and otherwise—is to teach what a program can do and let users figure out and integrate for themselves the information that fits their individual purposes and frames of reference (Jonassen and Grabinger 1990). In fact, learners are demonstrably less likely to learn when they rather than teachers (documentation writers) control instructional variables—provided, that is, that teachers control and structure information effectively for users' actual context-based purposes. Also, learning occurs best when instruction progressively builds explanations throughout task interactions, at first perhaps offering conceptual and procedural knowledge about the task and then establishing frameworks for interrelated problems to help learners clarify what to do, how, when, and why (Collins 1987).

In their information needs for complex tasks, users are more specific and selective than for routine tasks; they resist comprehensiveness and want only the information useful to their purposes (which is not the same as saying that they want scant information; they want the array of information that suits the complexity, but they want it selected and framed in the right way at the right time for the right purpose. See, for example, the search-focusing approach for work in context in Girill and Luk 1992; Granda, Helstead-Nussloch, and Winters 1990). Researchers in instructional design and interface development have proposed the following instructional strategies to accommodate users' needs for practical knowledge to perform complex tasks:

• Center instruction on pragmatic issues, addressing such questions as what early strategies are essential for later ones, what outcomes are worth what amounts of time and effort for specific situational conditions, or how revised task purposes alter choices and sequencing of functions (Jonassen and Wang 1993).

• Highlight the dynamic aspects of an interface in relation to holistic views of problem situations, for example, the effects of commands on each other or the short- and long-range consequences of each set of possible actions (Payne 1991; Kitajima and Polson 1992).

• Focus on a program triggering events relevant to users' social and organizational experiences of their work, highlighting what users do in their jobs, not what program functions do (for example, focusing on "looking for opportunities to share resources to stay on budget" rather than on generic querying and reporting) (Rheinfrank et al. 1992).

• Design dialogue and case study approaches as a rich means for capturing key patterns of possible approaches, with such instructional approaches helping users to move their tacit knowledge into the category of articulated heuristics and inferences (Collins 1987).

Minimalism

Minimalists' pragmatic bent is evident in their iterative and empirical methodology for testing and revising interfaces and instructions. This methodology, in turn, is based on the fundamental minimalist precept that instruction works only if users are motivated to learn and perform. Instruction itself should evoke and sustain this motivation. Minimalist principles for designing motivation into instruction stress the need to start users immediately on work that is meaningful to them. Implicitly, meaningful work is tied to users' pragmatic considerations and the extent to which they perceive they control decisions about pragmatic issues.

Another minimalist assumption that relates to users' pragmatic knowledge is the notion that users need useful, not comprehensive, information. Minimalist principles direct writers to focus on documenting program responses in relation to users' goals. In minimalist design, instructions strive to prompt users to coordinate screen displays with the documentation and to learn from the documentation how to interpret the flow of information from the interface for their purposes (Mayes et al. 1988). The challenge for writers is to discover and document what constitutes this useful information. This challenge drives the design methodology of iterative testing.

Minimalist views on iteratively testing and translating findings into texts rest on assumptions and philosophical leanings that are directly in line with pragmatic perspectives on performing complex tasks. Minimalists appreciate the unpredictability of human behavior. They do not set error-free performance as a goal. In design, they start with the premises that people come to computer-supported work with different levels and ranges of prior knowledge and experience, that users raise questions and seek solutions that software designers may not imagine, and that because of users' idiosyncratic interpretations and subsequent actions, they often get entangled in stacks of errors that defy preset foolproof procedures for resolution.

Minimalists understand tasks, user approaches, and the knowledge that users need by studying users' trial-and-error performances. Recently, another valued minimalist methodology has become scenario-based design. In scenario-based design, developers run or simulate numerous what-if cases of users' likely work-related goals and actions. From these use scenarios, developers determine the design decisions and trade-offs needed for accommodating projected, realistic use situations. For instance, a scenario for using a bibliographic program may be that a user wants the program to allow her to enter only partial information about a reference item because that is all the information that she has. The trade-off is that this user may lose track of her partial records if she retrieves a group of references related to a field that is still blank in some of the incomplete records (Rosson and Carroll 1995).

Nothing in the concept of scenario-based design ensures a focus on tasks at a higher level of detail than unit tasks. Some minimalist designers have experimented with usage scenarios for complex tasks (Rosson and Carroll 1995; Johnson, Johnson, and Wilson 1995). Yet many designers use narrow scenarios that simply present accounts of users' interacting with specific sets of computer operators for unit-level tasks, stripped of all social and cultural context. Bødker (1991) argues for a higher-level view of tasks, claiming that in instructions, one of the most underdeveloped areas is helping users to organize, control, and coordinate their real-world work, such as helping them to find and formulate problems or to manipulate output and determine which version comes closest to a goal. As a methodology, scenario-based design makes an important contribution to this challenge of documenting complex tasks regardless of the level at which designers describe a task. It reinforces the notion of design as a process of trade-offs tied to users' key concerns when they reason pragmatically about their task goals and methods.

Minimalist principles that run parallel to strategies for pragmatic instruction proposed by researchers in complex tasks and problem solving include the following (van der Meij and Carroll 1995):

• Choose an action-oriented approach and a focus on real goals and tasks to encourage users to get started immediately on meaningful work.
• Support reading-to-do by slashing verbiage so that users are not overwhelmed by excessive information that is comprehensive without being useful.

• Encourage and guide exploration, especially through wording that draws users' attention to the screen and links displays with instruction.

• Anchor the tool in the task domain by ensuring that components of instruction reflect the task structure and the trade-offs involved in the uses of various program operators.

7.3   Fostering Cognitive Flexibility

Elements of Complex Task Performance

The second element of performing complex tasks is that they demand cognitive flexibility—an ability to take multiple points of view, draw information from diverse sources and cases, and integrate knowledge in new ways.

Key characteristics of complex tasks are ill-structured goals, methods, or knowledge domains. Inseparable from the contexts in which they take place, complex tasks have problem spaces with broader and more ambiguous boundaries than routine tasks have. Numerous factors, relationships, and interpretations come into play. Uncertainty and flux surround users' choices and decisions. To figure out a course of action, users often compare their task situation with precedents, but one-to-one correspondences do not work. Slight variations across seemingly similar cases have significant meanings. For example, cost overruns in two different months may have everything in common except for one surrounding factor: in the second month, the organization introduced an automated effort reporting system. Based on this variation, program managers may generate an altogether new hypothesis about the cause for the second month, speculating that overruns resulted from a "buggy" effort system. The minor variation of a new effort system may signal the need to retrieve data across cost centers at a more detailed level than may at first seem warranted by the data in the financial statement alone. To deal with the multiple layers and nuances of complex problems, users need to develop flexible knowledge structures (Granda, Halstead-Nussloch, and Winters 1990). They need to be sensitive to these nuances and flexibly rearrange their plans and actions accordingly (Spiro et al. 1992; Feltovich, Spiro, and Coulson 1993).

This cognitive flexibility enables users to tackle one of the most confounding dimensions of complex problem solving: integrating knowledge in new ways, not just acquiring and applying it by rote. To integrate knowledge, people need to understand more than the separate composite pieces of information that make up a task in a formal modeling sense. Moreover, they need to "experience" the structures and logic that make ideas relate to each other, not simply read about these conceptual relationships in prose or visuals. As Jonassen and Wang (1993) find, "Merely providing structural cues ... merely browsing through a knowledge base does not engender deep enough processing to result in meaningful learning" (pp. 6–7). For the deep processing that occurs when people integrate new knowledge into prior learning, users must actively manipulate ideas, construct models and patterns themselves, and assess the implications of various versions. This interactivity fosters cognitive flexibility.

Users' choices for how to put ideas and processes together are shaped by situational priorities, opportunities, and costs. As Anderson et al. (1993) explain, the effect of introducing this "social dimension of action is that actions get freighted with meaning ... What someone is doing is open to interpretation ... the potential list of descriptions is endless ... [and finding] a stopping rule to fix what any task is [calls for] a foreshortening of ... the pragmatics of a task, the highly contextualized social descriptions of courses of action" (p. 1001).

For these socially defined tasks, users need to assemble and reassemble knowledge and techniques to fit circumstances and contingencies, and they need to be guided in setting boundaries and stopping points. They need what Salomon and Perkins (1989) call "high-road transfer": the ability to apply what they know to connected yet dissimilar cases by consciously selecting and abstracting relevant knowledge from one situation to another. For example, when users such as the project manager who argued for reallocating resources want to retrieve and relate data for persuasive purposes, they set boundaries according to what counts as evidence in a given situation as well at what ethically limits benefiting one project at the expense of another.

This high-road transfer differs from the "low-road transfer" that happens all the time in routine and automatically performed work. In low-road transfer, people unintentionally and spontaneously transfer well-practiced skills from one prototypical situation to another without needing to be mindful of the structure or consequences of their behavior. Many aspects of work run smoothly due to low-road transfer—for example, filling out administrative forms and generating routine summaries. Problems occur, however, when people apply low-road transfer inappropriately to complex tasks. For example, a project manager is unlikely to achieve the goal of getting a manager to reallocate resources if she simply gathers and presents stock facts and figures when the situation demands a more mindful approach to argument, support, and persuasion.

The instructional approaches and learning efforts required for automatic versus mindful transfer necessarily differ. Researchers have proposed the following instructional strategies to foster cognitive flexibility and a high-road transfer of learning:

• Develop users' situation perception, for instance, reminding them of previous or analogous types of problems or job-related tasks, highlighting exceptions and variations, or bringing interdependencies to the fore (Pea 1989; Miyata and Norman 1986).

• Highlight aspects of a task situation that are not prototypical so that users become more mindful of principles, ideas, or procedures that may be relevant to other situations (Salomon and Perkins 1989).

Minimalism

Minimalists have their own version of cognitive flexibility. It is tied to their belief that users do not need to acquire lockstep techniques and explanations as much as they need to concentrate on their task and software at the right level of representation. Even for routine tasks, minimalists presume that users do not necessarily follow sets of simple steps. Instead, users proceed through various procedures in any order, opening the way for unpredictable errors. Given this view, minimalists believe that the role of instruction is to help users see the meaning of a program for their work based on their actual experiences with the program.

For users to perceive this relationship between their goals and their program interactions, they must focus on the appropriate level of representation. The levels of generality describing tasks in instruction signal to users the corresponding mode and level of learning in which they should engage. Most minimalist manuals include high-level goals and plans, mid-level choices and methods, low-level commands, menu options, and (at times though rarely) keystrokes (Diaper and Johnson 1989). Recent minimalist instructions such as the View Matcher tutorial for Smalltalk programming expand on these representations of work to include rich contexts relevant to task activities as well (Carroll and Rosson 1996).

As minimalist testing reveals, users are more likely to gain control of a program and make inferences that transfer to other tasks if they move at the right time and in the right degree among many levels of representation—among exact steps, a larger picture of why a program responds as it, and task goals (Carroll and Aaronson 1989). By shifting back and forth from high to low levels of representation, users form different impressions of their experiences with a program and of their task goals than if they work consistently at the same step-by-step level. The minimalist concern with helping users to manipulate their points of view and knowledge structures captures many of the same issues of cognitive flexibility discussed by analysts of complex tasks and problem solving.

Yet the social dimension that Anderson et al. (1993) discuss—the dimension that freights actions with meaning and calls for cognitive flexibility—is missing from minimalist design perspectives. For minimalists, the main context for studying users' attention, actions, and shifts in perspective is the technological context: its potentially confusing program states, the extent to which "invisible" interdependencies cause tangled errors. Minimalists do not address the social, political, and cultural contexts in which users work, but minimalist documentation does strive to model the level of representation that helps users move back and forth from detailed to global views of their work. Instruction aims at helping users generalize from their specific program experiences the behaviors associated with competent task performance, the unexpected display situations or impasses that arise when performing that task, and strategies for overcoming them.

From a minimalist perspective, even when users perform routine tasks, they shift their goals, subgoals, operations, and methods according to what they see on screen displays, how they interpret what they see, and how their subsequent actions change the display once again. Minimalists are keenly aware that users do not notice aspects of screens that are irrelevant to their goals or expectations. This neglect by users reinforces the need for instructions to direct users' attention to the right level and focus of inquiry (Carroll 1990). This assumed interplay between instruction and users' trial-and-error and sensemaking at the interface underlies what has become an adage of minimalism: design for learning by doing.

Minimalist design principles that focus on coordinating users' attention between program operations and the documentation involve two of the principles noted above as being relevant to practical knowledge as well:

• Guide exploration to draw users' attention to the screen and to link it to the instruction.

• Anchor the tool in the task domain, with an emphasis this time on representing knowledge at a high enough level to facilitate actions and on representing multiple views of the same issue.

A central issue related to cognitive complexity but not yet covered by minimalism is:

• A need to expand instructions to include knowledge representations related to the social and cultural contexts of users' work.

7.4   Advanced Learning Objectives and Obstacles to Achieving Them

Elements of Complex Task Performance
The third element is that once people seek software support for complex tasks and nondeterministic problems, they need advanced, not introductory, instruction so that they learn to reason flexibly and integrate multiple levels and types of knowledge.

Complex tasks require advanced learning, and users' success in these tasks actually is thwarted if the instruction they receive keeps them at an introductory level (Feltovich, Spiro, and Coulson 1993). Introductory instruction typically teaches users discrete and basic concepts, principles, and processes, and it incrementally builds to larger, subsuming ideas or repertoires of action. It is hierarchical and teaches knowledge in pieces, with the whole being equal to the sum of the parts. By contrast, advanced learning involves creating relationships across knowledge domains (networks or heterarchies rather than hierarchies) (Jonassen and Wang 1993). For example, to evaluate product quality and customer satisfaction, users may define quality and satisfaction through a number of variables and diverse relationships, in the process drawing data from diverse sources. Advanced learning also involves discovering exceptions rather than rules and responding with flexibility to messy situations (Pea 1989).

For problem-solving computing, users need advanced learning. They need to learn to construct multiple approaches to a problem or goal and to draw on data from numerous sources based on the demands of situational variables. They also need to speculate on solutions tied to different points of view, draw a wide range of inferences, and interpret multiple metaphors or analogies for a single situation (Jacobson and Spiro 1995). In addition, users need to understand unintuitive relationships and dependencies between program functions and the implications of these relationships for their purposes. Finally, they need to hypothesize many possible causes for errors or causal chains, including causes that may have occurred well before they detected them. In sum, for complex tasks and problems, users need to explore a richly textured landscape of knowledge, charting different courses for different occasions and creating what Spiro et al. (1992) call a "criss-crossed landscape of knowledge." This landscape is multidimensional and replete with meaning, unlike the single dimensionality and literalism of rule-driven unit tasks, the common focus of conventional documentation.

Attempts to introduce advanced learning often stymie learners. Studies show that learners are impeded in their efforts to solve open-ended problems or ill-structured tasks by their tendency to misconceive complex situations because they oversimplify problems, a habit of thought assimilated from introductory learning. Users oversimplify when they separate concepts that are actually connected, understand an activity from only one point of view, and assume that program modes are static instead of seeing them as the result of dynamic unseen, interlinked processes (Feltovich, Spiro, and Coulson 1993). To accomplish complex tasks and inquire into complicated problems, users need to overcome their misconceptions, no small feat since they often are unaware that their ideas are mistaken in the first place. Yet the "cognitive disequilibrium" of challenging accepted beliefs and conceptions is a necessary and vital part of advanced learning (Pea 1989).

Other obstacles that impede users from learning and performing complex tasks include inert knowledge (an inability to apply knowledge flexibly to a given situation) and lost knowledge (a failure to retain prior learning) (Pea 1989). Instructionally, these obstacles cannot be overcome by writers' redoubling their efforts to be comprehensive. Users need guidance in posing the right questions and in constructing and using the right knowledge for a given set of circumstances. Instructional designers and interface developers offer the following strategies for developing training for advanced learning and for overcoming the obstacles that may thwart it:

• Provide multiple examples and cross-cutting cases; link cases thematically so that learners may assemble concepts and procedures in diverse ways and create different meanings for different purposes (Jacobson and Spiro 1995).

• Teach users to anticipate and manage errors, helping them to understand misconceptions that underlie impasses and provoking them to resist quick fixes and instead entertain many possibilities at once (Frese and Altmann 1989).

• Directly challenge users' misconceptions, creating the cognitive disequilibrium necessary for people to tackle complexity, for instance, highlight contradictions, paradoxes, and trade-offs (Pea 1989).

Minimalism

Minimalism has not usually been applied to designs for advanced learning, nor do minimalist assumptions and principles overtly address this learning. In fact, most minimalist manuals target program-defined tasks and introductory learning. This focus on unit tasks can be seen in a recently produced minimalist manual for a speech recognition program. In this manual, procedures for correcting errors are suggestive and exploratory rather than rote, as is customary in minimalist instruction. But they are nonetheless introductory, providing discrete procedures and repairs rather than guiding users to manage many hypotheses. The manual tells readers, "What you have to do is understand what action did occur and how to tell Speech Manager what the correct action should be" (Karat 1995). In introductory fashion, these instructions are not concerned with uncovering and challenging misconceptions.

Two recent trends associated with minimalist perspectives reveal contributions that minimalism can make to instruction for advanced learning. First, some advocates of minimalism have investigated (from the perspective of a technological context) the aspects of tasks that instructions should represent for different levels of learning. Black, Kay, and Soloway (1989) find that new users need introductory learning and benefit from instructions that teach program operators, commands, and repertoires—that is, what a program does and how to map goals to the actions that the program allows.

Advanced users, by contrast need instruction in combining clusters of actions or methods into purposeful plans and in constructing compound plans that address the contingencies and decisions of open-ended tasks and problems. For complex tasks, users often have to reorganize their knowledge into new "links between goals and plans" (Black, Kay, and Soloway 1989, p. 49). For instance, for the goal of proving the benefits of reallocating resources, users may have several plans for retrieving and relating data. They need help in assembling these plans and assigning priorities in ways that will best achieve their goal. Often the strategies that people use depend on software constraints and capabilities. Managing contextual plans and goals and the technology becomes a critical focus in this instruction for advanced learning. Instead of providing rote actions and rules for discrete, context-free tasks, advanced instruction needs to help users figure out what to attend to when many different things are going on at once, what factors and relationships are salient in this field of attention, and how this salience affects goals, plans, and methods.

A second trend that more concretely reveals the potential of minimalist approaches for advanced learning involves recent efforts to design minimalist-inspired interfaces and online tutorials for complex tasks and subject matters. Rosson, Carroll, and Sweeney (1991), for example, have used minimalist principles to develop the View Matcher tutorial for Smalltalk programming, also called the Minimalist Tutorial and Tools for Smalltalk (MiTTS). This tutorial, framed as games with scenario episodes and vignettes, is presented through split windows. Each window is divided into four panes, offering users four different perspectives on any single episode. MiTTS promotes advanced learning by prompting users to deliberate about trade-offs and encouraging them to explore the effects of arranging perspectives in one way rather than another. Carlson (1992) similarly uses multipane windows to present online instruction for difficult scientific subjects, citing minimalism as a strong influence on her multiperspective design.

These trends tie minimalist instruction to complex tasks and advanced learning. Minimalism also bridges to complexity in its notions about learning through error. These notions overlap with the precepts of advanced learning. Because users perform tasks and interpret the flow of information from the interface idiosyncratically, minimalists have no illusions about foolproof instructions. Errors are inevitable; in fact, they are intrinsic to tasks, even to seemingly formulaic and formalistically foolproof tasks. Empirical studies show that at least a third of users' time is spent in error recovery, with users often needing to untangle a series or stack of mistakes that have accumulated well before users ever recognize that a problem has occurred (Carroll 1990). This prominence of errors leads minimalists to place a high priority on documenting specific error recovery information, stressing that this information should be based on an inventory of demonstrated user impasses.

Minimalist design principles relevant to advanced learning include the following:

• Accommodate users' needs to reorganize knowledge repeatedly for their shifting interpretations of plans, goals, actions, and situations, stressing, for instance, conditions for pursuing one plan rather than another.
• Help users monitor their own activities by providing multiple perspectives and by cueing or flagging where to search for answers, what knowledge is needed, whether a method or outcome satisfies targeted circumstances, and what to look for to be sure that outcomes are "close enough" (Briggs 1990; van der Meij and Carroll 1995).
• Support error recognition and recovery by providing the specific information that users need for demonstrated, error-prone actions. Studies have shown that neither how-a-system-works explanations nor how-to-do-it procedures alone are adequate for error recovery (Carroll and Aaronson 1989; Black, Kay, and Soloway 1989). Given only how-it-works explanations, users often fail to infer the right procedures; procedures alone result in users generating faulty rationales for why they are doing what they are doing. Slashing the verbiage does not involve outlawing one type of information or another. Users need both: compound yet brief help on what to do and why to do it.

Minimalism has not yet addressed several advanced learning objectives and obstacles as follows:

• A need to articulate explicitly and challenge underlying misconceptions or contending beliefs so that users strengthen their abilities to diagnose or anticipate errors and to abstract and transfer insights to other situations.
• Cues for self-monitoring that raise questions about what constitutes an answerable problem and how certain goals and methods bind users to certain people, practices, and interests.
• A move away from instructions that reflect the design rationales for program functions and a move toward documentation structured around types of business problems or job-related tasks, perhaps in the form of rich organizational scenarios.

7.5   Summarizing the Relevance of Minimalism for Complex Tasks

Minimalist assumptions and design principles are compatible with many of the qualities associated with learning and performing complex tasks. Minimalism is not usually applied for these purposes, but it overlaps with many of the instructional strategies that other researchers propose for complexity:

• Task pragmatics receiving a prominent position, with learning tied to doing and with instructional information based on demonstrated usefulness and significance, not coverage and one universal best system.
• Users coordinating the flow of information from a display with the levels of inquiry and learning represented in the documentation.
• Instruction evoking and supporting inference making, interpretations, and generalization—all mindful abstractions dependent on users dynamically representing their work on a micro- and macrolevel, thereby laying the groundwork for high-road transfer.
• Instruction helping users learn through anomalies and speculations about what to do about them.
• Instruction providing multiple perspectives on a single issue at hand.

Minimalist assumptions and principles, however, are silent about some important elements of complex task performance. Minimalism does not focus on tasks as work in context, and design rationales remain fixed on the technological context and program functions. Minimalism does not articulate strategies for avoiding oversimplification and for helping users experience and overcome cognitive disequilibrium. Nor does it explicitly encourage writers to guide users in integrating knowledge in new ways in response to social, political, cultural, or historical constraints and opportunities. Yet minimalist principles do not militate against applying these instructional strategies either. Such principles as "Guide learners in reasoning, exploring, and improvising with questions and other hints" along with other principles for detecting, diagnosing, and recovering from errors are broad enough to be interpreted as support for inquiry into misconceptions. In all, minimalist principles in conjunction with other researchers' insights from studies on complex tasks lay a firm foundation for designing documentation for problem-solving computing. Writers now need to apply this foundation to actual instructional situations.

7.6 Complex Tasks and Minimalist Directions for the Future

Most documentation specialists would agree that complex task performance is synergistic, but many of them object that it may not be feasible for documentation to teach to that synergy. First, critics question whether it is valid to focus on the many factors, conditions, and points of view that intertwine to shape users' knowledge, approaches, and choices—something that documentation does not usually target. These critics point out that even complex tasks must devolve into a series of operations, the province in which documentation excels. Admittedly, even complex tasks and problems, especially in hindsight, can be described as composite sets of actions and expert strategies (Borland personal communication 1994). But the complexity of a task cannot be traced either to the number or the knowing of the actions per se. The complexity comes from needing to figure out how to get from one set of actions to another in a task or problem that is never the same every time. It is in this context-laden "figuring out" that users need to integrate and transfer knowledge actively so that they experience the deep processing needed for learning. Rote procedures or predetermined paths cannot capture the integration and problem solving that gets users from here to there. To develop competence in complexity, people need case-based guidance for handling multiple factors, perspectives, and levels of knowledge, not generic steps and context-free truths about program operators.

A second objection is that it seems impossible to represent all the cultural, organizational, political, social, and cognitive differences that lead users to take distinct approaches to the same complex, job-related task. To customize documentation for users' task approaches, writers would need to work in every business office and project group, a tantalizing pipe dream for anyone in this profession but a pipe dream nonetheless. Documenting complex tasks need not be reduced to this either-or choice between generic or personalized instruction. In between, improvement by degree is a worthy aim. Given that instruction in generic unit tasks fails to help people learn complex, computer-supported tasks adequately, something better is needed. Research underscores that improvement begins by representing tasks at a higher than unit task level so that users can see their conceptions of their work described in the documentation. Complex tasks may be shaped by context, but writers can still describe them by classes of tasks or inquiries, representing types of job activities or business-related problems, recognizable to users as the class of activity in which they are engaged.

Finally, critics claim that writers should be in the business of documenting users' activities with programs, not addressing their instructional needs for work-related problem solving. Otherwise they are doing something other than documentation.[3] For complex tasks, program interactions are tied to the technological, social, and cultural context of work. Very likely, documentation for complex tasks will need to look like something other than conventional documentation because it targets something new: experienced users, advanced learning, and tasks that are replete with meaning. As Richard Rorty notes, when people attempt to change an ongoing, conventional conversation—as documentation for complex tasks will do in a discussion dominated by unit-task-oriented documentation—they need nonnormal discourse.

Some themes, forms, and content for this nonnormal discourse are suggested by recent developments in the fields of instructional design and human factors. The following five themes should become a directing force in the development of documentation for complex tasks. Each theme marks a significant departure from unit task-oriented documentation.

Theme 1 is to *develop rich scenarios about activity in context rather than narrow scenarios about unit tasks*. Researchers are making progress in analyzing and developing categories of job-related tasks or problems (Nielsen et al. 1992; Brooks 1991; Mirel 1992). Writers could use these categories as the organizing themes of help topics and manual chapters. In addition, interface designers have been experimenting with ways to support people's work in context, for instance, by letting users specify their desired patterns of action (sequenced, interleaved, conditional) or by visualizing three-dimensional rooms that are filled with groupings of real-world task objects and actions for users to enter, manipulate and assemble for their circumstances (Johnson, Johnson, and Wilson 1995; Card, Robertson, and Mackinlay 1991). Another recent approach in interface design that writers could adapt to documentation is to let users define their relevant cognitive modes. For example, users could "turn on" the types of arguments that they want to pursue in an idea processing application or the levels of edit that they want to perform in a text processing program (Streitz 1992; Smith and Lansman 1992).

Theme 2 is to *build interactivity into instruction instead of presenting, for example, view-only semantic maps and graphic browsers.* Interactivity for learning, and not simply for navigation, is crucial to complex task performance. To understand their computing choices, users need to construct and then reassemble ideas and relationships and experience the effects. Recent innovations in interfaces encourage such interactivity, allowing users to move around or rename the links that join modules of information. Another model of interactivity can be seen in View Matcher for Smalltalk (Rosson and Carroll 1991). As mentioned earlier, in this tutorial, each screen represents an episode from four different perspectives, enabling users to experiment with arranging and rearranging these perspectives—manipulating objects, vignettes, and messages in various way. This interactivity has a deep learning effect (Jonassen and Wang 1993). Writers could adapt this learning-based interactivity to online help systems. One more promising experiment is the design of an intelligent help system that creates and stores a user profile from an individual's patterns of action for repeated tasks (Boy 1992). From this profile, a program automatically customizes and presents instruction to the level of learning implied by these patterns. One may argue that interactive help is already available through such tools as Cue Cards or Wizards. But the interactivity evoked by these tools is more akin to fill-in-the-blank exercises than to hands-on exploration for advanced learning. These tools do the hard work of manipulating processes behind the scenes based on user input. Users are blocked from interrupting the Wizards' routine and customizing it to their idiosyncratic needs. They do not learn for transfer, and they experience no cognitive dissonance.

Theme 3 is to *provide multiple cases that are thematically linked and not just single cases (elaborated examples)*. In some learning support systems for complex tasks, sets of hypertextually related cases are organized by shared themes, offering learners opportunities to call up information by these themes and see the distinct significance of a single theme in various cases (Spiro et al. 1992; Jacobson and Spiro 1995; Bransford et al. 1990; Schank 1992; Slator and Riesbeck 1991). MiTTS illustrates another way of involving users in relating cases (Rosson and Carroll 1991). True to the minimalist principle of being useful but not comprehensive, this tutorial concentrates on only a small set of existing Smalltalk class hierarchies. It frames them into core episodes and vignettes that represent a large proportion of the concepts and strategies that programmers need for real-world coding in Smalltalk. In spiral fashion, these concepts and strategies are replayed in each scenario episode in slightly different ways. Whether in cross-cutting or spiraling themes, researchers have found that instructions work best if they help users turn their pragmatic knowledge into explicable heuristic strategies, for instance, identifying the conditions under which certain clusters of rules and inferences apply (Cheng et al. 1986). Some documentation developers have experimented with cross-cutting cases in the form of electronic performance systems with linked task scenarios. But these scenarios usually only represent routine, program-defined tasks (Dicks and Lind 1995).

Theme 4 is to *bring misconceptions to the surface and examine them as part of instructing users in detecting, diagnosing, and recovering from errors*. Instructional designers offer writers important strategies for helping users to experience cognitive disequilibrium, described by some human factors specialists as teaching users to know what they do not know but ought to (Briggs 1990). One example of electronic support for learners to work through their misconceptions is an application that encourages users to work collaboratively on a task, having collaborators gather impressions of the task into an electronic community knowledge base (Scardamalia and Bereiter 1994). Using this knowledge base, instructors guide learners in moving from their own ideas to relating them to others' impressions, thereby recognizing underlying assumptions and misconceptions in order to define problems and tasks in new ways. Another shift in focus for documentation writers to consider—a shift intrinsic to minimalist principles—is to place error management at the center of instruction rather than relegating it to a self-contained troubleshooting section. According to some human factors researchers, advanced users may need to learn primarily from experiences with impasses (Frese and Altmann 1989).

Theme 5 is to *develop multiple analogies, metaphors, and examples that mutually support a single point or purpose and not merely one analogy, metaphor, or example per point.* Offering users sets of related cases may foster their abilities to take different angles on the same activities (Rosson, Carroll, and Sweeney 1991). Theoretically, multiple analogies and examples should operate on the same principle. They should provide robust grounds for relating the unfamiliar to the familiar and avoid the consequence of single analogies outliving their usefulness. Yet research findings suggest that the cumulative effect of diverse analogies and examples is that they may cause confusion and misunderstanding (Carroll and Rosson 1995). Success seems to depend on writers understanding and representing key details of the traits that composite sets of analogies should have in order to achieve their intended effects.

In the 1980s, Carroll countered the dominant formal mapping views that shaped (and still shape) user documentation by seeking to infuse instruction with educational principles of inquiry, experiential learning, and motivation. This perspective was valid almost twenty years ago and is still valid today. It is exactly the foundation on which writers now need to build in order to develop documentation for complex tasks and problem-solving computing. Moreover, writers need the same experimental spirit and quest for innovative products as many interface developers and instructional designers currently demonstrate.

As a bridge between routine and complex tasks, minimalist principles offer documentation developers vital support for moving from the familiar to the unknown. These principles need to be supplemented with constructivist perspectives that situate tasks in social contexts and learning by doing in a network of organizational and collective endeavors. This more expansive view of minimalism will give rise to new instructional forms and content.

Writers will make only partial progress toward documenting complex tasks and supporting advanced learning if they do not make critical distinctions: distinguishing between routine and complex tasks, between introductory and advanced learning, between interactivity for navigation and for learning, between single case examples and sets of cases linked thematically, between rich contextual and narrow program-oriented scenarios, and, finally, between error correction and error management. If writers do not make these distinctions, they are likely to remain tied to the world of program-defined unit tasks. Users, in the meantime, will continue to gain computing experience and quickly outgrow introductory instruction. If writers fail to explore new approaches to documentation for these users and their complex, computer-supported work, they will worsen the problem of documentation not meeting users' genuine needs.

By contrast, if writers make the distinctions I have noted and test new discourses inspired by minimalism, constructivism, and situated cognition, they will begin to satisfy the needs of experienced users for advanced learning. Ideally, once a number of documentation developers venture into this uncharted territory, they will test their innovations and produce and share empirical results so that others may better understanding the key issues and trade-offs intrinsic to designing documentation for complex tasks.

Acknowledgments

I thank everyone at the symposium. I particularly am grateful to a number of colleagues for reading earlier versions of this chapter and providing extensive and very helpful suggestions and comments, including Russell Borland, Lee Brasseur, Jack Carroll, Steve Draper, JoAnn Hackos, Ginny Redish, Christine Abbott.

Notes

1. These qualities assume a complexity related to information-processing tasks for nontechnical, business purposes (for instance, analyzing productivity or managing costs). A complex task from a technical—computer professional's—point of view often means something different. It implies, for example, a programming task of great scope with numerous parts and many levels of detail to attend to simultaneously. It implies different teams working on different parts of a complicated application, with teams ultimately needing to coordinate their modules into a coherent and consistent whole. Missing from this view of complex tasks is a direct and ongoing influence of social and contextual forces and contingencies, an influence continuously at work in complex business tasks. The context of professional computing tasks is the technological environment, not the internal business organization and its external environment.

2. The use of advanced program functions such as macros or print-merge is another example in which writers often mistakenly call tasks complex because they are difficult for novices to learn. For instance, "Using Macros," a unit-level how-to-execute-a-macro task, has few of the qualities of complex tasks. It requires advanced technical knowledge and a grasp of certain fundamental concepts about macros and how and why they work. But this conceptual learning does not call for multiple points of view or creating new perspectives for novel purposes. In addition, procedures for executing macros are generic and fairly normative, not open-ended, situational, and contingent.

3. I have deliberately omitted issues of feasibility related to critical questions about adequate time and resources, such as whether companies are willing to invest in writers' efforts to build intelligent tutoring systems to foster advanced learning. These issues are outside the scope of this inquiry. They are tied, I believe, to a need for structural changes in writers' workplaces—changes in the distribution of labor, authority, and methods for assessing productivity, quality, and value-added. Smart (this volume, chapter 11) addresses them in part.

References

Anderson, R. J. 1994. "Representation and Requirements: The Value of Ethnography in System Design." *Human-Computer Interaction* 9:151–182.

Anderson, R. J., C. C. Heath, P. Luff, and T. P. Moran. 1993. "The Social and the Cognitive in Human-Computer Interaction." *International Journal of Man-Machine Studies* 38:999–1016.

Bereiter, Carl. 1991. "Implications of Connectionism for Thinking About Rules." *Educational Researcher* 20:10–16.

Berger, Peter, and Thomas Luckmann. 1967. *The Social Construction of Reality: A Treatise in the Sociology of Knowledge.* Garden City, NY: Doubleday.

Bikson, Tora, and J. D. Eveland. 1987. *Implementing Computerized Procedures in Offices' Settings: Influences and Outcomes.* Santa Monica: RAND.

Black, John, Dana Kay, and Elliot Soloway. 1989. "Goal and Plan Knowledge Representations: From Stories to Text Editors and Programs." In John, M. Carroll (ed.), *Interfacing Thought: Cognitive Aspects of Human-Computer Interaction,* pp. 36–79. Cambridge, MA: MIT Press.

Bødker, Susanne. 1991. *Through the Interface: A Human Activity Approach to User Interface Design.* Hillsdale, NJ: Erlbaum.

Boy, Guy. 1992. "Computer Integrated Documentation." In E. Barrett (ed.), *Sociomedia,* pp. 508–531. Cambridge, MA: MIT Press.

Bransford, J., R. Sherwood, T. Hasselbring, C. Kinzer, and S. Williams. 1990. "Anchored Instructions: Why We Need it and How Technology Can Help." In D. Nix and J. Spiro (eds.), *Cognition, Education and Multimedia,* pp. 115–140. Hillsdale, NJ: Erlbaum.

Briggs, Pamela. 1990. "The Role of the User Model in Learning as an Internally and Externally Directed Activity." In D. Ackermann and M. Tauber (eds.), *Human-Computer Interaction,* pp. 195–208. Amsterdam: North-Holland.

Brooks, Ruven. 1991. "Comparative Task Analysis: An Alternative Direction for Human-Computer Interaction Science." In John M. Carroll (ed.), *Designing Interactions,* pp. 162–202. Cambridge: Cambridge University Press.

Brown, J. S., A. Collins, and P. Duguid. 1989. "Situated Cognition and the Culture of Learning." *Educational Researcher* 18(1):32–42.

Card, Stuart, George Robertson, and Jack Mackinlay. 1991. "The Information Visualizer, and Information Workspace." *CHI91 Proceedings,* pp. 181–188.

Carlson, Patricia. 1992. "From Document to Knowledge Base: Intelligent Hypertext as Minimalist Instruction." *Journal of Computer Documentation* 16:17–31.

Carroll, John M. 1990. *The Nurnberg Funnel.* Cambridge, MA: MIT Press.

Carroll, John M., and Amy Aaronson. 1989. "Learning by Doing with Simulated Intelligent Help." In E. Barrett (ed.), *The Society of Text: Hypertext, Hypermedia, and the Social Construction of Information,* pp. 423–452. Cambridge, MA: MIT Press.

Carroll, John M., and Mary Beth Rosson. 1989. "Paradox of the Active User." In John M. Carroll (ed.), *Interfacing Thought: Cognitive Aspects of Human-Computer Interaction.* Cambridge, MA: MIT Press.

Carroll, John M., and Mary Beth Rosson. 1995. "Managing Evaluation Goals for Training." Presentation at STC Currents Conference, Atlanta.

Carroll, John M., and Mary Beth Rosson. 1996. "Deliberated Evolution: Stalking the View Matcher in Design Space." In Thomas Moran and John M. Carroll (eds.), *Design Rationale: Concepts, Techniques, and Use,* pp. 107–145. Mahwah, NJ: Erlbaum.

Cheng, Patricia, Keith Loyoak, Richard Nisbett, and Lindsay Oliver. 1986. "Pragmatic Versus Syntactic Approaches to Training Deductive Reasoning." *Cognitive Psychology* 18:293–328.

Collins, H. M. 1987. "Expert Systems and the Science of Knowledge." In W. E. Bijker, T. Hughes, and T. Pinch (eds.), *The Social Construction of Technological Systems*, pp. 329–348. Cambridge, MA: MIT Press.

Diaper, Dan, and Peter Johnson. 1989. "Task Analysis for Knowledge Descriptions: Theory and Application in Training. In J. Long and A. Whitefield (eds.), *Cognitive Ergonomics and Human-Computer Interaction*, pp. 191–224. Cambridge: Cambridge University Press.

Dicks, R. Stanley, and Scott Lind. 1995. "Logistics of Integrating Online Help, Documentation, and Training: A Practical Example." *SIGDOC95 Proceedings*, pp. 34–38. New York: ACM.

Ehn, Pelle. 1988. *Work-Oriented Design of Computer Artifacts*. Stockholm: Arbetslivscentrum.

Ehn, Pelle. 1992. "Scandinavian Design: On Participation and Skill." In P. Adler and T. Winograd (eds.), *Usability: Turning Technologies into Tools*, pp. 96–132. New York: Oxford University Press.

Feltovich, P., R. Spiro, and R. Coulson. 1993. "Learning, Teaching, and Testing for Complex Conceptual Understanding." In N. Fredericksen, R. Mislevy, and I. Behar (eds.), *Test Theory for a New Generation of Test*, pp. 181–217. Hillsdale, NJ: Erlbaum.

Frese, Michael. 1987. "A Theory of Control and Complexity." In M. Frese, E. Ulich, and W. Dzida (eds.), *Psychological Issues of Human Computer Interaction in the Work Place*, pp. 313–337. Amsterdam: Elsevier Science Publishers.

Frese, M., and A. Altmann. 1989. "The Treatment of Errors in Learning and Training." In L. Bainbridge and S. A. Ruiz Quintanilla (eds.), *Developing Skills with Information Technology*, pp. 65–86. New York: Wiley.

Girill, T. R., and Clement H. Luk. 1992. "Hierarchical Search Support for Hypertext On-Line Documentation." *International Journal of Man-Machine Studies* 36:571–585.

Granda, Richard, Richard Halstead-Nussloch, and Joan Winters. 1990. "The Perceived Usefulness of Computer Information Sources: A Field Study." *SIGCHI Bulletin* 21:35–43.

Green, Thomas, Franz Schiele, and Stephen Payne. 1986. "Formalisable Models of User Knowledge." In G. VanderVeer, T. Green, J. M Hoc, and D. Murray (eds.), *Working with Computers: Theory vs. Outcome*, pp. 3–41. London: Academic Press.

Greeno, J., and H. Simon. 1988. "Problem-Solving and Reasoning." In R. Atkinson, R. Heistein, G. Lindzey, and D. Luce (eds.), *Steven's Handbook of Experimental Psychology* 2:589–671. New York: Wiley.

Human-Computer Interaction 9, 1994. Special Issue on Borderline Issues: Social and Material Aspects of Design.

Jacobson, Michael, and Rand Spiro. 1995. "Hypertext Learning Environments, Cognitive Flexiblity, and the Transfer of Complex Knowledge." *Journal of Education Computing Research.*

Johnson, P., H. Johnson, and S. Wilson. 1995. "Rapid Prototyping of User Interfaces Driven by Task Models." In John M. Carroll (ed.), *Scenario-Based Design: Envisioning Work and Technology in System Development*, pp. 209–246. New York: Wiley.

Jonassen, David, and R. Scott Grabinger. 1990. "Problems and Issues in Designing Hypertext/Hypermedia for Learning. "In D. Jonassen and H. Mandl (eds.), *Designing Hypermedia for Learning*, pp. 1.1–1.23. New York: Springer Verlag.

Jonassen, David, and Sherwood Wang. 1993. "Acquiring Structural Knowledge from Semantically Structured Hypertext." *Journal of Computer-Based Instruction* 20:1–8.

Karat, John. 1995. "Scenario Use in the Design of a Speech Recognition System." In John M. Carroll (ed.), *Scenario-Based Design: Envisioning Work and Technology in System Development*, pp. 109–134. New York: Wiley.

Kieras, David. 1990. *Learning About Equipment from Technical Documentation.* Technical Report FR-89-ONR-31. Washington, DC: Office of Naval Research. (ERIC ED 315 455)

Kitajima, Muneo, and Peter Polson. 1992. "A Computerized Model of Skilled Use of a Graphical User Interface." *CHI92 Proceedings*, pp. 241–249. New York: ACM.

Mayes, J. Terry, Stephen Draper, Alison McGregor and Keith Oatley. 1988. "Information Flow in a User Interface: The Effect of Experience and Context on the Recall of MacWrite Screens." In D. Jones and R. Winder (eds.), *People and Computers*, pp. 275–289. Cambridge: Cambridge University Press.

Mirel, Barbara. 1992. "Analyzing Audiences for Software Manuals: A Survey of Instructional Needs for 'Real World Tasks." *Technical Communication Quarterly* 1:13–38.

Miyata, Yoshiro, and Donald Norman. 1986. "Psychological Issues in Support of Multiple Activities." In S. Draper and D. Norman (eds.), *User-Centered Design*, pp. 271–290. Hillsdale, NJ: Erlbaum.

Nielsen, Jakob, Rita Bush, Tom Dayton, Nancy Mond, Michael Muller, and Robert Root. 1992. "Teaching Experienced Developers to Design Graphical User Interfaces." *CHI92 Proceedings*, pp. 557–564. New York: ACM.

Nielsen, Jakob, Robert Mack, Keith Bergendorff, and Nancy Gischkowsky. 1986. "Integrated Software Usage in the Professional Work Environment: Evidence from Questionnaires and Interviews." *CHI86 Proceedings*, pp. 162–167.

Norman, Donald. 1986. "Cognitive Engineering." In D. Norman and S. Draper (eds.), *User Centered System Design*, pp. 31–61. Hillsdale, NJ: Erlbaum.

Payne, Stephen. 1991. "Display-Based Action at the User Interface." *International Journal of Man-Machine Studies* 35:275–289.

Pea, R. 1989. "Putting Knowledge to Use." In R. Nickerson and P. Zodhiates (eds.), *Technology in Education: Looking Toward 2020*, pp. 35–64. New York: Wiley.

Rheinfrank, J., W. Hartman, and A. Wasserman. 1992. "Design for Usability." In P. Adler and T Winograd (eds.), *Usability: Turning Technologies into Tools*, pp. 15–40. New York: Oxford University Press.

Rorty, Richard. 1989. *Contingency, Irony, and Solidarity*. Cambridge: Cambridge University Press.

Rosson, Mary Beth, and John M. Carroll. 1995. "Narrowing the Specification-Implementation Gap in Scenario-Based Design." In John M. Carroll (ed.), *Scenario-Based Design: Envisioning Work and Technology in System Development*, pp. 247–278. New York: Wiley.

Rosson, Mary Beth, John M. Carroll, and Christine Sweeney. 1991. "A View Matcher for Reusing Smalltalk Classes." *CHI91 Proceedings*, pp. 277–283. New York: ACM Press.

Russell, Daniel, Mark Stefik, Peter Pirolli, and Stuart Card. 1993. "The Cost Structure of Sensemaking." *INTERCHI93 Proceedings*, pp. 269–276.

Salomon, G., and D. Perkins. 1989. "Rocky Roads to Transfer: Rethinking Mechanisms of a Neglected Phenomenon." *Educational Psychologist* 24:113–142.

Scardamalia, Marlene, and Carl Bereiter. 1994. "Developing a Progressive Curriculum Through Collaborative Environments." Presentation at American Educational Research Association.

Schank, Roger. 1992. *Goal-Based Scenarios*. Technical Report. Office of Naval Research. Evanston, IL: Institute of Learning Sciences, Northwestern University.

Schön, Donald. 1983. *The Reflective Practitioner*. New York: Basic Books.

Slator, Brian, and Christopher Riesbeck. 1991. *Taxops: Giving Expert Advice to Experts*. Technical Report 19. Office of Naval Research. Evanston, IL: Institute of Learning Sciences, 1991.

Smith, John B., and Marcy Lansman. 1992. "Designing Theory-Based Systems: A Case Study." *CHI92 Proceedings*, pp. 479–488. New York: ACM.

Spiro, R., P. Feltovich, M. Jacobson, and R. Coulson. 1992. "Cognitive Flexibility, Constructivism, and Hypertext." In T. Duffy and D. Jonassen (eds.), *Constructivism and the Technology of Instruction*, pp. 58–72. Hillsdale, NJ: Erlbaum.

Standard and Poors. 1994. Industrial surveys. Vol. 2. C75–C149.

Strassman, Paul. 1990. *The Business Value of Computers*. New Canaan, CT: Information Economics Press.

Streitz, Norbert. 1992. "Hypertext and Research at GMD-IPSI." *SIGLINK Newsletter* 1:13–16.

Thomas, J. C. 1989. "Problem-Solving by Human-Machine Interaction." In K. J. Gilhooly (ed.), *Human and Machine Problem Solving*, pp. 317–362. New York: Plenum Press.

Van der Meij, Hans. 1992. "A Critical Assessment of the Minimalist Approach to Documentation." *SIGDOC92 Proceedings*, pp. 7–17.

Van der Meij, H., and J. M. Carroll. 1995. "Principles and Heuristics for Designing Minimalist Instruction." *Technical Communication* 42:243–261.

Varela, Francisco, Evan Thompson, and Eleanor Rosch. 1991. *Embodied Minds: Cognitive Science and Human Experience*. Cambridge, MA: MIT Press.

Winograd, Terry, and F. Flores. 1986. *Understanding Computers and Cognition*. Reading, MA: Addison-Wesley.

Woods, D., and E. Hollnagel. 1988. "Mapping Cognitive Demands in Complex Problem-Worlds." *International Journal of Man-Machine Studies* 29:257.

Wright, Patricia. 1990. "Hypertexts as an Interface for Learners: Some Human Factors Issues." In D. Jonassen and H. Mandl (eds.), *Designing Hypermedia for Learning*, pp. 10.1–10.16. New York: Springer Verlag.

8

Minimalism in Technical Communication: Some Issues to Consider

Janice Redish

The first association that many people make to "minimalism" is "slash the verbiage." While shorter is almost always better, that is not the main point of minimalism, despite the obvious link to the name. As Draper and Oatley (1992) point out, slashing the verbiage is, in fact, a heuristic derived from a more fundamental principle: "Be action oriented."

Indeed, being action oriented is the first of the four principles in Van der Meij and Carroll (this volume, chapter 2):

1. Choose an action-oriented approach.
2. Anchor the tool in the task domain.
3. Support error recognition and recovery.
4. Support reading to do, study, and locate.

Being action oriented is itself a consequence of an even more fundamental principle: Be user oriented. Being user oriented means both writing for the user, not about the system, and understanding what users are like so that you can write for them.

The most important contribution that minimalism has made is the model of the user that emerged from the experiments of the minimalist research group during the 1980s. Certainly, other people were adopting similar approaches to documentation at the same time. Patricia Wright in England; myself and colleagues at the Document Design Center; Hayes, Schriver, and others at Carnegie Mellon University; and several other groups were studying how people interact with documents and were finding that cognitive psychology theory and research apply well to documentation. But the research results from Jack Carroll and his colleagues, their clear statements of the meaning of those results, and their critical insights about users were a significant part of the profound change in the overall approach to documentation that took place in the 1980s.

The model that came out of the early minimalist studies was of users who:

• Constantly try to make meaning of what they see and hear and read and do.
• Rely on prior experience, even when it may be inappropriate.
• Follow their own hypotheses, even when evidence may contradict it.
• Are eager to act, with a tendency to jump right in and to jump around.
• Are primarily interested in accomplishing real tasks (Carroll and Mack 1984; Carroll and Rosson 1987; Carroll 1990).

Based on this model of the user, Carroll and his colleagues evolved and tested specific principles and heuristics for instructional materials aimed at new users of large-scale software programs (a word processor and an object-oriented programming language). The model of the user that came out of their studies confirmed what others in cognitive psychology were uncovering about how people learn, read, and think. The minimalist model of the user matches two key principles of cognitive psychology, constructivism and active learning:

1. Users construct their own mental models (schemas), combining new information from what they see in interfaces and documentation with what they already have in their minds from earlier experiences.
2. Users learn best when they are actively involved, when they are doing for themselves, not just following rote instructions (Suchman 1987; Charney, Reder, and Wells 1988).

To implement these principles, Carroll and his colleagues developed heuristics for minimalist documentation, including these three:

1. Give users opportunities to form their own models. Invite them to explore and discover for themselves rather than always leading them step by step through an example.
2. Do not tell them what they already know or can infer. However, arbitrarily dropping information is not going to succeed. Incomplete information has to be based on knowing the users and on matching the documentation to what users can readily see in the interface.
3. Assume that users will make errors because they do. Certainly work to prevent errors, but also find out what types of errors users are likely to

make at a given point and help them recognize and recover from them. While they are learning, protect users from errors that will lead them too far afield (Carroll's training-wheels interfaces, Carroll 1990; Carroll and Rosson 1987).

My own experiences and research support the constructivist, action-oriented principles on which minimalism is based (Redish 1988, 1993). However, issues remain in the practical application of these principles. In this chapter, I raise two sets of issues.

First, users are not all the same, all the time, in all situations. We need an expanded model of the user that takes diversity into consideration. In the next section of this chapter, I discuss the implications of three ways that users differ: in the mode they are in at a given time (learning versus doing), in their personalities and learning styles, and in the types of problem domains they are working in.

Second, as we develop documents for users, we are constantly making specific practical decisions about what to include, how to organize, and how to write for users. In the last section of this chapter, I raise three concerns about decisions that technical communicators are making today:

• Do the headings we write really reflect *users'* tasks?
• Are we focusing too much on low-level tasks and not enough on helping users move from goals to tasks?
• Are we misinterpreting the minimalist view on overviews and thereby missing opportunities to help users develop useful mental models?

8.1   Expanding the Minimalist Model of the User

Although all users share the five characteristics that I listed in the chapter introduction, they also differ. Consider the implications of these three differences:

1. Users come to documentation in different modes at different times (learning mode versus doing mode).
2. Users differ in personality and learning styles (risk takers, non-risk takers).
3. Users work in different problem domains (with different products, in different domains in one product).

Different Modes at Different Times

Minimalism, as Van der Meij and Carroll write (this volume, chapter 2), has been primarily concerned with "*instruction* of the *novice* learner or of users who are *becoming acquainted* with a new application or tool" (italics added). However, we must be concerned not only with a user's first acquaintance with a product, but with supporting users in all their interactions with the product. An important issue to consider, then, is whether minimalism is applicable only to learning materials—to tutorials and getting-started guides. How applicable is minimalism to what many users see as the major parts of a documentation set, the user's guide and online help, which they primarily use for reference?

A decade ago, Carroll and Rosson (1987) pointed out the paradox of the user whose "paramount goal is throughput," that is doing, but who would be better off in the long run by learning. At about the same time, I wrote about the need to create materials that serve a purpose that I called *reading-to-learn-to-do* (Redish 1988). Carroll and Rosson and I were recognizing that users of software and hardware are action oriented, focused on tasks, and seldom in a study mode. Carroll and Rosson's answers, as well as those I focused on in my 1988 paper, were how to create learning materials (i.e., tutorials) that would be satisfying and successful with users who were focused on doing.

When Do Users Go to Manuals?   Users are not always in a learning mode, not even a learning-to-do mode. The same user turns to documentation at different times for different reasons. Perhaps early on, some users take time away from accomplishing their regular tasks and put themselves into a learning-to-do mode. They take a training class, turn to a product's online tutorials, or play and explore on their own. When they have a few minutes free, some users may browse the interface or online help, play around with the program, or skim a manual, and again be in a leaning-to-do mode.

Much of the time, however, users only want to do their own work. They may be under the pressure of a deadline or in the middle of a task when the need for new information or the need to solve a problem arises. These people want to use manuals or online help for reference. They want to get in, grab the relevant information, and get out and back to their work as quickly as possible.

People go to reference materials when:

• They do not know what tasks to do to accomplish a goal. (How do I send a formatted paper through my e-mail program?)
• They do not know the steps to take to do a specific task. (How do I change what the bullet looks like on this page?)
• They have a problem that can be specified fairly clearly. (I don't understand the choices that this message is giving me.)
• They have a problem but do not know what it is. (This program seems to be automatically numbering my paragraphs, and I don't want it to do that.)

Some users at some times go to user's manuals to look for conceptual information, just to see what the program is about, or to find out about new tips and new features. I suggest, however, that such uses are much rarer than we would hope for and are not the primary reasons or times that users go to user's manuals and online help.

What Do Users Want in Reference Manuals?   Minimalism so far has not dealt much with reference materials, so we may ask: Which principles of minimalism are relevant for reference materials? I suspect that users want reference material to:

• Be action oriented. (Help them to do.)
• Be anchored in the task. (Help them achieve their goals.)
• Support error recognition and recovery. (Help them recognize and identify what the problem is and then solve it.)
• Support locating (immediately) and doing. (Have the information be easy to find, that is, with headings that match the goals and tasks they are trying to achieve and index items that match their words.)
• Be modular. (Have the relevant information together in one place and not require reading other parts to deal with the specific issue at hand.)

This list of what users want in reference materials matches the four principles Van der Meij and Carroll identified, with the exception of a need to support studying. However, in implementing the four principles, minimalism also emphasizes encouraging users to explore and discover. To encourage users' active involvement in exploring, discovering, and figuring out for themselves, minimalism suggests that incomplete instructions are appropriate, based, of course, on understanding what can be left out for users as they are learning.

How Much Do Users Want to Explore in Reference Manuals?
Exploration and incomplete instructions are the elements of minimalism that I question for reference material. I suspect that when in a doing mode, users do not always want to be told to be innovative and to explore. In fact, they may be far less tolerant of incomplete instructions that expect them to discover much of the way to do things on their own.

Of course, as Jack Carroll has pointed out to me, all instructions are incomplete at some level. No document, whether meant as tutorial or reference, can cover all instances that any user might ever need. Also, minimalism may still be struggling with defining appropriate levels of exploration. The issue that needs further discussion and research is whether different levels or kinds of incompleteness and exploration are appropriate in getting-started (learning or learning to do) materials and in reference (doing) materials.

The same person may be both an explorer and a non-explorer, depending on the mode or goals. Even users who are otherwise explorers may want quick answers with step-by-step instructions, as well as error recognition and recovery information, from a user's guide or online help.

Who Is Most Likely to Explore?   The issue of minimalism and reference materials may be especially critical because I suspect that fewer people go to tutorials or any kind of training materials today than was true when Carroll and his colleagues and many of the rest of us started to study these issues. Most users today do not see themselves as novices even when they are totally new to a program. They see themselves as transfer users even if they do not know the term. Many people plunge right into using a product and go to any kind of documentation, be it a print manual or online help, only when they run into trouble.

Furthermore, users differ in their personal learning styles. Some are by nature more prone to explore than others. A paradox for minimalism is that the people with the greatest propensity to explore are also those who are least likely to go to tutorials. They are the most likely to plunge into working with the product without looking at any documentation and thus to bypass any time in learning mode.

From the problems that Carroll and his colleagues saw in early studies of minimalism, they adopted techniques like training wheels and structuring minimal manuals to reflect specific goals that should make sense to users as they first encounter a product. In the real world, however, users get programs without training wheels and are free to start with their own goals, which may not be the easiest or wisest to take on as initial learning.

What Can Studies of Minimalism Tell Us about Exploratory Learning?
Most studies of minimalism have been done in experimental settings. Unfortunately, studying the effectiveness of any type of documentation in an experimental setting does not tell us how much the document will actually be used in the exigencies of the real world. Iterative usability testing, for example, can be very informative (Dumas and Redish 1993). We can learn a great deal about how to develop a manual that works for people *if they will use it*. We can even learn how to develop materials that more people are more likely to use. The setting of either a controlled experiment or a usability test is, however, somewhat artificial and may not reflect why, how often, and how people will use the same documents when they are doing their own work with all the interruptions and deadlines of typical work environments.

Let us consider two experimental studies of minimalist manuals. Weidenbeck, Zila, and McConnell (1995) compared the effectiveness of minimalist manuals that differed only in the type of practice they included. I will discuss their results in the next section of this chapter. Here I point out that what they learned may be true but might have little effect in the real world. Their participants, university students with strong technological skills, were told to work through the manual from beginning to end, and in the experimental university setting, they did as they were asked to, practicing or exploring depending on the manual that they had. We can wonder, however, whether these technologically skilled students would in fact have actually used any version of the manual outside of the experimental setting. And if they did use the manual in their own work, would they have used it in the same way that they did in the study?

In another study, Van der Meij (1992) compared a minimal manual to a conventional manual for learning a word processing program. After up to six hours of using the manual and practicing by themselves, the participants were given an hour's worth of tasks to do with the program. They could refer to the manual when doing the tasks. Participants who had the minimal manual completed the near-transfer tasks (ones just like the ones in the manual) faster and made fewer errors than those who had the conventional manual. (Interestingly, neither manual seems to have helped with far-transfer tasks—complex tasks that participants had not practiced and were not covered in the manual.)

These users were volunteers in a study "to get to know how people learn how to work with a word processor." Thus, they were people who had chosen to spend a day learning a new product. They were told to "do as they might do at home." However, they had chosen to be away from their homes or offices for the day. They did not have the distractions or pressures of home or office, and thus could be in a learning-to-do mode all day. This study shows that if people have the time and will to spend learning, a minimalist manual helps more—and possibly maintains motivation and interest more—than a conventional manual. This study and others that have shown the success of minimalist training manuals are very important, but they do not cover all the issues that we must consider.

We need studies of minimalist manuals being used in the realities of home or office. We need studies of minimalist manuals that are used as user's guides for reference when people are trying to accomplish their own tasks quickly. We need to see how different types of manuals and other innovative ways to communicate promote incidental learning while doing, that is, how they help users learn while they are doing without even realizing they are learning.

Different Personality and Learning Styles
Users differ not only in the mode they are in but also in their personal learning and working styles. Modern software products have become

incredibly complex in part because developers are building in flexibility to satisfy users from an ever broader and more diverse range of backgrounds and styles (Redish 1995).

We have to distinguish between two meanings of "active learner." As I have written elsewhere: "All readers are active in the sense that they use their prior knowledge and experience to understand a new document. Every reader is a thinking human being. Every reader is involved in making meaning for himself or herself by invoking and building on his or her schemata.... Not all readers are active, however, in the sense that they want to explore new documents or products" (Redish 1993, 26).

Anyone who has watched users in a usability lab or elsewhere realizes that some people enjoy learning by exploring, while others want more direct instruction. Some people are risk takers; others want their hands held. Carroll found that although they performed better with Guided Exploration cards than with more traditional tutorials, some of the participants in his early studies did not like the very minimal Guided Exploration cards that only gave hints for procedures and some error recovery information (Carroll 1990, 135–136).

What Has Research Shown about Differences in Learning Styles?   The educational community has an extensive literature about learning styles. (See Claxton and Murrell 1987 for a review of this literature.) It is reasonable to assume that the differences seen among students also hold for adult learners working with computers. Hester Glasbeek did a small study that seems to confirm both the existence of different learning styles among computer users and the effect that different styles have on performance and preference (Glasbeek 1994; also discussed in Jansen 1993).

Glasbeek developed a list of statements that discriminate between users with a propensity to explore and those with a desire for more direct instruction. The questionnaire included statements like these: "I usually learn to work with a program by trying things on my own" and "I usually learn to work with a new program by using the manuals." From the thirty-one responses she received, she selected ten participants for her study: the five people with the highest scores on exploratory statements and the five with the highest scores on what she calls "receptive statements."

All were given an exploratory manual and a program that was new to them. They were told to learn and practice as much as they wanted and then were given tasks to perform. The explorers went to the manual primarily when they got stuck. They spent 30 percent less time in practice mode than the other group did and were still slightly faster at doing the tasks. They liked the manual; four of the five preferred it to conventional manuals they had seen.

The nonexplorers, however, were not happy. They tried to use the manual in ways in which it did not work. They read almost everything. They tried to practice everything, including the error recovery information. This is reminiscent of the way that some of the participants in Carroll's early studies tried to use the Guided Exploration cards (Carroll 1990, 136–137), and the reactions of Glasbeek's participants were similar to the reactions of some of the users of the early Guided Exploration cards.

Glasbeek says the nonexplorers had "more, and more serious, problems than the explorative subjects. Most of these problems were caused by lack of introductory material and by the incompleteness of some of the instructions." The nonexplorers did not like the manual. Four of the five rated it as difficult or rather difficult. The differences in attitude and approach to documentation between those who like to explore and those who do not are real. Manual developers must take these differences into account.

What Should "Exploratory" Mean?   As Van der Meij and Carroll write (this volume, chapter 2), minimalism is not about unguided exploration. It never was. But originally it was certainly about much less guided or much less structured exploration than has been evident in recent minimalist manuals. Over time, at least some examples of minimalist instruction guides have reduced the level of incompleteness and the level of exploration expected of users and have become much more structured. For example, in the Norstar manual (see figure 2.3), the user is led to very specific tasks, such as adjusting ring volume. Within that task, the user is encouraged to "try using some of these buttons now to set the volume of your phone's ring." The invitation is followed by instructions for doing the task. This example is more like an invitation to act on one's own than like the level of exploration required of users in early minimalist documentation.

In his response to Farkas and Williams (1990), Carroll (1991) wrote, "I do in fact see [learning by exploration] as a key theme in the minimalist approach." Perhaps, however, the term should not be "exploratory learning" but "invitations to act."

What Type of Activity or Exploration Works Best?   Weidenbeck, Zila, and McConnell (1995) compared three types of practice within a minimalist manual. All three manuals had the same organization, content, and style, except for the practice sections. At various points in the manual, users were given either an exercise, a suggestion for guided exploration, or both the exercise and the guided exploration. After they had gone through the manual and practiced, they were given tasks to do without the manual. Those who had either version with exercises were able to do the tasks faster and with fewer errors than those who had the version with only guided exploration. The exercises that were successful were like usability-testing scenarios. Each exercise suggested a specific set of tasks to do without telling the user any of the steps for doing the tasks. The less successful guided exploration in this manual was much vaguer and required users to create their own scenarios. Users who had just the suggestion to explore did not succeed in creating adequate practice for themselves.

The question remains, therefore, how much exploration should be built into manuals and what exploration should be like. The question also remains whether exploration is necessary or appropriate for all users in all types of documentation and in all types of products, that is, in all problem domains.

Different Problem Domains
Users differ in both the mode they are in and their personal styles. Products also differ in the complexity of the problem domains that they cover and the work that users want to do with them. Even within one product, the problems that users set for themselves may be of different levels of complexity.

In the earlier days of minimalism, the thought was that minimalist documentation, particularly exploratory learning, would be most appropriate for novices and simple problem domains and less appropriate for experts or complex problem domains (Carroll 1990, 1991; Farkas and Williams 1990). In fact, the opposite may be true.

Do Users Want to Explore for Simple Tasks?   When the problem domain is simple and straightforward, users may have little patience for exploratory learning. For example, I have no great desire to have to explore to learn how to put the paper into a fax machine. The first time that I do it, I want clear step-by-step instructions with words and pictures, and I want a machine that "affords itself," that makes those instructions obvious. I am actively involved as I am doing the task. When I have to change the paper later, I want to be able to find those clear, step-by-step instructions as quickly as possible if I need them, but I want not to need them. If the machine affords itself well enough, I should need only instructions to avoid errors that users typically make. The fax machine I own, in fact, does this very well with an instruction inside the machine. At the one place where I am always confused, it says on the piece of metal in question: "Pass the recording paper under this guide." Assuming that the developers of the fax machine put that instruction on the guide as a result of usability testing, it is a good example of all four of Van der Meij and Carroll's principles of minimalist documentation, but there is no exploratory learning involved.

Is Exploratory Learning More Valuable for Complex Tasks? Exploratory learning may be even more important in complex problem domains than in simple ones. But what is a simple problem domain, and what is a complex problem domain?

When Carroll and his colleagues were studying office temporaries who were learning word processing, that was considered a simple problem domain. Programming, particularly object-oriented programming, was considered a complex problem domain.

Is word processing a simple problem domain? It may have been fifteen years ago. Or perhaps the early minimalist studies worked with a restricted set of word processing tasks. Is word processing a simple problem domain today?

How Might We Define Types of Problem Domains?   Perhaps we need a typology of problem domains to help us plan to help all users learn and do. JoAnn Hackos (this volume, chapter 6) and Barbara Mirel (this volume, chapter 7) have helped with insights on this issue. Hackos suggests that there are important differences between these two types of software: open products, in which users may have many different goals and may put together the subtasks that the product supports in many different ways, and constrained products, in which users typically have a well-defined set of goals and are expected to perform the subtasks that the product supports in limited and straightforward ways.

As Hackos points out, the "canonical" products that come to mind when we think of software are the first type—word processors, spreadsheets, programming languages—but most developers are creating products that exemplify the second type, such as the programs used in most companies for accounting, personnel, or inventory. Hackos asks whether many developers are relying too much on the open programs as models and making decisions about interfaces and architecture that adversely affect the usability of the more constrained products they are creating. We can also ask whether the documentation needs of users of the two types of products differ.

Also, both products that have been the primary focus of the minimalist research program—word processing and object-oriented programming —are examples of the first type. Is exploratory learning more necessary and appropriate for open software products like word processors and programming languages than for more constrained software products like accounting or inventory programs?

Mirel suggests that we build a matrix of the work users do and the complexity of the domains they are dealing with. The matrix would have columns for different types of problem domains and rows for different users' goals (doing or learning). The cells would include notes about documentation features that would best serve the needs of those users. The columns (different problem domains) might be:

- Straightforward. (Example: clerks doing payroll, inventory.)
- Complex (tactical). (Example: managers doing budgets or staffing.)
- Complex (strategic). (Example: managers allocating resources, making investment decisions, or modeling what-ifs for other types of decisions.)

The rows (different users' goals or needs) might be:

- Doing routine work
- Doing enhanced or extended work
- Learning with low-level transfer
- Learning with high-level transfer

With Mirel's matrix, we can ask whether payroll clerks who will be performing the same constrained set of routine tasks with the software application over and over need the same type of materials as managers who are using software for modeling.

We must be careful, however, about ascribing routine tasks to certain types of work and certain types of workers without investigating what these people actually do. The reality of their situations might surprise us. For example, Muller et al. (1995) found that telephone operators (the people who answer calls for directory assistance) are, in fact, knowledge workers. Directory assistance operators often work with customers to refine the customer's request. The operators use their knowledge of the cities in their area code and the directories available in their computers. They make educated guesses about where else in the directory to search. They translate the customer's words into the words listed in the directories. They make decisions about how to conduct the call. And on most calls, they do it all in less than half a minute.

The variety of online aids that computer companies are now developing may be attempts to help people who see themselves in different problem domains even in large-scale, open-ended products. I was curious about how people use the new online aids, like Wizards and Cue Cards, and whether they help people learn, so I turned to a former colleague who is now a usability manager at Microsoft. Here is what he said about Wizards: "People who use them, like them. In fact, they rely on them. They continue to use them, rather than learning from them and going on to doing the task on their own" (Marshall McClintock, personal communication, 1995). Thus, Wizards may be succeeding very well as an aid to doing but may not be promoting learning while doing.

Hackos explains the success of Wizards by saying that they take one goal that users have within an open program and create a more constrained program to handle that goal. For the user who wants to meet a particular goal as quickly and easily as possible in that more constrained problem domain (for example, create a chart from a given set of data), the Wizard may be a heaven-sent solution. The user who relies on a Wizard wants only to do, is in a doing mode, and, at least at that time and for that goal, is not interested in being an explorer.

8.2   Developing User-Oriented Documentation

At the start of this chapter, I said that being user oriented means both writing for the user, not about the system, and understanding what users are like so that you can write for them. In the previous section, I suggested some ways that we should expand our understanding of what users are like, adding to the minimalist model of the user. In this section, I want to raise three issues about writing for the user that affect both minimalist manuals and the more typical user-oriented, task-oriented manuals that are part of the typical contemporary documentation set:

1. Are writers really describing tasks in users' terms?
2. Are writers focusing on tasks at too low a level?
3. Are writers misunderstanding what minimalism says about overviews?

Are Writers Really Describing Tasks in Users' Terms?
The guiding principles of minimalism include focusing on the user, not the system, and organizing the manual by realistic users' tasks. These two principles are basic to what many of us have been advocating and teaching for the past fifteen years. (For example, see Price 1984; Brockmann 1986; Redish, Battison, and Gold 1985; Redish 1989.)

Even today, unfortunately, not all documents exemplify these principles. Some training materials and user's guides are still organized by the program's menu structure or functionality. In other cases, writers who truly believe that they are preparing user-oriented, task-oriented manuals fall all too often into a trap of creating tasks for their manuals that we might call *pseudo–user oriented*. They are still documenting system tasks. They just make them look like users' tasks.

I do not believe that writers are doing this deliberately, which makes it all the more insidious a problem. If they are working from functional specifications, they may have no users' words for the tasks. If they do not get to do early field studies or conduct iterative usability testing, they may never get to hear users' words or see a user flounder over the headings in their documents. If they are well integrated into the development team, in many ways a step forward, they may not realize how much they have adopted the developers' view of the tasks.

An Example of a Pseudo-User-Oriented Heading The manual for my fax machine is in many ways an excellent example of a user's manual. It is action oriented, seems to be anchored in users' tasks, supports error recognition and recovery, and supports easily locating information and doing the tasks. Information is in clear procedures with words and pictures supporting each other. However, one of the major sections in the manual has the heading "Using Polling."

This looks like a user-oriented, task-oriented heading. "Using" is an action verb, and I, the user, am doing the action. But this is really a system-oriented heading. It makes no connection to any task or goal that typical users would come to the manual wanting to do or learn to do. It violates minimalist principles in that it does not mesh with users' prior experiences or the expectations that they bring.

For most users, "polling" is more likely to bring associations to someone calling on the telephone and asking who the person is going to vote for in the next election than to doing something with the fax machine. If the section were called, "Setting Up the Fax Machine So Someone Can Get a Fax from It When You're Not There" more users might go to the section and use the feature.

A Study in Which This Problem May Have Occurred This particular example is interesting because it came up in a study by Scholtz and Hansen (1993), who compared two versions of the manual for a fax modem: the original manual and a minimalist version. In this experiment, users were put into a doing mode, not a learning mode. That is, they were given tasks to do in a typical usability lab setting with (1) no manual, or (2) the original manual, or (3) the minimalist manual available to them. Those who had access to a manual typically used it only when they were having trouble.

The results showed that either manual was better than no manual. The minimalist manual did as well as but not better than the original manual. A more detailed look at the manuals might suggest that the minimal manual was short but was not a true example of a minimalist document, and thus could have been improved. However, what particularly interests me for the discussion here is that all the users had most of their problems in the same three places: with the first task and then with the last two tasks, which were "Do a polled send" and "Do a polled receive."

Scholtz and Hansen do not tell us how the scenarios were worded for the users, but we can gather from the description in the article that the headings for these tasks in both manuals were about "polling." Apparently, neither the interface developers nor the writers of either manual realized that the word *polling* would not match the users' mental model.

More Examples of Pseudo-User-Oriented Headings   The problem of pseudo user-oriented headings is common in user manuals and is something that technical communicators must guard against. Here are other examples gleaned from just a few minutes of perusing manuals on my shelf:

"Tagging with the Wildcard Option"
"Using the Hand Tool"
"Applying Line Styles"
"Grouping Objects"

The first is clearly system oriented. What user's task does it represent?

The second might be appropriate if I were looking at an icon of a hand on the screen and could get directly to an online help screen for that icon. However, it is in the manual as the heading for the section that gives procedures for accomplishing the task that the hand represents.

The third is not as bad as the others, but it is still system oriented. Line styles are part of the program. The user's goal is not to apply a line style.

It may be to change what the line looks like, put arrows on the line, change the thickness of the line, or something else.

The fourth, "Grouping Objects," is not only system oriented. It illustrates my next issue: Are we doing enough to help users move from goals to tasks? "Grouping Objects" may be the right heading for users who understand the concept of grouping in a software program and just need procedures or practice in doing it. If users do not know why they would group objects, however, it is not the right heading. The manual this came from has no section entitled "Working with Several Objects at the Same Time," which might be a better heading for many users.

Headings Should Reflect Users' Tasks in Users' Words   Whether the philosophy behind a manual is traditional task orientation or minimalism, the headings in it will be meaningful to users only if they reflect work that users want to do in the way that users would describe that work. To understand users' work and users' words requires iterative interactions with users. Minimalists stress not only principles and heuristics for organizing and writing manuals, but also the process required to develop a good manual. Many of us have been preaching for many years the importance of a coherent user-centered process for documentation—that extensive, iterative interactions with users and making use of what is learned in those interactions is critical to successful documentation. However, that message from minimalism is not being heeded nearly as much as the message to slash the verbiage.

Are Technical Writers Concentrating on Tasks at Too Low a Level?
One of the principles of minimalism is to focus on tasks that are realistic to users, but knowing what level of task is appropriate is not always easy. The early work on minimalism argued against focusing on tasks that were trivial and system related, such as providing practice in just moving the cursor. That was a reaction against earlier instructional design methodologies, such as programmed instruction, in which students were expected to master explicit subskills in isolation before they were allowed to work on realistic tasks that combined the subskills. Most technical communicators and instructional designers have gotten that point. They use realistic tasks like editing a letter to teach the necessary subskills of navigating around the screen and selecting from menus.

The more difficult question today is at the other end of the spectrum: Are many technical communicators, including those writing minimalist documentation, focusing on real tasks but still starting at the wrong level: focusing on tasks when users need help moving from a larger goal to those task?

Davida Charney and her colleagues (Charney, Reder, and Wells 1988) showed that when users know what they want to do, just giving procedural instructions is sufficient. If users do not know the tasks to do, however, introductory, overview information that helps them select appropriate tasks is useful.

Users May Need Help to Move from Goals to Tasks   As figure 8.1 shows, users start with goals. To meet these goals, they must decide what tasks to do. Only when they know what tasks to do can they attend to the steps and decisions that make up those tasks. For example, users may

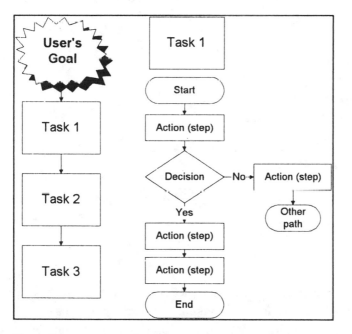

Figure 8.1
To achieve a goal, users have to figure out what tasks to do. Then they have to figure out the steps and decisions needed for each task.

want to send the same e-mail message to several people. That is the goal. To use the e-mail program efficiently, users first have to know that they can set up distribution lists. Then they have to find out how to do tasks they may not have even thought about: how to set up a distribution list and how to use the list as an address in an e-mail message. If the section "Sending an E-mail Message" does not even mention the functionality or have a cross-reference to how to set up a list, users may continue to work in a frustratingly inefficient way, writing the same message over and over.

As products become more complex and as there is more to document, some companies are eliminating all goal-level information and concentrating strictly on task-level procedures. Whether intended or not, misrepresented or not, minimalism has had an influence on eliminating overviews and other structural information that help users move from larger goals to specific tasks.

To understand the point that I am making, consider the first three steps in Donald Norman's seven-step action cycle. Interpreting Norman's (1988, 47–48) stages of execution for a user of a software program might look like this:

Using a program (or a document)
1. Form a goal.
2. Form an intention. (Select tasks to do.)
3. Specify actions to take.

We might then ask these questions:

Using a program (or a document)
1. Form a goal.
   Is the user here?
2. Form an intention. (Select tasks to do.)
   Or is the user here?
3. Specify actions to take.

Tables of Contents and Indexes May Help Users   How do we help users move from goals to tasks? In print manuals, we can make the goal the title of a chapter; write task headings with user-oriented action verbs; and organize those headings in a logical order for meeting the goal. Then, as Philippa Benson and I pointed out in a tutorial for technical writers:

"The headings become the table of contents and the table of contents not only shows users where information is, it also gives them an overview of the task" (Redish and Benson 1986, 269). Van der Meij and Carroll (this volume, chapter 2) make this point strongly in heuristic 2.2: Components of the Instruction Should Reflect the Task Structure, where they say, "The headings should be crafted to convey deliberately and clearly the major procedural elements in the instructional tasks. Such headings help the user keep in view the big picture of the skill being learned."

Some writers have misinterpreted this aspect of minimalism. If the minimal manual has no index, the writers may be concerned about users' needing an alphabetical way to search for their tasks. In some cases, writers have tried to meet this need by organizing the table of contents of the minimal manual with the headings under each main topic in alphabetical order. In listing all the headings under a topic alphabetically, however, writers lose the opportunity to use the table of contents to convey that big picture to users. As Van der Meij and Carroll point out, even minimal manuals that are meant primarily for instruction should be organized logically so that the table of contents shows the overall sequence of tasks needed to reach a goal.

Minimal manuals that are used not just as training materials but also for reference need both a logically organized table of contents and an index. Moreover, although early minimalist guidelines (Carroll 1990; Carroll et al. 1987–1988) suggested dropping almost all supporting information including the index, Carroll more recently has acknowledged that an index is often necessary to facilitate searching and matching users' prior knowledge (conference discussion, November 1995).

Another way to help users grasp the big picture and move from goals to tasks is to provide brief overviews at the beginnings of chapters and sections.

Are Writers Misunderstanding What Minimalism Says about Overviews?
Many readers of Carroll's research believe that minimalism rejects overviews of any kind. However, "less" is not zero, and we should look more closely at what minimalists say and do. Van der Meij and Carroll (this volume, chapter 2) do not say, "Eliminate overviews." They do say,

"Provide an immediate opportunity for users to act" and "An alternative approach [to traditional documentation] is to begin by giving the user less to read and more to do." They are contrasting minimalist documentation with tutorials that begin with fifteen or fifty-six pages of introductory material, not with having a sentence or two at the beginning of a section. In fact, the example they show (figure 2.3) has an overall introduction (one paragraph) and an introduction to each task (one paragraph for each task, focusing, in fact, on the system itself with the headings "Telephone Buttons" and "Display and Display buttons," respectively). The exploratory tasks come as subheads under each of these introductory paragraphs.

A Study on the Value of Brief Overviews   One of the striking and perhaps unexpected results of a research project that Joseph Dumas and I conducted in the early 1990s was that brief overviews can have a significant beneficial effect for people in their first encounter with a new product. The result was part of a large project that we conducted on what makes a user's manual easy to use.

We began by asking six experts for the principles and heuristics (factors and features) that they use in evaluating manuals. They responded with virtually identical factors and features. For the factors, they said a manual must:

• Help users grasp the big picture of the product, that is, help users develop a mental model that helps them predict what to do.
• Make it easy for users to find just the information they need quickly.
• Make it easy for users to understand the information immediately.
• Help users recognize errors and recover from them.

For example, for factor 2, helping users find information quickly, all the experts said that one of the features would be a table of contents that reflects real users' tasks in users' words.

To test the experts' factors and features, we constructed five versions of the user's manual for a new product (a debugger), varying the factors and features systematically. Versions that were high on factor 1, helping users grasp the big picture of the product, had some questions and answers at the beginning of the manual and where relevant elsewhere in the manual. They also had brief overviews at the beginning of chapters and some sections, with short, active sentences or lists, and sometimes pictures. Versions that were low on factor 1 did not have the questions and answers. They either had no overviews or a few overviews with single noun headings, paragraphs instead of lists, and passive sentences.

Fifty programmers who were potential users of the product participated in the study. Each attempted to complete eleven tasks in a usability lab with the product and one of the manuals. The manuals were given out in cyclical order so that person 1 got manual version 1, person 2 got manual version 2, and so on. Each manual was used by ten participants. Participants thought that they were doing a usability evaluation of the product and the manual they were given. They did not know there were other versions of the manual.

What We Learned   The results strongly support the value of the entire group of factors and features. One of the most interesting results was that users who had manuals that were high on factor 1 completed the last half of the tasks faster and the last three tasks much faster than users who had manuals that were low on factor 1. Table 8.1 compares the two manuals that differed only in the presence or absence of overviews.

Total task time did not differ for the two groups. Users of manual 1 spent time reading the mental model information that was not in manual 2. But they made up that time in doing the last few tasks, which took them only 58 percent of the time it took those who had not had any overview information.

Table 8.1
Comparing manuals with and without overviews

Measure	Manual 1 HHHH	Manual 2 LHHH
Total time	1:14:43	1:14:23
Time for last 5 tasks	27:05	30:04
Time for last 3 tasks	8:06	13:53

Table 8.2
Comparing all the manuals on the last few tasks

Measure	Manual 1 H ... HHH	Manual 3 H ... LLH	Manual 2 L ... HHH	Manual 4 L ... HLL	Manual 5 L ... LLL
Time for last 5 tasks	27:05	27:09	30:04	42:12	32:41
Time for last 3 tasks	8:06	8:07	13:53	14:54	12:32

This large difference holds for factor 1 across all the manuals. You can see the differences in table 8.2. The first *H* or *L* under the manual number indicates, respectively, high on factor 1 (overviews) and low on factor 1 (no overviews or a few, poorly written overviews). We interpret this result to mean that providing some questions and answers and very brief overviews, even in a manual that users only consult, that is, in a manual they use while doing, helps users learn, even in the hour or so of their first encounter with the product.

(This study, like others that I have discussed in this chapter, was done in a usability lab. Because we were comparing different versions of a manual, we asked participants to use the manual. As with the other studies, we do not know how much these users, who were computer programmers, would actually use any version of the manual on the job. Therefore, we can only say that if users go to manuals, brief overviews seem to help by promoting incidental learning while doing.)

More Research Is Needed   Questions remain about what even very brief overviews should look like and what information they should contain. In this project, some of the overviews were questions that users are likely to ask and short answers to the questions. Some of the overviews were brief procedural signposts, which seemed to work well. Participants who read them did not jump ahead to act.

But we know that users do sometimes jump the gun and act as soon as they see anything that looks like an instruction (Carroll 1990; Redish 1988). So we still need to ask questions like these: How do we create overviews that help users but that do not encourage them to jump the gun? How short must an overview be to keep users engaged without having them act? How conceptual or procedural should overviews be? How relevant are the findings from Charney and her colleagues today when that work was done with command-based programs and in a mode in which users studied manuals and then did tasks without the manuals rather than in the mode in which typical users actually work?

8.3   Conclusion: What Now for Minimalism?

With this book, the identification of minimalism with slashing the verbiage will perhaps be replaced by a more appropriate identification with being action centered (Draper and Oatley 1992). Nevertheless, more attention still needs to be paid to carrying over the model of the user and the principles of minimalism to the much broader domain of user's guides and online help for entire products, not just instructional materials for new users. In doing so, modifications may be needed to minimalist heuristics. How exploratory should reference manuals be? Isn't an index likely to be useful? Wouldn't short overviews be appropriate?

More attention also needs to be paid to the diversity of users within the general model of the user that Carroll and his colleagues have helped us see so clearly. Not only are all people actively involved in making meaning, each individual is different, and users act differently at different times, have different learning styles, and have different needs to deal with different types of products and problem domains. Technical communicators have been creating new types of both print and online documentation. They have been creating modular documentation to meet the needs of their many user groups and to meet the needs that even one user has at different times and in different situations. How and where does minimalism fit into this broader view of users and their documentation needs?

Moreover, we must appreciate the process needed to develop truly user-oriented, action-oriented documentation. To avoid writing pseudo-user-oriented headings, to understand users' goals, to know how to make the connections to prior experience that users need, and to understand the errors typical users make, we must involve users throughout the process, watch and listen to users, and draft and test iteratively with users.

This process is necessary for any type of documentation—indeed for any software or hardware, as well as for documentation.

References

Brockmann, R. J. 1986. *Writing Better Computer User Documentation: From Paper to Online*. New York: Wiley.

Carroll, J. M. 1990. *The Nurnberg Funnel*. Cambridge, MA: MIT Press.

Carroll, J. M. 1991. Author's reply to Farkas and William's review. *IEEE Transactions on Professional Communication* 34:58.

Carroll, J. M., and Mack, R. L. 1984. Learning to use a word processor: By doing, by thinking, and by knowing. In J. C. Thomas and M. L. Schneider (eds.), *Human Factors in Computer Systems*, pp. 13–15. Norwood, NJ: Ablex.

Carroll, J. M., and Rosson, M. B. 1987. The paradox of the active user. In J. M. Carroll (ed.), *Interfacing Thought: Cognitive Aspects of Human-Computer Interaction*, pp. 80–111. Cambridge, MA: MIT Press.

Carroll, J. M., Smith-Kerker, P., Ford, J., and Mazur-Rimetz, S. 1987–1988. The minimal manual. *Human-Computer Interaction* 3:123–153.

Charney, D. H., Reder, L. M., and Wells, G. W. 1988. Studies of elaboration in instructional texts. In S. Doheny-Farina (ed.), *Effective Documentation: What We Have Learned from Research*, pp. 47–72. Cambridge, MA: MIT Press.

Claxton, C. S., and Murrell, P. H. 1987. *Learning Styles: Implications for Improving Education Practices*. ASHE-ERIC Higher Education Report 4. Washington, DC: Association for the Study of Higher Education.

Draper, S. W., and Oatley, K. 1992. Action centered manuals or minimalist instruction? Alternative theories for Carroll's minimal manuals. In P. O. Holt and N. Williams (eds.), *Computers and Writing: State of the Art*, pp. 222–243. Norwell, MA: Kluwer.

Dumas, J. S., and Redish, J. C. 1993. *A Practical Guide to Usability Testing*. Greenwich CT: Ablex.

Farkas, D. K., and Williams, T. R. 1990. John Carroll's *The Nurnberg Funnel* and minimalist documentation. *IEEE Transactions on Professional Communication* 33:182–187.

Glasbeek, H. 1994. Improving the quality of tutorials: Does minimalism always help? In M. Steehouder, C. Jansen, P. Van der Poort, and R. Verheijen (eds.), *Quality of Technical Documentation*, pp. 77–83. Atlanta, GA: Rodolpi.

Jansen, C. 1993. Research in technical communication in the Netherlands. *Technical Communication* 41:234–239.

Muller, M. J., Carr, R., Ashworth, C., Diekmann, B., Wharton, C., Eickstaedt, C., and Clonts, J. 1995. Telephone operators as knowledge workers: Consultants who meet customer needs. *Human Factors in Computing Systems, CHI '95*

Conference Proceedings, pp. 130–137. New York: Association for Computing Machinery.

Norman, D. A. 1988. *The Design of Everyday Things*. New York: Basic Books.

Price, J. 1984. *How to Write a Computer Manual*. Menlo Park, CA: Benjamin/Cummings.

Price, J., and Korman, H. 1993. *How to Communicate Technical Information*. Menlo Park, CA: Benjamin/Cummings.

Redish, J. C. 1988. Reading to learn to do. *Technical Writing Teacher* 15:223–233.

Redish, J. C. 1989. Writing in organizations. In M. Kogen (ed.), *Writing in the Business Professions*, pp. 97–124. Urbana, IL: National Council of Teachers of English.

Redish, J. C. 1993. Understanding readers. In C. Barnum and S. Carliner (eds.), *Techniques for Technical Communicators*, pp. 14–41. New York: Macmillan.

Redish, J. C. 1995. Are we really entering a post-usability era? *Journal of Computer Documentation* 19:18–24.

Redish, J. C., Battison, R. M., and Gold, E. S. 1985. Making information accessible to readers. In L. Odell and D. G. Goswami (eds.), *Writing in Nonacademic Settings*, pp. 129–153. New York: Guilford Press.

Redish, J. C., and Benson, P. 1986. Planning and producing manuals that really help users. *Proceedings of the Seventh Annual Conference and Exposition, Vol. 1: Tutorials*, pp. 260–285. Fairfax, VA: National Computer Graphics Association.

Scholtz, J., and Hansen, M. 1993. Usability testing a minimal manual for the Intel SatisFAXtion Faxmodem. *IEEE Transactions on Professional Communication* 36:7–11.

Suchman, L. 1987. *Plans and Situated Actions: The Problem of Human Machine Communication*. New York: Cambridge University Press.

Van der Meij, H. 1994. Catching the user in the act. In M. Steehouder, C. Jansen, P. Van der Poort, and R. Verheijen (eds.), *Quality of Technical Documentation*, pp. 201–210. Atlanta, GA: Rodolpi.

Van der Meij, H. 1992. A critical assessment of the Minimalist approach to documentation. *SIGDOC Proceedings*, pp. 7–17. New York: Association for Computing Machinery.

Weidenbeck, S., Zila, P. L., and McConnell, D. S. 1995. End-user training: An empirical study comparing on-line practice methods. *Human Factors in Computing Systems, CHI '95 Conference Proceedings*, pp. 74–81. New York: Association for Computing Machinery.

9

Layering as a Safety Net for Minimalist Documentation

David K. Farkas

In this chapter I argue the value of adding supplementary material to minimalist documentation so as to provide a safety net for users. We can, in other words, use the rhetorical technique of layering to give users access to extra information that they may need if minimalist documentation does not provide all the information they require.

In making this argument, I look broadly at computer documentation. I classify the various forms of computer documentation and consider the degree to which the various categories are minimalist (or can be minimalist) in character and how amenable each category is to the layering strategy. Although there are various ways to classify computer documentation, I have found it most useful to delineate these four fundamental categories:

1. Procedures (found in help systems, user's guides, and minimalist tutorials)
2. Standard print and online tutorials
3. Performance support help (wizards and coaches)
4. Balloon help and other forms of interface-based documentation

All but the performance support category exist in both the print and online media, but throughout this chapter I emphasize online documentation. This is because the online medium has become dominant and because the dynamic nature of online text and graphics is more suitable than is print to layering.

Of the four categories, I focus heavily on procedures, by far the most prevalent category of documentation and the category that minimalist designers have most often worked with. Standard tutorial documentation and performance support, I believe, have less affinity with minimalism than the other two categories, and so I treat them in less depth. Balloon help is covered in detail because it is an inherently minimalist form of documentation, because it is a useful and flexible form of help, and because it can be effectively layered.

The first three categories, although distinct from each another, share one trait: they are task based. They list, in an online table of contents, index, and other places, tasks that users will want to perform and then guide the user through completing these tasks. Balloon help is interface based. Users who explore the interface looking for an interface element relevant to their goals get explanations of the functions of the various interface elements. The chapter closes with a look at Microsoft's "ghosted" help topics, an intriguing design that combines balloon help with task-based procedural help and at times includes elements of performance support help.

9.1   The Risk in Minimalist Documentation

Minimalism is an action-oriented strategy that attempts to accommodate the desire of many users to focus on the interface rather than on the documentation, to experiment, and to exercise their problem-solving skills. To achieve this goal, minimalist documentation is brief and excludes or abridges some of the components found in procedures and standard tutorials. It does include information to assist users in recognizing and recovering from the errors that users are likely to commit when they experiment with the interface.

Minimalism addresses a problem well known in the documentation community and computer industry in general: the reluctance of many users to read documentation (Carroll 1990; Horton 1993; Brockmann 1990; Mirel 1991). When users are unable to accomplish a task or are confused by what they see on the screen, they often try to solve the problem on their own. If they do consult a user's guide or help system, they are likely to scan for just the item of information they hope will solve their problem; if they cannot get the desired information quickly, they will likely abandon the documentation. Often users simply give up on what they were trying to accomplish and look for a workaround. Users' resistance to documentation and related aspects of user behavior were first analyzed by Carroll and Rosson (1987) and provided much of the impetus for the minimalist strategy.

Minimalism is not without risks. Several commentators have expressed concern with reducing the information that users receive (Brockmann 1990; Farkas and Williams 1990; Redish, this volume, chapter 8). Carroll himself acknowledges a potential problem: "learners might not have access to enough information to reason successfully and might be anxious about bearing such responsibilities" (this volume, chapter 1). The risks, as I see them, are these:

1. The user may be unable to complete the task successfully.
2. The user may complete the task but expend more time and energy than he or she wished to.
3. In the process of completing the task (or attempting to), the user may develop an incorrect mental model of the system that will cause difficulties later.

The degree of risk depends on how radically information is cut and just what is cut and how. Carroll's more recent formulations of minimalism (Van der Meij and Carroll, this volume, chapter 2) are more cautious in this regard than earlier formulations of minimalism (Carroll et al. 1987–1988; Carroll 1990). Still, this risk, though different in each minimalist design, is always present.

Reiterative usability testing has always been a core requirement of minimalism (Carroll 1990; Carroll and Van der Meij, this volume, chapter 3), and so one minimalist response to those concerned about sparse information is that first-rate design skills and reiterative usability testing should enable documentors to provide *just* the information that users need and no more. Maybe so, but as Carroll and van der Meij themselves recognize, providing just the right amount of information is a challenging endeavor. Furthermore, because documentation departments tend to be understaffed and software development schedules are often demanding, documentors often lack the opportunity to test and retest their documentation.

Another minimalist response is that learning from errors can be a productive experience. In particular, reasoning about errors increases understanding and promotes retention. This is certainly true to a point, and minimalist designers should attempt to help users learn from their errors. But the efficacy of errors is highly situational. Users will not learn if they get seriously confused, and they may not appreciate this kind of learning if they are under work pressure or have no interest in remembering how the task is performed (Williams and Farkas 1992).

Another complication for minimalism is that often documentors (in my experience, at least) believe that they do not have a fully adequate profile of their users. This situation comes about when documentors are cut off from marketers and others who are closer to the customers, or when the company as a whole has a fuzzy view of its customers.

Finally, we have the issue of diverse audiences. If the users of a software product are composed of diverse groups, the safest approach is usually to create separate documentation for the major groups. But the diversity of the audiences often exceeds the willingness of software companies to create separate documentation components. In fact, commonly a single document set seeks to serve the needs of a diverse audience. The need to write documentation for diverse audiences, which is inadequately addressed by minimalists, severely complicates the task of providing just the information that is necessary. For all these reasons, minimalist designers walk the tightrope or, more precisely, skirt the precipice of insufficient information.

9.2   Layering in Print and Electronic Documents

Layering, a familiar concept in technical communication, means providing clearly marked and useful reading choices, alternative channels through the information that accommodate different needs. Layering can be provided for novices who need more basic information and for experts who need more advanced information. It can also be provided for segments of an audience with special concerns. For example, a report might include an appendix of legal details intended primarily for the organization's attorneys. The concept of layering presents at least some theoretical difficulty because in many print and electronic documents, headings and subheadings only approximate a layering strategy. A clarifying perspective is to say that true layering exists when the channels through the document are part of an explicit strategy for accommodating selective reading. (For a careful analysis of layering, though it uses the term *compartmentalization*, see Holland, Charrow, and Wright 1988.)

As Horton (1994) has noted, layering is more effective online than in print. This is because in the online medium, layering can be accomplished through various kinds of hypertext links (or "jumps") that keep the supplemental information out of the way until it is needed. We will now examine each of the categories of documentation set forth above with an eye to its minimalist character and potential for layering.

9.3 Procedures

Procedural discourse is all around us. Recipes, travel directions, administrative procedures, and instructions for assembling and operating all kinds of equipment are just some of the forms of procedural discourse. Within the world of computer documentation, procedures make up the central part of most help systems and user's guides. Procedures, however, are often closely associated with conceptual overviews, definitions, and other kinds of information. The basic components of computer procedures are briefly described below and are shown in figure 9.1. For a more complete discussion of the components of procedures, see Boggan, Farkas, and Welinske 1996.

The starting point of procedures is the task that users want to accomplish—in other words, the user's goal or purpose. The purpose of the procedure is almost always expressed in the procedure's title. Documentors often elaborate on the procedure title in a brief paragraph or two, sometimes called the conceptual element. The conceptual element clarifies the purpose of the procedure, states any conditions that must be met before the procedure can be carried out, and makes clear any major implications ("side effects") of carrying out the procedure.

The information in the title and conceptual element enables users to decide whether they want to carry out the procedure. If they decide to, they need to know the specific actions they must take. These actions are described in a set of steps (or, on occasion, a single step). Steps often consist of nothing more than straightforward actions: "Under Pagination, click Keep with Next."

```
┌──────────────────────────────────────────────────────────────────────┐
│ ⟨⟩ Microsoft Imager Help                                    [_][□][X]  │
├──────────────────────────────────────────────────────────────────────┤
│ File  Edit  Bookmark  Options  Help                                    │
├──────────────────────────────────────────────────────────────────────┤
│ ┌────────┐┌────────┐┌────────┐┌────────┐                              │
│ │Contents││ Search ││  Back  ││ Print  │                              │
│ └────────┘└────────┘└────────┘└────────┘                              │
├──────────────────────────────────────────────────────────────────────┤
│  Pasting an image                                                      │
│ ───────────────────────────────────────────────────────────────────── │
│  You can insert all or part of an image from the Windows Clipboard into the active. │
│  document.                                                             │
│                                                                        │
│   1. Cut or copy the information you want to paste.                     │
│      If you are pasting to a document in a different application, start the application. │
│   2. Open the document you want to paste into, and then choose Paste from the Edit │
│      menu.                                                              │
│      Imager pastes the upper-left corner of the image in the upper-left corner of the │
│      active document.                                                  │
│                                                                        │
│  Note                                                                  │
│  Not all images can be pasted into documents of all image classes. Images from │
│  another application must be of the same image class as the Imager document into │
│  which you are pasting the image. See Paste command (Edit menu).       │
│                                                                        │
└──────────────────────────────────────────────────────────────────────┘
```

Figure 9.1
A simple procedure with a topic title, a one-sentence conceptual element, two steps (with feedback after step 2), and a note

Other steps are more complex. For example, they may describe optional actions that users may or may not want to take: "To download your files in compressed form, click Compression."

Some steps describe conditions and their associated actions. In other words, they ask users to test for a condition and, if it is operative, to take the action that is necessary to address the condition: "If your view of the tape icon is not expanded, double click on the icon to display its tape volumes."

Documentors sometimes choose to provide a feedback statement to assist the user in verifying that the correct action has been taken and that the system has responded appropriately: "Click the vertex whose position you want to change (the vertex turns magenta, and the pointer changes to a four-headed arrow)."

Many procedures utilize notes, usually located after the final step. Notes convey less important information—usually options that few users will care about and noncritical conditions that few users will encounter. The use of notes, a form of layering, enables the help author to keep the main body of the procedure shorter and less cluttered.

Help Topics

The term *help topic* is often used to describe the physical unit of help information. In other words, a help topic consists of all the information that appears in a single window (whether or not it scrolls) or other display area. Generally procedure topics contain a single procedure, although multiple short procedures can be placed together in a single procedure topic. In addition to procedure topics, there are often topics for overviews, definitions, and descriptions of command options.

Overview Topics

Overview topics are used when help authors want to present more conceptual information than they wish to include in a procedure topic. In addition, an overview topic is often broad enough in scope to serve as the overview for a cluster of procedure topics—for example, an overview topic on document styles, which might run several paragraphs and include one or more graphics, could be accessible from several procedure topics dealing with styles. Not only can users jump from a procedure topic to its associated overview topic, overview topics are often accessible directly from the online contents and online index so that users can choose to read an overview topic prior to looking at an associated procedure topic. Overviews and overview topics figure significantly in the layering of minimalist documentation.

9.4   Layering Minimalist Procedures

Procedure topics are highly amenable to layering, and there are many ways to use layering to provide a safety net for minimalist procedures. Such procedure topics might have, at the initial level of presentation, the following characteristics:

- No conceptual information other than the topic title.
- Steps written at a high level of generality.

• Omission of "note material" (little-used options and noncritical, infrequently encountered conditions).

Through these means, documentation becomes briefer and less intimidating than conventional procedures. Also, users are encouraged to explore the user interface and exercise their problem-solving skills. At the same time, complete information is available through layering for users who want the extra support.

This plan does not challenge or subvert minimalism. Rather, it is a sensible addition. From a certain perspective, backup information can be regarded as information for error recognition and correction (a part of minimalist theory), although users are at least as likely to display backup information to avoid making errors. Moreover, if it turns out that a minimalist help system or manual is perfectly on target with regard to the needs of its audience, the backup information will rarely be used. Assuming designers can carefully monitor how users work with the documentation, the designers might ultimately discard little-used backup topics. Alternatively, if they discover instances in which many users must resort to the backup topics, they can move this information into the initial topics that users encounter. Layering, then, might serve as a means of refining minimalist documentation in the early stages of its use, a substitute for extensive usability testing. We can explore layering in minimalist procedures by examining some layered help systems.

Layering with a How-To Button
A highly effective layering technique, shown in figure 9.2, is to write a step at a high level of generality for users who do not need more detail, but to make this detail available with a how-to button. To layer procedure components other than steps, however, more comprehensive designs are needed.

Layering with Tabs
Microsoft Works 4.0 is an integrated suite of business applications intended for entry-level users. Works help (and certain other Microsoft help systems) uses a distinctive tabbed design to layer various kinds of information. Two portions of a typical topic are shown in figures 9.3 and 9.4. The procedure for creating a numbered list that the user initially

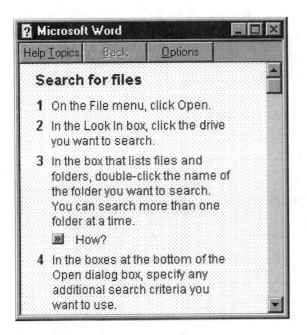

Figure 9.2
Layering with a how-to button

encounters is moderately minimalist; there is no conceptual element, the high-level procedure does not explain how to highlight, and some user options are not addressed. Certainly this is an uncluttered, unintimidating topic that is more action oriented and demands greater involvement from users than traditional procedures. A user who wants more support need only click the More Info tab. Now an overview topic, detailed steps on how to highlight, and information on two special formatting options become available. There are, as we shall see, pitfalls and drawbacks in this kind of design, but the fundamental strategy is sound.

Layering with Multiple Windows
This minimalist help system for a shareware application known as Address Book was created by an undergraduate technical communication major at the University of Washington. Figure 9.5 shows the initial topic that users encounter for an important Address Book task. This

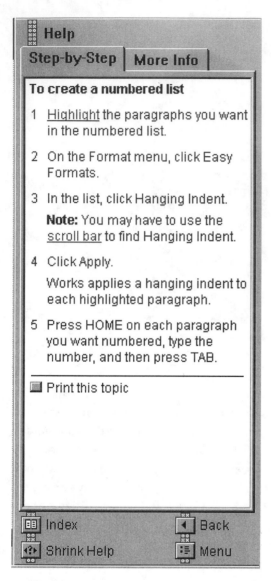

Figure 9.3
A minimalist procedure topic in a tabbed help system

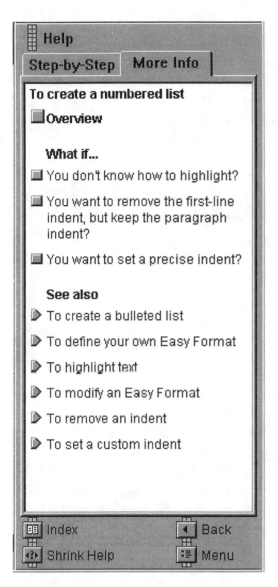

Figure 9.4
More complete information available through layering

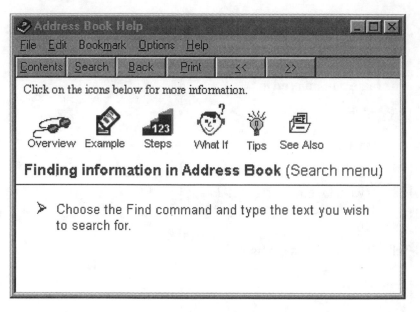

Figure 9.5
A minimalist procedure topic with hot-spot graphics that display more detailed information

topic is decidedly minimalist in character: there is no purpose information other than the topic title, and there is only a single, very general step
(although including the appropriate menu with the topic title is akin to a
step). When the user chooses the Find command, the Find dialog box will
display. In addition to typing text into the text box, the user must also
make selections from a cluster of checkboxes and must choose the OK
or Cancel button. The designer is assuming that many users will be able
to interpret the labels on the checkboxes and so has avoided lengthy
steps (or possibly a table) explaining these choices. The design goal is
that a proficient computer user or a novice with a yen for experimentation should succeed in many tasks using only the initial, minimalist
topic. Layering, however, makes extensive backup information readily
available. Six graphical hot spots provide supplementary information for
users who want (1) conceptual information, (2) an example, (3) detailed
steps, (4) explanations of little-used options and infrequently encountered conditions, (5) tips for the more efficient use of the command, and

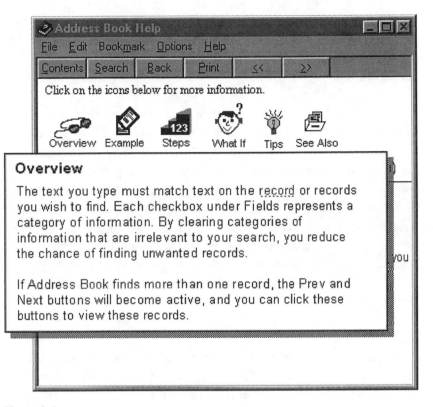

Figure 9.6
Layering with an overview topic displayed as a pop-up window

(6) jumps to related topics. Figure 9.6 shows this topic after the user has clicked the overview hot spot to display a pop-up overview topic.

Layering is not an ideal solution; it tends to make documentation more complex to create and more complex to use. In the case of Address Book help, the help author must write and code a cluster of help topics for each task. Because not every procedure will need the full set of backup topics (for example, in some procedures there will be no need for a What-If topic), the help author must also create grayed-out hot spots. This complexity creates barriers for users. Users of Address Book help must learn that the graphics are hot spots, must learn what kind of information each graphic represents, and must learn not to click the grayed-out hot spots. In the case of the Microsoft Works help system, the tabbed design makes implementation more complex, and some users have had difficulty understanding the operation of the tabs (Lenocker 1996).

9.5   Tutorials

Procedures are instrumental documentation. They enable users to perform a task while reading the procedure, but they do not explicitly support retention. Even so, when users follow traditional procedures, they are likely to remember something. Moreover, they may achieve high levels of retention if they transfer the information to long-term memory by reasoning about the procedure and the task (elaboration) or if they have reason to repeat the task (rehearsal). Procedures, however, do not include special components or special strategies intended to promote retention. In contrast, promoting retention is the defining feature of tutorial documentation, although standard tutorials and minimalist tutorials embody very different strategies for doing so.

Standard Tutorials

Standard tutorials provide a slow-paced, high-comfort learning environment (Price and Korman 1993). They are often geared to relatively inexperienced computer users and to patient and timid learners. More aggressive learners often skip tutorials altogether (Mirel 1991). To provide this highly supportive, high-comfort learning environment, tutorials offer rich conceptual information, steps more detailed than we see in any other form of documentation, and feedback following almost every action the user takes. Standard tutorials are also highly visual. Print tutorials employ many graphics to explain concepts, show the user where to act, and provide feedback. Online tutorials simulate a user's interaction with the software product. One further benefit of online tutorials is that they incorporate routines that can block or efficiently correct user errors.

Standard tutorials seek to achieve retention through transfer. In other words, users do not work on their own tasks. Rather, they work on predefined, canned tasks and then transfer what they have learned to their own work. The benefit of canned tasks is that the tutorial designer determines the tasks that the user will work on and the sequence in which the user will undertake these tasks. On the other hand, there is the considerable risk that the canned task will not be very similar to the user's actual goals, which frustrates both learning and transfer.

Standard tutorials promote retention through rehearsal and elaboration. For this reason, they tend to have components beyond those used in standard procedures—for example, behavioral objectives, previews, reviews, and exercises. Sometimes the exercises are rote drill and practice; other times they are more meaningful. In standard tutorials, layering, at least in the usual sense, is not a central strategy. Tutorials, especially online tutorials, do feature alternative pathways, remedial pathways for users who make errors, and fast-track pathways for users who are moving quickly. Often, however, the choice of pathways is managed by the tutorial rather than the user.

Minimalist Tutorials

Minimalists reject the standard tutorial model. First, minimalists want users to work on their own tasks and so try to avoid canned tasks. When the domain is sufficiently complex that they feel the need to manage the instructional environment for users, they create canned tasks that are as realistic as possible (Carroll, this volume, chapter 1; Van der Meij and Carroll 1995). Furthermore, minimalists reject the slow-paced, highly elaborated form of instruction characteristic of standard tutorials. Minimalist tutorials do not provide rich conceptual information, extensive feedback, and highly detailed steps. Instead, they try to achieve retention through deeper-level processing. In other words, durable learning results from sparse information and other strategies intended to engage and challenge the user.

To a large degree, the minimalist strategy in tutorial documentation is much like the strategy employed in other kinds of minimalist manuals and minimalist help systems. For example, minimalist documentation, whether or not it is labeled tutorial documentation, is likely to include components for recognizing and correcting errors and components that invite users to practice what they have learned. Furthermore, in encouraging users to pursue their own tasks and, hence, jump around in the documentation, minimalist tutorials are akin to user's guides and help systems and are quite unlike standard tutorials (Carroll 1990; Carroll and Van der Meij, this volume, chapter 3). Minimalists do not in fact distinguish crisply between instrumental and instructional discourse. Because the minimalist model for tutorial documentation is not greatly different from the model for procedures, the arguments and design techniques for layering minimalist tutorials are much like those for layering minimalist procedures. For this same reason, I regard minimalist tutorials as a kind of procedural documentation.

9.6   Performance Support Help

Performance support help, a relatively new form of user assistance, attempts to provide the high level of support characteristic of standard tutorials while transcending the great limitation of tutorials by enabling users to undertake their own work. Performance support systems do this by maintaining an ongoing dialogue with the user, in effect walking the user through the tasks she wishes to accomplish. Because branching logic is built into this dialogue, the tasks can be made easier for the user and the amount of text can be reduced. For example, if the user chooses an optional action that makes a subsequent step inapplicable, the system does not display the inapplicable step. Also, performance support help systems are often tightly integrated with the system, so, for example, rather than presenting the user with steps that ask the user to test for a certain condition and, if necessary, perform a required action, the performance support system tests for the condition itself and, if necessary, performs the action for the user.

Performance support consists of two categories: wizards and coaches. Neither is strongly minimalist in character, and so my treatment of performance support is brief. I explain the two forms of performance support help, indicate what I think is their relationship to minimalism, and discuss their use of layering. (For a more complete treatment of performance support help, see Gery 1995; Boggan, Farkas, and Welinske 1996; and Microsoft 1995.)

Wizards
Wizards are increasingly prevalent in contemporary software. Whether or not they are truly help, they are definitely an aspect of the user inter-

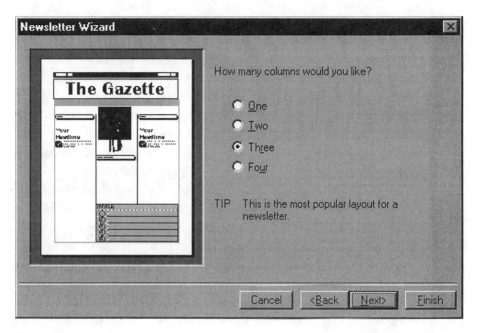

Figure 9.7
A wizard

face that, like help, is highly advisory in nature. A wizard provides a simple, single-purpose interface that enables the user to produce a useful end result quickly. For example, in RayDream's Add Depth, a product for creating 3D display text and copying that text into documents, a wizard enables the user to create the 3D text using a limited set of Add Depth's features with virtually no investment in time. Another example is the Newsletter wizard in Microsoft Word, shown in figure 9.7. This wizard allows a user to create a newsletter layout easily and rapidly, choosing from a limited set of format options. Other wizards perform tasks that would be difficult or impossible to do otherwise; in such cases, the wizard may be the sole means of carrying out the task. Installation software is an example.

Wizards usually consist of panels. A typical wizard panel consists of explanatory information and a simple set of choices (user options), usually provided by option buttons or checkboxes. When the user completes the panel, she can click the Next button and proceed to the next panel.

Wizards accord with minimalism because, unlike standard tutorials, users accomplish actual work. Also, they are action oriented in the sense that the user begins making choices right away. But wizards are antithetical to minimalism in important ways. By providing ample conceptual information, shielding users from the complexities of the product's regular interface, and restricting what the user is able to do, wizards do not encourage exploration, experimentation, or problem solving.

It is possible to layer wizards. For example, a wizard panel can contain a More Info button linked to a panel of supplementary information. But because the initial sequence of wizard panels, the main channel of information, is likely to provide fully adequate explanations of each decision the user will make, More Info buttons and other forms of layering are not typical.

Coach Help

Coach help systems consist of sequences of brief help topics that walk the user through a task. The defining feature of coach help is that users work with the product's regular interface. The typical sequence is this: the user chooses a coach-supported task from some kind of list, reads the first coach topic, performs an action (or a few closely related actions) with the product's regular interface, clicks the coach help topic's Next button or chooses from a set of options, reads the next coach help topic, and continues. Coach help systems are often tightly integrated with the application so that the coach can block user errors and indicate the correct action (as in the Cue Card coach help for Microsoft Publisher 2.0) or else can carry out a task if the user encounters difficulty (as in Macintosh Guide coach help for Apple's System 7.5 operating system).

Coaches are more in tune with minimalism than wizards because users are not shielded from the product's regular interface. Also, whereas errors are impossible with the simplified wizard interface, coaches allow errors and then attempt to provide comprehensive error correction. Furthermore, more so than in wizards, coach topics may provide relatively sparse information, and so there is more likely to be layering. As shown in figure 9.8, many Macintosh Guide coach topics have a "Huh?" button that allows users to display more detailed actions or supplementary conceptual information. Still, coaches, like wizards, dictate the

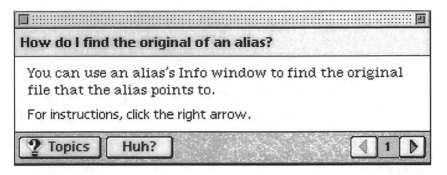

Figure 9.8
Layering in Macintosh Guide help

order in which users will carry out tasks and in general do not encourage exploration.

9.7   Task-Based versus Interface-Based Documentation

We have now considered three of the four categories of documentation in the classification I employ in this chapter. All three are similar in that they are based on procedures. Procedures themselves make up one category. Standard tutorial documentation consists of procedures augmented by elements designed to create a high-comfort environment for the user and to promote retention. Performance support also consists of procedures, though the procedures are decomposed into a sequence of wizard panels or coach topics.

These three categories can be described as task based. They have as their starting point tasks that the user wants to perform. Usually the user is shown a list of tasks, such as the entries in a table of contents. The user chooses the task that corresponds to his or her current goal. (In the case of tutorials, the situation is somewhat different; often the user performs the task chosen by the tutorial designer.) To sum up, we can say that in task-based documentation, the user encounters a task, asks the question, "How do I do this?" and is shown steps and other information that provide an answer to that question (Sellen and Mchol 1990).

The fourth category is interface-based documentation, of which balloon help is the most important kind. Here the user does not begin with a goal set forth in some kind of list. Rather the user examines the various parts of the interface asking, "What is this, and what is this for?" (Sellen and Nichol 1990). Interface-based documentation provides brief answers to these questions. It serves users who are simply exploring, trying to understand better what the software product can do. More frequently, the user has a goal in mind but has formulated this goal on her own rather than from a list of tasks.

Balloon Help

Although there were precursors, balloon help was introduced to most of the computer world in 1991 by Apple Computer as part of the System 7.0 release of the Macintosh operating system. Balloon help has now been widely adopted in the computer industry and modified in various ways. This form of help has been given various names, including Bubble Help (Lotus), What's This? Help and Tool Tips (Microsoft), and Object Help (Borland). Amid all these names, however, *balloon help* remains a serviceable and prevalent general term. Currently, Microsoft's What's This? Help (figure 9.9) is the most complete implementation of balloon help, and so it is the implementation I describe here.

A What's This? Help topic consists of a (usually) small, nonscrolling window that appears next to an element of interest on the user interface. This window has no controls, although jumps to other topics can be implemented. Simplifying somewhat, these topics are displayed when the user clicks on the element of interest or, in certain circumstances, presses the F1 key (Microsoft 1995). They are dismissed by a click anywhere on the screen. Other forms of balloon help display a balloon when the user pauses the pointer over an interface element for which a balloon topic has been written. This mechanism can result in a barrage of unwanted balloons, which was the case in Apple's original implementation.

Balloon help's brief descriptions of interface elements can take various forms. Often the user simply learns the purpose of the interface element: "Saves the document you are working with." The documentor can also explain how to act on the interface element: "Click here to save the document you are working with." At times, brief conceptual information is included: "Increases or decreases the amount of information that appears on your screen. Your monitor and display adapter determine whether you can change the setting. This is sometimes referred to as

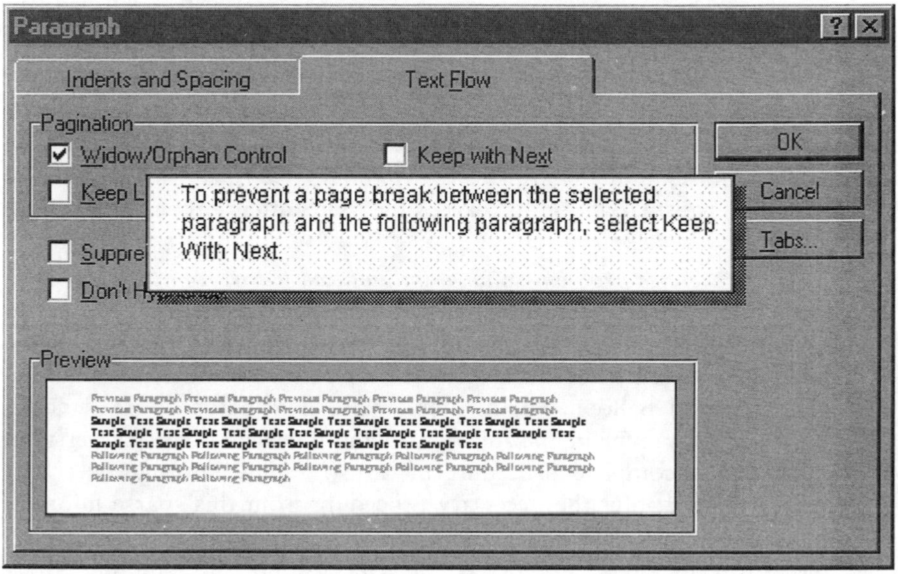

Figure 9.9
A What's This? help topic

'resolution.'" Finally, some balloons (e.g., Tool Tips) provide the names of tool-bar buttons (or similar elements) that have icons rather than text to identify them. These balloons are typically displayed when the user pauses the mouse over the button.

The power of the balloon help model lies in the speed and convenience with which users can get just the information they want (Farkas 1993). Often users need nothing more than an elaboration on the necessarily brief labels that appear on many interface elements. For example, the labels on checkboxes and option buttons typically do not exceed two or three words, and so if a user sees the checkbox label "Keep with Next," the user may well wonder what is being kept with what. A one-sentence explanation of the checkbox's function, rapidly displayed and easily dismissed, resolves the problem.

Balloon Help and Minimalism
Balloon help is inherently minimalist in nature and indeed is perhaps the most prevalent form of minimalism. The minimalist principles that balloon help most fully accords with follow:

1. *Action oriented.*   A central principal of minimalism is that documentation should be action oriented and let the user work with the software interface immediately (Van der Meij and Carroll, this volume, chapter 2). Balloon help follows this principle. It never stands between the user and the interface. Indeed, it is an extension of the interface.

2. *Users focus on the interface and explore the interface.*   In accordance with minimalism, balloon help keeps the user's attention on the interface and encourages exploration.

3. *Users exercise problem-solving abilities and learn from problem solving.*   In accordance with minimalism, balloon help encourages users to exercise their problem-solving abilities. Users must find the part of the interface relevant to the task they wish to perform before they can display a helpful balloon. Furthermore, balloon help topics are typically brief and only explain the function of the interface object rather than presenting a complete procedure or any overview information. Users therefore must infer the necessary procedure from this sparse information. We should remember, however, that requiring users to exercise their problem-solving abilities is not always desirable. Some users may not succeed in figuring out the procedure from balloons or may prefer following the steps of an explicit procedure.

4. *Error correction.*   Minimalism traditionally provides means for users to detect and recover from errors, highly desirable when users learn by exploring the interface. The convenience and speed with which balloons can be displayed can be viewed as a kind of error correction (Carroll 1995). For example, a user who chooses a checkbox in a dialog box and gets the wrong result can easily display that checkbox's balloon and will likely learn why that checkbox was the wrong choice. Then, by displaying the balloons of the other controls on the dialogue box, she will very possibly get on the right track.

Layering Balloon Help to Provide a Safety Net for Users

Although balloon help is an effective form of minimalist documentation, it is easy to envision instances in which users will want more detailed information than balloon help topics usually provide. For example, users might want some kind of conceptual overview; or if the particular control is typically used as part of a complex task involving other parts of the interface, the user might want a complete procedure (Clark 1992). Thus, just as balloons themselves can be seen as a kind of layering, a more communicative extension of the user interface, there is much to say for layering balloon help topics with supplementary information. This can be accomplished in various ways. For example, in some help systems, there are hypertext jumps from balloon help topics to topics providing supplementary information. What we want in balloon help and in documentation generally is a "least-first" strategy. In other words, users should be able to display easily the smallest amount of information that will, in most cases, suffice for the successful completion of the task, and they should be able to display more complete information quickly if the need arises.

Other Forms of Interface-Based Help

In addition to balloon help, the category of interface-based help includes status-line help messages, command topics, and printed command references. Status-line help messages consist usually of brief descriptions of the function of an interface element displayed—often in rapid succession and without any intention on the user's part—at the bottom of a window as the user moves the pointer over various elements of the interface (Microsoft 1995). Because they do not appear near the element of interest, status-line help messages are not obtrusive. On the other hand, a user unattuned to their presence is likely to miss them altogether.

Command topics (figure 9.10) are the online successor to printed command references. They are full-size help topics that explain the function of each of the interface elements on a dialog box. Users generally access command topics from an open dialog box by pressing the F1 key or clicking a special help button on the dialog box. Command topics are now facing stiff competition from balloon help. Balloon help topics are superior to command topics because users can display a balloon explaining just the interface element that interests them, whereas command topics require users to scan the command topic for the text pertaining to the element of interest. On the other hand, with command topics it is easy and natural to write an overview paragraph that explains or introduces the explanations of all the specific interface elements. Command topics are also favored by software companies because coding a single command topic for a dialog box requires much less effort than coding multiple balloon topics.

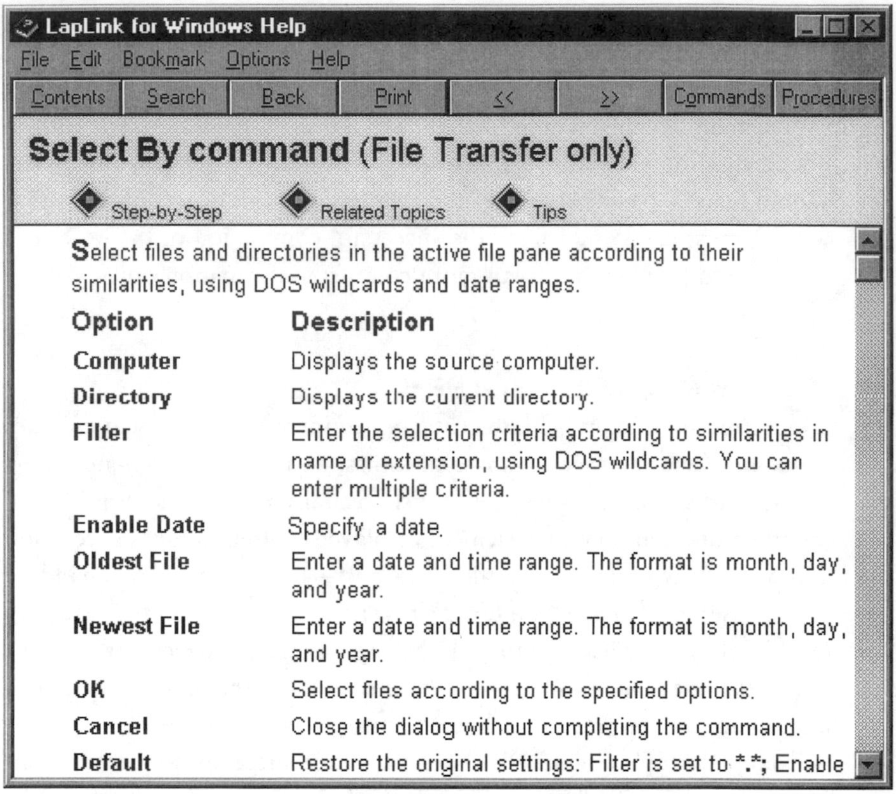

Figure 9.10
A command help topic

9.8   Ghosted Topic: A Hybrid Help Design

There is always the potential for complex hybrids that borrow elements from more than one fundamental help model. An intriguing hybrid can be seen in the "ghosted topics" created by Microsoft for Word 7.0 and other applications in Microsoft Office 95 for Windows. These topics are "ghosted" because there seems to be a ghost at work behind the scenes.

If a user of Word for Windows goes to the online contents and chooses the entry "Finding text and formatting" (in the Editing branch of the contents hierarchy), something unusual happens: the Edit menu drops from Word's menu bar, the commands on this menu highlight succes-

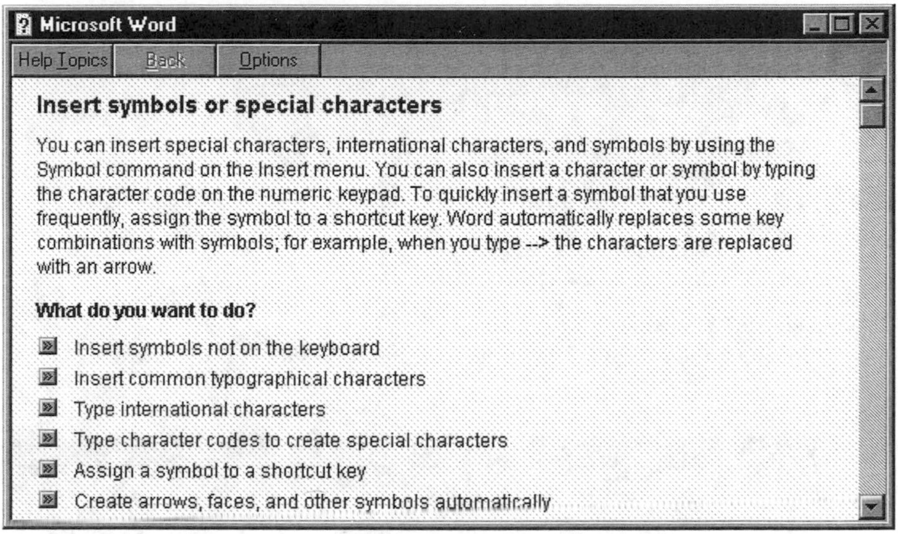

Figure 9.11
Prompting the user to clarify what should be inserted

sively until the Find command is reached, the find dialog box displays, and a What's This? help topic associated with this dialog box displays. What we have is a surprising synthesis of balloon help and procedure help. Although the user is looking at a standard balloon help topic, the user accessed this topic from the contents (or from the index) rather than directly from the interface. Also, the means with which this balloon topic is displayed provides kinds of information that users normally get from procedure topics. First, the entry in the contents (or index), "Finding text and formatting," is a brief statement of purpose. Traditionally this entry more or less duplicates the title of a procedure topic (which is a brief statement of purpose). In the case of ghosted topics, this statement of purpose nicely complements the more specific purpose information usually found in balloon help topics. In addition, by opening the Find dialog box automatically, this ghosted topic eliminates what is usually the first step of a procedure topic, "From the X menu, choose the Y command." A balloon help topic, in effect, is functioning as a minimalist procedure topic.

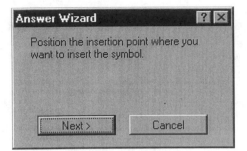

Figure 9.12
Prompting the user to indicate where the insertion should take place.

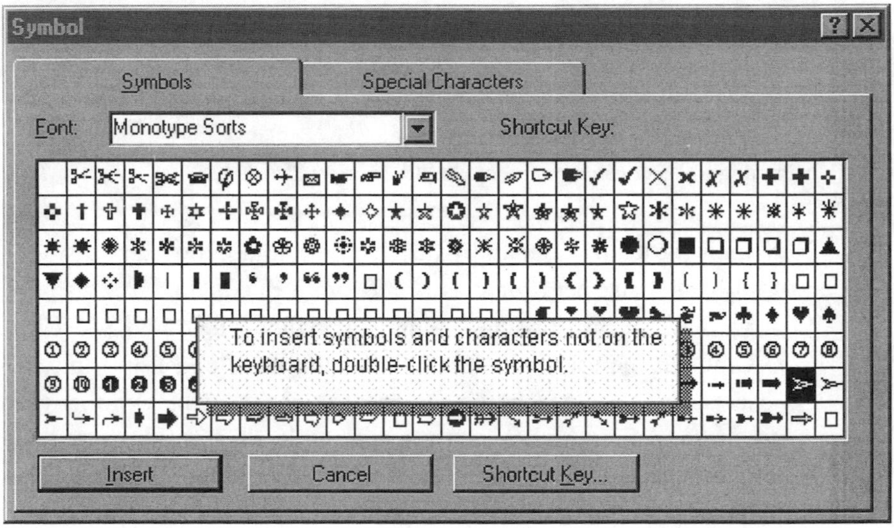

Figure 9.13
The insert symbol dialog box and a What's This? help topic

In some instances, ghosted topics exhibit an additional behavior that borrows from performance support help. When the Word user chooses "Inserting symbols or special characters" from the contents (under Typing) or from the index, the Word help system, functioning as a form of coach help, prompts the user to specify what kind of symbol or special character the user wants to insert (figure 9.11). If the user indicates, by making a choice from a menu, that she wants to insert a symbol not on the keyboard, the help system maintains this ongoing dialog by asking the user to indicate where in the document she wishes to insert the symbol (figure 9.12). Finally, the Insert Symbols dialog box (which includes an array of available symbols) displays along with an explanatory What's This? topic (figure 9.13).

Ghosted topics have significant drawbacks. They are difficult to implement, and they can be implemented only for certain tasks.

In the current implementation, users are often startled when ghosting occurs. Even so, ghosted topics are a very promising innovation in help design, a sophisticated melding of several documentation strategies, minimalism most certainly among them.

References

Boggan, S., Farkas, D. K., and Welinske, J. 1996. *Developing Online Help for Windows 95*. Boston: International Thomson Computer Press.

Brockmann, R. J. 1990. *Writing Better Computer Documentation: From Paper to Hypertext*. New York: Wiley.

Carroll, J. M. 1990. *The Nurnberg Funnel: Designing Minimalist Instruction for Practical Computer Skill*. Cambridge, MA: MIT Press.

Carroll, J. M. 1995. Workshop discussion, Blacksburg, VA, November 18.

Carroll, J. M., and Rosson, M. B. 1987. "The Paradox of the Active User." In J. M. Carroll (ed.), *Interfacing Thought: Cognitive Aspects of Human-Computer Interaction*, pp. 80–111. Cambridge, MA: MIT Press.

Carroll, J. M., Smith-Kerker, P. A., Ford, J. R., and Mazur-Rimetz, S. A. 1987–1988. "The Minimal Manual." *Human-Computer Interaction* 3:123–153.

Clark, D. 1992. "Object-Lessons from Self-Explanatory Objects." *Computers and Education* 18:11–22.

Farkas, D. K. 1993. "The Role of Balloon Help in the Documentation Set." *Journal of Computer Documentation* 17, no. 2:3–20.

Farkas, D. K., and Williams, T. R. 1990. "John Carroll's *Nurnberg Funnel* and Minimalist Documentation." *IEEE Transactions in Professional Communication* 33, no. 4:182–187.

Gery, G., ed. 1995. *Performance Improvement Quarterly* 8, no. 1 (special issue on performance support).

Holland, V. M., Charrow, V. R., and Wright, W. W. 1988. "How Can Technical Writers Write Effectively for Several Audiences at Once?" in L. Beene and P. White (eds.), *Solving Problems in Technical Writing*. Oxford: Oxford University Press.

Horton, W. 1993. "Let's Do Away with Manuals Before They Do Away with Us." *Technical Communication* 40, no. 1:26–34.

Horton, W. 1994. *Designing and Writing Online Documentation: Hypermedia for Self-Supporting Products*. 2d ed. New York: Wiley.

Lenocker, G. 1996. Personal communication, Redmond, WA, May 31. (Lenocker is the Microsoft Works documentation manager).

Microsoft. 1995. *The Windows Interface Guidelines for Software Design*. Redmond, WA: Microsoft Press.

Mirel, B. 1991. "Designing Manuals for Active Learning Styles." *Technical Communication* 38, no. 1:75–88.

Price, J., and Korman H. 1993. *How to Communicate Technical Information: A Handbook of Software and Hardware Documentation*. Redwood City, CA: Benjamin/Cummings.

Sellen, A., and Nichol, A. 1990. "Building User-Centered On-line Help." In B. Laurel (ed.), *The Art of Human-Computer Interface Design*. Reading, MA: Addison-Wesley.

Williams, T. R., and Farkas, D. K. 1992. "Minimalism Reconsidered: Should We Design Documentation for Exploratory Learning?" *SIGCHI Bulletin* 24, no. 2:41–50.

10

Optimizing the Joint Handling of Manual and Screen

Hans van der Meij

The user of a manual generally engages in some reading, some doing, some problem solving, and some switching back and forth between manual and screen. For example, the user may read various task descriptions, execute the actions needed to realize these tasks, correct mistakes, and coordinate or harmonize the processing of the manual with the handling of keyboard and screen. To support these user behaviors, the writer of a manual presents background information, action information, error information and coordinative information (Van der Meij 1994; Van der Meij and Carroll, this volume, chapter 2). Figure 10.1 characterizes these main information types.

In minimalism there has been research on action information (Black, Bechtold, Mitrani, and Carroll 1989; Black, Carroll, and McGuigan 1987; Frese et al. 1988; Gong and Elkerton 1990; VanderLinden, Cocklin, and McKita 1988; Wendel and Frese 1987; Wiedenbeck, Zila, and McConnell, 1995) and on error information (Frese et al. 1991; Gong and Elkerton 1990; Lazonder and Van der Meij 1994, 1995). The role and design of coordinative information (CI) within a minimalist approach has not yet been examined. It is the focus of this chapter.

10.1 Coordinative Information

The user of a manual must pay attention to three distinct sources of information: the paper manual, the screen, and an input device. The separate handling of each of these sources generally falls well within what most users can comfortably deal with. It is their joint processing that is taxing. And yet this is what users must do frequently: users must

Action information
Purposes: Primary support for goal-directed actions; primary role in constructive
              knowledge and skills development
Appearances: Methods (procedures), action steps, commands, prompts

Error information
Purposes: Primary support for troubleshooting actions; primary role in corrective
              knowledge and skills development
Appearances: Warnings, problem-solving information (components: detection, definition,
              diagnosis, correction)

Background information
Purposes: Primary support for goal setting, planning, and all other decision making;
              secondary support in general knowledge and skills development
Appearances: Goals, plans, selection rules, conceptual information (advance organizers,
              summaries, decision tables)

Coordinative information
Purposes: General support for handling of information from manual, keyboard, and
              screen; specific support for: paying attention to, identifying, locating, and
              verifying; secondary support in general knowledge and skills development,
              and for motivation
Appearances: Input devices (keys, mouse, trackball), full screens or partial screens
              (buttons, menu options, icons); variations in: content (complete or
              incomplete), position (before, within, or after) and form (textual or visual)

Figure 10.1
The four main information types in minimal manuals

coordinate (one could also say harmonize or synchronize) the processing of multiple sources of information.

Quite a number of mistakes of users seem to stem from coordination problems (split-attention problems, in the terminology of Sweller and Chandler 1994). For example, it is probably a coordination problem that causes users to skip one or two instructions when they have to search for the right key on the keyboard. Coordination problems probably also partly account for the asynchrony mistakes that result from the nose-in-the-book phenomenon. Users sometimes literally do not see the effects of their actions because they attend mainly to the manual. The result may be that the user is already trying to execute a new command while the program is still processing an earlier command.

In minimalism the coordination problem has long been recognized as an important obstacle for users. All minimal manuals therefore frequently give CI to help users deal with this obstacle. Most of the CI in these manuals supports the handling of information appearing on the screen. Support for handling input devices such as a keyboard or mouse is scarce. Apparently the audiences involved have been found skilled enough for the writer to leave out that information. This chapter too pays relatively little attention to the role and design of CI for handling input devices. It concentrates on the support that users can be given for optimizing the joint handling of manual and screen. The two main variations in form will be examined: text (or pointers) and pictures (or screen captures).

10.2   Coordinative Information as Text

In most minimal manuals the CI that should support the joint handling of manual and screen is given textually. Users are given a pointer such as, "Look at the status bar to see the message WordPerfect sends you," to call their attention to something appearing on the screen. Henceforth this textual variant for dealing with coordination obstacles will be referred to as CI-T, or as pointer(s).

Users can also be given pictorial support for the handling of manual and screen. In most cases the picture is a screen capture, or a screen dump, screen (snap)shot, or clip as it is sometimes called. In various manuals screen captures are the only pictures used (Horton 1991, 1993; Houghton-Alico 1985). Since pictures rarely appear without text, the study examines the role and design of a combination of text and picture. This combination will henceforth be referred to as CI-TP as text and screen capture(s), or simply as text and picture.

CI-T and CI-TP can serve the same goals, and their design may vary along the same dimensions. For example, both variants aim to reduce coordination obstacles, and both may give the user incomplete information for support. CI-TP thus shares the same roles and design variations with CI-T. However, it also has some unique characteristics that set it apart from CI-T. Wherein the two differ will become clear shortly. First, the role and design of CI-T will be discussed. Then CI-TP is examined, and an experiment is reported in which the effects of these two variants are assessed.

Pay attention to
"The program asks you whether you really would like to remove the file."
"Have you seen the two clearly distinguishable parts on the screen?"
"From here on WordPerfect tells you what to do next."

Identify
"A printer icon appears on your screen. It blinks."
"See how this changes the shape of the cursor."
"You are now using the font that is preceded by an *."

Locate
"WordPerfect asks a question. See where it appears on the screen."
"The Recipe Status always appears in the last column."
"Look at the statusbar to see the message WordPerfect sends you."

Verify
"Make sure your screen is empty before starting this exercise."
"You should now see the Composition screen."
"Check if the following question appears on the screen: Document to be saved:"

Figure 10.2
A pointer may stimulate or simplify four specific cognitive purposes.

Roles of CI-T

The main goal of CI-T is to synchronize the processing of multiple sources of information. All pointers together should help users handle coordination obstacles. In addition, each pointer has other uses besides harmonizing the joint processing of manual and screen. On a lower, individual level, each pointer should support one or more of the following cognitive processes: paying attention to, identifying, locating, and verifying (see figure 10.2).

Pointers may also serve another general goal: contribute to user motivation (self-confidence). Pointers can raise self-confidence in two ways. First, a pointer can enable the user to complete a task that is otherwise too difficult to realize. A pointer can make a task feasible. Because most pointers are deliberately incomplete, the tasks remain challenging; users must put in some cognitive effort to achieve their goal. Pointers can also contribute to self-confidence by reassuring the user. A pointer typically communicates something like, "If you see x or can do x, you are still on the right track, continue onward." In general, this reassuring effect is considered most important for tutorials and for anxious novices (Horton 1993; Price 1984; Price and Korman 1993).

Design of CI-T

There are many different ways for presenting pointers (CI-T). Variations depend on the specific cognitive process(es) the pointer is intended to support, as well as general design considerations. Main variations have to do with their content, position, and form.

Variations in content result from two design decisions: the kind(s) of cognitive process(es) the pointer should support and the level of completeness.

The decision about what cognitive process(es) to support partly follows logically from the way in which most task scenarios develop. At the beginning of a new task, the user's attention often must be drawn, or it may be necessary for the user to verify whether he or she is in the right starting position. Thus, the pointers may simply be asking the user to pay attention to (an object on) the screen or to check the presence of an object on the screen. During task execution, the user often needs some support in dealing with complex instructions and crowded screens. Typically this suggests that the user must be given a pointer for help in finding an object, such as a menu option, a window, a button, or a dialogue. Verification is always needed after task completion. Users should engage in such checks routinely, and pointers can help them develop this habit. At the end of a task, one often finds pointers that name the screen or screen part that the user should be facing (e.g., "You should now see the Recipe Screen").

As always, it is difficult the find the right level of completeness. The writer who wishes to apply the heuristic to be brief and not spell out everything faces the tough task of giving just the right amount of support—neither too much nor too little. The delicate balance is easily disturbed; the writer must carefully consider when and why it is useful to omit something (see misconception 2 in chapter 3). Most of the pointers in minimal manuals are incomplete. They do not specify everything. This is illustrated in the two examples from a minimal manual shown figure 10.3.

In deciding about the level of completeness, one should take into account the main function of the manual. Most minimal manuals are tutorials, primarily designed to support learning to do. For this purpose, incomplete CI is optimal; the pointers stimulate the thinking vital for

Type 1
Control manual: The next question appears on the status bar: "Document to be saved:"
Minimal manual: Check if the following question appears on the screen: "Document to be saved:"
Type 2
Control manual: On the status bar you will see the following comment: "Move cursor; Press Enter to retrieve"
Minimal manual: WordPerfect asks a question. See where it appears on the screen.

Figure 10.3
Linguistic variations and differences in completeness in the pointers examined by Van der Meij (1992)

learning. But if the manual is a reference guide, primarily serving to support doing, the writer may want to decide to give fewer incomplete instructions to speed up task execution.

Variations in position are constrained by the fact that nearly all pointers appear in the immediate vicinity of action information. They can be found right before, within, or after instructions. Positioning and content are often intertwined. There is a regularity in the way in which the positioning and specific functions of the pointers interact. That is, the "before-within-after" positioning often coincides with an "attend/verify–identify/locate–verify" functionality. (Instructions with many action steps may involve a repetition of this cycle.)

Pointers positioned before an instruction often prompt the user to pay attention to something on the screen, or they stimulate the user to verify whether the right starting conditions have been met: "To start right here, you should be facing the homepage of the program." Most of the pointers within instructions stimulate the user to identify or locate an object on the screen. The user might thus receive a pointer such as, "Please look at the Instructor window on your screen," or "See where the new icon appears." When all instructions have been completed, the pointer often suggests that the user verify the outcome: "You have completed the exercise successfully if, after a few seconds, a 'document changed' reaction appears."

For pointers, the variations in form concern only linguistic variations. Whenever possible, pointers should be written so that they stimulate the user to look up from the manual to examine the screen. In one study pointers were found to have exactly this effect on users (Van der Meij 1992). That study examined the effects of CI-T on users of a minimal manual with the effects of CI-T on users of a control manual. The main variations in the CI-T presented in these two manuals are shown in figure 10.3.

Observations revealed that the coordinative information in the minimal manual often had the intended effect (van der Meij 1992). Nearly 80 percent of the pointers made users examine their screen. The users of the control manual also used the majority of the pointers (69 percent) for switching back and forth between manual and screen; however, this percentage was significantly lower than for the users of the minimal manual ($F(1, 23) = 5.45$, $p < .05$). It is unclear what caused this difference. Was it the variation in content and form of the CI-T, or the more active processing of the minimal manual in general that also made its CI-T more engaging?

10.3   Coordinative Information as Text and Picture

The role and design of screen captures, alone or in combination with text, are unknown by and large. Detailed conceptual and experimental work is virtually nonexistent. For example, the most elaborate conceptual view presented in the literature is a three-page discussion by Horton (1993), and the only experiment on screen captures, the study of Nowaczyk and James (1993), is plagued with a number of serious flaws (see Van der Meij 1996a).

Horton (1993) suggests that screen captures are useful because they offer visual relief from pages of just text. In addition, they may improve verification and can help build an imagine of using the system. Horton also mentions two main design issues: size of reproduction—50 percent actual size is generally best—and displayed object—showing part of the screen is often preferable to showing the whole screen.

Text and screen capture in combination (CI-TP) can serve more roles, and there are more design issues to deal with than Horton (1993) described. Among others, a comprehensive analysis of some visual manuals was conducted to unearth the special functions and design issues. This section summarizes the outcomes from that analysis, providing ample information on the role and design of CI-TP (see Van der Grijspaarde 1995a; Van der Meij 1996b).

CI-TP can serve the same roles as CI-T. And just as for CI-T, its design variations also depend on decisions about content, position, and form. These shared aspects are discussed only briefly here. Mainly the unique aspects of CI-TP are addressed. With a combination of text and screen captures, it is possible to satisfy distinct roles that pointers alone cannot realize. The combination of text and screen captures also leads to important, special issues of design: those concerning page design and balancing of picture and text.

Shared Roles of CI-T and CI-TP

With a combination of text and screen capture, it is possible to realize the same general goal of reducing coordination obstacles and also to support the same specific cognitive process(es) as pointers do. In this sense, CI-T and CI-TP may be said to share the general goal of all CI and to share the specific goals of helping users to pay attention to, identify, locate, and verify objects (e.g., menus, windows, buttons, screens). This does not mean that the two also have the same effect.

Indeed, two opposite predictions exist about their general support for handling coordination obstacles (Sweller and Chandler 1994). According to one view, CI-TP is less helpful than CI-T because it adds information to an already overloaded user. The other view suggests that CI-TP is more helpful than CI-T because it better allows the user to handle the information that is presented. Only the latter view will be detailed here. That is, I will argue why CI-TP may have a beneficial effect on the specific cognitive processes of paying attention to, identifying locating, and verifying.

A screen capture automatically draws the user's attention. It catches the user's eye more easily than a pointer—in general, an important advantage of pictures over text (White 1987). Since users are more likely to notice pictures, CI-TP may be more effective than CI-T in attracting the users' attention.

A combination of text and picture is probably a better help than a pointer alone when the user needs to identify or locate an object in a complex display (e.g., a screen with many overlays, buttons, variables, or open spaces to be filled in). For simple displays such as a blank screen with a menu bar, the form variation probably does not matter since the user can identify the relevant object nearly instantaneously, regardless of the form in which the prompt is given. For complex displays, however, the added presence of a screen capture can increase the speed of detection because the user needs merely to compare images. Screen captures may also increase accuracy. They may help prevent confusion by identifying the right button, window, screen, or variable (see figure 10.4a).

A combination of text and picture is probably also more helpful than a pointer alone when users must verify task progression. Screen captures "confirm a reader's progress in learning a tutorial" (Price and Korman 1993, 202; Horton 1993). After people press a key, they want to know they have done the right thing. Screen captures support verification by showing a screen, or part of it, that should be the same as on the user's monitor. Thus, a screen capture serves as a bridge between the textual description of an outcome (e.g., "You should now see *x* on your screen") and the real outcome on the screen (see figure 10.4b).

Unique Roles of CI-TP

CI-TP can affect users in ways that are impossible to realize with pointers alone. One unique contribution of CI-TP is that the user can be instructed to do something and simultaneously be given some support for handling the screen (or input device; see Krull 1994). The contribution is best exemplified by contrasting figure 10.5 with figure 10.6. Some of the design options for directly coupling instructions and pictures are probably quite effective for reducing cognitive load because users are presented with the image of the object they should be looking for. The coupling of instruction and picture can also be realized indirectly by drawing a hairline between a described object in an instruction and a screen capture (see figure 10.7).

Another unique possibility of CI-TP is that it may contribute to image formation. All of the pictures together can give users the look of a program. Image formation is probably best served when the manual offers full screens that illustrate the major displays that users encounter during

Identify & locate

Type 1

> You are now using the font
> that is preceded by an *.

Type 2

> The hidden code for
> underline is shown in your
> underwater screen.

a

Figure 10.4

(*a*) A combination of text and picture can help users quickly identify and locate the right object(s) on the screen. (*b*) A combination of text and picture can help users quickly verify program states at the start, in the middle, or at the end of a procedure.

Verify

Type 1

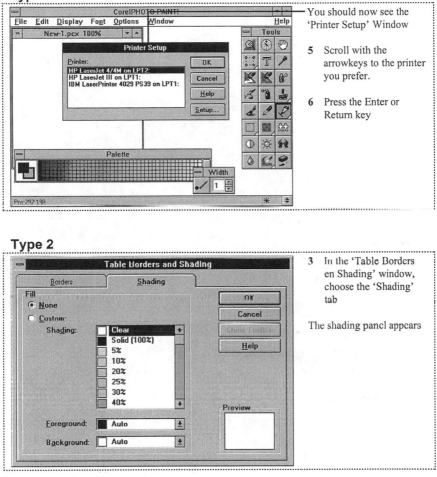

You should now see the 'Printer Setup' Window

5 Scroll with the arrowkeys to the printer you prefer.

6 Press the Enter or Return key

Type 2

3 In the 'Table Borders en Shading' window, choose the 'Shading' tab

The shading panel appears

b

Figure 10.4 (continued)

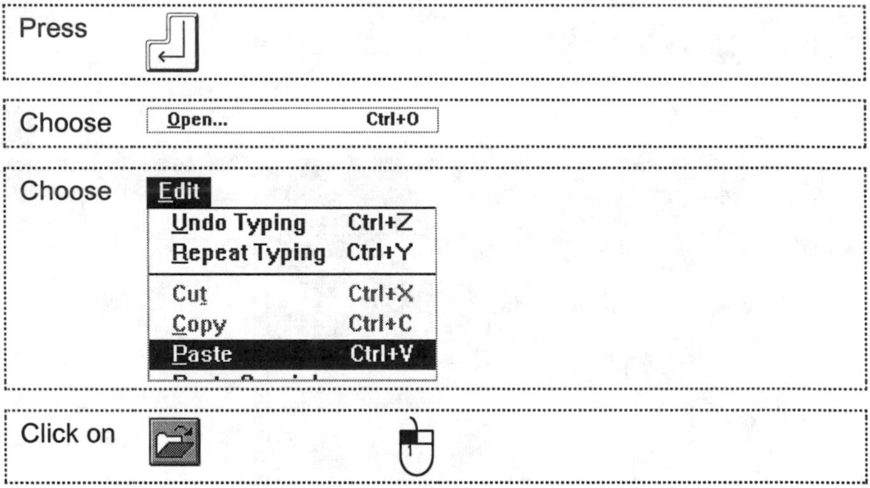

Figure 10.6
Instructions with a direct coupling of text and picture

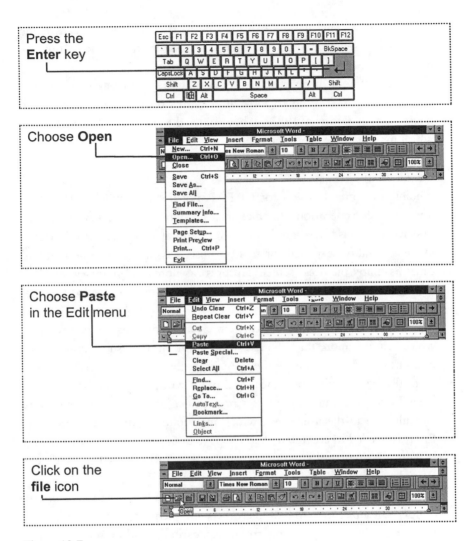

Figure 10.7
Instructions with an indirect coupling of text and picture

task execution. The manual can then be used as a book to read. Being more or less self-contained, the user can study it without activating the program.

A third, unique benefit of CI-TP is that the pictures can make the manual more interesting to look at. Pictures offer visual relief on full pages of text (Horton 1993). They make the manual more attractive, which may increase user motivation.

Design of CI-TP

Finding an optimal design for CI-TP is not a simple matter. There are numerous considerations to take into account. To unearth the major design variations, an analysis of visual manuals was conducted. Visual manuals qualify very well for this purpose, having fifty to one hundred times as many pictures (screen captures) as nonvisual manuals do. Following is a brief summary of that analysis (Van der Grijspaarde 1995a; Van der Meij 1996b).

One of the critical design features in visual manuals is the *page design*, which requires more than the usual attention. In nonvisual manuals, the user knows where to start and end reading; the user's eye is drawn automatically by the titles, headings, and other words that stand out on the page. In visual manuals, the frequent presence of pictures makes it more difficult to lead the user's eye, which may follow a more diverse route. Effort is needed to create an effective page design; the writer must attend to how the joint presentation of text and pictures leads the user's eye (Van der Meij 1996b).

Another critical design feature in visual manuals concerns the *tuning* of text with pictures and of pictures with pictures. For example, the writer may decide to give only full screen captures and present these at a 50 percent reduction of the actual size. The pictures then all give a similar view of the program, and the user does not have to rescale images mentally.

These and other design issues for creating effective combinations of text and picture are illustrated below in a discussion of the two main variants of visual manuals: the guided tour manual and the step-by-step manual.

Guided Tour Manuals   In these manuals, screen captures are used to group together all information that belongs to a (sub)task. The pictures show the main events, displaying important changes on the screen. Armchair reading already gives an impression of what happens during task execution; users can easily get the look of a program.

A prototypical example of this kind of manual is the visual learning guide, now a trademarked name (Gardner and Beatty 1993a, 1993b). Mostly full screens (in reduced format) are shown (see figure 10.8). Colored hairlines are used to draw the users' attention to the relevant part of the screen capture and to connect textual and visual information.

Guided tour manuals are aimed at adult users with a few basic computer skills. Gardner and Beatty (1993a) claim that their visual learning guides are very effective, but no scientific report has yet substantiated this claim.

Step-by-Step Manuals   These manuals (Stuur 1992, 1993) differ in three important ways from guided tour manuals: (1) all actions and all effects of actions are supported with a screen capture, (2) many actions for which the user must handle the mouse are visualized, and (3) there is a mixture of full- and partial-screen captures, with the latter being more frequent.

Figure 10.9 shows a section from a step-by-step manual (Stuur 1992). The coupling of actions to screen captures supports the action-reaction mode typical in human-computer interaction. The icon with the input device supports the execution of the correct physical action. Full-screen captures are typically displayed only at the start and end of an instruction. Partial-screen captures (menus and menu options) are shown at each intermediate stage.

Step-by-step manuals have a minimalist design. They are task oriented, users are given realistic tasks, error information appears regularly and timely, there are "on your own" sections at the end of short chapters, and so on. The manuals are written for a specific audience: children and adults over age fifty-five.

Step-by-step manuals are highly acclaimed in the Netherlands; one even won first prize as best book for children. The manuals also sell extremely well and have been translated into English, French, German,

Moving text

With this paragraph you remove a part of the text of one part of the memo and replace it somewhere else.

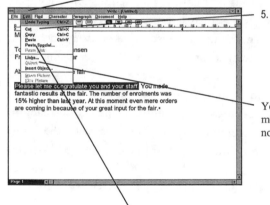

1. **Put** the mouse pointer in front of **the word Please**.

2. **Click** to put the insertion point here.

3. **Press the mouse button and keep it pressed** while **dragging** the **marking** over the complete sentence and the spacing behind. Relieve the mouse button.

4. **Click Edit** from the menu bar to open this menu.

5. **Choose Cut**. The marked text disappears and is sent to the clipboard, where it will stay until you paste it somewhere else or replace it by other data on the clipboard.

You see that several options of the menu are grey, which means they are not available at this moment.

If you have cut or copied data from a Windows program before performing this action, the clipboard will already contain data. This will make available the Pasting option, which is therefore darkened.

Figure 10.8
An example from a guided tour type of visual manual (from Gardner and Beatty 1993b)

Cutting

You can cut a part of text. It will be put automatically on the clipboard.

You have to select the part of text first, before you are able to cut it.

⇨ **Watch out!**

Think about this: Select first ...before action.

☞ **Select the word** *Holland*

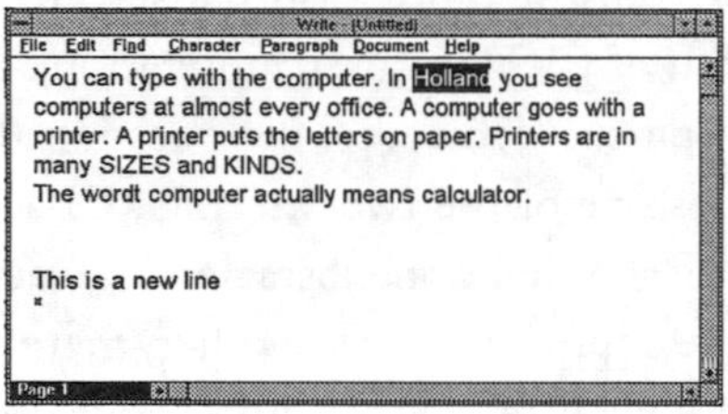

☞ **Click Edit**

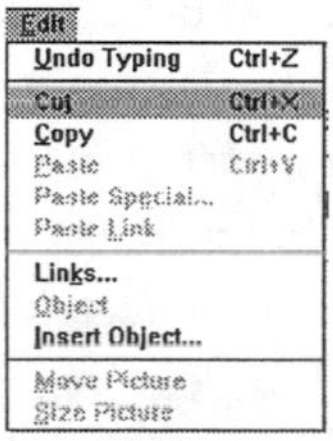

☞ **Click Cut**

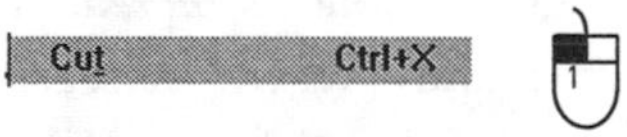

The word *Holland* is cut of the text:

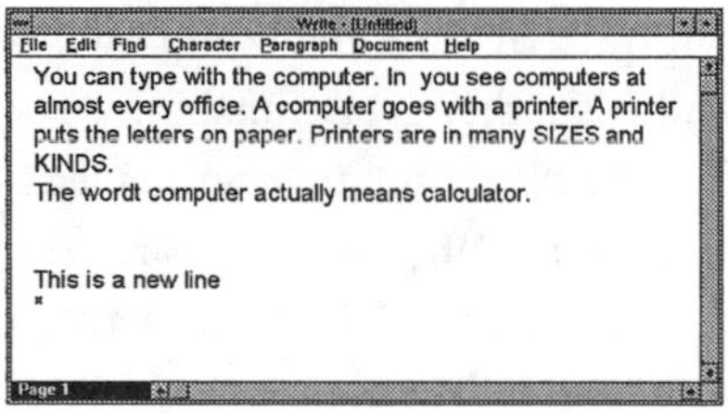

Holland is on the clipboard now. You can paste Holland back in the text:

Figure 10.9
An example for a step-by-step type of visual manual (from Stuur 1992)

Japanese, Polish, and Portuguese. No research on their effectiveness has yet been published.

10.4   Empirical Study

The various discussions on the role and design of CI allow for detailed experiments. For example, one could study how CI-T, or CI-TP, affects the cognitive processes of paying attention to, identifying, locating, and verifying screens or objects on the screen. One could also examine the contribution of CI-TP to user motivation. These are all quite interesting options to pursue. However, the question that should be dealt with first is this: Does one of the two variants, CI-T or CI-TP, better support the handling of coordination obstacles?" If different tests show no advantages of one approach over the other, there is probably little to be gained from examining detailed roles and designs of either CI-T or CI-TP.

It is impossible to answer this question from theory alone. There are advantages and disadvantages to presenting users a combination of text and picture (CI-TP) rather than just some text (pointers or CI-T), or no information at all for handling coordination obstacles. And there are two opposite predictions on the general effects of CI-T and CI-TP on users.

The prediction that CI-TP is less helpful than CI-T rests on the assumption that cognitive load is *increased*. According to this view, the combination of text and picture increases the problems of the user because there is more information to attend to. Instead of just the textual information, the user now must pay attention to the text and the screen capture, and also their relationship. This assumption, known as the redundancy hypothesis, hinges on the idea that the pictures merely repeat the textual information and therefore are considered to be redundant (Sweller and Chandler 1994). A moderate expression of the redundancy hypothesis is that only screen captures that share goals with pointers, or screen captures that visualize the obvious (simple screens), have a negative effect on users.

The prediction that CI-TP is more helpful than CI-T rests on the assumption that cognitive load is *reduced*. According to this view, pictures help the user in handling coordination obstacles. One supporting argument is that the user no longer has to translate text into an image;

the user can simply compare the screen capture with the actual screen display. Another supporting argument is that the parallel presentation on paper supports parallel processing. When text and picture are clearly connected—for example, when a pointer and a screen capture are presented side by side on paper—the user sees the two in tandem, and they are then automatically associated with one another.

The experiment was set up as a comparative study, assessing the effects of two manuals that differ only in the kind of support given for coordination. In the CI-T manual, this support was given textually (with pointers). In the CI-TP manual, there were combinations of text and pictures to support the user. The CI-TP manual is a guided tour typed manual. Some of the pictures, screen captures, are connected to the pointers, and some are linked to instructions.

The manuals are identical in all other respects. Their design is minimalist, they have the same number of pages, describe the same tasks, give the same background information and so forth. Both have a two-column layout. In the CI-T manual, the left column is used only to present headings. The CI-TP minimal manual uses this column for the pictures (see figure 10.10).

Both manuals are designed to support reading to do. The general hypothesis is that the CI-TP manual is better suited for this purpose than is the CI-T manual. The arguments for this prediction have been given earlier. The tested prediction is that users of the CI-TP manual complete tasks faster and more accurately than do users of the CI-T manual.

Users are observed to see how they process the coordinative information. The main prediction is that the combination of pointer and picture in the CI-TP manual invites more reading. It is not as strong a stimulus for users to switch back and forth between manual and screen as is the pointer in the CI-T manual because the pictures reduce the need to examine the actual screen.

Method

Subjects   Thirty adult volunteers participated in the study. Fifteen participants received the CI-T manual; the other fifteen received the CI-TP manual. All subjects were experienced computer users, having worked

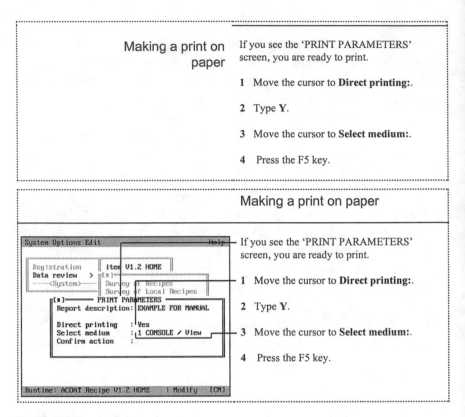

Figure 10.10
A paragraph from the textual minimal manual (CI-T) and its visual counterpart
(CI-TP) (from Van der Grijspaarde 1995b)

with computers for seven and a half years on average. None had any
prior experience with the database program tested.

All of the participants were employees of a large international chemical
company for whose database program the manuals were developed. The
participants had some knowledge of the coating recipes contained by the
database. These recipes for making all kinds of paints show the number
of ingredients, the kinds of ingredients, the amount needed of each ingredient, the temperatures needed, the place of storage, and so on.

Procedure   The participants were seated in front of a personal computer
and given a manual and a booklet. They were asked to complete the
seven tasks described in the booklet with the aid of the manual.

For each task, the user is given a chapter number, an assignment, and some data codes. The chapter number informs the user of the relevant chapter in the manual. It is given to gain time; the general search strategies of users are not of interest in the study. Assignments consist of one or two sentences that inform the user about the task. For all tasks, the user must know some data codes. Normally, users carry these codes to the job themselves, or they are given to them. In this study they are given to the user. An example of a task description is: "Chapter: 5. Assignment: Your goal is to print the Recipe Card with code 01322/000000 from the Recipe Sample. Data codes: Alias type = Akzo Coatings, Local Code = 01322/000000."

The seven tasks are typical jobs of database users. For example, participants were asked to start the database program, request a recipe, request a list of recipes from a particular location, add a new recipe, add an ingredient to an existing recipe, and print a recipe.

The participants were not informed of the presence of another type of manual or of the specific focus of the study. They were simply told that we wanted to find out how they would do on the assigned tasks. They were asked to think aloud during the session.

Materials   For the experiment two different kinds materials were developed: the two minimal manuals and an observation instrument.

Users of the database program found the existing documentation inadequate. They complained about the information's being inaccessible, and they criticized the lack of support for task execution and problem solving. To create documentation that would fit better the various user needs, it was decided to follow a minimalist approach.

The first step in the design of the minimal manuals was a needs and task analysis. This led to a detailed view of the audience, information needs, and the typical uses of the database. An important outcome of the inventory was the finding that the main audience would have considerable computer knowledge and skills and that the manuals should primarily support reading to do.

In the next step choices were made about the content of the manuals and about layout and typography. The two manuals were given the same content and design, except for the pictures (screen captures). Two prototypes were created and subsequently tested and revised.

The CI-TP manual, designed as a guided tour type of visual manual, mainly shows full-screen captures in reduced format. The relevant parts of these screen captures are linked visually to the text through green hairlines (see figure 10.10). The use of color is important for the hairline to stand out clearly from the screen capture. As a reproduction in black and white, figure 10.10 shows too little contrast; one cannot follow the hairlines easily. If color is not possible, one might want to consider using crooked hairlines, such as those shown in figure 10.8.

The information in the two manuals is clearly demarcated into paragraphs. Nearly all of these paragraphs contain some background information about a goal, some action information, and some coordinative information. Occasionally error information is included. Some paragraphs contain a CI cluster in which all the information—minimally three consecutive units—is grouped around a single screen capture. Two CI clusters are shown in figure 10.11.

An observation instrument was developed to register the users' handling of the coordinative information and for recording time on task and error handling. A small part of the instrument is shown in figure 10.12. It depicts a paragraph including the coding for one of the CI clusters of figure 10.11. The instrument is fashioned after the ISTE approach (Van der Meij, 1994, 1997). ISTE-type instruments have been created for observing user behaviors for a variety of manuals, for which they have been found reliable and easy to use. In ISTE instruments each information (sub)type (IST) is coupled to some anticipated effects (E), which are specific, observable user acts. While the user processes the manual, the instrument allows the experimenter to follow along and register what the user does with each information (type) in the manual.

The ISTE instrument created for this study concentrates on the processing of coordinative information. Users tend to act in three different ways on such information: they skip, read, or switch. Skipping occurs when the user does not attend to the CI when he or she could have done so. Typically it means that the user jumps ahead a paragraph or one or two lines of text. The thinking aloud should reveal whether users read the CI. A "read" code is given for all kinds of reading behavior. Thus it may mean that the user reads aloud one or two words of the text or the complete sentence. The intended reaction is switching. It means that the CI

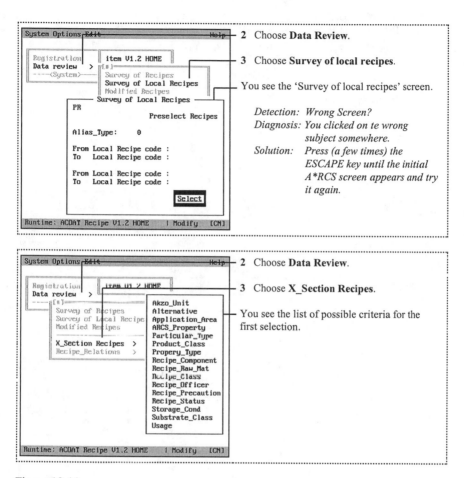

Figure 10.11
Two CI clusters in which three consecutive units of information are coupled to a single screen capture

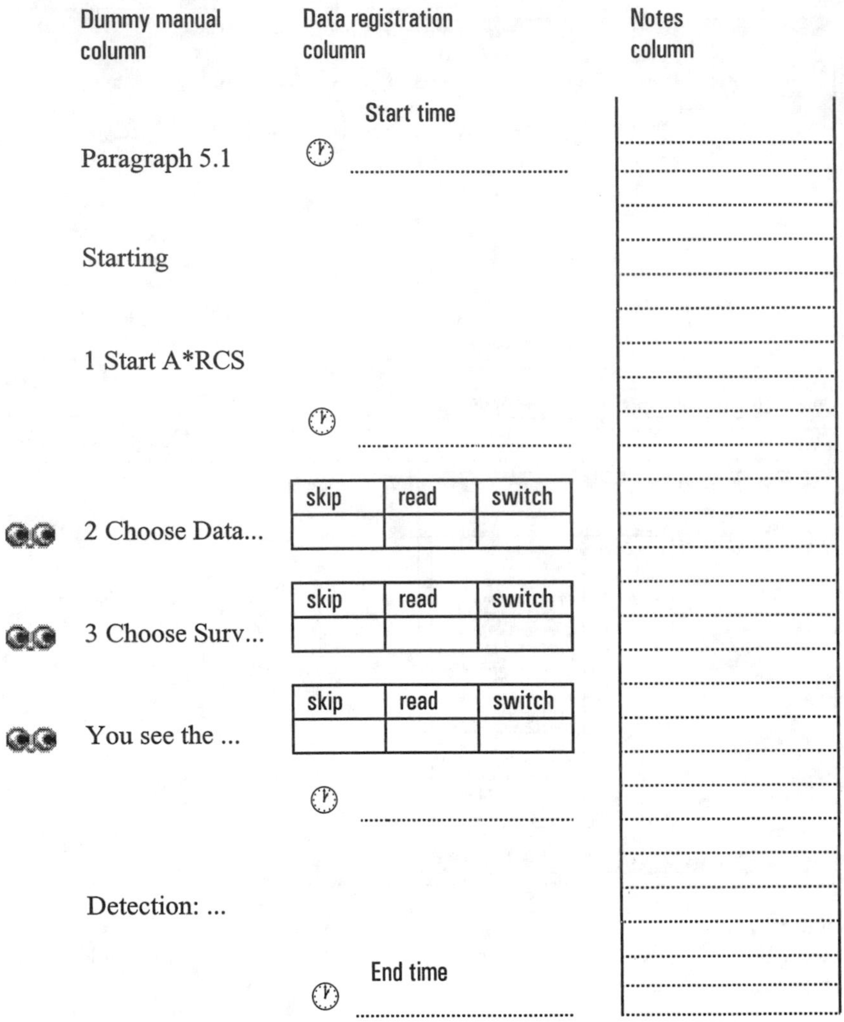

Dummy manual column	Data registration column	Notes column

Start time

Paragraph 5.1   🕐 ....

Starting

1 Start A*RCS

🕐 ....

	skip	read	switch
2 Choose Data...			

	skip	read	switch
3 Choose Surv...			

	skip	read	switch
You see the ...			

🕐 ....

Detection: ...

End time

🕐 ....

Figure 10.12
A paragraph from the ISTE type of observation instrument. The paragraph contains the coding for one of the CI clusters presented in figure 10.11.

prompts the user to examine both the screen and the manual. In most cases, switching is easy to observe. The usual positioning of manual and screen is such that the eye movements of the user tend to be accompanied by a gross movement of the head. The observation instrument has some open space after the place for coding the user behavior. In this study, it was used to time and record errors and error handling.

An important unit for time measurement is the paragraph. The experimenter is prompted to note the (real) time users need to complete a paragraph through a clock icon presented at the start and end of each paragraph (see figure 10.12). CI clusters provide clean views on the effects of pictures because each text segment is linked to the screen capture. Just as for paragraphs, the experimenter is prompted to note their start and end time with a clock icon.

Coding and Scoring   The dependent variables examined in the study are time, accuracy, and processing of the coordinative information.

Time registration concentrates on the time it takes users to complete paragraphs and CI clusters. CI cluster completion time gives the best, cleanest estimate of an effect of pictures because, unlike paragraphs, all information relates to the picture. Time on task is calculated by subtracting the start time from the end time for each of the twenty-one paragraphs and five clusters involved. (Clusters with pictures connecting three or more consecutive units of information were scarce. The majority of pictures were connected to a single action step, a pointer, or the two in combination. The background information given in between tended not to be visibly connected to the picture).

Accuracy is measured by coding the number and kind of mistakes made by the user. The experimenter also noted whether the mistake was corrected and the time it took to make the correction.

The observations should yield information on what users do—how they process the coordinative information. All observation data are noted immediately onto the observation instrument. The experimenter thus simply tags the code "skip," "read," or "switch" for each instance of CI.

If the user processes the same information more than once, the appropriate category is scored for each occurrence, but only the deepest level of processing is used in the data analyses. Thus, if a user first reads some CI and then examines it again while looking back and forth between manual and screen, both reading and switching are marked, but only the "switch" code is used for data analysis.

The default score is the "missing value." The experimenter marks each instance of CI only when it is absolutely clear that the user skips, reads, or switches. Missing values may thus have two different origins. A missing value may mean that the user has ignored a relatively large portion in the manual (e.g., a complete paragraph) or that the experimenter cannot with certainty score the user's behavior. This may be due to a slip of attention, but the experimenter may also be busy coding something else (e.g., time). The minimum number of valid observations is set at five. If there are fewer than five observations on how a user processes coordinative information, that user's observations are not used in data analyses.

Comparisons of the effects of manual type on the handling of coordinative information can be made only for shared text. In other words, one should compare the processing of the pointers in the CI-T manual only with the processing of the combination of pointers and pictures in the CI-TP manual. To complete all seven tasks, the user ought to process thirty-two pointers, or pointer and picture combinations, in each manual.

Analyses of the observations made for the CI-TP manual should indicate whether users react differently to combinations of instruction and picture than to combinations of pointer and picture. To complete all seven tasks, users of the CI-TP manual ought to process fifty-two combinations of instruction and picture. These combinations are a kind of "body double." Users must execute an action command and process the coordination information. The observer ignores the handling of the action information. The coding is therefore the same as for the combination of pointer and picture.

Data Analysis The effect of manual type on time and accuracy is assessed with univariate analyses of variance (ANOVA). For significant findings ($p < .05$, one-sided), an effect size (ES) is calculated to find out whether a difference has any practical significance. Effect size can be calculated by evaluating the proportion of variance explained in the analysis (e.g., R^2, eta^2, omega^2), or by standardized differences in statistics (e.g., means, as in the ES statistic). The eta^2 and the ES statistic are reported in this study. The meaning of eta is the same as for a correlation coefficient. For the ES statistic, values of 0.2, 0.5, and 0.8 correspond, respectively, to small, medium and large effects (Cohen 1977).

The effect of manual type on the processing of pointers and pictures is assessed with chi-square analyses (χ^2) with alpha set at 0.5 (one-sided). Paired sample t-tests ($p < .05$, two-sided) are calculated to test whether users of the CI-TP manual handle combinations of pointers and pictures differently from combinations of instructions and pictures.

Results

The screen captures had a strong effect on time on task. Users of the CI-TP manual completed their tasks much faster than did users of the CI manual. Statistically significant speed gains were measured for CI clusters as well as for paragraphs ($F(1, 28) = 9.82$, $p < .01$; $F(1, 28) = 3.61$, $p < .05$).

The biggest time gain was found for CI clusters in which the screen captures speeded up task completion by about 35 percent (see table 10.1). Both effect size measures indicate a large effect. The difference between the two manuals was more than one standard deviation (ES = 1.14), and it was reasonably well accounted for by the experimental manipulation (eta^2 = 0.26). A smaller but still statistically significant speed gain was found for paragraphs. Here the screen captures speeded up task completion by about 15 percent. Effect size was a bit lower for paragraphs than for CI clusters, but the screen captures still had a medium positive effect (ES = 0.69, eta^2 = 0.11).

The screen captures did not affect accuracy outcomes. Users of the CI-TP manual made as many mistakes, and needed as much time for

Table 10.1
Mean number of seconds needed to complete subtasks in the two manuals (standard deviation between parentheses).

	CI-T manual	CI-TP manual
CI clusters	89 (33)	59 (17)
Paragraphs	75 (17)	64 (14)

Table 10.2
Mean number of mistakes and mean number of seconds needed to recover from an error (standard deviation between parentheses).

	CI-T manual	CI-TP manual
Mistakes	2.3 (1.3)	1.8 (1.4)
Correction time	36 (29)	27 (27)

Table 10.3
User reactions to the pointers in the CI-T manual, and to the combinations of pointer and picture in the CI-TP manual (scores in percentages with standard deviation between parentheses).

	CI-T manual	CI-TP manual
Read	18 (17)	37 (13)
Switch	28 (9)	15 (14)

recovery, as did users of the CI-T manual ($F < 1$, n.s.; see table 10.2). The kinds of mistakes the users made were quite comparable. Typical errors were typing a response instead of selecting it, selecting the wrong key for navigation (e.g., pressing the Enter key instead of the TAB key), typing a response in the wrong place on the screen, and choosing an incorrect option.

Table 10.3 shows how the users processed the coordinative information—that is, how often they read it and how often they reacted to the pointers (CI-T) or to the combination of pointers and pictures by switching attention back and forth between manual and screen. The difference is statistically significant ($\chi^2 = 23.6$, $df = 1$, $p < .01$). It signals that the users of the CI-TP manual read the CI more often than do users of the CI-T manual, who switch attention more often. There were only eight observations of users' actually skipping some coordinative information, all of which found for the CI-TP manual. Table 10.3 summarizes the observations of ten users of the CI-T manual and seven users of the CI-TP manual. The mean percentage of missing observations for these seventeen users is about 50 percent. For thirteen users, there were five or fewer observations.

Comparisons were made for the handling of the two kinds of coordinative information within the CI-TP manual: pointers and pictures, instruction and pictures. There were no statistically differences for reading ($t = -1.98$, $df = 6$, $p < .10$) or for switching ($t = 1.72$, $df = 6$, n.s.). Users of the CI-TP manual reacted to the combinations of instruction and picture mainly by reading (47 percent, *s.d.* 20). Switching was rather uncommon (7 percent, *s.d.* 6).

10.5   Conclusion and Discussion

This chapter has explored the role and design of coordinative information whose main goal it is to help users harmonize the joint handling of manual and screen (and input device). The effects of two variations in form are compared: text (CI-T manual) versus text and picture (CI-TP manual).

The presence of pictures (screen captures) had a strong and statistically significant effect on the speed of task execution. Users who worked with the CI-TP manual completed tasks about 35 percent faster than did users of the CI-T manual. No effects on accuracy were found.

User observations confirmed the prediction that a combination of pointer and picture is less effective than a pointer alone for stimulating users to switch back and forth between manual and screen. Users of the CI-TP manual more often just read the coordinative information than did users of the CI-T manual. No differences were found for the handling of the two kinds of coordinative information in the CI-TP manual. Users reacted in a similar way to the combination of pointer and picture as to the combination of instruction and picture.

This chapter provides ample food for thought on the role and design of coordinative information in manuals; the ideas and findings invite various new studies. A prime candidate for future work is an independent replication. The study reported in this chapter is the first to examine the effects of screen captures on real users working with real manuals. Surely it is desirable to find out whether there is additional evidence for a supportive role of screen captures. Important extensions within such a replication study concern the main function(s) of the manual and the audience involved.

The tested manuals have been designed primarily to support doing. The screen captures in the CI-TP manual nicely fit that role by speeding up task execution. If the manual's primary role is to enhance learning, however, faster execution of tasks may not be so desirable. The manual should then preferably cause the user to pause and think frequently. One of the possible ways to achieve that is to present mainly incomplete screen captures—to have screen captures display only a part of the window, object, or screen. A step-by-step type manual may be optimal for this purpose because, unlike a guided tour manual, it is not self-contained. The frequent presence of incomplete screen captures calls for some thinking and inferencing by the user, which should make this type of visual manual more suited to learning to do.

It is not clear what audience is most likely to profit from the visual support for handling coordination obstacles. The participants in the experiment were experienced computer users. Upon first thought, one is inclined to believe that these users are not the most obvious beneficiaries of screen captures. Typically it is the novice who needs more motivational support; recall that screen captures may increase self-confidence. And typically it is also the novice who suffers more from coordination obstacles. Is the novice therefore the person to profit most from having screen captures added to the verbal information in a manual? The answer is not an unqualified yes.

It matters quite a bit how users handle the coordinative information, and novices and experienced users probably vary considerably in this respect. Maybe a user needs a fair amount of computer experience to deal effectively with the combination of textual and pictorial information. For example, experienced users may be more likely to recognize a correct screen more swiftly; maybe they even process some screen captures as singular icons. Thus, it may be the experienced user, and not the novice, who benefits most from a combination of textual and pictorial support (Sweller and Chandler 1994). Experienced users may also be more inclined to peek at the screen captures, glancing at them rather quickly; they know they do not have to remember such screen items as menu options or field locations because it is always there for reference (Payne 1991). Yet another possibility is that experienced users tend to ignore most of the screen captures because they are confident that they do not need these to perform (simple) tasks (Kern 1985; Mirel, Feinberg, and Allminger 1991).

These considerations suggest yet another important topic for research: user observations. How do users handle coordinative information? The observations from the experiment give some initial data. These findings should be looked at with caution, however, because, unlike other studies with ISTE-type observation instruments, there were many missing data. In part, this can be accounted for by the fact that the observer had to register time by writing down start and end times. In all other observation studies, time was registered automatically by a log registration program. Some of the missing values can also be accounted for by the conservative way of scoring. The default value is the code "missing." The observer is instructed to score the user's behavior only with absolute certainty. The observer scores the handling of coordinative information only when there is no doubt about the user's behavior.

With the ISTE approach it is relatively easy to observe and score the users' reactions to coordinative information (skip, read, or switch). The simplicity is vital for data recording. The observer can keep pace even when users process the information in their manuals swiftly (Van der Meij 1994, 1997). The observations may yield answers to questions such as, "Do the users act when they are supposed to?" and "Does the coordinative information prompt them to examine the screen?"

The ISTE approach is unfit for answering more detailed research questions. For example, switching now merely indicates that users look up from their manual to the screen and back from the screen to their manual again. Intriguing questions about switching acts that cannot be answered from these observation data are: "Do users verify screen captures, and, if so, do they do this accurately?" and "Do users look at the screen captures first, and then decide whether or not to ignore the pointer?" To catch these processes, one might want to consider using eye-movement registration, or include some deliberately incorrect screen capture in the manual.

Detailed user observations can also shed new light on the effects of screen captures on accuracy. In the experiment, the screen captures did not help prevent mistakes or speed up recovery. The latter finding is especially surprising. After all, screen captures almost immediately show when an error has been made, enabling the user to detect mistakes promptly and easily. Recovery too should be faster than in a nonvisual manual because the screen captures provide intermediate reentry points. Without a screen capture, the user frequently must start a task all over again from the start. Perhaps the nonsignificant finding for accuracy relates to the scarcity of error in the study. There may simply have been too few mistakes for detecting any difference.

The CI-TP manual has been fashioned after the guided tour type of visual manual. By following this genre, some design options for the presentation of the screen captures were decided on in advance. For example, it meant the usage of mainly full-screen captures displaying the main events. An important advantage of following such a genre approach is that it is very practical. The writer does not, for example, have to think very hard about different ways to support object verification, identification, or location since these processes are nearly always supported in the same way.

An intriguing side effect of getting to know better the genre of visual manuals is that this knowledge tends to affect the intermediate stages of manual writing and development as well. For example, in creating minimal manuals, my students and I are more and more creating visualized task scenarios. First drafts of manuals are becoming more like film scenarios organized around the major tasks and visually supported by screen captures.

This study focused on screen captures. This type of pictorial support was found to be a good means for helping users with coordination obstacles. Other information types presented in the manual are likely to benefit from some other kind of pictorial support. For example, for many action commands it can be very advantageous to support the manipulation of input devices such as a keyboard, mouse, or trackball visually (Krull 1994).

As a final note it is perhaps useful to address the question of how specifically this work pertains to minimalism—that is, beyond the fact that the study involved minimal manuals. The relation is twofold. First, minimalism has never expressed a strong opinion about visual design. Layout, typography, and the presentation of screen captures have received little attention. In this respect, the present study makes amends. Second, the study set out to examine the role and design of coordinative information in detail. In minimalism, the coordination obstacle has long been recognized as an important obstacle to users. The study supports this view. The experiment indicates that an important change in the presentation of this information can have a strong effect on user behavior. In essence, this is what minimalism is all about: finding optimal ways to help users.

Acknowledgment

I thank Linda van der Grijspaarde for her substantial contribution in creating and testing the two minimal manuals reported in this paper and Mark Gellevij for various discussions on this chapter.

References

Black, J. B., Bechtold, J. S., Mitrani, M., and Carroll, J. M. 1989. On-line tutorials: What kind of inference leads to the most effective learning? In T. Bice and C. H. Lewis (eds.), *Proceedings of CHI'89: Human factors in computing systems* (pp. 81–94). New York: Association for Computing Machinery.

Black, J. B., Carroll, J. M., and McGuigan, S. M. 1987. What kind of minimal instruction manual is the most effective? In H. J. Bullinger, B. Shackel, and K. Kornwachs (eds.), *Proceedings of the Second IFIP Conference on Human-Computer Interaction* (pp. 159–162). Amsterdam: Elsevier.

Cohen, J. 1977. *Statistical power analysis for the behavioral sciences.* New York: Academic Press.

Frese, M., Albrecht, K., Altmann, A., Lang, J., Von Papstein, P., Peyerl, R., Prümper, J., Schulte-Göcking, H., Wankmüller, I., and Wendel, R. 1988. The effect of an active development of the mental model in the training process: Experimental results in a word processing system. *Behavior and Information Technology* 7:295–304.

Frese, M., Brodbeck, F., Heinbokel, T., Mooser, C., Schleiffenbaum, E., and Thiemann, P. 1991. Errors in training computer skills: On the positive function of errors. *Human Computer Interaction* 6:77–93.

Gardner, D. C., and Beatty, G. J. 1993a. *WordPerfect 6 for Windows: The visual learning guide.* Rocklin, CA: Prima Publishers.

Gardner, D. C., and Beatty, G. J. 1993b. *Windows 3.1: The visual learning guide.* Rocklin, CA: Prima Publishers.

Gong, R., and Elkerton, J. 1990. Designing minimal documentation using a GOMS model: A usability evaluation of an engineering approach. In J. Carrasco

Chew and J. Whiteside (eds.), *Proceedings of the CHI'90 Conference* (pp. 99–106). New York: Association for Computing Machinery.

Horton, W. 1991. *Illustrating computer documentation: The art of presenting information graphically on paper and online*. New York: Wiley.

Horton, W. 1993. Dump the dumb screen dumps. *Technical Communication* 40(1):146–148.

Houghton-Alico, D. 1985. *Creating computer software user guides*. New York: McGraw-Hill.

Kern, R. P. 1985. Modeling users and their use of technical manuals. In T. M. Duffy and R. Waller (eds.), *Designing usable texts* (pp. 341–375). Orlando, FL: Academic Press.

Krull, R. 1994. Documentation for a physical world. *Journal of Technical Writing and Communication* 24(2):181–195.

Lazonder, A. W., and van der Meij, H. 1994. The effect of error-information in tutorial documentation. *Interacting with Computers* 6(1):23–40.

Lazonder, A. W., and van der Meij, H. 1995. Error-information in tutorial documentation: Supporting users' errors to facilitate initial skill learning. *International Journal of Human-Computer Studies* 42:185–206.

Mirel, B., Feinberg S., and Allmendinger, L. 1991. Designing manuals for active learning styles. *Technical Communication* 38(1):75–87.

Nowaczyk, R. H., and James, E. C. 1993. Applying minimal manual principles for documentation of graphical user interfaces. *Journal of Technical Writing and Communication* 23(4):379–388.

Payne, S. 1991. Display-based action at the user interface. *International Journal of Man Machine Studies* 35:275–289.

Price, J. 1984. *How to write a computer manual: A handbook of software documentation*. Menlo Park, CA: Benjamin/Cummings.

Price, J., and Korman, H. 1993. *How to communicate technical information*. Menlo Park, CA: Benjamin/Cummings.

Stuur, A. 1992. *Windows voor kinderen. Een stap-voor-stap methode voor iedereen vanaf 8 jaar* [Windows for children. A step-by-step method for anyone from eight years]. Utrecht: Bruna Informatica.

Stuur, A. 1993. *CorelDraw voor kinderen. Een stap-voor-stap methode voor iedereen vanaf 8 jaar* [CorelDraw for children. A step-by-step method for anyone from eight years]. Utrecht: Bruna Informatica.

Sweller, J., and Chandler, P. 1994. Why some material is difficult to learn. *Cognition and Instruction* 12(3):185–233.

Van der Grijspaarde, L. 1995a. *Analyse van visuele handleidingen*. [Analysis of visual manuals]. Literatuurverslag. Universiteit van Twente, Enschede.

Van der Grijspaarde, L. 1995b. *Viewing and registrating recipes with A*RCS*. Sassenheim: Akzo Nobel Coatings.

VanderLinden, G., Cocklin, T. G., and McKita, M. 1988. Testing and developing minimalist tutorials: A case history. In *Proceedings of the 35th International Technical Communications Conference* (pp. RET196–199). Washington, DC: Society for Technical Communication.

Van der Meij, H. 1992. A critical assessment of the minimalist approach to documentation. In *Conference proceedings of the 10th Annual International Conference on Systems Documentation (SIGDOC92)* (pp. 7–17). New York: Association for Computing Machinery.

Van der Meij, H. 1994. Catching the user in the act. In M. W. Steehouder, C. Jansen, P. van der Poort, and R. Verheyen (eds.), *Quality of technical documentation* (pp. 210–211). Amsterdam: Editions Rodopi.

Van der Meij, H. 1996a. Examining the role of screen captures in manuals. *InterCom* 43(4):35–38.

Van der Meij, H. 1996b. Visuele handleidingen: ik zie ik zie wat jij niet ziet. [Visual manuals: Do you see what I see?]. *Opleiding & Ontwikkeling*, 9(11), 21–26.

Van der Meij, H. 1997. "The ISTE-approach to usability testing." *IEEE Transactions on Professional Communication* 40(3):209–223.

Wendel, R., and Frese, M. 1987. Developing exploratory strategies in training: The general approach and a specific example for manual use. In H. J. Bullinger, B. Shackeland, and K. Kornwachs (eds.), *Proceedings of the Second IFIP Conference on Human-Computer Interaction* (pp. 943–948). Amsterdam: Elsevier.

White, J. 1987. *The grid book. A guide to page planning*. Paramus, NJ: Letraset.

Wiedenbeck, S., Zila, P. L., and McConnell, D. S. 1995. End-user training: An empirical study comparing on-line practice methods. *In Proceedings of the CHI'95 Conference* (pp. 74–81) New York: Association for Computing Machinery.

11

Minimalism: A Quality Strategy for Success

Karl L. Smart

Several years ago I worked as a technical writer for a major software company. Our documentation department discovered minimalism about the time major decisions confronted us as to the amount and type of documentation we would provide. Through the early years of the company, a standard encyclopedic reference manual had become the major component of our documentation set. With small, relatively simple applications; unlimited free telephone customer support; and generous profit margins for each product sold, little concern existed as to the amount—and to some degree the kind—of documentation we produced.

As our applications became more sophisticated, the amount of documentation we shipped with products correspondingly increased. The once small reference manual of three hundred pages became a large, unwieldy behemoth of nearly two thousand pages. The pieces of documentation shipped with a product also proliferated: a reference manual, a getting-started manual, a tutorial workbook, and several other small pieces of documentation, such as a function key template and an easy reference sheet. One release of a major product contained sixteen separate pieces of documentation.

About this time, several forces precipitated a careful examination of how we approached the task of supporting users of our software. Keen competition forced retail prices down; profit margins similarly declined. The company began to limit and charge for its telephone support. Out of necessity, the company looked seriously at what documentation users really wanted and needed and how much documentation we could afford to produce.

A happy, fairy-tale ending would be that our documentation department began using minimalist principles, we reduced the amount of documentation we shipped, customers raved about the documentation, and we saved the company millions of dollars. Unfortunately, fairy tales seldom reflect life as it is. Although many of us were convinced that we should adopt a minimalist approach to documentation, we encountered strong resistance from several important decision makers within the company. In retrospect, we failed to adopt minimalism not because it lacked a solid theoretical foundation or because research failed to show improved customer performance and satisfaction. Neither did our failure stem from technical writers who could not learn and apply the principles. Rather, we confronted organizational reluctance to change. Many considered minimalism too radical a departure to the way we had always worked and to the type of documentation we had provided customers. They feared minimalist manuals would hurt sales and increase customer dissatisfaction.

No doubt many readers may ask, "If minimalism is as good as folks say it is, if it really does benefit users and potentially save a company money, why isn't everyone producing minimalist documentation?" This chapter attempts to respond to this question in a way very different from the other chapters. As Rosenbaum (this volume, chapter 5) noted in her follow-up interviews with those who had attended her minimalism seminars, individuals found that implementing minimalism in their own organizations proved a difficult task. Although some received support from coworkers and managers, others found indifference or even strong opposition to their efforts to produce minimalist documentation. My experience suggests that minimalism has not become more widespread because as technical communicators we fail to present it convincingly to those who make implementation decisions.

Although technical communicators and even users may be convinced of minimalism's benefit, commitment to minimalism will come more readily when managers and others see the cost benefits of the approach. If my documentation group could have helped resistant decision makers to see minimalism as a quality issue, a strategy to compete more cost-effectively and gain a competitive advantage, we would have more likely received support. This chapter therefore focuses on corporate advantages of adopting a minimalist approach to documentation. With an added emphasis given to product and service quality in many businesses, I look at minimalism as a quality issue and a component of strategic managerial decision making. I discuss documentation in relationship to quality and minimalism as a specific quality initiative. The chapter ends by addressing some of the issues involved in implementing minimalism and other quality initiatives.

11.1 Approaches to Quality and to Documentation

Quality has become a focus of organizational management, yet prescriptive quality formulas and tools have met with varying success due to differing organizational needs and methods used in implementing quality. Some failure has resulted from how companies have applied quality. Too often quality appropriates a narrowly defined meaning or becomes synonymous with a particular organizational tool or process. Like minimalism, quality consists of principles that individuals use to make informed decisions, not specific rules and tools applied indiscriminately.

To see the relationship between varying approaches to quality, different emphases can be arranged on a continuum. Figure 11.1 illustrates the

Design based	Product based	Customer based	Value based	Strategic quality
Conformance to predetermined design specifications	Measured product attributes— such as durability, reliability, or usability	Satisfied customer expectations and needs	Satisfied customers through product excellence at an acceptable price	Differentiated product that provides a competitive advantage

Internal		External

Figure 11.1
A quality continuum, with a definition of each emphasis (from Seawright and Young 1996)

primary emphases of quality as five categories along the continuum and gives a brief definition of each emphasis. An internal focus on quality represents an emphasis on improving processes and setting internal standards. Conversely, an external focus concentrates on the results of effective design and production processes that result in customer satisfaction.

Many approaches to quality concentrate on one of these emphases. For instance, some tools managers use focus on the internal application of quality surrounding design and production, resulting in design specifications or quality metrics that identify errors in production processes. Although this focus and these applications have an impact on the quality of products, increased focus has centered on the external dimensions of quality: customer satisfaction and strategic advantage. Increasingly, organizations have found that unless customer involvement drives the internal focus, the end result fails to satisfy customer needs and expectations (Chase, Kumar, and Youngdahl 1995).

As an approach to documentation, minimalism reflects the focus on fulfilling customer needs and expectations, and it addresses other issues that arise in quality management. We can review varying approaches to documentation to see how documentation relates to the quality continuum. I would note, however, that not every category along the continuum has a corresponding type of documentation. Some approaches to documentation use several of the emphases. But providing a brief description of each dimension and showing examples of documentation that fit into one or more of these categories helps us see how quality issues apply to documentation.

Design-based quality includes establishing predetermined design specification before production. These specifications then become a standard to judge the product. Many technical writers work with some type of specifications. For instance, most documentation groups have style guides and specs to provide guidelines for writers and to ensure consistency in their documentation. Style guides and specs provide consistency in such matters as what fonts writers use, how heading levels appear, and how users approach tasks—whether they use a mouse, pull-down menus, or keystrokes.

Product-based quality emphasizes features or characteristics of a product. Systems-based documentation reflects the structure of the product it supports and most closely relates to product-based quality. For instance, if an application has nine menus, a systems-based manual accompanying the product would have nine chapters—one chapter for each menu. Each chapter describes in detail the function of the options of each menu.

Another approach to documentation reflects a more traditional instructional design orientation (Gagne and Briggs 1979) and represents an emphasis of both design-based and product-based quality. Identifying a target skill to teach users, a systems approach decomposes the skill into sequential tasks and subtasks. Each task may have an accompanying objective or specification to indicate if the user has successfully learned the task. Such an analysis becomes the basis for an instructional sequence users need to accomplish. The documentation sequentially presents information, assuming users will follow each step to achieve the desired outcome, mastering the first skill before working on more advanced ones. Similar to design-based quality where design specifications and conformance requirements drive production processes, this approach to documentation assumes that all users accomplish tasks in a specific way and that they will follow steps outlined to complete their work. Although comprehensive, this approach to documentation fails to acknowledge differences in user needs and user learning styles. For instance, users may want to know only about moving the cursor with the mouse. The documentation, however, may lead the user through understanding cursor concepts, explaining default cursor settings, and changing cursor options before covering the basics of simple cursor usage. The documentation may contain the information the users want; however, users may have difficulty in locating the information or recognizing the relevance of the information to the task at hand.

Task-oriented documentation provides a more user-centered or customer-based approach to quality. A task-oriented manual would not organize information around features, such Styles or Font, nor would it teach decomposed, system-oriented skills, such as moving the cursor. Instead, task-oriented documentation helps users in doing their own work. If a user wanted to learn how to move text in a document, a task-oriented manual would not organize information around features (such as Select, Cut, Paste) but would have an action-oriented section ("Moving

Text in Your Document") that discusses the features in terms of accomplishing the action desired by the user.

Documentation that embodies value-based or strategic quality may employ any or all aspects of the previous quality emphases. However, documentation that implements value-based quality achieves customer satisfaction with acceptable cost as a component. For example, documentation that focuses on value-based quality may use product specifications similar to design-based documentation, but the specifications come from assessing users' needs. The success of the documentation and its specifications is judged by the degree of customer satisfaction that results in using the documentation. Also, with value-based documentation, both the company producing the documentation and the customers purchasing it must find the cost acceptable.

Strategic quality as applied to documentation goes a step further. Documentation becomes strategic when satisfied customers differentiate documentation to the extent that they will select the product over competing brands. For example, the use of balloon help with Macintosh computers and wizards in Microsoft products initially served to differentiate them from their competitors. Differentiating features become more important when competitors cannot easily duplicate the features in their own products. Balloon help differentiated Macintosh systems initially, but context-sensitive help using the right mouse button quickly became standard in Windows products. Competitors of Microsoft soon provided equivalents of wizards, such as cue cards and coaches. As documentation becomes a differentiating feature in software products, its strategic value increases.

Minimalist documentation serves as an example of documentation that integrates both value-based and strategic quality. If minimalist documentation satisfies the needs of computer users at a cost acceptable to the company (and likely with less expense than other forms of documentation), it can function strategically as part of a product's differentiation and overall success. Because customer satisfaction and costs play such an important role in implementing quality efforts, a more in-depth discussion of these topics provides a broader understanding of how we can view minimalism as a quality initiative. Although I focus more on external aspects of quality, I do not mean to gloss over the internal dimensions of quality related to design-based and product-based quality. However, these dimensions of quality become more strategically important when viewed in the context of cost considerations and customer satisfaction.

11.2 Documentation as a Quality Issue

Like quality, minimalism focuses on customer needs. Achieving customer satisfaction is essential to creating quality products and services (Juran 1988). Satisfaction is often measured as the difference between expectations of product characteristics and actual experience with a product (Oliver 1980; Olson and Dover 1979). Satisfaction results when products or services meet or exceed expectations; dissatisfaction results when products fail to meet expectations. In addition to customer expectations, customer desires also play a significant role in customer satisfaction (Olshavsky and Spreng 1989; Spreng, Dixon, and Olshavsky 1993). Dissatisfaction can result even when expectations of a product are met but desires are not.

Often customers view product characteristics—such as performance, reliability, or usability—as the product itself (Dodds and Monroe 1985; Garvin 1987). How well these characteristics meet customers' desires and expectations, in combination with product cost, determines satisfaction or dissatisfaction. Product cost becomes important in that customers may be satisfied with a low-quality product if they have a low expectation of the product due to a low price. Cost also plays a significant role in organizational decisions, especially those involving documentation. Increasingly, managers scrutinize documentation to see if they can cost justify the resources devoted to it. Technical communicators must show the dollar value that good documentation adds in competitive and economically constrained times.

Issues of quality directly affect documentation. Establishing the cost value of documentation can help establish its strategic value to an organization. Technical communicators face tremendous, often opposing, organizational pressures when designing documentation. Many organizations still view documentation as peripheral, something apart from product development. Managers often fail to cost justify documentation when it is not a direct revenue producer. In such organizations, quality often means creating documentation as quickly and inexpensively as possible (Schriver 1993).

In response to such an attitude, technical communicators have sought to replace limited views of documentation quality by quantifying the value they add to organizations and the value of the documentation they produce (Redish 1995). Recent studies have shown that inadequate documentation incurs greater costs for organizations, and good documentation reduces costs (Blackwell 1995; Spencer and Yates 1995). Furthermore, additional research suggests that documentation has become an important product characteristic in determining customer satisfaction (Schriver 1993; Smart, Madrigal, and Seawright 1996). In being able to discuss documentation in terms of corporate cost benefits, technical communicators can show that documentation is not an expendable luxury but has become a demand of customers who want more usable documentation that meets their needs.

11.3   Minimalism as a Quality Response

Minimalism is an approach to documentation that emerged in response to changing customer needs and expectations. Technical communicators can show greater cost benefits of minimalist documentation than documentation produced with other approaches. The principles of minimalism correlate with many of the elements necessary to achieve customer satisfaction, the goal of any product. As a set of principles that serve to guide design rather than prescribe answers for every situation, minimalism encompasses principles affecting customer satisfaction and cost: an action orientation, an anchor in the task domain, a strategy for error recognition and recovery, and a support for reading to do (Van der Meij and Carroll, this volume, chapter 2). Although most research places these principles in a context of learning theory, they also relate to issues of customer satisfaction, costs, and product differentiation as well.

Minimalism and Customer Satisfaction
As an approach to document design, minimalism developed in response to users' getting the help they needed from documentation. Much of the research connected with minimalism has focused on cognitive psychology

and adult learning, exploring how individuals best learn information and determining what information users need when confronted with learning to use computer hardware and software (Ramsay and Oatley 1992; Ramey 1988; Van der Meij 1993). Fundamentally, minimalism advocates user-centered documentation. Research has shown that users both understand and retain information better and complete tasks in less time with minimalist documentation (Carroll 1990).

In a real sense, minimalism is an approach to customer satisfaction, striving to meet users' need for assistance with computers. Research has provided a profile of adult learners, the primary user base of computers (Carroll 1990): adults lack of patience, want to work with real tasks that have meaning, like to explore and figure out things on their own, and need help recognizing and recovering from errors. From such a profile we can infer several needs users have when learning new tasks. Minimalism advocates documentation designed in content and structure to meet these needs. In other words, minimalist documentation provides immediate opportunities to act or do, focuses on real tasks for instructional activities, encourages exploration, and attempts to prevent errors while providing on-the-spot information to help in error recovery (Van der Meij and Carroll, this volume, chapter 2). In responding to these user needs and desires, minimalist documentation can foster significant customer satisfaction.

Minimalism and Costs

Another important element of customer satisfaction and quality relates to cost. Costs serve as a primary factor in determining a company's competitive advantage (Porter 1985). In viewing documentation in terms of quality management, costs can be classified in two major categories: costs of improvement and costs of failure. Improvement costs come from quality improvement efforts: the resources committed to producing good documentation. In designing minimalist documentation, companies must incur certain expenses. Such a willingness suggests a commitment to hiring professional technical communicators who can create user profiles, assess user needs, perform usability testing, and write concise, readable prose. Unfortunately, recent industry trends have seen increasing numbers of technical communicators downsized. In competitive times of mandated cost reduction, reducing or eliminating resources for documentation may result in short-term savings at the expense of long-term growth and profitability.

Failure costs relate to expenses incurred from less than perfect quality. Technical communicators can help demonstrate failure costs resulting from poor documentation. These costs relate to the consequences of inaccurate or inadequate documentation and the loss of customer satisfaction resulting from poor documentation. Failure costs include out-of-pocket and lost opportunity costs. Out-of-pocket expenses could include having manuals rewritten to correct errors as well as paying for help desks to assist users in tasks they cannot perform because of poor documentation.

Several principles of minimalism relate directly to these cost issues. Although the primary objective of minimalist documentation is not to produce a smaller manual, the notion of selectively giving users only information they really need—not comprehensive information on systems or system operations but task-oriented information needed to assist users in completing real work—generally results in smaller manuals. Smaller manuals have a direct impact on cost of goods related to delivering product. A greater margin of profit is possible if cost of goods can be decreased, and documentation can significantly reduce cost of goods (Porter 1985).

Minimalist documentation also has important cost implications for organizations using products documented with a minimalist approach. Although less obvious and harder to measure, these costs are real nonetheless. The adoption of new technology creates enormous costs for organizations, not just in the purchase of the technology but in a training and conversion period. During such transitions, the issue is less about the gains concomitant with change than the loses inevitably tied to new tools and processes (de Jager 1994).

In most instances, productivity decreases at the initial adoption of a new technology as workers spend less time devoted to work-related tasks and more time understanding how to use the technology. If documentation can reduce the learning curve and provide recovery assistance with problems encountered, users can devote more time to real work. Additionally, when the learning involves tasks in the users' domain rather than contrived situations, users learn as they perform their work. If minimalist documentation helps a company reduce costs of training and adopting new technology, that company will likely experience greater customer satisfaction.

Both those companies using minimalist documentation and those providing it enjoy cost benefits. Minimalist documentation has the potential of generating substantial savings through increased user productivity, decreased user error, and decreased training costs. Additionally, decreased help desk and support costs net even greater savings (Mayhew and Mantei 1993). One study suggests that for every dollar spent on formal support in approved budgets, another three dollars is spent on "informal" support. An estimated $6,000 to $15,000 is associated with annual informal support for each end-user workstation (LaBounty 1994). Minimalist documentation can reduce the need for both formal and informal support. Such estimated benefits and savings become convincing arguments for committing the necessary resources to produce minimalist documentation.

Minimalism and Product Differentiation

In addition to customer satisfaction and cost, product differentation— offering a product that provides unique benefits for customers in areas they value (Porter 1985)—emerges as a significant factor in determining profitability. The means to differentiate differs for every product, just as the documentation needs for products differ. Minimalism attempts to provide precise documentation that users need and desire. This type of documentation is best achieved through a nonprescriptive, principle-oriented approach like minimalism that views document design as an iterative process, assessing the needs of users and how well documentation meets those needs again and again.

We can see the degree to which documentation has become a differentiating product characteristic in the reviews of computer products in trade journals and magazines. Documentation has become a standard category that reviewers use in rating the quality of hardware and software. Otherwise-good products often receive poor reviews when the documentation is poor or inadequate. In an increasingly competitive marketplace, with companies vying for market share, poor documentation has begun to affect product sales. A customer-driven approach like minimalism can function as a significant component in satisfying customers, reducing costs, and improving strategic planning through product differentiation.

11.4   Implementing Quality and Minimalism in Documentation

Although an understanding of the principles of quality may not have changed the outcome of my company's decision against adopting minimalism, I feel that we would have had a greater chance to garner more support if we could have argued more persuasively that the changes we proposed would have saved the company money and increased customer satisfaction. The question remains, "How do we make a difference in our companies? How do we get others to let us implement minimalism or other quality processes?"

No single answer will magically make a difference in our ability to implement minimalism. I do believe that through education and advocacy, we will bring about changes. Education begins with us. We need to understand business issues that decision makers face. We need to understand how documentation affects these issues. We need a solid understanding of what we are proposing, such as a minimalist approach to documentation, and make the effort to educate others about it.

With an understanding of minimalism along with business and quality issues, we can become advocates for change. Even if we do not receive financial support or official work time to track our progress or implement quality measures, we can informally measure documentation's impact on a company. We can gather information to show how documentation increases our company's profitability through cost savings or increased customer satisfaction.

While attending a recent conference of technical communicators, I heard a compelling account of how a small documentation group got approval and support to implement many of the principles of quality and of minimalism I have discussed. They also followed through with customers and obtained compelling data that justified any expense spent in their documentation efforts (Merritt 1997).

A title company wanted to create a large hypertext application to provide title insurance agents, lenders, and attorneys with the reference information they need to make good decisions about issuing title insurance. A competitor of the company had developed a similar product, and the title company hoped that a superior product would increase its business.

The documentation team proceeded to perform user assessments and developed design standards that would guide their creation of the interface (using elements of customer-based and design-based quality). They determined certain product characteristics that the application must have (applying product-based quality), such as a three-level system that allowed customers to find information in three or fewer clicks.

Although the company had a commitment to quality, some managers were unsure if revenues generated by the sale of the product would offset the final cost of $500,000. Upon release, the product received three prestigious awards and favorable press. The documentation group, however, anxious to justify the expense of the documentation they produced, wanted more specific feedback and followed through to get individual customer feedback on the product.

One month after the product's release, they received a letter from a customer thanking them for considering his needs. He said that in the future his company would be ordering an additional forty to fifty copies of the application a month. This order represented approximately $100,000 a month revenue for the company. One satisfied customer paid for the cost of developing the hypertext application in five months. In the first year after release, the company sold five thousand copies of the application, an application that was primarily a piece of documentation.

This story shows how effective documentation serves as a strategic tool in garnering customer satisfaction and increasing a company's competitive edge. For this company, quality documentation reaped substantial rewards. Not all stories will be as dramatic as this one, and not all good documentation adheres to all the principles of minimalism. But as technical communicators, we need to advocate the advantage of good documentation and be vigilant in gathering evidence that shows the organizational benefits of what we do.

As documentation and as customer needs and expectations continue to change, we have an opportunity to play an even more significant role within organizations and in promoting customer satisfaction. For example, the line between product and documentation will continue to grow thinner as we develop more sophisticated systems of delivering online information and as we better assist users with intelligent agents and other smart systems. Documentation, the communication component of products, will become an increasingly important dimension of these new systems. As an approach to documentation, minimalism provides technical communicators with effective tools for meeting the challenges of the future.

Minimalism, like quality, is a process in which no final solution to any documentation or quality problem can ever be reached. Customers' needs and expectations change. Minimalism does not claim to have one solution that applies to all situations. Rather, it embodies a set of principles that aid technical communicators in creating usable documentation. The iterative nature of the minimalist approach accommodates varying situations and changing needs.

Certainly enough evidence exists for technical communicators to argue persuasively that a minimalist approach to documentation can be a strategy for achieving quality documentation, a significant factor in increasing profitability while realizing a competitive advantage. Failure to assess the corporate benefit of a minimalist approach will inhibit, if not prevent, its acceptance and implementation. Meeting users' desires and expectations —the intent of minimalism—creates users who are satisfied customers, and satisfying customers remains a key to succeeding in an increasingly competitive global market.

References

Blackwell, C. A. 1995. A good installation guide means fewer support calls and lower support costs. *Technical Communication* 42:56–60.

Carroll, J. M. 1990. *The Nurnberg Funnel: Designing Minimalist Instruction for Practical Computer Skill*. Cambridge MA: MIT Press.

Chase, R B., K. R. Kumar, and W. E. Youngdahl. 1995. Service-based manufacturing: The service factory. *Production Operations Management Journal* 1(2).

de Jager, P. 1994. Communicating in times of change. *Journal of Systems Management*, June, pp. 28–30.

Dodds, W. B., and K. B. Monroe. 1985. The effects of brand and price information on subjective product evaluations. In *Advances in Consumer Research*, 12:85–90. Provo, UT: E. C. Hirschman and M. B. Holbrook, Association for Consumer Research.

Flynn, B. B., R. G. Schroeder, and S. Sukakibara. 1994. A framework for quality management research and an associated measurement instrument. *Journal of Operations Management* 11:339–366.

Gagne, R. M., and L. J. Briggs. 1979. *Principles of Instructional Design*. New York: Holt, Rinehart, and Winston.

Garvin, D. A. 1987. Competing on the eight dimensions of quality. *Harvard Business Review* 65:101–109.

Juran, J. M. 1988. *Juran on Planning for Quality*. New York: Free Press.

LaBounty, C. 1994. Help desk industry trends: The crisis heats up. *Microcomputer Trainer*, November.

Mayhew, D. J., and M. Mantei. 1993. A basic framework for cost-justifying usability. In R. G. Bias and D. J. Mayhew (eds.), *Cost-justifying Usability*, pp, 9–13. San Diego: Academic Press.

Merritt, L. 1997. Is quality worth it? *Intercom*. June 1997:39–41.

Oliver, R. L. 1980. A cognitive model of the antecedents and consequences of satisfaction decisions. *Journal of Marketing Research* 17:460–469.

Olshavsky, R. W., and R. A. Spreng. 1989. A desires as standard. *Journal of Consumer Satisfaction, Dissatisfaction, and Complaining Behavior* 2:49–54.

Olson, J. C., and P. A. Dover. 1979. Disconfirmation of consumer expectations through product trial. *Journal of Applied Psychology* 64(2):179–189.

Porter, M. E. 1985. *Competitive Advantage: Creating and Sustaining Superior Performance*. New York: Free Press.

Ramey, J. 1988. How people use computer documentation: Implications for book design. In *Effective documentation: What we have learned from research*, pp. 143–158. Cambridge, MA: MIT Press.

Ramsay, J. E., and K. Oatley. 1992. Designing minimal computer manuals from scratch. *Instructional Science* 21:85–98.

Redish, J. 1995. Adding value as a professional communicator. *Technical Communication* 42:26–39.

Schriver, K. A. 1993. Quality in document design: Issues and controversies. *Technical Communication* 40:239–254.

Smart, K. 1994. Traversing the great divide: Documentation challenges of the 90s. In *Conference Proceedings of 12th Annual SIGDOC Conference*, pp. 246–250. New York: Association of Computing Machinery.

Smart, K., J. L. Madrigal, and K. K. Seawright. 1996. The impact of documentation on customer satisfaction. *IEEE Transactions on Professional Communication* 39(3):157–162.

Spencer, C. J., and D. K. Yates. 1995. A good user's guide means fewer support calls and lower support costs. *Technical Communication* 42:52–55.

Spreng, R. A., A. L. Dixon, and R. W. Olshavsky. 1993. The impact of perceived value on consumer satisfaction. *Journal of Consumer Satisfaction, Dissatisfaction, and Complaint Behavior* 6:50–55.

Van der Meij, H. 1993. Learning by doing it on your own. *Performance and Instruction* 32(10)18–20.

12

The Art of Minimalism: Constructing a Rhetorical Theory of Computer Documentation

Robert R. Johnson

The user, or, in other words, the master, of the house will even be a better judge than the builder, just as the pilot will judge better of the rudder than the carpenter, and the guest will judge better of the feast than the cook.
—Aristotle, *Politica*, 1282a 21-2

During the past decade or so, the problem of writing user-centered computer documentation has been one of the most talked-about problems in professional communication. The reasons for this widespread dialogue are many, and the scope of this chapter will not be to expound on all of the debates regarding the processes and techniques for creating computer user instructional materials. Instead, I will limit the focus by examining one general question that in many ways has driven the multitude of discussions surrounding computer documentation development: Why can't users use computer documentation, whether in print or online form?

Minimalism has dealt successfully with this question to a great degree. It is no secret that the very problem of users' difficulty with learning how to use computers spawned the initial research that has come to be known as the minimalist approach. By itself, however, minimalism cannot fully answer the question of user difficulties with computer documentation and interface design. Grounded in the empirical methods of cognitive psychology, the original research of minimalism answers significant portions of the problem, but there is a need to enrich the conception of minimalism so that it can more successfully approach the whole problem of usable instructional materials.

Such an expansion of the notion of minimalism is clearly a primary goal of this book. To this effort, I hope to contribute in two specific ways. First, I seek to foreground the user-centered goals of minimalism. Minimalism has been without a doubt a user-centered concept from the outset, but I will argue that the user-centered goals have often been over-shadowed by a stronger emphasis on the products rather than the process of minimalism. That is, I believe that the user often gets lost because we move too quickly to the textual solution. To illuminate the importance of user-centered development processes, I will present what is my second contribution: the incorporation of the history and theory of rhetoric into the minimalist approach. Minimalism is grounded in a strong empirical and psychological soil. My intent is to add to the depth and richness of the soil by introducing relevant interdisciplinary nutrients from the historical tradition of rhetoric.

12.1   Discovering Minimalism: Promises and Problems for User Documentation

I first encountered minimalism while I was in a problem-solving mode. I was teaching a course in computer documentation in the late 1980s, and I was continually frustrated by the lack of coherent theory that seemed to drive the various approaches in textbooks and how-to articles. Some of the approaches offered practical advice gleaned from the authors' experiences in writing for the computer industry. Others presented some theoretical foundations, like storyboarding or modular design, and thus provided a partial rationale that, like practical experience, presented students with something to go on as they worked in the murky waters of documentation writing. However, I found the approaches lacking in a grounded theory that could be more generalizable and flexible.[1] Although the approaches were helpful, they tended to offer static guide-lines that were recipe-like—almost as if there were some sort of "truth" or "right or wrong" as far as computer documentation was concerned. In addition, the numerous approaches were in scattered pieces that begged to be pulled together.

To alleviate my frustration, I began digging into the issues of human-computer interaction research in the hope that somewhere in this inter-disciplinary swamp I could find some solutions. It was here that I discovered Carroll's work on the minimal manual. The approach seemed to coincide with a number of my own goals. I wanted the students to value user needs, engage with user learning problems, and learn strategies for eliminating unnecessary information. The minimalist approach afforded me some strong possibilities for strengthening my approach to teaching computer documentation.

From my perspective as a technical communicator, though, there were still some apparent gaps that the minimalist perspective failed to fill. Chief among these was the integration of minimalist concepts with writing and document design processes. The minimalist researchers were interested in development processes due to their intimate connection with the software and interface design interests at IBM. However, the translation of minimalist concepts to actual writing processes was unclear. Most technical communicators I spoke to about minimalism were more interested in the manuals themselves—the products, not the process. I would hear questions like, "Oh, so you're interested in minimal manuals! What do they look like? Have you seen any? Where can I get one to look at?" There seemed to be quite a bit of interest in finding models or formats but little in developing a process for producing the products.

Another significant gap for technical communicators was what I would call "portability"—the potential for the minimalist research to be distilled into a usable terminology or set of heuristic that writers could use in their everyday practices. The problem of portability was, in my view, important not only for the practicing writers but for my students as well because they needed some formalized system that would aid in their struggle to learn how to produce documentation. Thus, "teachability" became an issue closely linked to that of "portability."

Finally, I perceived a problem with the role of usability in minimalism when it was applied by technical communicators. Clearly usability is a cornerstone of minimalism. The entire project, in fact, appears to have evolved from questions that arose from user observation and testing. Technical communicators I encountered, though, rarely mentioned the link between minimal manuals and usability methods. This was possibly the largest of the gaps that I saw, and at the same time I thought that a solution to it might be the most fruitful for technical communicators. I hypothesized that if minimalist concepts could inform a reasonable approach to documentation writing that incorporated usability throughout the designing and development process, then I would have something substantial for my students and practicing writers too.

In the remainder of this chapter, I elaborate a solution that I have developed over the past several years regarding applications of minimalism to computer documentation development. Drawing on theories from various disciplines—primarily rhetoric, composition, and usability studies—I provide a rationale for the approach and an overview of the approach as I present it to my graduate students in technical communication and to practicing writers when I consult outside the academy.

12.2   Refiguring Minimalism as a Rhetorical Art: A Theoretical Rationale

In modern times, the term *rhetoric* often has a negative connotation, as when someone refers to "the politician's rhetoric" or when we label someone's speech as being "mere rhetoric." This common but limited definition of rhetoric nevertheless has a long history. Usually traced to the ancient Greeks, especially the dialogues of Plato, this pejorative connotation has laid a foundation throughout Western history of rhetoric as the art of deception: the instrument of devious and self-serving individuals who use language to achieve their own selfish ends. Socrates' descriptions of rhetoric as "cookery" in the *Gorgias* or as the use of language to deceive in the *Phaedrus* are but two examples of this fundamental skepticism regarding rhetorics.[2]

Rhetoric, however, has another meaning—one that is positive and productive. In this sense, rhetoric is the art of inventing, arranging, and delivering language for the purpose of persuading, and in some cases evoking action from an audience. That is, rhetoric can be defined as the knowledge of techniques that make the production and dissemination of language strategic for orators or writers. In addition, due to rhetoric's systematic and thus transferable nature, it allows these techniques, or arts, of language to be taught.[3] Consequently, rhetoric in this uplifted sense has the power to persuade and to distribute the power of language to others.

A key difference between these two definitions of rhetoric (as deceit or as the strategic application of language) is, like technology, based on the perceived ends. When the end is deceit or deception, the possibility that rhetoric might be used for unethical purposes presupposes that the rhetor will use rhetoric only toward his or her own gain. The definition of rhetoric as strategy, however, clearly defines the end of rhetoric much differently because in this sense rhetoric is defined as an art: "The end of an art is *not* a product, but the use made of an artistic construct. The end of the art of housebuilding, for example, is neither the builder's use of the art nor the house itself, but rather the use made of the house by those for whom it was constructed. Similarly, the end of rhetoric is an active response in the auditor not the speech itself" (Lauer and Atwill 1995).

Drawn from the Aristotelian concept of productive knowledge,[4] this definition of art places an ethical and moral responsibility on the rhetor-maker-artisan to make artifacts that suit the needs of the audience or, in the case of technology, the user. Hence, the end of rhetoric as art is in the hearer, or as the analogy to house building demonstrates, the end of any kind of human activity involving making or producing artifacts (material or discursive) is in the receiver or user of the product. To use the analogy of the house, if the house would collapse upon the user of it, or if the user simply finds the house unusable due to poor planning on the part of the builder, then the builder (maker) has created a product that is unusable and, it can be argued, even unethical.

To act as rhetoricians, then, technical communicators should develop arts that will aid them in better understanding the needs of and, ultimately, the production of useful products for their hearers (the users of documentation). Let me be clear that the arts to which I refer are not rules or recipes (as Plato claimed them to be). Instead, they are flexible, general, and transferable, thus forwarding the causes of portability and teachability. To these ends, I will first provide a conceptual framework that offers a generalizable approach for ultimately applying minimalist principles to computer documentation processes.

12.3 The Rhetorical Complex of Technology: A Conceptual Framework for the Art of Minimalist Documentation

All technologies emerge and eventually are disseminated within a rhetorical complex of situational constraints. These situational constraints vary from artifact to artifact, and thus descriptions of how technological development and dissemination occur will vary depending on the artifact under consideration. Language itself can be considered a technology or artifact. Language is an artifact of human creation that is used to achieve some end, even though the ends might be quite different within given situations. For example, the end of an essay might be to convince, the end of an instructional document might be to a demonstrate how to do something, and the end of a poem might be to delight. The ends of the arts of language may vary from context to context or from audience to audience, but the nature of language is still clearly that of a technological artifact. Given this perspective of language as technology, I offer figure 12.1 as a representation of technology development for the pur-

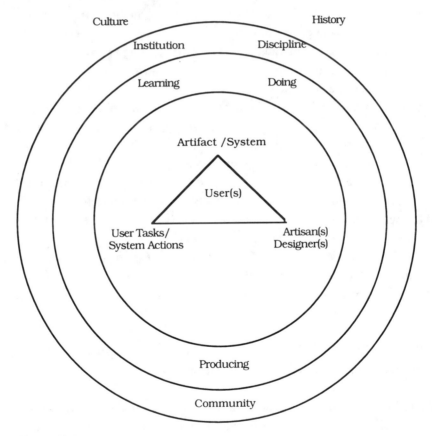

Figure 12.1
The rhetorical complex of technology

pose of introducing the minimalist documentation process as a technological development process—a process that includes much more than
just the writer, the user, and a text.

The triangle at the center of the rhetorical complex been used by various people to describe communication activities (Richards and Ogden
1935; Lakoff 1990), but the most relevant use of the triangle within
rhetoric (and thus within the arts of language) has been the work of
James Kinneavy (1970). In Kinneavy's conception, the three points of
the triangle consist of reader/writer/reality (subject matter) with the text
residing in the center.

I have taken the metaphor of the rhetorical triangle and rearranged
and renamed these constituent parts to make them more relevant to technological development. The reader becomes the user and is placed in the
center of the triangle to depict the importance of centering on users
(instead of artifacts or designers) when we are either actively designing or
reflectively studying technology. Around the perimeter of the triangle, the
writer is replaced by the *artisan/designer*, as these terms more accurately
represent the role of the creator in technological development. The *text*
becomes the *artifact/system* because the text of technology can indeed be
textual in the traditional sense (such as a book or user manual), but the
terms *artifact* and *system* expand the potential scope of analysis. Finally,
reality is changed to *user tasks/system actions* to describe the two different ways that technologies are represented by designers or artisans on the
one hand and by users on the other. In other words, user tasks/system
actions represents the point of contact between the designers' and the
users' perspective—what we often refer to as the interface.[5]

In the first ring, the context of the users' activity is represented by
the three activities of *learning, doing*, and *producing*. These three terms
define global activities that users are likely to be involved with during the
design, dissemination, or end use of technological systems or artifacts.
Learning and *doing* are most closely associated with end-use activities,
and they have been documented to a great degree by researchers in
disciplines involving technology development and use. (These two components are closely allied with the concepts of reading to learn and
reading to do; however I am not limiting the definition to the act of

reading texts but rather have expanded it to encompass the broader scope of technology use).[6]

Learning is associated with knowledge for knowledge's sake: users learn about the functionality of a computer system, for instance, so that they can understand the material components of the system. An example of this activity would be classroom-based learning where the user may even be removed from the actual activity of working with the computer, instead to engage with memorizing the elements of the system or learn how the elements conceptually work together. *Doing* is the activity a user actually carries out while using the computer system. In the doing context, the user is rarely interested in learning for the sake of learning but instead wants to get on with the task at hand (an obviously central concept to minimalist design). Thus, in the situation of doing, reflection or memorization is often not a central concern as in the situation of learning.

Producing is an activity rarely associated with modern users but is integral to a fuller understanding of the role of users in technological development. In essence, producing is the activity of knowledge creation that a user brings to technology. In the postindustrial age we have tended to forget the knowledge that users have of artifacts. Michel de Certeau (1984), for instance, claims that in the preindustrial age, everyday users of artifacts constantly revealed their knowledge of artifacts because they had to rely essentially on their own wits to make things work in those days before standardization and machine-driven processing. The knowledge of everyday knowledge production, De Certeau insists, has been "handed over" in modern times to the experts, who make everything for us. Thus, the knowledge associated with artifact usage has become lost. Our job, he argues, is to learn to hear that forgotten language so that we can put it back into our everyday experience. In terms of minimalism, as we will see in the upcoming examples, a significant part of the *art* of minimalist processes is learning to listen to the users' knowledge.[7]

The next ring outward describes those constraints that larger human networks place on technological use. These networks—depicted here as *disciplines, institutions*, and *communities*—do not constitute a complete list but nevertheless cover much of the ground. In addition, these networks could easily overlap and create complexes within and among themselves. One example would be the institution of the academy: various disciplines constitute its structure (e.g., the sciences, the arts, education, engineering), but there is also an overriding institutional structure that defines its purpose, objectives, proclivities, and so on. These activities all impinge on technology, and ultimately on the various users of the technologies within the disciplinary and organizational boundaries. The term *community*, as well, is complex in itself, and here it can be used as broadly and completely as necessary. For instance, it can refer to well-defined communities like towns or organizations, but it can also refer to more ill-defined (or less formal) constituencies, like communities of discourse, such as those discussed by social construction theorists.[8]

Residing on the outer edges of the rhetorical complex are the factors of *culture* and *history*. These often invisible forces are nonetheless impossible to ignore (nor should any attempt be made to do so). Cultural forces define nearly every human action, and in a world more dependent than ever on international communication and technology transfer, the element of culture is without question essential when defining the use of a technology. History, although of course integrally related to culture, refers to the reflective aspect of understanding human action, particularly in terms of ethics and responsibility. Thus, history informs our understanding of technology in unique and indispensable ways.

It is not my purpose here to elaborate fully the rhetorical complex of technology in the upcoming discussion of minimalism and computer documentation processes.[9] Rather, I wish to use the rhetorical complex in two specific ways. First, I present it as a conceptual framework within which I can discuss the relationship between rhetorical theory and minimalism as they apply to technical communication, and in particular computer documentation. Second, the rhetorical complex provides a vocabulary through which I can discuss the art of minimalist documentation.

12.4   A Minimalist-Aid Art of User-Centered Computer Documentation

In this section I will activate the theoretical discussion through an example of a minimalist-driven documentation process that incorporates the concept of rhetorical art. More specifically, the following case will be couched in a structure that I hope will illuminate the flexible process—the art or technique—that can evolve from a wedding of minimalist principles, usability methods, and rhetorical theory.

Step 1:   Presenting Minimalism

I introduce minimalism by asking writers to discard many of their notions about computer documentation development. I assure them that they will eventually rely heavily on their previous knowledge once a project is underway, but in the beginning I want them to start with an open mind and a clean slate. (Many of them are experienced writers, and although this is advantageous because there are fundamentals that I can skip or gloss over, there are also the problems associated with teaching new tricks.) Before we begin, I have given them several articles to read about minimalism, usually summary articles of the approach written by Carroll or some of his associates.

Drawing upon the rhetorical complex, we use the minimalist approach to center on users—not on manual design, style sheets, or chapter outlines. (We eventually get to these important matters of actual text production soon, but to concentrate on those textual matters too quickly can dilute the focus on users that the minimalist approach advocates.) To accomplish this, we glean defining terminology from the minimalist readings so that we can begin to frame questions that will guide the project.

For example, we often pull such key phrases as "slashing the verbiage," "letting the learner lead," "focusing on error recovery," or "focusing on user tasks" to develop guiding questions that propel this early research stage of the development cycle. These questions can be wide ranging depending on the context or scope of the project, but they might include questions like, "What does the user call or term action X?" "What does the user already know?" "Does the user have a sense of common or problematic errors?" "What does the user *not* need to know?" These questions will be used in interviews or surveys, but also can help provide the writers with specific goals to drive their observation of the users during talking-aloud protocol sessions.

We go beyond the minimalist vocabulary per se and ask the users questions regarding their perception of the goals of their work activities (learning or doing). We try to get at their role as they perceive it within their particular social or institutional context. For example, we might ask users to describe their work tasks as they understand them so that we can compare the users' task vocabulary with the task vocabulary that the system displays. Additionally, we may want to find out how the organization or institution defines the user's tasks. "Where does the user reside on the workplace hierarchy?" "What political factors might be embedded in any of the perspectives that we reveal?" Such information can prove helpful later when we begin to experience user breakdowns during the testing phase of the proJect because, in part, we will have some sense of the users' relationship to their larger work context. All of this early exploration of minimalist concepts and how they might be employed in a documentation project prepares us for the next stage of user needs evaluation.

Step 2: Evaluating Users' Needs

Involving actual users in design and development is one of the fundamental strengths of minimalism. Therefore, we exploit this attribute of minimalism by taking our research questions to the intended users in the form of interviews, focus groups, and observation sessions. The use of the empirically derived minimalist vocabulary is of great service in this second phase because the constrained vocabulary allows us to investigate the users' situation in a focused manner, and sometimes it provides us with surprising results.

For instance, in one recent experience, we found that early analysis of errors helped us to define better which tasks to document. Working in a somewhat backward fashion, we used the error information collected from interviews and observations to determine which tasks should be focused on in the manual. The errors served as pathways to the tasks that troubled the users. Thus, we managed to uncover to some degree the knowledge of the system that the user produces. The users, in other words, produced knowledge of the system through error, and we were able to reconstruct these error pathways and turn that knowledge into useful tasks for the users to follow. This discovery not only saved time, because we were able to document what was really troublesome in the system, but eventually it helped provide users with a relevant product because the documentation was designed around *their* perception—*their* knowledge—of the system.

A project where we developed instructions for a new voice mail system at Miami University is a case that helps to concretize this stage of the process. The automated voice mail system had been in use at Miami University for several years, but it was not receiving the level of new subscriptions that the university had anticipated. The documentation that accompanied the system was rough, to say the least; it consisted of some cursory instructions written by an overworked clerical staff member because no other documentation existed. The director of telecommunications felt that better instructions might help to advertise the system, so we were asked to help in the endeavor.

We began with an analysis of the system's prerecorded phone instructions: a woman's voice that took a first-time user step by step through the process of setting up the mail system. We thought that the recorded instructions might provide us with a basis for the print documents that we were going to develop, especially since the existing print documents were in such rough condition. In addition, the prerecorded instructions were supposedly of good quality, at least according to the developers of the system and the manager of telecommunications. As we were told by one of the developers, they had "never found any bugs in the instructions." The secretaries who work in the telecommunications office, however, had received a number of calls by frustrated users of the system during their initial setup. This was enough to convince us to investigate the prerecorded instructions from a users' point of view by observing a few users as they used the instructions.

To frame the analysis, we borrowed from the minimalist terminology, especially the concepts of "letting the learner lead," "focusing on error recovery," and "focusing on user tasks." These fundamental goals of minimalism appeared to be most appropriate for the learning and doing contexts of the prerecorded messages. That is, in the initial setup of the voice mail system, the users were learning essential characteristics of the system that they would need to recall at a later time, but they were also engaged with doing the tasks at the same time. Consequently, we took the situation of initial voice mailbox setup as an opportunity to find out what the documentation might contain that would contribute to both learning and doing.

We observed several users as they followed the voice prompts, and we simultaneously listened to the prompts on an adjacent phone set up for the purpose of the usability project. We found that the users were doing quite well with the initial steps, which involved linking a private phone to the voice mail system and then creating a password. We soon discovered, however, that the users were having difficulty when they were asked to choose among various options of the system.

For example, the voice prompt asked the user to choose one of three options regarding the activation of the recording function that allows an incoming caller to leave a message. The user could choose to have the system (1) transfer an incoming call after several rings, (2) transfer the call after only one ring, or (3) transfer the call immediately to the message recording function if the line is busy. To choose one of the options, the voice prompt instructed the user to "go to the top of the menu for option X."

The users, having only a touch-tone phone interface to look at, were baffled by the phrase "top of the menu." (This terminology, of course, was "developer talk" describing a hierarchical tree structure that was in the voice system's central computer but not evident in any way on the telephone interface.) Thus, users would try pushing the top three buttons on the phone interface or push other buttons hoping to receive further instructions. The result, in most cases, was that the users would be inadvertently transferred to another level of the voice mail system, leaving them hopelessly lost in a sort of hyperspace—a hyperspace that was more intimidating than that of the computer interface because they had no visual markers indicating their whereabouts in the system. The ability to return "home," for instance, was not evident to the uninitiated user of the voice mail system.

Our discovery of this conceptual and visual problem of the voice mail instructional prompts compelled us to build into the print documentation constant reminders of how to return to a familiar place if the user got lost. As the project proceeded, this general understanding of the system-centered ideology driving the system's design enabled us to seek other system-centered flaws in the voice mail system, thus making our job somewhat easier and more focused.

Step 3: Designing and Testing a Prototype Module

In this phase the writers begin to feel more at home because they start to do what they do best: write documents. However, they write only a short part of the eventual document at this stage—one task or a single chapter. The rationale is to develop a short, testable piece before producing a whole text that might ultimately be unusable.

Minimalism continues to be visible to a great degree as we often return to the research findings of minimalism to assist in document design decisions. One of the most hotly debated in my experience has been the issue of eliminating the table of contents (something that Carroll and his associates tested in their research). Many of the writers resist this idea, but I have experienced several cases where the elimination of a traditional table of contents has sparked some creative document design decisions, such as hybrid solutions that combine tables of contents with cover design or some that include error recovery information within a refigured table of contents.

To structure the testing of the module, we once again turn to the minimalist vocabulary as a device to guide the test design. Similar to the inquiry method used in the initial phase, we pose questions based on the minimalist vocabulary to drive the design of the test. Thus, we continue to use the common terminology and concepts provided by minimalism to thread the process together. The terminology in essence serves as a benchmark against which we can evaluate and interpret our findings. The interpretation of qualitative data is difficult, and the grounded vocabulary offers some sense of direction in this often slippery task. For instance, we were able to see if some of our assumptions of letting the learner lead in the voice mail documentation were actually working or to what extent they were working.

Step 4: Revising the Module, Testing Again, and Completing the Document Draft

The final phase is in many ways a repetition of the earlier parts of the process. We complete the drafting of the document, test it iteratively, and then eventually compile a final product. Throughout the process, the minimalist concepts help to check the goals of the product, either when the writers use the vocabulary to reflect on the product or when the iterative testing is carried out in line with the minimalist objectives. Key to the success of the document in this last stage, I believe, is the continual contact the writers have with the users during the iterative testing. Obviously, the testing of document pieces all along has the potential to increase document quality. More important, the users are drawn into the process in a way that helps them value the manuals as actual work tools—as artifacts that they might use meaningfully on a regular basis. Because the users take part in the document production process, they see the minimal manuals as something useful: something that they have had a hand in making, unlike the throwaway tutorials that come shrink-wrapped with the system or the software.

I also have a hunch that this level of user involvement may have a profound effect on the knowledge, comfort level, and expertise of the users. It seems that because the users actually see and take part in the document production process, they are better able to understand how the system works. In addition, the users have much to offer concerning concep tualization of the system. They, of course, often see systems from unique perspectives that could inform the development of systems. (Isn't that what usability in a large, theoretical sense is all about?)

The ancient Greeks referred to this as the knowledge of "building *and* driving." Athena, for instance, knew how to fell the trees and shape the wood for her chariot. She also knew how to drive (use) it. I am not suggesting that users must become hackers who make and then use their computer systems. I am, however, wondering what situations there might be concerning user involvement beyond just the evaluation and testing of documents and systems. Again, I refer to the rhetorical complex of technology to point out that users are producers of knowledge and that such user-derived knowledge is essential to usable systems. The work of many Scandinavian computer designers comes to mind here (Ehn 1988; Bødker 1991). Users in some of the Scandinavian projects play roles that encourage input on civic and cultural ramifications of computer dissemination. Consequently, these users are not just involved with the development of stand-alone artifacts, but instead have a voice in how the proposed system might affect such global concerns as education, public welfare, or the environment. Their knowledge and know-how of the technological artifacts are built into the systems. Thus, they become decision makers in the design and development process—a goal that is essential to technology development, be it minimalist inspired or otherwise.

12.5   Potential Pitfalls and Places for Growth

In this final section I note some issues and questions that arise as we move forward with the tasks of expanding the notion and application of minimalism. I also attempt a few clarifications that occur to me as I think about the complications of developing theoretical positions, especially when such positions must be placed directly against practical implications.

Can minimalist approaches to documentation be applied to large audiences? It is evident that the manuals I am discussing have been developed for relatively small audiences. In fact, most of these projects are customized manuals for specific institutions or offices. In other words, the question might be raised, "But how could this type of intensive user evaluation and testing be used to create manuals for large software markets?" My answer is twofold. First, I believe that usability must be thought of as a long-term project that over time can build longitudinal understandings of user knowledge and know-how. With the potential models that would be constructed of users, it might then be possible to apply minimalist principles to broad-based audiences. Second, however, I fear that we might lose sight of the local nature of user knowledge if we attend to merely building universal models. It is hard to solve all of the problems all of the time, and I worry that we could fall into such a trap—a trap of universalist definitions—if we do not admit to the issue of the localization of knowledge.

I realize that some of my colleagues, most likely some chapter authors in this book, will take issue with me concerning the immediate broad-based appeal of a minimalist approach. The approach I present is directed toward in-house or single-client consulting projects for the purpose of developing manuals or online documentation for customized use. (In many cases we are not even minimalizing a large manual, but instead start from scratch by just documenting user actions.) I have no problem with developing manuals for small audiences. Such an approach pays close attention to the institutional or community constraints depicted in the rhetorical complex—constraints that are usually invisible to broad-based documentation. In addition, I would suggest that the case could be made for more companies, institutions, and organizations to hire technical communicators who can produce training materials for their own contexts; institutions of higher education, in fact, are some of the most negligent in this regard. Minimalist approaches, in other words, should be able to do more than just benefit users, and I believe that minimalism is well suited to address this significant challenge.

Is the approach I advocate too time-consuming and too costly? It is commonly argued that usability is just too expensive. The approach I advocate certainly argues for a significant amount of usability research. The problem of determining how much usability should be implemented, however, is contextual in that the amount of usability evaluation and testing changes depending on the complexity or newness of the project. The ongoing development of vocabulary like that which minimalism offers could help alleviate the amount of time spent planning and pilot-testing usability studies. I again see the approach as an argument for long-term thinking by companies and institutions to build users into their design and development cycles. In the long run, less time will be spent figuring out why no one can learn the system. Instead, we will have some common evidence to fall back on—some heuristics that writers and developers can flexibly apply to different situations.

Is the minimalist approach too controlling? It has been said, especially in the realm of rhetoric and composition studies, that the use of empirically derived vocabulary could be too constraining and too controlling. Minimalism, as we know, has already been criticized for possibly being too controlling because it gets users only the base amount of information they need, and little more. These are criticisms that we should take seriously. Several researchers have written in recent years concerning the issue of control and communication (Yates 1994; Beniger 1986), and their research clearly documents the desire by organizations or cultures to limit communication for sometimes questionable ideological reasons. I think my approach deflects some of these worries to an extent. That is, I see the users as having more to say over the control aspect because they are allowed to have a central voice in the design and development of the products. However, I am also aware that such user-driven control could be only an illusion in certain contexts. As the rhetorical complex once again demonstrates, the institutional, historical, and cultural constraints are forever present in technological development.

Is minimalism applicable to contexts other than the computer? I believe that it would be unfortunate if minimalist approaches to documentation were relegated solely to the realm of the computer. The development of user-oriented technologies is needed across a wide swath of user environments, such as those that contain medical or environmental information. For instance, medical patient information is closely akin to computer documentation. The medical establishment can certainly be likened to the blackbox of the computer. When a medical patient encounters the interface of the medical establishment, there are parallels to the computer user regarding such things as access to information, readability of the information, and even definitions of what constitutes literacy. The expansion of minimalist principles and processes to other areas of use is an exciting prospect indeed.

12.6   Conclusion

In *The Origins of Greek Thought* (1982) Jean-Pierre Vernant points to the concept of the *polis* as a turning point in Western culture. During this formative period (roughly the eighth and seventh centuries B.C.E.) Western culture witnessed, among other things, the development of the foundations of Western philosophy and the shift from oligarchy to democracy. Most strikingly, however, he points to one phenomenon that was more influential than any other during this period, the emergence of rhetoric and the arts of oratory: "The system of the polis implied ... the extraordinary preeminence of speech over all other instruments of power. Speech became the political tool par excellence, the key to all authority in the state, the means of commanding and dominating others.... All questions of general concern that the sovereign had to settle ... were now submitted to the art of oratory" (pp. 49–50).

It is interesting to speculate at our moment in Western culture whether there is a similar phenomenon occurring in regard to the computer and the currently emerging *polis* of electronic networks. Computers, and the information they contain, certainly are significant instruments of power; their power as a rhetorical tool is similarly substantial. I think it is important that we keep this rhetorical perspective in mind as we develop methods for the teaching and learning of computer technology. Technical communicators are rhetoricians, and we are and can continue to be important players in the computer technology game. We also are intimate with that impressionable audience of users who might come to rely on the documents we create. I conclude by implicitly returning to the question I posed at the beginning and leave you with another question (as unanswerable as it may be). If strategies and processes like minimalism help users to use computers more effectively, then what is our responsibility to them after that?

Notes

1. By "grounded theory" I mean a theoretical rationale or construct girded by empirical or other "practical" evidence. Such evidence can be qualitative or quantitative in nature depending on the context of the problem being studied. For more on "grounded theory" see Flower (1989); for more on the rationale of empirical research see Lauer and Asher (1988).

2. In the *Gorgias* I am referring to the moment when Socrates tells Callicles that rhetoric is like cookery in that it has no knowledge or epistemology of its own, but merely copies what is already known. The example from the *Phaedrus* refers to the example of selling a mule to someone who has been convinced, through rhetorical means, that he or she has bought a horse.

3. A distinction between the classical and modern definitions of art might be helpful here. In the modern sense, art usually refers to the fine arts, or the artifacts of creative activity like paintings, sculptures, or poetry. The ancient term (and one used in some contexts today) refers to systematic techniques or crafts that an artisan uses to create an artifact. An example would be, "There is really an *art* to that!"

4. In "Refiguring Rhetoric as an Art: Aristotle's Concept of *Techne*," Janice Lauer and James Atwill describe the epistemological taxonomy of Aristotle as having three parts: theoretical (episteme), practical (praxis), and productive (techne) knowledge. They go on to explain that "the taxonomy explicitly locates the study of mathematics, the natural sciences and philosophy in the domain of theoretical knowledge, ethics and politics in the domain of practical knowledge, and the *arts* [my italics] in the domain of productive knowledge. Throughout the corpus, medicine and housebuilding are used as examples of arts" (p. 6).

5. Another way of defining user tasks/system actions is Dumas and Redish's (1994) concept of usability and functionality. Usability is the measure of how well a system is designed to meet user needs; functionality measures the ability for the system itself to run smoothly.

6. See, for example, Sticht (1977) or Redish (1988).

7. See chapter 5 of de Certeau's *The Practice of Everyday Life* (1984) for an elaboration of the loss of the knowledge of arts.

8. For a summary of communities of discourse, see Porter (1992).

9. For a in-depth discussion of "the complex" see my forthcoming book, *User-centered: A Rhetorical Theory of Technology for Technical Communicators*, SUNY Press.

References

Aristotle. 1952. *The works of Aristotle, Vol. 2.* Ed. R. M. Hutchins. Chicago: Encyclopedia Brittannica, University of Chicago Press.

Atwill, Janet. 1993. Instituting the art of rhetoric: Theory, practice and productive knowledge in interpretations of Aristotle's *Rhetoric*. In Takis Poulakis (ed.), *Rethinking the history of rhetoric: Multidisciplinary essays on the rhetorical tradition* (pp. 91–118). Boulder, CO: Westview Press.

Benig -, James R. 1986. *The control revolution: Technological and economic origins of the information society*. Cambridge, MA: Harvard University Press.

Bizzell, Patricia, and Herzberg, Bruce. 1990. *The rhetorical tradition: Readings from classical times to the present*. New York: St. Martins Press.

Bødker, Susanne. 1991. *Through the interface: A human activity approach to user interface design*. Hillsdale, NJ: Erlbaum.

Carroll, J. M. 1990. *The Nurnberg funnel: Designing minimalist instruction for practical computer skill*. Cambridge, MA: MIT Press.

Carroll, J. M. and Rosson, M. B. 1987a. The paradox of the active user. In J. M. Carroll (ed.), *Interfacing thought: Cognitive aspects of human-computer interaction*, pp. 80–111. Cambridge, MA: MIT Press.

de Certeau, Michel. 1984. *The practice of everyday life*. Berkeley, CA: University of California Press.

Detienne, Marcel. and Vernant, Jean-Pierre. 1974. *Cunning intelligence in Greek culture and society*. Trans. Janet Lloyd. Chicago: University of Chicago Press.

Dumas, Joseph S., and Redish, Janice C. 1994. *A practical guide to usability testing*. Norwood, NJ: Ablex.

Ehn, Pelle. 1988. *Work-oriented design of computer artifacts*. Stockholm: Arbetslivscebtrum.

Flower, L. 1989. Cognition, context and theory building. *College Composition and Communication*, 40(3), 282–311.

Kinneavy, J. L. 1971. *A theory of discourse*. New York: Norton.

Lakoff, Robin. 1990. *Talking power*. New York: Basic Books.

Lauer, J. M., and Asher, J. W. 1988. *Composition research: Empirical designs*. New York, Oxford University Press.

Lauer, J., and Atwill, J. 1995. Refiguring rhetoric: Aristotle's concept of techne. In R. Gabin (ed.), *Discourse studies in honor of James Kinneavy*, pp. 25–40. Maryland: Scripta Humanistica.

Porter, J. 1992. *Audience and rhetoric: An archaeological composition of the discourse community*. Englewood Cliffs, NJ: Prentice Hall.

Redish, J. C. 1988. Reading to learn to do. *Technical Writing Teacher, 15*, 223–233.

Richards, I. A., and Ogden, C. K. 1923. The meaning of meaning. In P. Bizzell and B. Herzberg (eds.), *The rhetorical tradition: Readings from classical times to the present*, pp. 967–974. New York: St. Martin's.

Sticht, T. 1985. Understanding readers and their uses of text. In T. M. Duffy and R. Waller (eds.), *Designing usable text*, pp. 315–340. Orlando, FL: Academic Press.

Sticht, T. G. 1977. Comprehending reading at work. In M. A. Just and P. A. Carpenter (eds.), *Cognitive processes in comprehension*. Hillsdale, NJ: Erlbaum.

Vernant, Jean-Pierre. 1982. *The origins of Greek thought*. Ithaca, NY: Cornell University Press.

Yates, JoAnne. 1989. *Control through communication: The rise of system American management*. Baltimore, MD: Johns Hopkins University Press.

13

Practical Problems and Proposed Solutions in Designing Action-Centered Documentation

Stephen W. Draper

This chapter examines and attempts to develop current conceptions of minimalist instruction in four related ways: looking back to our experience so far, looking down to discern and articulate its foundations, looking forward at the problems of complex domains that seem beyond the reach of the original simple minimalist techniques, and proposing an organization for the design of manuals in terms of three levels of structure and four key types of design decision.

In looking back, I draw on my own experience with minimal manuals, based on lecturing on them to classes in a human-computer interaction (HCI) course, on supervising a series of student projects that developed and tested such manuals, on writing one or two myself for introducing classes of students to various bits of software, and on writing a paper with Keith Oatley about them (Draper and Oatley 1992). This experience convinced me of the great power and robustness of the technique, since it was usually easy to show superiority over the manufacturer's manual even though each student author probably did not follow the minimalist technique exactly and was far from optimizing the manual. It also made me aware of difficulties that my students and I would come up against when writing a minimal manual.

The chapter attempts to improve and extend the minimalist approach by analyzing theoretical and practical problems with it, and then suggesting applications of the analysis. But what do we know about it? First, it is one of the very few techniques in HCI that directly and demonstrably benefit users: you can take a piece of software that gives users trouble, write a minimal manual for it, and see them have a much better experience. Second, both task gains in time and errors and learning gains have been repeatedly demonstrated: minimal manuals are good for both immediate use and supporting learning. Third, the technique is transferable. I have repeatedly taken Carroll's writings and got students to produce measurably improved manuals. Thus, however vague the minimalist "principles" may seem to a theorist, stated as they are in informal English in phrases that vary from paper to paper, they have proved to be sufficient to transfer a successful practice. Fourth, the effect is robust: the manuals produced by my students have varied widely in appearance, and I am sure have not been optimized, and yet they have been sufficient to show gains for users relative to existing manuals. Thus the effect must be big and insensitive to suboptimal implementation.

In what follows I assume that whatever the practical realities may be of writing manuals after the software is fixed, the success and quality of the resulting user experience depend on the joint effect of manual and user interface. To a considerable extent, we can think of writing a minimal manual as supplementing the deficiencies of the interface's display. A perfectly designed interface does not require a manual at all (in an increasing number of cases, users succeed without ever consulting a manual). On the other hand, a sufficiently bad interface not only makes the manual designer's job more difficult but may leave the final user experience poor. However, we should not admit this as an established fact: we may just not have developed manual design sufficiently. Claiming that the user interface design prevents a good manual from being written is close to admitting that manual writers are useless. If good interfaces do not require manuals and bad interfaces cannot have good manuals, why bother with manuals at all? The rational approach is to consider the design of interface and manual together, in order to minimize the total effort and allow rational trade-offs (e.g., save screen space at the cost of providing permanent "cheat sheet" quick reference cards for all users). In designing a manual we are really producing a new part of the overall interface (with a printed manual acting as a second parallel display for the user).

13.1   Practical Problems

This section lists some of the commonly occurring problems from the viewpoint of a manual writer.

Preminimalism Problems

The classic problems of preminimalism writing, also represent issues of continuing importance in minimalism.

Telling Users Nothing An early attitude to (or rather against) documentation was that truly educated and skilled computer users can discover things for themselves; only the incompetent need manuals. Originally documentation was often omitted because users', particularly unskilled users', needs were little regarded. Now that is much less acceptable as a principle, but as user interfaces have become much easier to use, omitting documentation can in fact have some success. For instance, the recent explosion of use of the World Wide Web since visual interfaces to it have spread has occurred almost entirely independent of user documentation. The half truth behind the tactic of omitting documentation is that learning by exploration is often a successful alternative to documenting information (it is a large part of what makes minimalism successful). The fallacies behind the idea of omitting all documentation are that often a user has to know something about how to learn by exploration from a given system and that usually some information cannot easily be obtained in that mode. Thus, the central problem for users posed by this approach is that of missing information. This problem lingers on, as Thimbleby (Thimbleby and Ladkin 1995) emphasizes, in manuals that are incomplete or incorrect in their information. Minimal manuals that choose to cover only a subset of commands are also open to this criticism. Omitting information is an important tactic but can fail the user if it is unobtainable by any other route. The issue is ensuring that all functionally necessary information is available by some route (not necessarily by describing it in the manual).

Documentation as a Brain Dump from the Designer A first reaction against telling the users nothing is to tell them everything. This results in the classic preminimalism manual that tries to record everything and results in an unusable manual. It is seen in discursive introductory manuals that seem to have been written as if a new user had just said, "Tell me about this software" and settled down for a good read, as one might spend an evening reading a travel book. Its central problem is that it is not organized for users who are actively engaged in using the software and makes it hard for them to access the information needed. The information is present but inaccessible. Information presence is not enough; accessibility in practice is equally crucial.

Documentation Organized by Feature   Documentation organized by software function or feature as one kind of reference manual forms another common preminimalism format. This is actually of considerable use, but the organization still reflects designers', not users', main preoccupations. Thus it is useful but only if the user already knows the existence and name of a function (the same problem as dictionaries have: you can only verify spellings you already know or find meanings for terms you have come across elsewhere; you cannot look up a word given its meaning). Its central problem is that access is limited to one method (from name to task), and one little needed by new users or users driven by a goal of getting a job done, who need to go from task meaning to name. The information is present but accessible to only a minority of users who already have the right prerequisite partial knowledge. Access by feature does not serve all, or even most, user needs.

Common Problems with Minimalism

Some of the most commonly occurring problems from the viewpoint of a writer of minimal manuals represent frequently asked questions by students who are trying to write manuals, but equally problems that I find hard to decide upon when I am writing a manual. These are problems mainly because of apparent clashes between minimalist principles.

Maximize Learning or Maximize Getting Work Done?   Are we trying to get users to succeed at their immediate tasks or to learn the maximum? If the former, then we generally want to provide every bit of information they need, removing the motivation for learning; if the latter, then we went to set them puzzles that may slow them up but will result in greater retention (a well-known learning principle).

The strength of the minimalist approach is that at either extreme there is no conflict: if the puzzle is too difficult, the user neither succeeds at the task nor learns anything, and if the instructions are too detailed and complete, then users lose more time and make more errors in interpreting them than they gain in extra information. Nevertheless in the central region in which a minimalist approach places a documentation author, there is a real tension. For instance, consider sitting in a car and directing the driver where to go. Telling her where the next turn is in terms of immediate local marks (e.g., the second intersection from here) generally works the best, but the driver is less likely to be able to find the place again than if she had been given more global instructions and made to work out their meaning on the ground. Similarly users who are given fairly detailed recipes (e.g., "Edit menu; Select All command") are less likely to remember them later. It may be true that people do not follow all dictated recipes accurately, but if our goal is to maximize task success, then we will develop a skill at giving the recipes in ways that minimize those deviations, comparable to choices of how to tell the driver which turn to make. On the other hand, if we want to maximize learning, then we must first decide if it is retention of items (e.g., memorizing command names) or discovering generalizations we are aiming for, and then devise techniques for that pedagogic goal (e.g., "Find the menu command that will highlight all the text at once"). The measures we would use to check on our success as authors would also be different: time to first successful task completion versus success at performing without the minimal manual on later occasions.

Tutorial Activities or Efficient Job Support?   Similarly, is a minimal manual aiming to be a reference manual to support work or a tutorial that can direct the user to do tasks to achieve an optimal training sequence? People hired as experimental subjects for research labs and users on a training course for software may have some patience for tutorial instructions. Many others do not; they expect to get useful work done from the start.

This matters, because an issue for authors is whether they can instruct users what task to do, just for the learning experience. In many interfaces, it is very hard to explain something without reference to some other task. If the user encounters tasks in one order, it can all seem easy and natural, but in another order it can seem hopelessly obscure (e.g., explaining "paste" before "cut," or the point of those little triangles before the user has used the tab key, or the effect of right margin controls before the user has typed in enough text to fill a line). This argument really applies mainly to learning by exploration, but that possibility is one of the most important enablers of minimalism. If the user can learn by experiment, the manual need describe nothing. However, in many contemporary interfaces, learning by exploration depends in practice on the sequence of user actions, so a crucial issue for authors is whether they allow themselves the presumption of directing the sequence of a user's exploratory actions.

Explanations   Should manuals contain explanations, as opposed to direct support for actions (e.g., should they explain what the clipboard is or other hidden buffers)? A truly minimalist approach has no explanations at all (and boasts of avoiding long descriptive introductions), but sometimes learning (although perhaps not doing) is likely to be greatly aided by explanation. Note that none of Carroll's summary statements of minimalist principles (van der Meij and Carroll, this volume, chapter 2) have anything that would promote the inclusion of explanations, and his experimental results tell against them (Carroll 1990, 178–180), but elsewhere he reports that users complained about their absence. As an author, my intuition is that there are a few cases where they are vital to allow the user to understand some hidden pattern in action procedures (e.g., the hidden storage buffers linking the effects of cut and paste), and the Task Action Grammar work on consistency and learning time might support this (Payne and Green 1986), but there seems to be no direct evidence.

Addressing Misconceptions as an Additional Requirement   Barbara Mirel (this volume, chapter 7) suggests that preventing misconceptions is an important additional requirement. This is in the basic tradition of observing actual problems users have and trying to address them, and it is furthermore recognizable as compatible with experiences in the education field, where it has become clear that it is not enough to present information for learning; instead at times educators must explicitly address misconceptions known to recur. The tension for minimalism is the same as that for explanatory material: it will add more material, and unlike in education, users may not recognize that they need to use it.

Necessary Detail for Whom?   How can an author decide on the level of detail? A big saving in verbiage is to omit all details that the user does not need, but omitting any detail that a user does need is disastrous (for that user). There is a big tension in practice between supporting novice users and achieving minimal text (and so supporting users who do not need the greater detail). In general, the principle is that a manual must be targeted for a particular user, and there can be no such thing as a single manual for all users but ultimately a library full of different manuals: minimalism in reading for an individual user but an explosion of material per product.

The immediate problem is that you can write much slimmer manuals for experienced users than for novices, but for complete novices you have to include material on how to use the mouse, where to find the menus, and so forth. One solution I have tried is to write a graded series of manuals, omitting more and more detail but including more and more functions as the series goes from introductory to expert in its target audience. For the first (getting-started) manual, the important point is to include a complete set of functionality but no more than the minimum (e.g., in a word processor, a way of adding and removing text and some very basic formatting). Later manuals can introduce faster but logically redundant commands (e.g., a way of moving text instead of deleting it and retyping it in a different place). For the users, this graded series is minimalist since each manual is by itself usefully minimal (either few functions or few procedural details), although for the author and manager it is not, as there are now several documents instead of one.

Organizing by Task versus Avoiding Repetition   In some cases at least there is material, typically error recovery information, that apparently cannot be put in a task-organized manual, because the problems could arise in any context. For instance in the UNIX editor **vi**, observations of problems users have show that there is a set of baffling error states, any of which may arise at any time. These stem from the editor itself and general features of the UNIX environment interacting with it. For instance, the editor allows the number of lines displayed to be set; if it is accidentally set to 1, then it is hard to understand what has happened as the screen is mostly blank. Similarly, if the user ever presses ⟨control⟩S, then all screen output is suppressed, making it appear that the keyboard has gone dead. There are at least nine different such cases where an accidental keystroke or two can throw the machine into a baffling state, requiring special error recovery actions. Duplication of this material for every normal user task seems unthinkable, but putting it in a separate place is a dangerous lapse from having the material in the exact place in the text that a user needs it. That is, minimizing verbiage can conflict with organizing the manual by task.

It is actually a consequence of consistency that makes such error recovery actions (and the accidental actions that cause the problems) valid in all or most states. This general applicability also makes it apparently sensible to put such universal error recovery task procedures in a single place in a manual. However, as the minimalism literature tells us, this approach has a poor record of serving users in practice, probably because when an apparent problem occurs, users naturally tend to suspect it has to do with what they just did and the particular task they were in the middle of. It is not obvious to them that this is a general problem and might be addressed in another part of the manual, under a general heading of problems and error recovery. One solution is to instruct beginners to induce such a problem state deliberately and then to use the error recovery procedures. This solves this problem only by trading it for the problem already described of persuading all users to go through a tutorial before they experience the need for it.

The Unnaturalness of the Writing Task   It is hard for people to learn to write minimal manuals because it goes against the basic approach to writing that we have all (painfully) learned from childhood: that in most writing, the difficulty is in describing everything that you (the writer) know and can see to someone who is not there. The easy use of language is in human-human dialogue. However, in most writing, we face the essential difficulty of achieving clarity and nonambiguity for a piece of paper standing alone. This is difficult for children, but eventually writers develop the skill of including enough explanations and background context in their writing so that readers can understand descriptions without being there and without asking questions.

With a manual for supporting a practical task, however, we face a third situation where what we are describing is there, physically present. The writing is like speaking to someone present with both you and the machine but who cannot question you—monologue but with copresence of what is discussed. You do not need to describe what is obvious and visible, and anyway you probably cannot do so very well.

People do not read but try things out, partly because the text is not comprehensible without looking at the machine. The minimalist approach notes that you cannot fight this, but that actually it is also an advantage, allowing great brevity. Thus this writing is not like most other writing (letters, novels, etc.) that is for making present something remote from the reader. It is not an encyclopedia for recording everything known about a device (although technicians may need this kind of manual). In most writing, the main problem is being explicit enough to overcome differences in the prior knowledge and perspectives of writer and reader, but here we can and should use the actual device as much as possible to show what we mean. This is more like a conversation about something we are standing beside than it is like most other types of writing. Could we devise special training techniques for authors?

Counterexamples to Minimalism   How are we to understand very successful cases that are the opposite of minimalist? For instance, a printed telephone directory at home is very usable: you can often find the entry you want in seconds, yet it has an extraordinarily low ratio of useful (to you) entries to useless ones. Perhaps in the two-year life of a directory, you might refer to only ten numbers, yet a fairly small directory has hundreds of thousands of numbers. This is extreme antiminimalism, yet very successful. Presumably it works because people can easily skip text they do not need, provided they know they do not need it. When can we use this principle in our manuals? In fact, minimal manuals already do use this in a small way by structuring the parts of each entry to separate task description, procedural instructions, and error recovery material (say), so users do not have to read the error recovery entries unless and until they need them.

Another example is that of command reference manuals (e.g., the UNIX online manual). These are not successes for new users, but they are successful some of the time, as you can observe by watching system experts at work: these experts use such manuals frequently and often successfully. On the occasions they succeed, their lack of minimalism (their sheer bulk) is clearly not a drawback.

13.2 Identifying Underlying Principles for Minimalism

The central feature of the minimalist technique for designing manuals is that it is empirical, not theoretical. The sequence of studies that culminated in minimalism (Carroll 1990) was, unusually for both HCI and experimental psychology, driven not by prior theories but by responding to the observations at each phase by creating another version of the technique intended to overcome problems observed with the earlier versions. The bottom-up empiricism of the research program is echoed in the method for developing each new manual, where first designs are tested on real users and modified in the light of observed problems. In order to communicate the method to new practitioners, about six heuristic principles (such as "slash the verbiage") have been extracted from the successful applications and experiments. These can be handed in written form to new practitioners, who are then generally able to create new manuals that show the expected advantages. I have been able to do this with a sequence of students, so I know firsthand that this is a technique transferable through these principles written in English.

The principles have been presented in various forms. For instance Carroll (1989), in relating minimalist principles to features of human learning, listed these:

- Allow the user to get started fast.
- Rely on the user to think and improvise.
- Direct training to real tasks.
- Exploit what people already know.
- Support error recognition and recovery.

Earlier versions had, in combination with some or all of those, the following:

- Slash the verbiage.
- Guide exploration.
- Promote coordination of display and manual.

In Carroll (1990) the section headings reveal this variation on the list:

- Training on real tasks
- Getting started fast
- Reasoning and improvising
- Reading in any order
- Coordinating system and training
- Supporting error recognition and recovery
- Exploiting prior knowledge

The most recent presentation, by van der Meij and Carroll, has eleven heuristic principles, structured under four main principles (see chapter 2, this volume).

It is clear that the exact statement of the principles is important for communicating enough to new practitioners for successful manuals with demonstrably high performance to be created. Conversely, there must be a very powerful and robust effect underlying the minimalist approach, as some statements of principles must be better than others, and almost certainly some practitioners are better than others. This means that many minimal manuals actually produced must be less than optimal and yet show good performance. Nevertheless, it might be useful to reanalyze the principles, both to attempt a better statement of them for new practitioners and also to resolve some of the practical problems and apparent contradictions that arise, some of which were described above. Draper and Oatley (1992) offered one attempt at this. Here I offer a revised version that incorporates the connection Johnson (this volume, chapter 12) draws between the study of rhetoric, user centeredness, and minimal manuals.

This analysis is presented from proposed underlying principles through a series of derivations toward the practical prescriptive principles usually listed. It covers five or six levels, each derived from or generated by the previous one, the last two being the levels of practical heuristics. My claim is that these minimalist prescriptive principles can be derived solely from the notion of action centeredness, which in turn derives from the user-centered or usability testing approach of focusing on optimizing support for observed user performance at their work.

A Derivation

Level 1: User Centeredness   The most basic principle that of user centeredness in the sense that the overriding criterion for manuals in the minimalist approach is how well the user performs with them: their length, their use of language and format, their consistency, whether they look nice, whether they use correct English. None of these matters except to the extent that observations show they affect the user's ability to succeed in this particular case. Everything else follows from that. The corollary associated with this principle is the use of usability methods and testing in designing documentation, in particular, iterative design based on testing versions on real users and modifying the design as a result.

In the context of writing, this corresponds to being reader centered rather than text centered; to writing to achieve a specific (rhetorical) effect on the reader and to get them to act as a result, rather than on producing a text whose interpretation and effect depend as much on the context and the reader; to an emphasis on the process of writing and still more on the net effect of the process of reading rather than on the text as product. This is related to a speech act view of language (speaking to produce an instrumental effect), as opposed to the use of texts for bills of lading, legislation, rules of a game, or novels in all of which applications the effect of the text and indeed its meaning depend a lot on the reader and is relatively independent of the intentions of the writer. (See Johnson, this volume, chapter 12, for a related, fuller discussion of this point.)

Level 2: Action-Centered Manual   It follows from taking a usability approach that manuals are designed to support successful user action and are judged by how well they do that. Hence, their essential characteristic is to be action centered, and "minimal" only if and when that best supports action.

Level 3: Two Aspects of Action Centeredness   The two aspects are to organize the manual to support doing tasks with the software and organize it to be used during action, as a resource—not to be read like a text-book. In other words, aim at learning by doing, not learning by study of an exposition.

Level 4: Three "Super" Principles About What to Include and Omit
Level 3 in turn leads to one principle of what to cover and two principles of what to leave out, given the additional observation that users act in a context of knowledge and information from sources other than the manual, they do not suspend disbelief and read manuals like fairy tales. The principles are:

1. Organize the design around user activity.
2. Design around the effect of users' prior knowledge (and beliefs and desires).
3. Design around the effect of users' (future) knowledge during action (i.e., exploit the information available from the interface at the relevant moment).

Levels 5 and 6: Specific Practical Principles   All the specific practical principles in their various versions (level 6) and their (level 5) groupings in the van der Meij and Carroll form (this volume, chapter 2) can be derived from the above. Only a couple of examples are discussed here. For example "provide on-the-spot error information" follows because errors occur during user activity and recovering from them is part of that activity, and error information needs to be supplied on the spot (as part of the task information in the manual) since reading the manual is itself part of the task the user is executing, but placing the information else-where will demand a new task of searching for it. Similarly the older "slash the verbiage" heuristic follows from avoiding creating extra user tasks of reading a lot by designing around the user's prior and action-supplied knowledge. The higher-level principles can suggest when to apply this heuristic (when the user has other sources of information) and when not (e.g., leave out error information only when the user can re-cover just by responding to the software's error messages). Similarly in considering the question of whether to duplicate material so as to ensure it is present where needed, we can see that the underlying principles imply that the true rule is to minimize reading for the user. One way to do this is to minimize the printed material, but another is to organize the material (cf. phone directories) so that users do not have to search through what they do not need.

Is the Technique Essentially Minimalist or Action Centered?

Two important issues can be brought out by the above analysis. The first is that, although the approach is called "minimal manuals" or "minimalist instruction," it might more accurately be called "action-centered manuals." The usual names are good for selling the idea to managers, but I have found them distinctly counterproductive in teaching the technique to would-be manual writers. This shows up most acutely in that one of the most important aspects of the technique is the inclusion of error detection and recovery information, which usually involves adding, not deleting, material relative to conventional manuals. The analysis gives priority to action support over verbiage reduction, as is required for successful manual design, and it would save time in training practitioners if the technique's name reflected this.

Is the Goal of Manuals to Support Learning or Doing?

The above change of analysis can also be seen as a claim that minimal manuals are about supporting user doing, not user learning, which implies that we can look to theories of doing, such as Norman's (1986) theory of action, rather than to theories of learning. In reality, however, users do both, inextricably combined, and manuals when successful support this mixture. Hence, we should not ignore learning, but it is essential to realize that doing is at least as important an outcome to support as learning, and furthermore the indissoluble mixture raises issues of its own that are central to understanding how to design manuals.

Common sense, much of design, and much of psychology all presuppose that learning and doing are separate: done by different people (novices versus experts) at different times (e.g., training versus doing the job) by different parts of the mind (learning versus problem solving) and supported by different parts of the user interface (meaningful menu labels versus learned menu positions or keystrokes). A little reflection shows that this tacit view is deeply mistaken. A more nearly correct view is that all human activity involves both doing and learning. Such a statement, however, does not capture the entailed key problems for the design of both user interfaces and manuals, problems that make this both a theoretical puzzle and an important and difficult practical tension. The problems are what knowledge is actually used in operating an interface, what knowledge is learned by experts, and the large effect on learning of a person's decisions about what to learn.

We know rather little about how much knowledge (and so learning) in fact underpins successful human action. If you shut your eyes, you will not be able to travel to work or even move around your own home with anything like the skill you normally show. Thus, you do not know your way over these familiar routes in the sense of having a self-sufficient knowledge of the route in your head; instead you have some partial traces that are sufficient to complement perceptual input during the task. Similarly people have been shown not to be able either to recall or recognize many of the features of the coins and banknotes they use every day (Nickerson and Adams 1979). This also applies to users' memory for the menus of the programs they use (Mayes et al. 1988). Prolonged skilled use does not lead to anything approaching complete knowledge of the objects being used. Doing, even skilled doing, does not require learning in the most obvious sense of knowing the main attributes. Thus, even if we were to take learning as the goal of manual design, we know little of what users need to learn. In minimalism, this appears as exploiting coordination of display and manual to omit text, but this principle labels the existence of an opportunity rather than telling us what people either use or learn.

A tempting hypothesis is that people learn only those attributes necessary for the tasks they are doing. Although this is a good first attempt to counteract the assumption that people remember every obvious feature, it is turning out to be a poor approximation to the facts (Kaptelinin 1993; Moyes 1995). People do do some "incidental learning" and accumulate knowledge of some apparently nonfunctional attributes, but on the other hand they do not always learn apparently useful ones. For instance, mouse-driven menu systems require the use of position information as part of users' actions, and most users do start to learn some positions and can move to some menu commands without using their eyes, but they do not learn the positions of most of the menu commands they use.

All people, then, whether in computer use or in other domains, from first-time use to world-class expertise, employ some mixture of prior knowledge and reference to external information sources. Librarians do not know all the books in their library, but instead are characterized by special skills for getting the information they need. The same applies to Smalltalk programmers who do not know thousands of Smalltalk classes by heart but have skills at finding them. The use of preflight checklists by aircraft pilots is another example of the use of reference material in expert practice to avoid reliance on human memory. Expert users of large systems depend on reference manuals, and the aim of those manuals must be to promote not user learning but user doing. Effective use of reference manuals is part of what constitutes expertise in many domains (Draper 1985).

In summary, then, all human activity comprises a mixture of learning and doing, drawing on a mixture of internal memory and external information. Remarkably little is known about these mixtures, although the success of information sources such as manuals must depend on it. Learning never stops (even after thousands of trials, people are still improving a skill), yet many "obvious" features apparently go unlearned despite daily exposure or even use.

There is a further important issue here: the mixture of doing and learning is strongly affected by the intentions of the person. Learning is not an automatic side effect of doing (as some theories seem to assume), except possibly at the lowest level. This is because what people do is determined by their goals: if their goal is to learn, they do different things (e.g., deliberate exploration), while if their goal is to get the job done, they act differently and so learn differently and much less. This is most obvious in higher education, where almost all learning depends on student effort, which in turn depends on their decisions about where to expend it. Sitting through a lecture or video without wanting to learn results in very low retention, as in most evening TV watching, whereas the same external experiences coupled with a goal of learning (whether derived from personal interest or institutional coercion through exams) results in quite high retention. The ratio of material retained in these two cases may perhaps be of the order of one hundred to one—This is a big effect, bigger than almost all effects ever reported in the literature from varying learning materials or methods.

When users confront an interface, they will apply their own goal priorities. On a training course, this goal may be to learn; in their office, it may be to do a job and they may have as little patience for activities justified only by learning as I would have if I was trying to use a new toaster for my kitchen, or to drive an automobile I had just hired at an airport. It is not obvious, and probably not true, that we can assume that one kind of manual will do for all. Taking the goal of minimal manuals to be learning by users would be tantamount to saying that minimalism has no contribution to make to manuals for most workplaces other than training courses; but in fact minimal manuals seem to do quite well for users who only want to get tasks done. Thus, I believe that minimal manuals are more than just learning aids, and our conscious design objectives should be to support work as much as or more than to support learning.

In summary, the interaction of learning and doing leads to three issues in the design of manuals, and in fact in HCI in general:

1. What information do users actually use in operating an interface, and, for manuals, what information in addition to that supplied by the interface and common knowledge? For instance, if a command is recognized as having the longest name on the menu or being at the top, should that be how it is described in manuals?

2. What information will expert users normally learn? It is only this subset that we might be justified in writing tutorial material for.

3. Learning is strongly controlled by the user's intention: to learn or just to achieve a material task. This is not under the designer's control. Both alternatives must usually be served. One way to develop this idea is to add learning to the set of tasks used in analyzing what manuals (and user interfaces) must be designed to support.

13.3 Extending Minimalism to More Difficult Cases

Given the many successes in designing minimalist documentation for applications like word processors and the various analyses of the principles underlying these successes, it becomes natural to ask how far we could extend its application. In the years since minimalist work began, changes in technology have affected the challenge of designing action-centered documentation. The two main changes are that on the one hand user interfaces have become easier to use, and so providing documentation is easier or even unnecessary, and on the other hand instructing the user in the task domain as opposed to merely the user interface has become more important, which makes documentation more challenging to design. This has tended to move the focus of design for manuals up from the lowest to the highest level in terms of the three levels of structure implicit in most minimalist designs.

The Three Levels Within Minimal Manuals

Minimal manuals typically have three levels of structure:

1. *The level of individual actions* is the lowest (e.g., "Press ⟨control⟩V— the selected text will disappear").

2. *The level of a single user task* is the middle level and the chief unit in minimal manuals. Each such unit describes a multistep procedure for a single user task, complete with associated error recovery and success recognition information (e.g., select the text, delete it, select the new position, do "put").

3. *The set of user tasks* forms the top level. The main design difficulty is how to organize the complete set of alternative tasks so that users can find the one they need and recognize that they have found it. Part of this problem is how to name or describe each task (e.g., do you describe the task as "moving text" or "cut and paste"); the other part is how to support the user's search over the set. One approach is to add an index, or contents list, or a hierarchical structure of user task (e.g., group tasks under topic headings).

This three-level structure was clear in the Guided Exploration cards approach (Carroll 1990, ch. 5). Here the set of cards formed level 3 (there was no index; users just flipped through the cards), a single card corresponded to level 2 with the different aspects (e.g., actions versus error recovery) labeled separately within a card, and level 1 corresponded to one instruction, typically represented by one or two lines.

Minimalism operates separately at each level. At the lowest level (of individual actions), it is about being sparse in the amount of detail for each instruction step by coordinating display and manual (i.e., exploiting all the clues in the screen display), and the observation is that this not only reduces problems in finding and following printed instructions, it also seems to reduce many comprehension problems. At the middle level of the entry for a single task, there is the structural system of subdividing entries into standard parts (e.g., description of the outcome and purpose of the task, procedure, error recognition, and recovery) with standard headers or graphic symbols. This allows users to skip parts they do not need at any given moment, and so achieves minimal reading by the user, although not minimal printing of words. Presumably to the extent that this works, we could add more parts to an entry without harm (e.g., extra optional explanations).

At the top level is the issue of how a user is to find the right entry. The problem here is that manual writers and users do not in general have a pre-agreed language in common for naming or describing tasks, so in practice users have to scan the whole list of entries looking for a best match to their need. This is what is so different from phone directories, where if you know the person's name, you can skip right to the entry you need by exploiting the alphabetic ordering and without having to read and consider every name. Minimalism is more problematic here. One approach is to remove all lists (contents and index), which works if the whole manual can be fit on to one sheet so that the user can scan it all without turning a page. When this is possible, it works well (one reason that one-sheet reference cards are so popular). Because the user must scan all entry titles to find the sought task, there is great pressure to apply the other minimalist tactic at this level, and to reduce the number of tasks described as radically as possible. This leads to one aspect of a training-wheels approach, where only a specially selected subset of tasks and machine features is covered. This top level is often the hardest to do well, and some manuals manage to apply minimalism only to the lower two levels, while leaving the top level organized essentially like a conventional manual with one entry per software command or feature and indexed by command name.

Interfaces Are Often Easier to Use

A lot of user interfaces today need no manual (e.g., bank cash machines, many public information system). Many users of the World Wide Web have never consulted documentation for their Web browser, essentially because the two other sources of what the user knows (on-screen information delivery and previous experience of similar interfaces) are often sufficient so that a manual has nothing to add. This affects all levels, but has had the most effect on the lowest level of individual actions.

As user interfaces have become broadly easier to use in the years since minimalist work began, so has writing manuals. We should perhaps use that spare capacity somewhere else. If we could create successful minimalist manuals for keyboard command interfaces, then perhaps we could succeed in cases with a simple graphical interface but a more complex kind of software.

The Increasing Need for Task Domain Instruction

Partly because the surface of user interfaces has become easier to use, the greatest limitation on user performance—the goal by which we judge our documentation's performance, just as we judge a user interface—becomes the user's knowledge of the domain and its work tasks. Direct evidence of this can be found in an experiment by Baxter and Oatley (1991). They measured the time to learn two spreadsheets and found no difference between two rather different commercial designs, but a large difference in learning time between subjects who had used some other spreadsheet before and those who had not. Clearly a large part of the learning burden concerned knowledge about the kind of thing a spreadsheet is and what it is useful for. Although it may be that the original users of spreadsheets had long experience of adding up columns of figures, many learners now do not, and they have to be prompted into both thinking of a task that is meaningful to them and into using a column or matrix layout, and into typing a formula to calculate. Pocket calculators, now familiar to all, do simple arithmetic in a rather different way (with no separation of numbers and formulas).

Domain knowledge frequently seems to be the main barrier to wider user success (and so wider use of the software). Why don't more people use databases (now a mature technology) routinely in their work? Mainly because relatively few people understand how a database would fit in with their work, or rather how to describe their work in terms of a consistent data model that could be represented by a database.

This issue is part of a broader trend for computer systems to be seen not as a central piece of equipment around which the work is structured, but as part of an overall work pattern. It is that overall work pattern that is the real topic to be supported by documentation (because it is what matters to users), just as more and more computer systems, if they are to succeed, must be designed not as devices in themselves, but as one component among many in a wider pattern of work.

Whether documentation authors are prepared to write a manual to instruct users in a new external task domain rather than in how to operate a user interface depends on their job remit. If they do take it on, then this is mandated by minimalist principles of supporting user action in any way required, being action centered, and as matching the documentation to a user's real tasks; and they will face problems that were always present in minimalist approaches, even if with a different balance. Supporting users' learning about new task domains means focusing on the top structural level of the set of user tasks and addressing it successfully. Obviously the more complex the domain, the harder this becomes (e.g., "balancing your accounts" versus "pasting a special function"; see Mirel, this volume, chapter 7, for discussion of complex task domains).

13.4   Key Design Decisions for Action-Centered Documentation

This chapter has reviewed the main problems that have arisen in minimalist documentation so far, looked at the direction that future work is likely to have to tackle, and discussed the relative priorities of the various principles underpinning minimalism—not least of which is that designing around user action takes priority over minimizing words. It has also introduced the notion that such documentation is structured into three levels, each with its own problems and solution techniques. In this section, I suggest that the design of a manual consists of four main types of decision and that future progress depends on improving solutions for these problems.

What Information to Include?
The earliest question for documentation is what information to include. Minimalism offers a novel compromise answer between the first two

obvious approaches of supplying no information or all possible information. However, deciding the exact balance remains an active issue, different for each case.

A lot of manual design is driven by compiling a list of commands or features, although omissions are by no means unknown. However, users need things to be organized by task. This leads to further issues of how to decide what tasks to include. Below the level of the software's main commands are all the subprocedures or articulatory procedures of how to execute those commands: how to open a menu, how to operate the mouse, and so on. Should these be included? Do you have to include how to use a mouse in every section? Too much information undermines delivery (making it even harder for users to follow instructions), but too little undermines the whole enterprise. My conclusion is that I have to design a different manual for each type of user as defined by the typical user's prior knowledge. Online manuals delivered by software, however, could try dynamically adjusted amounts of detail (cf. the contingent tutoring technique of Wood, Wood, and Middleton 1978).

Beside the main commands are other issues that are not the responsibility of the software package designer, but an effective manual writer must deal with them; they have to do with the environment the software operates in, such as switching on, firing up the application, and dealing with switching between applications. For instance stray mouse clicks just outside a window often cause a switch to another application and cause trouble for new users.

Above the main commands is an indefinite hierarchy of larger tasks for which the software is a means to an end. Should a manual for a word processor deal with how to manage the writing of a book, interfaces to software for managing bibliographies, and so forth? If these are the tasks that users are engaged in and motivated them to use the software, then it seems hard to avoid, but there seems no obvious boundary, so this threatens an explosion of content and the defeat of minimalism. New work is perhaps needed most in this area. There are also other grounds for expanding the tasks covered. For instance, offering learning as a possible explicit user task might be one way of handling the problem of whether to offer pedagogic activities or only immediate work tasks.

Access Mechanisms

A crucial aspect of manuals, as with any other information resource, is its index or access mechanisms. Having the information present but not in practice accessible by the user is as bad as omitting it. The bottom level has none below it, and so no access design issue. At the middle level of an entry for a task, the access issue is about how the user can move between the parts of an entry, for example, skipping the error recovery information unless it is needed. Standard headings or other page layout mechanisms have been made to work repeatedly to solve this problem. The top level of providing efficient access to the right entry from within the whole set of tasks is the most problematic case, and one that seems to require new work to support an extension into supporting work domain instruction.

The first element is to describe each task in a way the user will recognize, such as "typing in some text" rather than "using the Insert command." The second element is to allow the user to search through these descriptions to find the best match to the need. This is typically done by an exhaustive scanning of either separate pages (flipping through looking at the titles of each entry) or possibly in a list (an index or contents list). Because the task descriptions are largely unpredictable by the user, they are effectively unordered, and the scan must be exhaustive—a technique that does not scale up well to manuals with many tasks. Progress here is needed. For instance, online manuals with free text matching from users' free text request to the task descriptions in each manual entry might be one way forward. Another might be graphical maps of task hierarchies to provide more structure to what users scan while searching for a correspondence with their internal mental descriptions of what they want to do.

Information Delivery

When the user has found the item, how should it best convey what the user needs to know? Minimalism is striking here in being terse and relying on coordination with the display and in effect forcing a little local learning by exploration. This is probably important for speed and for improving both comprehension and learning, independent of reducing volume to facilitate finding by scanning. The issue is about how to describe an action in a way that works in conjunction with the display. Iterative design and testing of the manual will remain necessary to debug these descriptions, but we are now confident that we will succeed at this.

Hans van der Meij (this volume, chapter 10) has explored using pictures of screen displays for information delivery here. Experience in other applications suggests, however, that similar issues, and minimalism, may well apply. For instance, simplified diagrams may do better than veridical screen snapshots (just as maps are usually better than aerial photographs for many tasks). And in extreme cases, special perceptual training could be needed: just showing medical X-rays does not tell you how to perceive the medically relevant features, so perhaps in some cases users must be trained in how to read screen displays.

Success Criteria for Manuals

When we test manuals in order to improve them, what should the criteria be: learning outcomes or success at material tasks? In practice, we often react most strongly as designers to neither of these but to evidence of breakdowns and user complaints. Perhaps we should consider how we imagine our users to be monitoring and controlling their activity. Are they judging by a feeling of understanding? Of certainty and confidence in the choice of actions? Of confidence in eventually achieving their goals?

Complaints about ultraminimalist manuals (e.g., the Guided Exploration cards) center on feeling anxious and underinformed. But too much certainty removes the motivation for learning. It is plausible that people try to understand only when confronted by a problem (a "breakdown"), and only when they try to understand is there an opportunity for learning. But giving users problems means raising their anxiety at least for a while and is likely to lead to complaints. We must decide not only whether our aim is to maximize learning or job completion, but whether to use breakdowns or user complaints as the main measure during testing.

13.5   Conclusion

The design of action-centered documentation can be seen as revolving around the three levels of structure and the four main types of design issue. This framework seems to apply to all such manuals, to let us describe which areas seem to be getting easier and which harder, and yet to cover the oldest problems in manual design. Most usefully, though, it identifies the hardest part in extending the approach to complex task domains—designing an effective access mechanism to a large collection of user tasks—and so suggests where innovation is most needed to extend the application of this approach to documentation.

References

Baxter, I., and Oatley, K. 1991. "Measuring the learnability of spreadsheets in inexperienced users and those with previous spreadsheet experience". *Behaviour and Information Technology* 10:475–490.

Carroll, J. M. 1989. "An overview of minimalist instruction." Technical report RC 15109. Yorktown Heights, NY: IBM.

Carroll, J. M. 1990. *The Nurnberg Funnel: Designing Minimalist Instruction for Practical Computer Skill.* Cambridge, MA: MIT Press.

Draper, S. W. 1985. "The nature of expertise in UNIX." In B. Shackel (ed.), *Interact '84: First IFIP Conference on Human-Computer Interaction*, pp. 465–471. Amsterdam: North-Holland.

Draper, S. W., and Oatley, K. 1992. "Action centered manuals or minimalist instruction? Alternative theories for Carroll's minimal manuals." In P. O. Holt and N. Williams (eds.), *Computers and Writing: State of the Art*. Norwell, MA: Kluwer.

Kaptelinin, V. 1993. "Item recognition in menu selection: The effect of practice." In S. Ashlund, K. Mullet, A. Henderson, E. Hollnagel, and T. White (eds.), *Interchi'93 Adjunct proceedings*, pp. 183–184. New York: Association for Computing Machinery.

Mayes, J. T., Draper, S. W., McGregor, A. M., and Oatley, K. 1988. "Information flow in a user interface: The effect of experience and context on the recall of MacWrite screens." In D. M. Jones and R. Winder (eds.), *People and Computers IV*, pp. 275–289. Cambridge: Cambridge University Press.

Moyes, J. 1995. "Putting icons into context: The influence of contextual cues on the usability of icons." Ph.D. dissertation, University of Glasgow.

Nickerson, R. S., and Adams, M. J. 1979. "Long-term memory for a common object." *Cognitive Psychology* 11:287–307.

Norman, D. A. 1986. "Cognitive engineering." In *User Centered System Design*, pp. 31–61. London: Erlbaum.

Payne, S. J., and Green, T. R. G. 1986. "Task-action grammars: A model of the mental representation of task language." *Human-Computer Interaction* 2:93–133.

Thimbleby, H., and Ladkin, P. B. 1995. "A proper explanation when you need one." In M. A. R. Kirby, A. J. Dix, and J. E. Finlay (eds.), *People and Computers X*, pp. 107–118. Cambridge: Cambridge University Press.

Wood, D., Wood, H., and Middleton, D. 1978. "An experimental evaluation of four face-to-face teaching strategies." *International Journal of Behavioral Development* 1:131–147.

14

Minimalism: A Case of Information Transfer in Technical Communication

R. John Brockmann

Usually it is the case that technical communicators introduce new technology or problem-solving methods to audiences who are either unaware of the novelties offered or are wary of their acceptance. Throughout the 1980s, for example, I was one of many technical communicators who sought to bring the hardware and software of personal computers to homes and offices. At times we found our efforts rewarded as products were understood and used; at other times, for many varied reasons, we found our efforts confounded by our audiences or even by our corporate home companies and organizations. For example, the first professional writer of computer documentation for Eckert-Mauchly (UNIVAC, Sperry-Rand UNIVAC, UNISYS), Joseph Chapline, had his manual for the BINAC in 1949 shelved by his own company because his managers thought it revealed too much too well to outsiders, not because it was poorly or incorrectly written. In a similar vein, Barbara Mirel documented the story of how a well-written manual in the 1980s was rejected by a group within the company because its process of development left out their input—the old "not invented here" gripe.[1]

Technical communicators have long focused on analyzing why other groups do not accept new information and how information transfer fails in other groups, professions, or organizations. Rarely, however, has such an analytic eye been turned on the profession of technical communication itself to see how it has or has not accepted novel information. Rarely has anyone examined the way in which novel information has been accepted and digested by the very profession that makes its living by helping others get novel information into their companies, organizations, or professions. The way in which the profession of technical communication has integrated minimalism into its philosophy and techniques proves to be a wonderful case study of information transfer replete with resistance, champions, selective apprehension, and content change during the very act of adoption.

14.1   Some Factors Suggesting How Minimalism Gained Entrée into Technical Communication

The set of ideas and beliefs called minimalism, invented outside the profession of technical communication, gained entrée into the profession because of four key events or features. First, minimalism appeared on the technical communication scene just at the time as a sea change of core ideas was taking place. Thus it was swept inside the door of technical communication like many other ideas and changes because so many others were coming in simultaneously. Second, minimalism was able to gain entrée because it had an attractive spokesperson with psychological and scientific cachet, as well as well-known advocates within the profession who had easy access to many within the profession. Third, it had an attractive moniker as well as a coherent program of theory, research, and practice to attract a wide variety of constituents within the profession—both practitioners and academics. Finally, minimalism had a distinctively radical edge.

Instigating Sea Change in the Profession

Information transfer opportunities require an instigating event so that a group is receptive to new information or new technologies. The shock of Pearl Harbor and the sweep of the Nazi blitzkrieg across Europe moved the United States and its allies to seek out and exploit a variety of new technologies, such as carrier-based naval battle, transfusable blood serum, radar, atomic energy, and digital electronic computers. In a similar way, in the 1970s, typical employers of technical communicators such as electronics and mechanical industries found their businesses under great pressure with the onslaught of foreign competition. Thus communicators were losing their typical corporate perches. At the same time as the typical perches diminished, wholly new industries dependent on the exploitation of the microchip appeared.[2] This moment was a sea change in the profession of technical communication, and it worked to make the profession open to a wide variety of new ideas and approaches. Desktop publishing supplanted dedicated print and typesetting shops, and thus the whole relationship of communicators, printers, and designers was altered. Writing teams began to supplant lone writers as perhaps one way to deal with the abbreviated life cycle of products and the ever diminishing time before a product's release to the market. With the rise of teams, there has been both an increase in the academic study of collaboration and a change in gender of the profession—from a profession of majority men to a profession of majority women. Scientifically verifiable usability findings supplanted both standard operating procedures dependent on tradition or the gut feelings of experienced writers or editors. This has led to advanced graduate programs in which the coursework looks more akin to psychology than to writing and editing.

Amid all these changes that swept in with the advent of the computer industry and its phenomenal growth during the 1980s came the concept package of testing/designing/audience-understanding called minimalism. The industry change, however, is just the general instigating incident to explain why minimalism was able to move into technical communication. More specifically, it was able to sweep in because its key spokesperson, John Carroll, worked at the IBM Watson Research Labs, one of the premier companies in the computer industry—one of the largest employer of technical communicators, as well as the publisher of earlier testing/designing/audience-understanding guidelines called task orientation.

Bethke, Dean, Kaiser, Ort, and Pessin published "Improving the Usability of Programming Publications" in a 1981 issue of the *IBM Systems Journal,* and in 1982 they released an internal corporate document, *Publications Guidelines, Designing Task-Oriented Libraries for Programming Products.* Between 1982 and 1990 there was an avalanche of conference presentations on task orientation design principles—at least sixteen conference presentations were given by IBMers on task orientation between 1982 and 1990.[3] A measure of how thoroughly the principles of this "Z" document intended for IBM internal eyes only[4] passed into the mainstream of technical communication can be see in Joanne

Hackos's 1994 textbook, *Managing Your Documentation Projects*.[5] Hackos, a former president of the largest technical communication organization, the Society for Technical Communication, did not feel the need to cite IBM or the *Publications Guidelines* as sources even though she spent sixteen pages discussing various aspects of task orientation design principles. Hence, by 1994, IBM's task orientation design principles had become an integral element of technical communication's paradigm.[6]

There are many reasons that task orientation was accepted so readily and completely into the profession of technical communication, and I have discussed these at length elsewhere.[7] Suffice it to say that task orientation—the testing/designing/audience-understanding guidelines that called for focusing on what the readers need to know in order to perform a task rather than focusing on the internal workings of the tools used to perform the task—built on a tradition of American instruction manuals reaching back to at least the 1850s. Task-oriented technical communication basically reached back and dusted off a style and approach that was familiar and customary. Moreover, this "new" methodology was coming from a source that was trusted, IBM in the early 1980s. Most of the speakers at the International Technical Communication Conferences who spoke on task orientation were indeed IBM employees, and most of their citations were self-referential; later task orientation articles merely cited earlier ones.

As the avalanche of articles on task orientation diminished, a number of articles on minimalism, twelve, began appearing in the professional journals and conference proceedings between 1988 and 1995 (see figure 14.1).[8] It is interesting to observe in the figure the similarity in the publications rise in both task orientation and minimalism as well as the sense of succession; publications in the two areas did not overlap except from 1987 to 1989. It is almost as if the earlier set of ideas had to be explored and adopted before the second set of ideas could be explored and adopted.

Thus the profession was made receptive for minimalism as a set of ideas by the large-scale sea change in the profession that made it open and accepting of new many ideas, the positioning of where minimalism came from, IBM, as well as the particular specifics of earlier testing/designing/audience-understanding guidelines called task orientation.

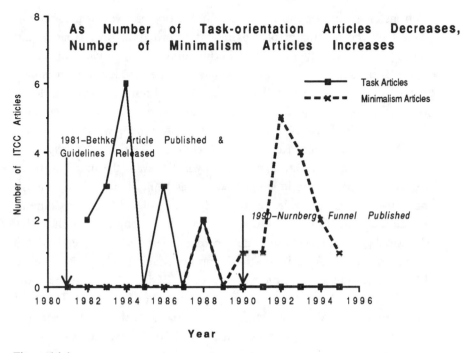

Figure 14.1
Number of task orientation and minimalism articles published, 1980–1995

What is interesting to note is the change in the corporate base of the authors as well as their citation practices. Whereas task orientation International Technical Communication Conference (ITCC) speakers came from the ranks of IBM and used primarily self-referential citations, ITCC speakers on minimalism came from the ranks of Hewlett-Packard[9] and largely referenced nontechnical communication sources, for example, John Carroll's 1984 seminal article in *Datamation*[10] and those in the human factors literature.[11]

Carolyn Miller has noted that in technology or information transfers, there is motivation on both ends: the supplier and the receiver of the information must believe they will be benefit by the transaction. Thus, early gun runners to the Native Americans were motivated by money, furs, or possible political alliances, while the Native American recipients were motivated by the possible warfare and hunting advantages such weapons would give them. One can only guess that Carroll was motivated in transferring information from human factors into technical communication by the possibility of moving his information on testing/design/audience understanding from within the ranks of human factors psychologists and computer software designers to a new audience of technical communicators. In early 1980 articles, he does not cite anything developed within the ranks of technical communication that could have some bearing on his efforts even when he uses quite similar words; for example, his and Mary Beth Rosson's 1985 chapter, "Usability Specifications as a Tool in Iterative Development," appeared just at the time that work on usability performed in similar ways was being done both by Redish and the American Institutes of Research and Carnegie Mellon's Communication Design Center.[12] However, Carroll's attempt at injecting his "outside" information into a new profession worked: he received the highest award the Association for Computer Machinery's Special Interest Group on Computer Documentation (ACM SIGDOC) gives in 1994, the RIGO award, and he has been widely discussed at Society for Technical Communication (STC) meetings, and it is the STC that underwrote the symposium on minimalism from which this book is derived.

In a similar way, there were those of us who were motivated to use and transfer Carroll's information. For example, the HP speakers could achieve the image of being cutting edge by going outside the customary boundaries of citation and to include him; rather than going head to head with the IBM task-oriented speakers, they simply headed out to new territory. Carroll returns the favor by discussing HP's use of minimalism as much as, if not more than, his own IBM's use in his 1990 book.

I was motivated to help move the outside information into technical communication. In 1989 when Carroll's book was in the final publishing process, I was also in my *Writing Better Computer Documentation: From Paper to Online, Version 2.0*. I had known of John Carroll's work in the area of human factors and interface design from his 1987 book, *Interfacing Thought: Cognitive Aspects of Human-Computer Interaction*, but I was unaware of the minimal manual information located in other articles. The 1986 version of my book had been somewhat successful and had launched a series of national and international seminars. Wanting to keep the seminars going as well as develop a book that was up to date and cutting edge, I was allowed to see Carroll's book in manuscript, and I immediately recognized that here was something novel—something to improve my seminars and book. Earlier in 1988, Philip Lillies from HP had presented a paper on minimalism and had made the connection that I saw only two years later: he connected Carroll's work on minimalism, the work on task orientation, and my book.[13] I was also personally flattered to find that my recommendations to use a rather traditional item, quick reference cards (a.k.a. "cheat sheets," or "job aids"), in my 1986 book found its way into Carroll's cutting-edge work as an example of minimalism. The connection was made, a new section on minimalism was added to both my book and seminar, and Carroll's work was carried by me within rather traditional technical communication vehicles so that his work became part of our profession. Thus, the specific instances of information transfer were motivated perhaps less by purely informational reasons and more by rhetorical jockeying within the profession of technical communication.

An Attractive Spokesperson and Inside Advocates with Access

In addition to instigating moments in information transfer that were especially propitious for minimalism, minimalism also had a champion and an advocate, the outsider, John Carroll, and the insiders, Ginny Redish and Stephanie Rosenbaum. Robert Horn had been able to foster his earlier testing/designing/audience-understanding guidelines called Informations Mapping and make it popular for many reasons in the early 1980s, but most especially because he was not a typical writer. He was an educational psychologist and spoke the language of science to a profession arising largely from the humanities. John Carroll, the author of *The Nurnberg Funnel*, the central text in minimalism, was also an attractive outsider. Like Horn, Carroll too had his primary training in cognitive psychology, and his book and articles used the language of scientific testing and science. He was not a member of any of the typical technical communication organizations, the STC, IEEE's Special Interest Group on Professional Communication (IEEE PC) or ACM's SIGDOC, and he was more likely to be found publishing in *Datamation*, *International Journal of Man-Machine Studies*, and *SIGCHI Proceedings*. All this allowed him a certain hard science cachet in a field grown weary of impassioned subjective arguments of editors over the use or misuse of various grammatical usages.

However attractive, Carroll's outsider status might have made him unknown to technical communicators. Consider that it was five years before architect Saul Wurman and his books, *Information Anxiety: What to Do When Information Doesn't Tell You What You Need to Know* (1990) and *Follow the Yellow Brick Road: Learning to Give, Take, and Use Instructions* (1992), were cited in STC proceedings and that a cover article on him in an STC organ did not appear until 1995.[14] STC articles citing Carroll, on the other hand, begin appearing the very year, 1988, that his article, "The Minimal Manual," appeared in *Human-Computer Interaction*.[15] What Carroll had as an outside champion of minimalism were some insider advocates.

Carroll's advocates had to be known in the field, trusted, and able to implement minimalism in a variety of constituencies within the profession. Like the honeybee cross-pollinating whole fields of plants because the bee can move from plant to plant, these advocates had to be far ranging in their influence. Early advocates such as Ginny Redish and Stephanie Rosenbaum helped bring Carroll's outsider ideas in. Redish's Document Design Center at the American Institutes for Research had begun to implement aspects of minimalism with clients as early as 1988.[16] Rosenbaum is one of the principles of Tec-Ed, a consulting firm with clients across the United States as well as a member of the governing boards of most, if not all, technical communication associations at one time or another. As early as 1986 in work Tec-Ed did with Xerox, Rosenbaum was using and demonstrating minimalist techniques, and as recently as 1995 she taught short courses on minimalism in university extension organizations.

Thus minimalism benefited from having both an attractive outsider as champion for its ideas as well as effective insider advocates.

A Bandwagon Moniker and a Coherent Program of Theory, Research, and Practice to Appeal to a Variety of Constituents

In the late 1970s, Leslie Matthies popularized a system of procedure writing called Playscript, and he traveled the country teaching seminars on this method and writing a newsletter, *Les Matthies' World of Sys-*

tems, that popularized his methodology.[17] At about the same time, Robert Horn created Information Mapping, as well as a company to present and license seminars on the program called Information Mapping Inc.[18] In the late 1970s and early 1980s, both systems of writing had large numbers of proponents, large numbers attended the seminars, and many companies used their systems.

Both Playscript and Information Mapping had short, easy-to-remember monikers that seemed to sum up the core of the two systems of writing: Playscript pushed for a type of outline procedural writing that looked like a play's script; Information Mapping sought to break content down into short modules, which then could be assembled into visually attractive page formats that would encourage reader comprehension and implementation by mapping information. Geoffrey James also created a catchy moniker for his novel documentation ideas—Document Databases—but unlike Playscript and Information Mapping, James had no publicity or distribution program to disseminate his ideas to the profession.[19] He did not create a company and marketing force to promote, teach, or license his ideas. Thus, his concept died young even though it had the catchy moniker and insights into what the profession needed to know.

In addition to catchy monikers and ways of distribution and promotion, innovative methods of technical communication need to be attractive to both practitioners and academics. Playscript did not have a program of theory and research that could make it attractive to both of these groups, who would teach the next generation of writers. There was basically nothing to research, and the citations to Playscript in the STC proceedings are rare. Information Mapping, on the other hand, drawing on Horn's earlier work in learning theory and training, as well as his work for the Department of Defense, offered a number of areas for both practitioners and research academics. Thus articles on Information Mapping, though rare in public books and journals, did appear in both the 1982 research-oriented collection, *The Technology of Text*, as well as in an early 1981 practitioner-oriented newsletter of ACM SIGDOC.[20]

Minimalism certainly has the short memorable moniker, and it picked up on echoes of modern architectural doctrine: "Less is more." John Carroll did not create his own company or newsletter to proselytize for minimalism, but he also kept it from being a proprietary system. For example, both the Playscript and Information Mapping seminars were strictly controlled, and access to information about them had to come from the presenting organizations. They were, in fact, closed system, not unlike the closed operating system of Apple's Macintosh that was designed to keep out clones. Carroll's open and public distribution of minimalism was much more like Bell Lab's open distribution of UNIX; many people could teach minimalism and use minimalism. It also proved attractive to researchers, as evidenced by some of the doctoral research done at the University of Twente in the Netherlands.[21]

Not only was minimalism packaged in a memorable way and not only did it prove attractive to both practitioners and academics, but the program of research, theory, and practice used tools that were familiar and popular in the field of technical communication. Reader protocols were popularized for over a decade by Flowers and Hayes and implemented in many companies in their usability labs.

A Distinctive Radical Edge

The final reason that minimalism was given entrée into the profession of technical communication was that it offered a distinct radical edge. Often to move a group to a new idea, the new idea must be radically stated; early feminists burned bras, and some African-American activists posed in black berets and black leather jackets, and held harpoons and guns. If compromise or syncretism seems possible from the very beginning, there is a serious possibility that the new movement or idea will be co-opted by the prevailing systems.

Minimalism's rhetoric of "no indexes" and "intentional incompleteness" was and is a radical notion to the prevailing paradigm of technical communication. But perhaps it was necessary to "talk" radical to get any kind of wedge in which to begin to move technical communicators to a new view of methods and techniques.

Thus, minimalism gained entrée because it was the right time in the profession overall; an attractive champion and well-known advocates moved its discussion and practice quickly into the mainstream of technical communication; it had an attractive moniker; a coherent program of theory, research, and practice to attract both practitioners and academics;

and it was able to keep a distinctive radical edge. With all these things going right for it, why isn't minimalism the current paradigm? The reason may lie in the fact that in information transfer, sometimes the very act of coming into a new organization meets resistance and uneven penetration.

14.2   Problems in How the Profession Has Digested the Outside Information of Minimalism

As with any other information transfer act, the new, outside information met with resistance and inertia. The result was that minimalism was only minimally digested, unevenly digested, and the original technical communication context of minimalism's introduction changed.

In the chapters of this book, the authors write that minimalism has been only minimally digested by many in the profession of technical communication; they have examined how the iterative testing elements of minimalism disappeared completely in a consultant's "minimalism" checklist, which bore an uncanny resemblance to traditional plain writing admonitions. The checklist represented one of many attempts to shift minimalism from a philosophical perspective and multidimensional program to discrete, measurable, printed, grammatical elements. In another instance, in a paper appearing in the *IEEE Transactions on Professional Communication*, the iterative testing elements of minimalism disappeared again in a side-by-side rewrite illustration of a page before minimalism and a page after minimalism was applied. Finally, some Indonesian technical communication translators got wind of the brevity aspects of minimalism and proceeded to delete every other paragraph. Each of these examples suggests that minimalism was repeatedly garbled when the profession came to apply what it thought was minimalism.

Most often the garbling came from technical communicators' overlaying the new techniques of minimalism over those that they were more accustomed to. For example, the elements of minimalism that were evidently most easily appropriated by technical communicators were those that most directly matched customary techniques. Minimalism's suggestions about cutting verbiage became the most memorable feature for many technical communicators because they fit quite nicely on the World War II technical communication adage KISS (keep it simple, stupid), a technique proceding *The Nurnberg Funnel* by some three decades. In a similar way, many of the minimalist techniques reportedly most used, beyond brevity, seem to be close kin to task orientation, that is, focus on doing, not explaining, as well as on the visual design of information—a focus of great interest in technical communication with the advent of desktop publishing. None of these areas of minimalism—the brevity, the task orientation, the visual design—really forces writers, their companies, or readers to let go of what is comfortable and traditional or to confront radically new approaches.

None of these selectively digested aspects of minimalism effectively faced and incorporated some of the most important aspects of minimalism's approach:

- Basing design on empirical data.
- Using an iterative approach to design.
- Making use of audiences' prior knowledge.
- Guiding user exploration.
- Using intentionally incomplete information.

Most important, the selective way in which technical communication as a profession has digested and recreated minimalism in its own traditional image has robbed minimalism of its tension and resistance to technical communication orthodoxy. In many ways, minimalism has ceased to be revolutionary and has been co-opted. For example, rather than fight revolutionists as revolutionists and risk the creation of a whole new nation, the British in 1870 Canada co-opted many of the Riél revolutionaries and made a number of them members of Parliament rather than martyrs. The result was that the revolutionary's ardor soon died down, and many of their more radical doctrines were forgotten.

To compound this problem of syncretism that robs minimalism of both its most unsettling elements as well as its tension and resistance, the constellation of forces and media and beliefs central to technical communication at the time of minimalism entrance has changed. Now the audiences of computer documentation must face the problem of "transfer" audiences, coming to learn after having had extensive experience with a similar or competitive product, rather than "new" audiences, who have little or no preconceptions or experiences. Now the audience is just as likely to be multinational rather than local, narrow, and limited. Now there is a great increase in the task complexity that perhaps will not lend itself so easily to intentionally incomplete instructions. Now the medium of communication has become the computer interface and not solely the printed page.

All of this means that although minimalism's outside information was admitted to the profession of technical communication, minimalism, like any other outside set of ideas, has had trouble in being integrated into technical communication or even in maintaining its distinctive qualities. Additionally, simply reintroducing the original minimalism ideas is inappropriate to the state of technical communication today. Many of the central communication needs present at the beginning of minimalism a decade ago have changed.

14.3   In Conclusion

The chapters in this book hold up a mirror for the technical communicators themselves to observe how they have functioned as an audience for information transfer. I think our actions as recipients of such novel outside information are nearly identical to those in any other profession or any other culture. We have observed that it required certain activities or people to be present for minimalism to be accepted into technical communication: a sea change of ideas in the profession, a champion of these new ideas who proved intellectually attractive to the members of the profession and inside advocates who could spread the ideas of minimalism, a euphonious moniker, and a radical edge.

When the profession of technical communication assimilated minimalism, it did so in ways in which any other group would assimilate new ideas: selectively, partially, and with resistance. Moreover, in the very act of assimilating this new outside information, the profession changed minimalism to be more like its own traditional ideas and techniques. The question now is: What must be done? Should minimalism be reconceived to maintain its tension or edge on technical communication orthodoxy? And if so, how? Does minimalism need to be reinvented to cope with the changed circumstances of the profession and its audiences and its work? Do we need new champions and new advocates?

Notes

Some of this article is based on earlier work of mine: *From Millwrights to Shipwrights to the 21st Century* (Cresskill, NJ: Hampton Press, 1997), chap. 9: A Historical Perspective on Technical Communication Paradigms, IBM's Task-Orientation and Minimalism"; "Protecting Technical Communication Innovations?" a RIGO Award address given at the *SIGDOC '86 Conference*, Ann Arbor, Michigan, November 1–2, 1986, and "The Why, Where and How of Minimalism," in *Proceedings of SIGDOC '90 Conference, Little Rock, Arkansas November 1–2 1990 (SIGDOC Asterisk* 14 (4)): 111–119.

1. Barbara Mirel, "The Politics of Usability: The Organizational Functions of an In-House Manual," in S. Doheny-Farina (ed.), *Effective Documentation: What We Have Learned from Research* (Cambridge, MA: MIT Press, 1988), 277–297.

2. See also Stephen Doheny-Farina, *Rhetoric, Innovation, Technology: Case Studies of Technical Communication in Technology Transfers* (Cambridge, MA: MIT Press, 1992), 31–34.

3. In *Proceedings of the 29th International Technical Communication Conference, May 1982* (Washington, DC: Society for Technical Communication, 1982): B. H. Hadley, "Designing Task-Oriented Documentation Using a Universal Architecture," C38–C40, and Georgina E. Mitchell, "Solving Problems of Information Gathering with Task-Oriented Library Design," C76–C78.

In *The Proceedings of the 30th International Technical Communication Conference, May 1983* (Washington, DC: Society for Technical Communication, 1983): Georgina E. Mitchell, "Need to Know: Bringing Task Analysis to the People Who Need It—Writers!" W&E102–W&E103, Allan Henderson, "Need to Know: Defining a Computer System's User Interface via Scenarios—A Methodological Cookbook," W&E104–W&E105, and Jarey L. Cortwright, "Workshop: Need to Know: The Way to Go, Experiences in Task Analysis," W&E159.

In *The Proceedings of the 31st International Technical Communication Conference, May 1984* (Washington, DC: Society for Technical Communication, 1984): Georgina E. Mitchell, "Task Analysis (Need to Know: The Way to Go)," WE84–WE85, Candace Sederston, "Task Analysis: Applying Composition Theory in an Industrial Forum," WE89–WE92, Robert G. Waite, "Organizing Computer Manuals on the Basis of User Tasks," WE38–WE40, Bob Ward, "A Task Analysis Primer for Technical Communicators," WE86–WE88, Eleanor Wight, "Need to Know: The Way to Go—Case Study in Task Analysis," WE93–WE96, and Jarey Lee Cortwright, "Need to Know: Way to Go—Two Forms of Task-Oriented Information," WE100–WE101.

In *The Proceedings of the 33rd International Technical Communication Conference, May 1986* (Washington, DC: Society for Technical Communication, 1986): George T. Bowman, "Applying Theory to Develop Task-Oriented Documents," 174–176, Esther Kando Odescalchi, "Productivity Gain Attained by Task-Oriented Information," 359–362, and Amy Simpson, "Task Oriented Writing: Using Action Sentences to Get the Job Done," 447–449.

In *The Proceedings of the 35th International Technical Communication Conference, May 1988* (Washington, DC: Society for Technical Communication, 1988): Richard Oppenheimer, "Introduction to the Task Analysis Panel," WE78–WE79; Annette N. Bradford, "What Is a Task Analysis Matrix," WE80–WE83. T. R. Girill, "Ease of Use and the Richness of Documentation Adequacy." *Journal of Computer Documentation* 15 (2)(September 1991): 22—"According to the Society for Technical Communication's comprehensive, annotated bibliography of technical writing papers published between 1966 and 1980, only four publications-related articles in that 15-year period had task analysis as their primary topic. Just six years later, the *Proceedings of the 34th International Technical Communication Conference* contained four papers on task analysis in its first 50 pages alone (Society for Technical Communication, 1987). It included dozens on that topic altogether."

4. The publication's ordering number was ZC28-2525-2, and the "Z" prefacing the number meant the document was for "IBM Internal Use Only."

5. Joanne Hackos, *Managing Your Documentation Projects* (New York: Wiley, 1994).

6. Thus, the final line of Bethke et al.'s paper introducing task orientation to IBM in 1981 functions today quite ironically: "Finally, we expect task-orientation concepts and their application to be widely accepted and grow far beyond their genesis in publications." F. J. Bethke, W. M. Dean, P. H. Kaiser, E. Ort, and F. H. Pessin, "Improving the Usability of Programming Publications" *IBM Systems Journal* 20 (3)(1981), reprinted in *Journal of Computer Documentation* 15 (2)(September 1991): 16.

7. Brockmann, op. cit., 1997: Chapter 9.

8. The thirteen articles in the publications of the Society for Technical Communication include: In *The Proceedings of the 34th International Technical Communication Conference, May 10–13 1988* (Washington, DC: Society for Technical Communication, 1988): Gay Vanderlinden, Thomas G. Cocklin, Martha McKita, "Testing and Developing Minimalist Tutorials," RET196–RET199; Philip Lillies, "Some Guidelines for Making a Computer Manual More Task-Oriented," WE46–WE48.

In *The Proceedings of the 37th International Technical Communication Conference, May 20–23, 1990, Santa Clara, California* (Washington, DC: Society for Technical Communication, 1990): Ann Hill Duin, "Minimal Manuals vs. Elaboration in Documentation: Centering on the Learner," RT77–RT80.

In *The 1992 Proceedings of the 39th Annual Conference, May 10–13, 1992* (Arlington, VA: Society for Technical Communication, 1992): Alice Chiang and Kevin McBride "TIRS Tutorial: New Techniques for Guided Exploration," 327–330; Alice Chiang, Kevin McBride, and Edmund Payne, "TIRS Tutorial: New Techniques for Guided Exploration," 331–334.

In *The 1993 Proceedings of the 40th Annual Conference, June 6–9, 1993* (Arlington, VA: Society for Technical Communication, 1993): Arthur G. Elser, "Minimalist Strategies for Improving User Documentation," 11–14, Karl Smart,

"Accommodating Active Learners in Software Documentation Decisions," 15–17, Robert Bringhurst, "Concrete Methods that Promote Active Learning in Software Manuals," 18–20, and Barbara Mirel, "A Study of Instructions for Information Systems: Variations on a Minimalist Theme," 363–366.

In *The 1994 Proceedings of the 41st Annual Conference, May 15–18, 1994* (Arlington, VA: Society for Technical Communication, 1994): Terri J. Miles, "Writing to Reduce Information," 29–31, and Arthur G. Elser, "Designing Minimalist Principles into User Interfaces," 95.

In *The 1995 Proceedings of the 42nd Annual Conference, April 23–26, 1995* (Arlington, VA: Society for Technical Communication, 1995): Arthur G. Elser, "Using Graphics to Help Users Build Mental Models," 345–347. See also Barbara Mirel, Susan Feinberg, and Leif Allmendinger, "Designing Manuals for Active Learning Styles," *Technical Communication* 38 (1) (First Quarter 1991): 75–87.

9. Half of the speakers come from Hewlett-Packard.

10. John Carroll, "Minimalist Training." *Datamation*, November 1, 1984) 125–136.

11. Carroll, J. and R. L. Mack, "Learning to Use a Word Processor: By Doing, by Thinking, and by Knowing," in J. C. Thomas and M. Schneider (eds.), *Human Factors in Computing Systems* (Norwood, NJ: Ablex, 1984); Carroll, J., R. L. Mack, C. H. Lewis, N. L. Grischknowsky, and S. R. Robertson, "Exploring a Word Processor," *Human-Computer Interaction* 1(1) (1985): 283–307; Carroll, J., P. A. Smith-Kerker, J. R. Ford, and S. A. Mazur-Rimetez, "The Minimal Manual," *Human-Computer Interaction* 3(1987–1988): 123–153.

12. John Carroll, and Mary Beth Rosson, "Usability Specifications as a Tool in Iterative Development," in H. Hartson (ed.), *Advances in Human-Computer Interaction* (Norwood, NJ: Ablex Publishing, 1985), 1:1–28.

13. Lillies, "Some Guidelines."

14. Saul Wurman, *Information Anxiety* (New York: Bantam Books, 1990), and *Follow the Yellow Brick Road* (New York: Bantam Books, 1992).

15. J. M. Carroll, P. S. Smith-Kerker, J. R. Ford, and S. A. Mazur-Rimetz, "The Minimal Manual," *Human-Computer Interaction* 3(1987/1988) 123–53. In *The Proceedings of the 34th International Technical Communication Conference, May 10–13, 1988* (Washington, DC: Society for Technical Communication, 1988), Gay Vanderlinden, Thomas G. Cocklin, and Martha McKita, "Testing and Developing Minimalist Tutorials," RET196–RET199, and Philip Lillies, "Some Guidelines for Making a Computer Manual More Task-Oriented," WE46–WE48.

16. V. C. Redish, "Learning to Read to Do," *Technical Writing Teacher* 15(1988): 223–233.

17. Leslie H. Matthies, *The New Playscript Procedure, Management Tool for Action* (Stamford, CT: Office Publications, 1977). See also *Les Matthies' World of System* newsletter from the late 1970s (numbers 104–106 are dated 1976).

System Planning Associates of Mountainside, New Jersey, has carried on the seminars into the 1990s.

18. A wide variety of books and articles on Information Mapping are available from Information Mapping Inc., Waltham, MA.

19. Geoffrey James, *Document Databases* (New York: Van Nostrand Reinhold, 1986).

20. David H. Jonassen (ed.), *The Technology of Text* (Englewood Cliffs, NJ: Educational Technology Publications, 1982); Robert E. Horn and John N. Kelley, "Structure Writing—An Approach to the Documentation of Computer Software," *ACM SIGDOC ASTERISK* * 7(4)(July 1981): 4–25.

21. See the work of H. van der Meij, "Catching the User in the Act," in M. Stee-houdern, C. Jansen, P. van der Poort, and R. Verheijen (eds.), *Quality of Technical Documentation* (Amsterdam, Netherlands, 1994), 201–210, and "Principles and Heuristics for Designing Minimalist Instruction," *Technical Communication* 42(2) (May 1995): 243–261. See also A. W. Lazonder, "Minimalist Computer Documentation: A Study on Constructive and Corrective Skills Development (dissertation, Enschede, the Netherlands, 1994).

15

Minimalism: An Agenda for Research and Practice

Greg Kearsley

My initial exposure to minimalism occurred in the early 1980s when I was involved in the development of training materials for dedicated word processing systems and later in the decade when I was teaching the fundamentals of user interface design to software developers in large corporations (most of them in the computer business). It was clear from the beginning that the prevailing methods of instructional design (the so-called systems approach) did not work well when applied to the computer domain. The training materials and documentation being developed at the time were not very good at helping users learn to use computer systems or products; indeed, the situation was pretty dismal.

Reading Carroll's early work on minimalism (such as Carroll 1982; Carroll and Mack 1984) stimulated some "aha" experiences for me. The basic principles of abandoning sequential instruction in favor of task-oriented exercises, leaving gaps for users to fill in on their own (instead of detailing every single step), and a focus on error recovery made a tremendous amount of sense. After our development team adopted the minimalist approach to the design of training and documentation, we got much better results and produced happier users and customers. (Alas, like most work in the commercial sector, this work was not publicly documented.) When *The Nurnberg Funnel* was published in 1990, it became the bible for the design of any computer-related training or documentation as far as I was concerned.

My second brush with minimalism came in the mid-1990s when I was working on a hypertext database of learning and instructional theory. This database contained descriptions of fifty major theoretical frameworks including minimalism: ⟨http://www.gwu.edu/ ~tip⟩. In creating this database, it appeared that minimalism faired well as a theoretical framework; its principles were clearly stated, its scope was well defined, it had accumulated a substantial amount of empirical support, and it had obvious practical applications. However, it was also evident that there were some significant theoretical lacunae in minimalism, particularly when compared to other theoretical frameworks. Indeed, these theoretical holes also mapped onto practical problems in applying minimalism.

In this chapter, I examine these gaps in the theory and practice of minimalism, drawing on the points made by the other chapter authors, with the eventual goal of generating a research agenda. I hope this will help to integrate and synthesize the many perspectives presented in earlier chapters and provide some direction for minimalism in the future.

15.1   The Theoretical Gaps

Let us begin by considering the theoretical foundation for minimalism as originally laid out in *The Nurnberg Funnel*, (primarily chapter 4). Carroll describes the fundamental basis for minimalism as the "paradox of sense-making"; when people learn to use computers, they attempt to make sense of the way the system behaves. They make inferences, perform experiments, and look for cause-and-effect relationships. What they do not do is follow step-by-step directions very well, especially since doing so tends to land them quickly in the middle of some puzzling situation.

Carroll builds a justification for the principles of minimalism (e.g., guided discovery, exploiting prior knowledge, action-oriented learning) based on the work of Jerome Bruner, Jean Piaget, and other cognitive psychologists. He also cites the work of Tom Sticht and Pat Wright on the design of technical documentation to support the principle of "getting started fast" and creating task-oriented materials. Although there are relatively few explicit references to the adult learning literature (the work of Cross, Knowles, Kolb, or Schön), minimalism clearly embraces the key ideas of this framework: learner-centered, experientially based, instrinsically motivated activities.

It was not just the theoretical foundations of minimalism that made it a potent framework but also its methodology: use of protocol analysis to uncover the details of user problems and what users were thinking while trying to learn to use computers. Up to that point, document and instructional design were based on the results of traditional experimental studies, which yielded relatively little understanding of what people were actually doing when learning complex tasks. Protocol analysis (and simple observation of user activity) revealed the variables that were important in learning to use computers.

Despite the solid theoretical basis for minimalism as outlined in *The Nurnberg Funnel* (and refined in Van der Meij and Carroll, this volume, chapter 2) there are some missing pieces. One of the biggest gaps is the failure to address the social context of learning, an aspect that has received a lot of attention in the "situated learning" movement (e.g. Brown, Collins and Duguid 1988; Lave 1988). Situated learning emphasizes the point that much learning takes place in a community of practice (as opposed to structured classroom settings). Obviously a great deal of computer learning occurs through observation or questioning of others. Indeed, asking someone else for help is probably the main form of learning how to use computers in workplaces. Any theory that purports to explain learning in this domain needs to address the social components, particularly behavior modeling and discourse strategies (i.e., context of usage).

Another shortcoming of minimalism is the failure to link it with other major cognitive and instructional theoretical frameworks (Brien and Eastman 1994; Wilson 1996). Although these frameworks have not emerged from study of the computer domain, they still have relevance in terms of understanding human learning. For example, Anderson's ACT* theory (Anderson 1990) provides a detailed explanation of memory processes, particularly the differences between declarative and procedural knowledge. This could be an important aspect of determining the appropriate balance of explanation and action in a given task description, an issue discussed in other chapters in this book. The work of Schank on language and story understanding (Schank, 1986, 1991) could be highly relevant to the directions given to users in exploratory learning sequences, an aspect of minimalism that is somewhat murky. And given the importance of visual information in most computer documentation, the dual coding theory of Paivio (1986) could provide valuable insights into the coordination of text and graphics, an area in which minimalism provides little guidance. These particular examples of potential theoretical links may or may not have merit, but I believe the point that minimalism could benefit from further analysis of cognitive theories is sound.

Contributors to this book have identified other theoretical issues. Barbara Mirel and Janice Redish discuss the extent to which minimalism applies to complex tasks involving higher-order cognitive skills (such as decision making, judgment, and problem solving). Most of the research associated with minimalism has focused on routine tasks—how to use the basic functions of a program. However, many professionals and managers use computers to perform planning and evaluation activities that involve ill-defined problems and unique solutions. JoAnn Hackos presents an application of minimalism for expert users that addresses this domain of more advanced applications. In his chapter, Carroll discusses his later work applying minimalism to Smalltalk programming, clearly an important step in this direction. However, it is not clear that programming activities represent the same kind of complexity as those involving decision making and judgment. We do not yet know how well minimalism works for more sophisticated computer-using tasks.

In her chapter, Redish introduces the issue of individual differences, particularly cognitive styles that may not be highly compatible with the guided exploration strategy that is fundamental to minimalism. For example, Pask (1975) identified two kinds of learning styles in his research: holists, who follow a top-down approach, and serialists, who prefer linear methods. Individuals with a holistic style would likely do well with a guided-exploration approach, but serialists would probably not. Gardner (1993) has discussed seven types of intelligence that individuals possess to varying degrees; minimalism may tap into only one or two of these different aspects of intelligence. Documentation and training developed according to current minimalist principles may not be well designed for certain individuals. There is also a question of how well minimalism works for individuals with disabilities, who have different kinds of learning needs and characteristics.

Actually, this issue is really much broader; minimalism needs to address cultural differences as well. Computer products (and their accompanying documentation and training materials) are distributed to a global marketplace spanning a diverse range of cultures. User interfaces need to accommodate differences across cultures (Nielsen 1990). We do not know whether guided exploration and the associated principles of minimalism apply equally well to all cultures. There is no reason to believe that they will not, but we do not know this until more research and practical applications are completed.

Finally, a major issue not addressed extensively in this book is how minimalism applies to different media, particularly printed documentation versus online systems. These two environments vary in many respects. Online documentation can be interactive and focused on specific user responses or actions. The amount of information available in an online system can be hidden since users see only what they select or what is currently relevant, whereas in the print environment, the physical size of the document and the amount of information provided are very evident. This bulk must affect the user's perception of amount to be learned. Also, the characteristics of print versus electronic displays in terms of readability, graphics, color, and multimedia components (audio and video) may have some significance for the application of minimalism. For example, the use of screen illustrations (with text captions) seems to be an important aspect of many minimal manuals, whereas in an online system, the user views the actual screen annotated by pop-up text boxes. The chapters by Farkas and van der Meij raise questions about these kind of variables and their significance for minimalism.

15.2   Practical Concerns

Many of the theoretical gaps just discussed have practical implications. Draper discusses a number of these issues, the foremost being whether minimalism is a theory of learning or action (doing). He points out that in many cases, users want documentation that helps them perform a task but are not necessarily interested in learning anything at the time. Documentation designed for the purpose of learning (such as tutorials) may not work well in an action setting, where reference materials or job aids are needed. On the other hand, a well-designed minimalist document might serve both needs simultaneously.

This raises the question of whether minimalism is equally suited to both learning and performance, and how its application might differ across the two. It can be argued that minimalism is best applied to the development of tutorial materials for novices who need a lean and uncluttered introductory path. But it can also be argued that minimalism is best applied to the design of advanced reference materials for experts who can better handle the guided-discovery approach. The chapter by Hackos is an illustration of this point. In fact, we do not know which kind of user state (novice versus expert) or type of documentation (tutorial versus reference) minimalism is most appropriate for. A related question is how to integrate minimal documentation with conventional manuals and online helps. Can they be complementary, or do they interfere with each other?

Another practical issue raised by Draper and others in this book is determining what information to include in minimal documentation. Minimalism gives clear direction to focus on tasks, but at what level of detail? In some circumstances, users might need very fine grained information (e.g., screen location), whereas in others, the information need might be quite high level (e.g., system characteristics). Within a particular task description, the user might need successive steps (depth) or relationships to other program functions (breadth). At present, there is no methodology (within minimalism or any other framework) to help developers figure out the appropriate level of detail when choosing and explaining tasks in a manual or online documentation.

A related issue is the use of explanatory overviews (or conceptual information in general). In her chapter, Redish claims that developers tend to focus on too much detail and fail to give users sufficient orientation to understand what they are doing. Adding overviews can provide this background information, but it goes against the grain of only providing task-oriented details. Again, the current methodology of minimalism does not provide much guidance about how to balance conceptual and procedural information, posing a fundamental dilemma for developers when they try to follow and apply the minimalist framework.

Farkas suggests that online helps can diminish the significance of these issues by putting responsibility for information selection in the hands of the user (or perhaps the system). To the extent that online help systems can provide many levels and types of information—particularly supplemental explanatory material, only when requested or needed by the user—the need for a minimal manual is eliminated. On the other hand, if we keep in mind that the real thrust of minimalism is providing user-oriented content, not just less material, online helps may or may not achieve the intended outcomes of the minimalist approach. If the content of an online help system is not well chosen and well presented, it will not be any more effective than traditional documentation.

Preparing technical writers to apply minimalism is a major issue discussed by a number of chapter authors. Adopting a user orientation is a significant problem for many technical writers. In their usual training, writers are prepared to write prose ("writing to read") rather than action sequences ("writing to do"). In their chapters, Johnson and Rosenbaum discuss what is involved in teaching technical writers to use minimalism. One aspect that seems to cause a lot of uncertainty is the perceived incompleteness that results from the guided-discovery strategy. Writing less instead of more is counterintuitive to many developers and is often not well received by members of the development team who expect exhaustive (not selective) coverage of product information.

In order to understand what users need to know, technical writers must have access to users through either direct contact or the results of usability studies. However, many writers and training developers do not have such access; the source of almost all their information is system designers or engineers. It is no surprise that writers have difficulty describing tasks in user terms or determining the appropriate level of detail for a task description; they have no opportunity to understand user behavior. This is really more of an implementation problem than one having to do with technical writers—a failure on the part of the organization to accept or understand the emphasis that minimalism places on user analysis. Usability studies consume time and resources, which are in short supply in the rush to get products to the marketplace and systems implemented. In his chapter, Smart argues that minimalism appeals to the quest for quality in organizations. This is true. But many organizations are not prepared to pay for quality in terms of the costs of usability studies.

This brings us to the most pragmatic of all considerations: the need for organizational change. The chapters by Anson, Hackos, and Smart present rationales for the adoption of minimalism in organizations that focus on reducing the cost of publications, better meeting user needs (creating a more satisfied customer), and reducing product and system support costs. Almost any manager would see these as very desirable outcomes and endorse minimalism on this basis. But to realize any of the benefits, a great deal of change may be required in the way documentation and product development are done. There must be a genuine commitment to user testing from early in the development cycle and one that involves all developers (including technical writers). A broad view of the documentation process is needed that spans all aspects of user support (print, online helps, hot lines, Web sites, etc.) in order for the cost/benefits of minimalism to make sense. But minimalism itself provides no real basis for these kind of paradigmatic changes needed in organizational culture. Perhaps it should.

15.3   Further Questions

Beyond the questions raised by the theoretical and practical issues discussed, there are some more fundamental considerations for minimalism.

Is computer documentation and online help even necessary? Over the years, we have seen vast improvements in the usability of computers systems, in no small part due to a tremendous amount of research in user interface design (Shneiderman 1997). Features such as pull-down menus, pop-up dialogues and "undo" have significantly reduced the learning time and problems associated with using computers. Indeed, we see public-access kiosks in building lobbies, shopping malls, and museums that involve no formal user training to use; the same is true for computer games and automated bank teller (ATM) machines. Clearly we can design computer programs and information systems that do not require any user documentation or training. Whether it is possible to design most or all systems in this fashion is not known. But it does raise the question of whether minimalism (or any other methodology for training and documentation) will be quite so important in the future. Perhaps minimalism was a product of an awkward time in the history of computing, a period that is quickly vanishing. On the other hand, if we think of minimalism as a user interface design methodology (as Carroll suggests in his introductory chapter), then it still has a major role to play in creating "walk up and use" computer systems, even if they do not involve documentation or formal training. Furthermore, it seems minimalism is highly relevant to the design of Electronic Performance Support Systems (e.g., Gery 1991), which are becoming increasingly common.

If minimalism is so good, why hasn't it been adopted more widely? While information about minimalism has been publicly accessible since the publication of *The Nurnberg Funnel* in 1990, there has been relatively little application of the ideas in the computer documentation or training world. Indeed, it appears that only a small percentage of technical writers or training developers have even heard of minimalism. It can be argued that this lack of widespread adoption is largely a function of insufficient publicity. There have been very few articles published or conference presentations made about minimalism. (Compare this with the kind of attention accorded to Information Mapping as a consequence of considerable publicity). On the other hand, there is enough of a literature on minimalism to launch it into the mainstream under the right circumstances. For example, is there a widely used (or award-winning) manual that provides a well-known demonstration of minimalism? And why haven't we seen many examples of commercial computer books using the minimalism framework? Perhaps it requires too much effort (time and money) on the part of authors or publishers to put minimalism into practice?

Does minimalism mesh with the power structure of the software development world? Minimalism addresses the technical considerations of computer documentation and training. But there is also a social and psychological side that dictates how things get done. The emphasis that minimalism places on user analysis usurps the role of the engineer or software developer as unchallenged content expert. In the classic documentation and training model, system experts provide the content and structure, which technical writers and training developers fashion into user materials. Minimalism puts system experts in a support role, subservient to user input. Ironically, this is exactly the same dilemma experienced by instructional developers trying to apply the principles of instructional systems design (ISD), which minimalism attempts to supplant. ISD was promoted as content free; developers were supposed to work with subject matter experts as partners to create well-designed training materials. But more often than not, content experts were unable or unwilling to establish the kind of partnership needed for the ISD model to work, and the resulting training was inadequate from a content or instructional point of view. Minimalism assumes that usability testing can refine materials generated by system experts. Perhaps this model is inherently unworkable. Or perhaps the adoption of a user-centered model for product development (dictated by competitive demands in the software business) will force a change in organizational power structures than makes minimalism much more acceptable.

How effective is minimalism? While there is ample empirical and anecdotal evidence that minimalism works, there are also plenty of questions about its effectiveness. For example, we know little about what aspects of minimalism produce the greatest effects. Is it the user analysis, the action orientation, the guided-discovery strategy, or just the brevity? Perhaps conventional documentation could be just as effective if it was more carefully tailored to user needs. And how does the effectiveness of minimalist materials compare to those developed with other alternative design methodologies such as Information Mapping or well-crafted online help systems? The rationale for minimalism is compelling, but exactly what are the specific payoffs of using the methodology in terms of user performance?

Where are the next generation of minimalists coming from? If minimalism is to grow and be more widely adopted (not to mention the conduct of research studies), it will need many more disciples and practitioners of the art. Should these individuals come from the ranks of computer science, technical writing, or instructional technology programs?

Is minimalism really a methodology for computer systems design, writing technical documents, or creating training materials? And what about current software developers, technical writers, and training developers? How can they learn to apply minimalism? Who will conduct the necessary workshops, publish relevant studies and guidelines, or convene research symposia? While professional organizations obviously have an influential role to play here, is that sufficient to reach such a large and diverse audience?

Questions such as these are not really answerable; they serve as probes to gauge the scope and direction of a broad theoretical framework such as minimalism. On the other hand, there are many specific research questions that could be addressed.

15.4   Research Needed

To address the current theoretical and practical limitations of minimalism, much more research is needed. Here are some specific ideas suggested by the contributors to this book:

• What is the range of programs, software applications, and types of users that minimalism is effective for? Given the tremendous diversity of computer learning tasks and people who use computers, it would be useful to know where minimalism is more or less effective. When is it worthwhile to use a minimalist approach, and when would it be better to use conventional methods?

• What exactly do users do when they use minimalist documentation? Although there has been intensive examination of user behavior in the development of minimalist documents, little detailed analysis exists of what people do when they use such documentation. For example, how well do they do with the guided-exploration strategy? How do they make use of error-handling information?

• How does the effectiveness of minimalism vary with user expertise? Is minimalism more suited to documentation for novices or experts? For a given computer learning task, should different aspects of minimalism be emphasized for novices and experts? What about individual and cultural differences?

• What are the skills and processes involved in developing minimalist documentation? Although the principles of minimalism are fairly well articulated, the procedures for applying it are not. It would be helpful to know in detail what is involved in applying minimalism to specific programs.

• What is the most effective way to train practitioners about minimalism? The successful application of minimalism depends on how well technical writers and developers understand the principles and processes. What are the consequences of good training in terms of user outcomes as well as development costs and time?

• What is the impact of minimalism on user support in organizations? There is a need to conduct longitudinal studies of user performance and problems on a range of products that involve minimalist documentation, along with baseline data on conventional documentation for comparison.

• How can the use of minimalism streamline the software development process? Iterative design based on continuous user testing is a fundamental tenet of minimalism. However, in practice, iterative design often makes product development lengthy and expensive (although it results in better quality). Consequently, the adoption of minimalism may be viewed as more of an obstacle to rapid software development than a way to expedite it. But minimalism ought to streamline the development process by producing a path that is more direct and with fewer dead-ends.

• Can minimalism be applied beyond the computer domain? Although minimalism was developed in the context of computer tasks, it should work just as well for any other kind of product documentation. What changes to the theory or practice of minimalism would be needed to make it useful beyond computers?

• How can minimalism be improved? What aspects of the theory or practice of minimalism are the least robust and in need of refinement? Do research results suggest changes to the theory or the way it is employed? Can we subject minimalism to iterative design itself?

As this list of research ideas make clear, there is a need to study minimalism in much more detail, particularly in the context of actual application settings.

The contributors to this book have summarized the research base for minimalism. It is an impressive beginning; now we need to push much further if minimalism is to have a significant impact. Minimalism represents one of the most advanced theoretical frameworks and methodologies we have today for the design of documentation and training; with further refinement, it could dramatically increase the usability of computer systems.

References

Anderson, J. 1990. *The Adaptive Character of Thought*. Hillsdale, NJ: Erlbaum.

Brien, R., and Eastman, N. 1994. *Cognitive Science and Instruction*. Englewood Cliffs, NJ: Educational Technology Publications.

Brown, J. S., Collins, A., and Duguid, S. 1989. Situated cognition and the culture of learning. *Educational Researcher*, 18(1), 32–42.

Carroll, J. M. 1982. The adventure of getting to know a computer. *IEEE Computer*, 15(11), 49–58.

Carroll, J. M., and Mack, R. L. 1984. Learning to use a word processor: By doing, by thinking, and by knowing. In J. C. Thomas and M. Schneider (eds.), *Human Factors in Computer Systems*. Norwood, NJ: Ablex.

Gardner, H. 1993. *Multiple Intelligences: The Theory in Practice*. New York: Basic Books.

Gery, G. 1991. *Electronic Performance Support Systems*. Tolland, MA: Gery Associates.

Lave, J. 1988. *Cognition in Practice*. Cambridge: Cambridge University Press.

Nielsen, J. 1990. *Designing User Interfaces for International Use*. Amsterdam: Elsevier.

Paivio, A. 1986. *Mental Representations*. New York: Oxford University Press.

Pask, G. 1975. *Conversation, Cognition, and Learning*. New York: Elsevier.

Schank, R. C. 1986. *Explanation Patterns: Understanding Mechanically and Creatively*. Hillsdale, NJ: Erlbaum.

Schank, R. C. 1991. *Tell Me a Story: A New Look at Real and Artificial Intelligence*. New York: Simon & Schuster.

Shneiderman, B. 1997. *Designing the User Interface* (3rd ed). Reading, MA: Addison-Wesley.

Wilson, B. G. 1996. *Constructivist Learning Environments: Case Studies in Instructional Design*. Englewood Cliffs, NJ: Educational Technology Publications.

Appendix: Reviews, General Discussions, and Applications of Minimalism Since 1990

Faith A. McCreary and John M. Carroll

Reviews

Becke, K. 1991. Review of *The Nurnberg Funnel*. *Library Software Journal* (September–October), 33.

Benyon, D. 1992. Review of *The Nurnberg Funnel*. *International Journal of Man-Machine Studies, 36*(3), 507–508.

Carroll, J. 1991. Author's reply to Farkas and William's review. *IEEE Transactions on Professional Communication, 34*(1), 58.

DeWeaver, M., and Bauman, J. 1992. *The Nurnberg Funnel*: Designing minimalist instruction for practical computer skill. *Performance and Instruction* (April), 25–26.

Etlinger, H. 1991. Teaching programming: The minimalist view. *IEEE Software* (March), 108–109.

Farkas, D., and Williams, T. 1990. Review article: John Carroll's *The Nurnberg Funnel* and minimalist documentation. *IEEE Transactions on Professional Communication, 33*(4), 188–192.

Grossman, W. 1991. Review of *The Nurnberg Funnel*. *Personal Computer World* (November) (United Kingdom).

Hallgren, C. 1992. *The Nurnberg Funnel*: A minimal collection. *Journal of Computer Documentation, 16*(1), 11–17.

Horn, R. 1992. Commentary on *The Nurnberg Funnel*. *Journal of Computer Documentation, 16*(1), 3–10.

Jacobson, N. 1991. Review of *The Nurnberg Funnel*. *Social Science Computer Review, 9*(4), 701–704.

Lyttle, T. 1991. Review of *The Nurnberg Funnel*. *Journal of Documentation, 47*(4), 412–413.

Nickerson, R. 1991. A minimalist approach to the "paradox of sense making." *Educational Researcher, 20*(9), 24–26.

Rockwell, R. 1990. Review of *The Nurnberg Funnel. Data Training* (October), 31.

Rothkopf, E. Z. 1991. Short and sweet computer skill instruction. *Contemporary Psychology, 36*(10), 834–836.

Tarka, M. 1991. Review of *The Nurnberg Funnel. Computing Reviews* (April), 185.

Tetzlaff, L. (1991). Review of *The Nurnberg Funnel. IBM Systems Journal, 30*(3), 410–411.

Tripp, S. 1990. Review of *The Nurnberg Funnel. Educational Research and Development, 38*(3), 87–90.

Zimmerman, M. 1991. Review of *The Nurnberg Funnel. Issues in Writing, 3*(2), 211–215.

General Discussions

Brockman, R. 1990. The why, where, and how of minimalism. *Journal of Computer Documentation, 14*(4), 111–119.

Carroll, J. 1992. Minimalist documentation. In H. D. Stolovitch and E. J. Keeps (eds.), *Handbook of human performance technology* (pp. 331–351). San Francisco: Jossey-Bass.

Carroll, J. 1994. Techniques for minimalist documentation and user interface design. In M. Steehouder, C. Jansen, P. van der Poort, and R. Verheijen (eds.), *Quality of technical documentation.* Amsterdam: Rodopi.

Carroll, J., and Van der Meij, H. 1996. Ten misconceptions about minimalism. *IEEE Transactions on Professional Communications, 39*(2), 72–86.

Draper, S. W., and Oatley, K. 1990. Action centered manuals or minimalist instruction? Alternative theories for Carroll's minimal manuals. In P. O. Holt and N. Williams (eds.), *Computers and writing: State of the art* (pp. 222–243). Oxford: Intellect Books.

Duin, A. 1992. Minimal manuals vs. elaboration in documentation: Centering on the learner. In *Proceedings of the 39th Annual Conference.* Arlington, VA: Society for Technical Communication.

Elser, A. 1993. Minimalist strategies for improving user documentation. In *Proceedings of the 40th Annual Conference* (pp. 11–14). Arlington, VA: Society for Technical Communication.

Elser, A. 1994. Designing minimalist principles into user interfaces. In *The 1994 Proceedings of the 41st Annual Conference* (p. 95). Arlington, VA: Society for Technical Communication.

Glasbeek, H. 1994. Improving the quality of tutorials: Does minimalism really help? In M. Steehouder, C. Jansen P. Van der Poort, and R. Verheijen (eds.), *Quality of technical documentation* (pp. 77–83). Amsterdam: Rodopi.

Gong, R., and Elkerton, J. 1990. Designing minimal documentation using a GOMS model. In *CHI'90: Human Factors in Computing Systems* (pp. 99–106).

Jansen, C. 1994. Research in technical communication in the Netherlands. *Technical Communication, 41*(2), 234.

Lazonder, A. 1994. "Minimalist computer documentation: A study on constructive and corrective skills development." Ph.D. dissertation, Twente University, The Netherlands.

Lazonder, A., and Van der Meij, H. 1993. The minimal manual: Is less really more? *International Journal of Man-Machine Studies, 39,* 729–752.

Mirel, B. A. 1993. Study of instructions for information systems: Variations on a minimalist theme. In *Proceedings of the 40th Annual Conference* (pp. 363–366). Arlington, VA: Society for Technical Communication.

Mirel, B., Feinberg, S., and Allmendinger, L. 1991. Designing manuals for active learning styles. *Technical Communication, 38*(1), 75–88.

Ummelen, N. 1997. *Procedural and declarative information in software manuals.* Amsterdam: Rodopi.

Van der Meij, H. 1992. A critical assessment of the minimalist approach to documentation. In *Conference Proceedings of the 10th Annual International Conference on Systems Documentation* (pp. 7–17). New York: ACM.

Van der Meij, H., and Carroll, J. 1995. Principles and heuristics for designing minimalist instruction. *Technical Communication, 42*(2), 243–261.

Van der Meij, H., and Lazonder, A. W. 1993. Assessment of the minimalist approach to computer user documentation. *Interacting with Computers, 5*(4), 355–370.

Williams, T., and Farkas, D. 1992. Minimalism reconsidered: Should we design documentation for exploratory learning? *SIGCHI Bulletin, 24*(2), 41–50.

Applications

Carlson, P. 1992. From document to knowledge base: Intelligent hypertext as minimalist instruction. *Journal of Computer Documentation, 16*(1), 17–31.

Carroll, J., and Rosson, M. 1995. Managing evaluation goals for training. *Communications of the ACM, 38*(7), 40–48.

Elser, A. 1994. Using graphics to support minimalist documentation. In *IPCC 94 Proceedings. Scaling New Heights in Technical Communication* (pp. 174–179).

Farkas, D., Talburt, J., Price, J., and Carroll, J. (1993). The role of balloon help. *Journal of Computer Documentation, 17*(2), 3–24.

Gong, R. 1990. The development of a task-oriented, minimal content user's manual. *SIGCHI Bulletin, 21*(3), 29–33.

Nowaczyk, R., and James, E. 1993. Applying minimal manual principles for documentation of graphical user interfaces. *Journal of Technical Writing and Communication, 23*(4), 379–388.

Oatey, M. 1993. Minimalism and quick reference documentation. In *IEE Colloquium on 'Issues in Computer Support for Documentation and Manuals'* (p. 55).

Oatley, K., Meldrum, M., and Draper, S. 1991. *Evaluating Self-instruction by minimal manual and by video for a feature of a word-processing system.* Glasgow, Scotland: University of Glasgow.

Ramsey, J., and Oatley, K. 1992. Designing minimal computer manuals from scratch. *Instructional Science, 21*, 85–98.

Reznich, C. B. 1996. Applying minimalist design principles to the problem of computer anxiety. *Computers in Human Behavior, 12*(2), 245–261.

Rosson, M. B., Carroll, J. M., and Bellamy, R. K. E. 1990. Smalltalk scaffolding: a case study of minimalist instruction. *SIGCHI Bulletin* (April spec. issue), 423–429.

Scholtz, J., and Hansen, M. 1993. Usability testing a minimal manual for the Intel SatisFAXtion Faxmodem. *IEEE Transactions on Professional Communication, 36*(1), 7–11.

Singley, M., and Carroll, J. 1990. Minimalist planning tools in an instructional system for Smalltalk. In D. Diaper et al. (eds.), *Proceedings of the Third Conference on Human-Computer Interaction* (937–944). Amsterdam: North-Holland.

Vanasse, S. 1994. Minimal manual and on-line examples for learning how to use interface construction toolkits. *Performance Improvement Quarterly, 7*(1), 80–96.

Contributors

Patricia A. H. Anson
International Business Machines
Corporation
2021 Coloma Way
Boise, Idaho 83712
tanson@VNET.IBM.COM

R. John Brockmann
English Department
University of Delaware
Newark, DE 19716
jbrockma@udel.edu

John M. Carroll
Department of Computer Science
Virginia Tech (VPI&SU)
Blacksburg, VA 24061-0106
carroll@cs.vt.edu
http://info.cs.vt.edu/vitae/Carroll.html

Stephen W. Draper
Department of Psychology
University of Glasgow
Glasgow G12 8QQ, Scotland
steve@psy.gla.ac.uk
http://www.psy.gla.ac.uk/~steve

David K. Farkas
Department of Technical
Communication
College of Engineering
University of Washington
Seattle, WA 98195-2195
farkas@u.washington.edu

JoAnn T. Hackos
Comtech Services, Inc.
710 Kipling St. Suite 400
Denver, CO 80215
joann.hackos@comtech-serv.com

Robert R. Johnson
Department of English
Miami University
Oxford, OH 45056
johnson_bob@msmail.muohio.edu

Greg Kearsley
Department of Educational Leadership
Graduate School of Education and
Human Development
The George Washington University
Washington, DC 20052
kearsley@gwis2.circ.gwu.edu

Hans van der Meij
Department of Instructional
Technology
University of Twente
P.O. Box 217
NL-7500 AE Enschede,
The Netherlands
meij@edte.utwente.nl

Barbara Mirel
School for New Learning
De Paul University
243 South Wabash
Chicago, Illinois 60604
bmirel@condor.depaul.edu

Janice (Ginny) Redish
Redish & Associates, Inc.
6820 Winterberry Lane
Bethesda, MD 20817
redish@ari.net

Stephanie Rosenbaum
Tec-Ed, Inc.
P.O. Box 1905
Ann Arbor, MI 48106
stephanie@teced.com /
stephani@conch.aa.msen.com

Karl L. Smart
Marriott School of Management
Brigham Young University
Provo, UT 84602
ucsnet.adena.kxsmart@byugate.
byu.edu

Index